David
Sturdge

OUT OF ARCADIA

BULLETIN OF THE INSTITUTE OF CLASSICAL STUDIES SUPPLEMENT 79

GENERAL EDITOR: GEOFFREY WAYWELL

OUT OF ARCADIA
CLASSICS AND POLITICS IN GERMANY IN THE AGE OF BURCKHARDT, NIETZSCHE AND WILAMOWITZ

EDITED BY
INGO GILDENHARD AND MARTIN RUEHL

INSTITUTE OF CLASSICAL STUDIES
SCHOOL OF ADVANCED STUDY
UNIVERSITY OF LONDON

2003

BICS SUPPLEMENT 79

ISBN 0 900587 90 3

First published in 2003 by the Institute of Classical Studies,
School of Advanced Study, University of London,
Senate House, Malet Street, London WC1E 7HU.

All rights reserved. No part of this publication may be reproduced, stored in a retrieval system, or transmitted, in any form or by any means, electronic, mechanical, photocopying, recording, or otherwise, without the prior permission of the publisher.

© Institute of Classical Studies,
School of Advanced Study, University of London, 2003

The right of the contributors to this work to be identified as the authors of the articles published here has been asserted by them in accordance with
the Copyright, Designs and Patents Act 1988.

Designed and computer typeset at the Institute of Classical Studies

Printed by Remous Limited, Milborne Port, Sherborne, Dorset DT95EP

Wenn wir von den Griechen reden, reden wir unwillkürlich zugleich von Heute und Gestern: ihre allbekannte Geschichte ist ein blanker Spiegel, der immer Etwas wiederstrahlt, das nicht im Spiegel selbst ist. Wir benützen die Freiheit, von ihnen zu reden, um von Anderen schweigen zu dürfen, – damit jene nun selber dem sinnenden Leser Etwas in's Ohr sagen.

Friedrich Nietzsche, *Menschliches, Allzumenschliches.*
Zweiter Band: Vermischte Meinungen und Sprüche (1879)

When we speak of the Greeks, we involuntarily also speak of today and yesterday. Their well-known history is a blank mirror which always reflects something that is not in the mirror itself. We avail ourselves of the liberty to speak of the Greeks so that we may be silent about others, and they may whisper something into the ear of the contemplative reader.

Friedrich Nietzsche, *Human, All Too Human* (1879)

CONTENTS

Abbreviations		viii
Ingo Gildenhard and Martin Ruehl	Introduction	1
Egon Flaig	Jacob Burckhardt, Greek culture, and modernity	7
	A comment on Egon Flaig's essay by Lionel Gossman	41
Lionel Gossman	*Per me si va nella città dolente*: Burckhardt and the *polis*	47
Martin Ruehl	*Politeia* 1871: Nietzsche *contra* Wagner on the Greek State	61
Andreas Urs Sommer	On the genealogy of the genealogical method: Overbeck, Nietzsche, and the search for origins	87
Egon Flaig	Towards '*Rassenhygiene*': Wilamowitz and the German New Right	105
Suzanne Marchand	From Liberalism to Neoromanticism: Albrecht Dieterich, Richard Reitzenstein, and the religious turn in *fin-de-siècle* German Classical Studies	129
Ingo Gildenhard	*Philologia perennis*? Classical scholarship and Functional Differentiation	161
Thematic Index		205
Index of Names		207

ABBREVIATIONS

BGStA   Berlin, Geheimes Staatsarchiv (Dahlem)

BSB   Berlin, Staatsbibliothek (Handschriftenabteilung)

GSD   R. Wagner, *Gesammelte Schriften und Dichtungen*, 10 vols (Leipzig 1871-83)

GW   J. Burckhardt, *Gesammelte Werke*, 10 vols (Basel and Stuttgart 1955-59)

JBB   J. Burckhardt, *Briefe. Vollständige und kritisch bearbeitete Ausgabe*, ed. M. Burckhardt, 9 vols (Basel 1949-94)

KSA   F. Nietzsche, *Sämtliche Werke: Kritische Studienausgabe*, ed. G. Colli and M. Montinari, 15 vols (Munich, Berlin, and New York 1980)

KSB   F. Nietzsche, *Sämtliche Briefe: Kritische Studienausgabe*, ed. G. Colli and M. Montinari, 8 vols (Berlin and New York 1986)

OC   A. de Tocqueville, *Œuvres, papiers et correspondance*, ed. J. P. Mayer (Paris 1952-)

OWN   F. Overbeck, *Werke und Nachlass*, ed. E. Stegemann *et al.* (Stuttgart and Weimar 1994)

INTRODUCTION

The German philhellenists of the Enlightenment era imagined Greek antiquity as a kind of pastoral idyll.[1] Throughout the second half of the eighteenth century, scholars and poets enthused about the innocent beauty of the ancients, glorified the 'noble simplicity' and 'calm grandeur' (Winckelmann)[2] of Hellenic art, and posited an elective affinity between the glory that was Greece and the future achievements of a German *Kulturnation*. Schiller's poem 'The Gods of Greece' (1788) held up the harmonious world of pagan antiquity as a moral and aesthetic model for a disenchanted, alienated modernity. The educational reforms initiated by Wilhelm von Humboldt between 1809-10 moved this model to the centre of school and university curricula. For members of the educated middle class (*Bildungsbürger*), classical philology became an integral part of their self-cultivation or *Bildung*. Through their identification with ancient Greece, however, many of them expressed hopes not just of cultural, but also political transformation. In the age of Winckelmann and Humboldt, Graecophilia was associated with a lofty (and often vaguely defined) liberalism.[3] Yet from the start, there were voices of doubt. In *Faust II* (1832), Goethe questioned the viability of a marriage between Romantic Germany and classical Greece – as well as the emancipatory elements of Graecophilia: Euphorion, product of Faust's union with Helen of Troy and an allegory of Byron's fateful commitment to the cause of Greek independence, met a significantly premature death in the play.[4]

Several decades later, these voices of doubt echoed ever more loudly through the philhellenists' Arcadian fields. For a variety of reasons, Humboldt's neohumanist 'paedagogical creed' (*Bildungsreligion*) lost its hold on the minds of the *Bildungsbürger*. Towards the end of the nineteenth century, the professionalization of classical studies,[5] the availability of new archaeological evidence,[6] and fundamental changes in Germany's political as well as cultural climate had all but eroded the belief of an earlier generation in the timeless, normative

---

1 For the eighteenth-century origins of German Graecophilia see S. Marchand, *Down from Olympus: Archaeology and Philhellenism in Germany, 1750-1970* (Princeton 1996) 3-74.
2 J. J. Winckelmann, *Gedanken über die Nachahmung der Griechischen Werke in der Malerei und Bildhauer-Kunst* (1755), in idem, *Kleine Schriften. Vorreden – Entwürfe*, ed. W. Rehm (Berlin 1968) 27-59 (43).
3 See C. Hauser, *Anfänge bürgerlicher Organisation: Philhellenismus und Frühliberalismus in Südwestdeutschland* (Göttingen 1990).
4 J. W. v. Goethe, *Faust. Zweiter Teil* (Act III), see *Goethes Werke*. Hamburger Ausgabe, 14 vols, 16th edn (Munich 1996), III, 290-98.
5 See A. Grafton, 'Polyhistor into *Philolog*: Notes on the Transformation of German Classical Scholarship, 1780-1850', *History of Universities* 3 (1983) 159-92, and A. La Vopa, 'Specialists against Specialization: Hellenism as Professional Ideology in German Classical Studies', in *German Professions, 1800-1950*, ed. G. Cocks and K. Jarausch (New York 1990).
6 See K. Bittel, 'The German Perspective and the German Archaeological Institute', *American Journal of Archaeology* 84 (1980) 271-77, and Marchand, *Down from Olympus* (n. 1 above) 51-115.

values of Greek antiquity. Once the exclusive gatekeepers to academe, the *Philologen* were now forced to leave their eyries on top of Mount Olympus and found themselves embroiled in protracted dogfights over the meaning and purpose of classical education in a modern, industrialized society.[7] Their dean, Ulrich von Wilamowitz-Moellendorf (1848-1931), gave an evocative description of the new situation in an 1897 public lecture, which presented the decline of classics as part of a larger cultural malaise. 'Culture can die', Wilamowitz warned his listeners, 'for it has died at least once before. The jackals howl in Ephesus, where Heraclitus and Paul preached; in the marble halls of hundreds of cities in Asia Minor, the thorns proliferate and only a handful of stunted barbarians cower.'[8]

The jackals howling in Ephesus – a thinly veiled allusion to the proletarian masses and their inability to appreciate the classical heritage – did not just preoccupy Wilamowitz. Two maverick scholars at the University of Basel, Jacob Burckhardt (1818-1897) and Friedrich Nietzsche (1844-1900), shared Wilamowitz's cultural pessimism and elitism. Their vision of ancient Greece, however, was radically different. Both believed that Hellenic civilization had been whitewashed by Winckelmann, Schiller, and other philhellenists. In their lectures and writings of the 1870s, they set out to correct the picture and explore the 'dark sides' (*Schattenseiten*)[9] of the ancients: their myths and cults, their bleak, violent worldview, their agonal conception of politics and proud aristocratic ethos.[10] Even though their interpretations of Greek culture were initially received with much scepticism by the guild, they exercised a powerful long-term effect and shaped popular perceptions as well as seminal scholarly research in the first decades of the twentieth century.[11] A new generation of classicists, investigating the irrational, transgressive aspects of antiquity and dissatisfied with the traditional empiricist methods preached by Wilamowitz, frequently turned to Nietzsche and Burckhardt for inspiration.[12]

---

7 See M. Landfester, *Humanismus und Gesellschaft im 19. Jahrhundert* (Darmstadt 1988); C. McClelland, *State, Society, and University in Germany, 1700-1914* (Cambridge 1980); U. Preuß, *Humanismus und Gesellschaft: Zur Geschichte des altsprachlichen Unterrichts in Deutschland von 1890-1933* (Frankfurt 1988).
8 U. v. Wilamowitz-Moellendorf, 'Weltperioden', in *idem, Reden und Vorträge*, 3rd edn (Berlin 1913) 122. Quoted in Marchand, *Down from Olympus* (n. 1, above) 139.
9 Burckhardt had originally used this term to describe the Machiavellian politics of the Florentine Republic: J. Burckhardt, *Die Kultur der Renaissance in Italien: Ein Versuch*, 10th edn (Stuttgart 1988) 63. For his comments on the 'Schattenseiten' of ancient Greece see L. Gossman, *Basel in the Age of Burckhardt: A Study in Unseasonable Ideas* (Chicago 2000) 328-29. The best examination to date of Nietzsche's interpretation of Greek antiquity is H. Cancik, *Nietzsches Antike: Vorlesung* (Stuttgart and Weimar 1995).
10 But see A. v. Martin, *Nietzsche und Burckhardt: Zwei geistige Welten im Dialog*, 4th edn (Munich 1947) 85-109, who points to crucial differences between Burckhardt's and Nietzsche's conception of Greek culture.
11 See J. Latacz, *Fruchtbares Ärgernis: Nietzsches 'Geburt der Tragödie' und die gräzistische Tragödienforschung* (Basel 1998) and W. Kaegi, *Jacob Burckhardt: Eine Biographie*, 7 vols, VII (Basel and Stuttgart 1982) 98-107. Stefan Bauer's bibliographical survey shows that after 1900, Burckhardt's *Griechische Kulturgeschichte* received increasingly favourable reviews: S. Bauer, *Polisbild und Demokratieverständnis in Jacob Burckhardts 'Griechischer Kulturgeschichte'* (Basel 2001) 263-64.
12 See, e.g., H. Cancik, 'Der Einfluss Nietzsches auf klassische Philologen in Deutschland bis 1945. Philologen am Nietzsche-Archiv (I)', in *Altertumswissenschaft in den 20er Jahren*, ed. H. Flashar (Stuttgart 1995) 381-402.

The sixty odd years between *c.* 1870 and 1930, thus, saw not only severe crises and doubts, but also dramatic transformations in German classical scholarship. Over the past decade, this period has attracted considerable attention in the fields of *Antikerezeption* (the history of the reception of classical antiquity) and *Wissenschaftsgeschichte* (the history of disciplines), both in Germany and abroad.[13] To assess the major recent shifts of focus and paradigm in these areas was the purpose of a conference held at Princeton University in April 1999. The conference brought together European and American specialists from different disciplines – classics, ancient and modern history, as well as literature – to address a central theme: the gradual erosion of the neohumanist, emancipatory legacy of philhellenism in the Wilhelmine era and the increasing susceptibility of classical scholars to illiberal, nationalist and – especially after World War I – racist beliefs.

The papers assembled here (which have been substantially revised since they were first presented at Princeton) hardly provide a unified analysis of this phase in German classical scholarship. Differences in method and interpretation will readily be apparent. The approaches range from the traditional biographical concern of *Wissenschaftsgeschichte* to agendas of enquiry that go decidedly beyond prosopography. All of the papers, however, share a strong 'geneaological' thrust in that they explore the manifold factors and forces conditioning the genesis and circulation of ideas and semantic patterns. The authors investigate networks and relations, *Gesprächsgemeinschaften* (discursive communities) of friends and scholars, intertextual appropriations as well as the affinities and affiliations of certain ideas with larger discursive formations. The 'fate' of ideas through later acts of reception and changing political circumstances constitutes another major preoccupation in the collection, not least in the two contributions by Egon Flaig.

Flaig's opening salvo, 'Jacob Burckhardt, Greek Culture, and Modernity', takes aim at the politics of Jacob Burckhardt's *Griechische Kulturgeschichte*. It focuses on three particular targets: Burckhardt's perception of democracy as a threat to civic society and cultural achievement; his view that the unrestrained pursuit of material interests corrodes the realm of 'the social'; and his conception of war as both a moral litmus-test and aesthetic phenomenon. Throughout, Flaig situates Burckhardt within the wider context of nineteenth-century conservative political thought (De Maistre, Bonald, Donoso Cortés), drawing particular attention to his, at times, verbatim reliance on Fustel de Coulanges' *The Ancient City* (1864). In a series of close intertextual readings, he shows that Burckhardt's dependence on Fustel

---

13 For the renewed interest in the history of German classical scholarship over the past fifteen years see the perceptive remarks by J. Porter in his review of W. Ludwig, *Hellas in Deutschland: Darstellungen der Gräzistik im deutschprachigen Raum aus dem 16. und 17. Jahrhundert* (Hamburg 1998), in *Bryn Mawr Classical Review* 2000.09.05. Some of the most influential work on the period in question has come from Arnaldo Momigliano, Karl Christ, and William Calder: see A. Momigliano, *Studies on Modern Scholarship*, ed. G. Bowersock and T. Cornell (Berkeley 1994); *L'Antichità nell' Ottocento in Italia e Germania*, ed. K. Christ and A. Momigliano (Bologna and Berlin 1988); K. Christ, *Hellas: Griechische Geschichte und deutsche Geschichtswissenschaft* (Munich 1999); *Wilamowitz nach 50 Jahren*, ed. W. Calder, H. Flashar, and T. Lindken (Darmstadt 1985); *Werner Jaeger Reconsidered*, ed. W. Calder (Atlanta 1992). See also W. Nippel, *Über das Studium der alten Geschichte* (Munich 1993); B. Näf, *Von Perikles zu Hitler? Die athenische Demokratie und die deutsche Althistorie bis 1945* (Bern 1986); H. Flashar, *Altertumswissenschaft in den 20er Jahren* (Stuttgart 1995); and *'Mehr Dionysos als Apoll': antiklassizistische Antike-Rezeption um 1900*, ed. A. Aurnhammer and T. Pittrof (Frankfurt a. M. 2002).

marks a significant break with his early work *The Age of Constantine*, in which biologistic concepts of cultural decline prevailed. In his *Griechische Kulturgeschichte*, by contrast, Burckhardt, drawing on Fustel, predominantly employed socio-political categories (such as class struggle) to explain cultural change. This interpretative shift is commensurate with the transformation of Burckhardt's political outlook in the 1860s. According to Flaig, *Griechische Kulturgeschichte* is imbued with deeply reactionary – at times, protofascist – concerns about cultural continuity, 'massification' and democratization, which cast doubt on its recently acquired status as a classic of nineteenth-century historiography.

Defending him against Flaig's charges, Lionel Gossman ('*Per me si va nella città dolente*: Burckhardt and the *polis*') presents Burckhardt as a sceptical *altliberal* humanist rather than a proponent of prefascist ideas. For Gossman, Burckhardt's *Griechische Kulturgeschichte* was marked by the Basel patriciate's preoccupation with centralization and democratization in the aftermath of the Swiss Civil War (1847) and the German Wars of Unification (1864-71). It was also a contribution, Gossman argues, to a very topical debate amongst nineteenth-century historians – including Droysen and Grote – about the political and cultural viability of the small Greek city-states. Finally, Burckhardt's lectures on Greek culture represented a comprehensive attack on the neo-humanist glorification of classical Greece. Athens in the fifth century BC, according to Burckhardt, by no means produced the happy, harmonious individuals described by Winckelmann and Schiller; on the contrary, its citizens were largely deprived of their individuality insofar as their lives were completely subordinated to the state, especially under democratic governments. Gossman concludes that Burckhardt's account of ancient Greece, though undoubtedly anti-democratic, was nonetheless a powerful re-statement, in the age of Bismarck and Cavour, of the classic liberal, anti-Machiavellian view of the state found in Constant and Montesquieu.

Martin Ruehl's paper, '*Politeia* 1871: Nietzsche *contra* Wagner on the Greek State', investigates Nietzsche's perhaps most straightforwardly political text, a short essay entitled 'The Greek State'. Originally conceived as part of the *Birth of Tragedy*, this essay was presented to Cosima Wagner in the winter of 1872 as one of the 'Five Prefaces to Five Unwritten Books'. It was an ambivalent gift (and considered as such by the recipients), for Nietzsche's vision of the Greek *polis* differed markedly from the one Wagner had projected in his Zurich Writings, most notably 'Art and Revolution'. In contrast to Wagner, Nietzsche idealized the ancient Greek city-state as an anti-socialist, anti-liberal archetype: a hierarch-ically structured, cruelly oppressive society, whose cultural excellence rested on the relentless exploitation of slave labour. Combining a close reading of Nietzsche's essay with careful historical contextualization, Ruehl argues that 'The Greek State' marked a transformation in Nietzsche's political thinking, from the potentially egalitarian concept of the Dionysian developed in the *Birth of Tragedy* to the notion of *Rangordnung* ('order of rank') elaborated in later writings. 'The Greek State' also reveals an early – and hitherto unnoticed – caesura in Nietzsche's relation to Wagner. At a time when Wagner still considered him a faithful disciple, Nietzsche, under the influence of Jacob Burckhardt, had already begun to revise the classicizing, republican image of the *polis* that played such a central role in the composer's revolutionary aesthetics. Ruehl traces the anti-humanist, illiberal ideas of 'The Greek State' in the rest of Nietzsche's œuvre to question the post-modernist portrait of Nietzsche as a cheerful, ironic relativist, whose 'perspectivism' ultimately subverts all forms of political domination.

'On the genealogy of the genealogical method: Overbeck, Nietzsche, and the search for origins' by Andreas Urs Sommer compares the development of the 'genealogical method' in the works of Nietzsche and the Basel Church historian Franz Overbeck. Hardly known in Anglo-American scholarship other than as 'Nietzsche's friend', Overbeck, Sommer argues, in fact anticipated (and probably influenced) his associate's abandonment of the search for normative origins in classical antiquity after the publication of the *Birth of Tragedy*. In the latter work, according to Sommer, Nietzsche still idealized pre-Socratic Greece as an archetype, an 'original' yardstick with which to measure the corruption of contemporary European culture. Overbeck's polemic *On the Christianity of Today's Theology* (1873), in like fashion, unfavourably compared modern Christian theology with the early stages of Christendom (*das Urchristentum*). While Nietzsche posited that Hellenism marked the fateful departure from the pure, tragic spirit of archaic Greece, Overbeck claimed that the contact with Graeco-Roman civilization lastingly contaminated the otherworldly religiosity of the ur-Christian communities. Overbeck's formalist critique of such myths of 'origin' (*Ursprünglichkeit*) in his later writings, Sommer contends, inspired Nietzsche's turn away from the Greek model and his genealogical approach to religion and morality after 1886.

'Towards "*Rassenhygiene*": Wilamowitz and the German New Right', Egon Flaig's second foray into the political unconscious of classical scholarship, tackles the problem of racism and antisemitism in Ulrich von Wilamowitz-Moellendorf's 'intellectual testament', his late *Faith of the Hellenes*. Flaig advances his argument in two steps. He begins with a critical analysis of Wilamowitz's pre-war essay 'State and Society of the Greeks', written in 1910, highlighting its contradictory uses of 'race' as a heuristic category. In some passages, Wilamowitz employed the notion of race as a crucial explanatory tool; in others, he explicitly rejected it. Contrasting this earlier publication with *Faith of the Hellenes*, Flaig demonstrates that Wilamowitz's political views underwent dramatic changes in the aftermath of the Great War. For one thing, 'race' became an essential category for him, as is evidenced by the book's preface, which attacked the comparativist ethnographic approach of the Usener School on the grounds that there existed fundamental cultural and racial differences between the ancient Greeks on the one hand and East African as well as Polynesian tribes on the other. Furthermore, Wilamowitz's interpretation of ancient Greek religion drew on a particularly racist discourse initiated by Droysen, which emphasized the Hellenic roots and affiliations of Christianity and denied its Judaic elements. However, unlike his predecessors – Droysen, Harnack, Reitzenstein – for whom Christianity was a genuine product of the Hellenistic period, Wilamowitz tried to establish a continuity between Christianity and the archaic Greek religion of Homer. He thereby radicalized the idea that Greek culture was the main source of Western civilization, in an effort to put 'antisemitism on a stronger footing'. Flaig concludes his essay with a close examination of the language Wilamowitz used in certain passages of *Faith of the Hellenes* – a language, he argues, that reverberates with Nazi rhetoric.

Suzanne Marchand's contribution ('From Liberalism to Neoromanticism: Albrecht Dieterich, Richard Reitzenstein, and the religious turn in *fin-de-siècle* German Classical Studies') offers a comprehensive discussion of the 'revolt against historicism' in German classical scholarship between 1890 and 1940. This was an important generational and interpretative transformation in the fields of philology and *Altertumswissenschaft*, which in many ways transcended purely methodological questions. What characterized the father figures of German classicism (Ulrich von Wilamowitz-Moellendorf, Eduard Meyer), according to Marchand, was not a particular political outlook – on the whole, their politics were as anti-democratic as those of the 'sons' – but an aestheticizing Graecophilia, a shared belief in the autonomy and rationality of Greek culture as well as a firm adherence to the principles of philological positivism. The new generation of classicists brought a set of decidedly different questions to their field of study. Inspired by Nietzsche, Burckhardt, and Bachofen, no less than by recent findings in neighbouring disciplines such as ethnology and comparative religious history, they investigated the oriental influences on Greek civilization as well as its 'dark passions': the sexual and the cultic. Marchand illustrates this paradigm shift by two penetrating case studies, examining in turn the research and careers of Albrecht Dieterich and Richard Reitzenstein. While considering the worrying aspects of their work, she highlights the new and fruitful directions in which they were moving – something that has largely been ignored by the most recent scholarship.

A kind of epilogue to the volume that brings the story up to the present, Ingo Gildenhard's essay '*Philologia perennis*? Classical Scholarship and Functional Differentiation', starts by surveying different views of philology and 'the philologist' in late nineteenth- and early twentieth-century German classical studies, notably those of Usener, Wilamowitz, and Jaeger, and proceeds to assess the various conceptions against the backdrop of the peculiar order of modern society, which he delineates with the help of contemporary social theory. The paper argues that many aspects of the – frequently self-contradictory – rhetoric employed by German classical scholars in their self-fashionings can be explained with reference to the complex and composite environment in which modern classicists have to manoeuvre. To illustrate this point, Gildenhard focuses on one aspect in particular, that is, the rise of modern science and its uneasy relationship with education. He concludes with some metacritical remarks about the explanatory schemes that prevail in the historiography of classical scholarship as well as current debates about the future of the field.

With the exception of Andreas Urs Sommer's contribution, the following essays are all products of the Princeton conference 'The Gods of Greece and their Prophets: Liberal and Illiberal Moments in German Classical Scholarship since Burckhardt and Nietzsche', held on 9 April 1999. Unfortunately, not all the conference papers could be included. Stefan Bauer's stimulating presentation, 'Between Athens and *Alteuropa*: Burckhardt's Liberal Anxieties', is mentioned with gratitude. The conference was organized by the editors, under the auspices of the Department of History and the Department of Classics, Princeton University. It was made possible by generous funding from Princeton's Modern Europe Colloquium. The editors would like to thank, in particular, Josiah Ober, Barry Strauss, Fritz Stern, Carl Schorske, and Alexander Nehamas for their intellectual input during the conference, and Lionel Gossman, James Diggle, and Richard Simpson for their friendly support in the preparation of this volume.

Ingo Gildenhard
Martin Ruehl

JACOB BURCKHARDT, GREEK CULTURE, AND MODERNITY[1]

EGON FLAIG

The masterpieces of nineteenth-century historiography are fraught with political agendas. Under the veneer of disinterested historical scholarship, their authors consistently pursue decidedly contemporary concerns. This essay offers a case study of one scholar who did so in an extreme fashion: Jacob Burckhardt. The extent to which his obsessive fear of current political developments determined the account of the crumbling of the Greek *polis* in his *Griechische Kulturgeschichte* is truly astonishing, yet rarely recognized.

I would like to emphasize at the outset that, in this essay, I am not primarily concerned with Burckhardt's comments on contemporary political affairs. Nor do I seek to explore the question of whether or not he was a 'liberal'.[2] A word that can be employed to refer to political theorists as diverse as Montesquieu and Friedrich von Hayek has ceased to be heuristically useful. Some of the worst defenders of slavery happened to be ardent champions of liberty and individuality, claiming these ideals as privileges both for themselves and 'the deserving few'. What have we actually gained if we call these men 'liberals'? What we have lost, or at least obscured, are genuinely important distinctions, like that between scholars and intellectuals who believed in the fundamental equality of all human beings, and those who did not. Professional historians are often reluctant to pursue such distinctions with the necessary rigour – not for lofty academic reasons but because interrogations of this kind almost inevitably result in harsh controversies over the politics of *contemporary* historical research.

This said, from a strictly methodological point of view, political catchwords such as 'liberal' simply lack the analytic exactitude necessary to bring out with precision the pertinent differences between the diverse political stances and discourses that shape the intellectual outlook of a period. They fail utterly in the case of a historian who, while never shying away from harsh political verdicts, refused from a certain point onwards to get involved in actual politics. Burckhardt assumed the elevated and ostensibly disinterested standpoint of the apolitical sage when commenting on the various periods and the overall fate of Western civilization. Yet while his self-fashioning may have made him relatively safe from political

---

[1] This essay is the expanded version of a lecture delivered at the History Department of Princeton University in April 1999. I am grateful to Suzanne Marchand, Josiah Ober, Lionel Gossman, and Barry Strauss for their criticisms, and to Ingo Gildenhard and Martin Ruehl who kindly translated my text and made many useful suggestions.

[2] In his wonderfully learned essay on 'Burckhardt and the *polis*' (pp. 47-59 in this volume), Lionel Gossman traces the literary genealogies by which important themes reached Burckhardt. His assessment of the politics inherent in Burckhardt's historiography takes a direction different from mine.

appropriations and critiques, the same cannot be said for the texts into which our seemingly apolitical Lynceus wove his verdicts – on history, culture, and contemporary society.

In terms of method and approach, then, this essay marks a departure from the traditional Burckhardt-philology and the intricacies of biographical criticism, from prosopographical questions of 'influence' and appraisals of 'the man' and his intellectual development over time. Instead, I wish to inquire into the guiding interests, unacknowledged presuppositions, and axiomatically stated premises Burckhardt marshalled to make sense of things – both in his historiographical and in his theoretical writings. Scrutiny of his works from this perspective reveals two pivotal concerns: an almost morbid obsession with those forces that seemed to threaten the continuity of traditional European culture at the time; and a related interest in the social processes that generated and sustained the sort of moral dispositions which Burckhardt deemed vital prerequisites for cultural achievement of the highest order.

The upshot of his anxiety about the survival of European civilization was a philosophy of history that brought four different factors into antagonistic correlation: on one side Burckhardt placed the trend towards democracy and the triumph of material interests; on the other the moral quality of war and an aesthetics of the sublime. The two parts of my essay follow this 'world-historical equation'. Part I sets out Burckhardt's construction of the 'problem'; part II his view of what a possible 'solution' might look like.

I Democracy – the downward spiral into the abyss of material interests

Burckhardt suffered from a paranoid fear of the masses – a delusory foreboding that occidental culture was under the real, even imminent threat of annihilation, to be effected either by a violent uprising of the masses or by a gradual decline of high culture due to 'massification'. I shall bypass discussion of the rather questionable concept of 'the masses', which, for almost a century, enjoyed a remarkable currency in European political thought. I simply note, that for Burckhardt, there existed a cast-iron law of history: the masses, once empowered in and through a democratic form of government, would go about destroying cultural achievements until stopped from doing so by the rise of a dictatorship. He thought the masses capable of depriving occidental culture of the vital space necessary for its continued existence, and firmly believed they would do so if given the chance.[3]

More specifically, Burckhardt's conception of history revolved around three premises that will form the focus of discussion in the first part of my essay. He postulated, first, that there was no distinction between direct and representative democracy: any kind of restraint that the principle of representation could impose on the will of the masses would ultimately fail to be effective, owing to the basic sovereignty of the people in *all* types of democratic government; second, that *political* equality inevitably produced the desire for *social* equality, and that the ensuing fight for social equality produced class struggles; and third, that class struggles

---

3 See JBB (= Jacob Burckhardt, *Briefe. Vollständige und kritisch bearbeitete Ausgabe*, ed. M. Burckhardt, 10 vols, Basel 1949-86), VII, 289, and IX, 125-26. See on this topic in general, W. Hardtwig, *Geschichtsschreibung zwischen Alteuropa und moderner Welt. Jacob Burckhardt in seiner Zeit* (Göttingen 1974). J. Wenzel, *Jacob Burckhardt in der Krise seiner Zeit* (East Berlin 1967) critically discusses the wider ideological implications, F. Jäger, *Bürgerliche Modernisierungskrise und historische Sinnbildung. Kulturgeschichte bei Droysen, Burckhardt und Max Weber* (Göttingen 1994) 134-81, addresses the issue of the increasing disciplinary and methodological autonomy of historical research.

dramatically lowered the moral standard of a society insofar as they generated a historical constellation in which social life fell increasingly under the sway of base material motives that lacked any cultural dimension whatsoever. This, in turn, posed the danger of civil wars that threatened to tear the very fabric of society to pieces. Let us consider the central arguments that Burckhardt adduced in support of this doomsday scenario.

I.i The untamable sovereignty of the people:
Burckhardt's historiographical de-legitimization of modern democracy

For an appraisal of Burckhardt's pronouncements on democracy, it is vital to map out briefly the main contours of political thought at the time, that is, the 'space of possibilities' within and against which he defined his own point of view. The cardinal point of reference in nineteenth-century political debates was, of course, the French Revolution. When formulating their political theories, self-proclaimed liberals, democrats, Bonapartists, legitimists, and reactionaries all argued their case with reference to this event. The most hotly debated issue, in this context, was the sovereignty of the people. The great counter-revolutionary thinkers – DeMaistre, Bonald, Donoso Cortés – shared the same fundamental objection to a form of government based on this principle: it would, they thought, result in chaos and the dissolution of society. How so? Quite simply: the sovereignty of the people would bring about the equality of all citizens; political equality would undermine social hierarchies; this would destroy the political authority of social institutions and lead to anarchy; and anarchy, finally, would plunge society into chaos and civil war. This chain-reaction was bound to happen, since the sovereign people were allegedly unable to maintain a stable order. After all, in a democracy, everything was at all times potentially up for discussion, transformation, and repeal – even the constitution itself.

In part, this line of reasoning was a backlash against some of the most widely-read theorists of the sovereignty of the people – Rousseau and the Abbé Sieyès – who had developed such radical versions of the concept that one could indeed draw anarchistic conclusions from their ideas. Rousseau's *Social Contract* of 1762 still struck a compromise. It is true that it rejected the concept of representation – the sovereign, that is, the people, Rousseau argued, could not transfer their will, only their power: 'le pouvoir peut bien se transmettre, mais non pas la volonté'.[4] But the claim that the people could transfer their power implied that a stable government was in fact a distinct possibility, indeed an absolute necessity. Still, a *representative* government, in Rousseau's eyes was absurd: the will of the sovereign simply had to express itself in direct, not in indirect fashion. The outcome of this line of reasoning was a system of government we would dub 'direct democracy', in which the will of the entire people was to be constantly polled.

In his famous pamphlet, *Qu'est-ce que le tiers état?*, Abbé Sieyès took Rousseau's thinking several steps further. He argued that the 'pouvoir constituant' was not bound to any single act of will; it could dissolve or reshuffle the 'pouvoir constitué', that is, the government and the constitution, at any time and in any way it considered fit. The nation, in other words, could perpetually re-create its societal conditions – when and as it pleased. At the time of the French

---

4 J. J. Rousseau, *Du Contrat social* II, 1.

Revolution, the Abbé Mably endorsed the same point of view.[5] This was precisely the line of thought against which the counter-revolutionary critics of democracy directed their harshest polemics.

In the beginning of the nineteenth century, a 'liberal' movement gradually took shape that defined itself against the forces of radical democracy as well as counter-revolutionary Catholicism and conservatism. These 'liberals' were outspoken proponents of the sovereignty of the people, while at the same time rebutting the ancient model of direct democracy. The best-known advocate of this *via media* was Benjamin Constant, who, in 1819, delivered a speech on 'two types of freedom' in the Athenaeum at Paris, in which he drew a sharp distinction between the individual freedom of modernity and the political freedom of antiquity.[6] He acknowledged the principle of sovereignty of the people (which he considered a good thing); yet at the same time he took the edge off its radical implications by claiming that the people should not govern directly, but *via* their elected representatives. Here we have, for the first time, a succinct political formula of modern representative democracy. Constant's writings were highly influential in the decades leading up to the 1848 revolutions.

In many ways, Burckhardt conducted a frontal attack on this notion of representative democracy. For him, the ultimate outcome of any democratic form of government, with or without an element of representation, was the tyranny of the masses. Representation in no way prevented those who were represented from gaining the upper hand over the representing body, because the masses ruthlessly and unconditionally pursued their own interests:

> Die guten liberalen und selbst radikalen Erwerblinge können lange vor den Volksführern auf die Knie fallen und sie anflehen, keine Dummheiten zu machen. Die Volksführer müssen eben, um wiedergewählt zu werden, die geschreilustigen Schichten der Volksmassen für sich haben, und diese verlangen, daß stets etwas geschehe, sonst glauben sie nicht, daß 'Fortschritt' vorhanden sei ... Aus diesem cercle vicieux kommt man beim suffrage universel überhaupt nicht mehr heraus. Eins nach dem Andern muß geopfert werden: Stellen, Habe, Religion, distinguierte Sitte, höhere Wissenschaft – so lange die Massen auf ihre meneurs drücken können und solange nicht irgend eine Gewalt drein ruft: Haltet's Maul! Wozu vor der Hand noch nicht die leiseste Aussicht vorhanden. Und... diese Gewalt kann beinahe nur aus den Bösesten hervorgehen und haarsträubend wirken.
> Burckhardt to Alioth, 10 September 1881, JBB (n. 3, above), VII, 288-89.[7]

The good liberals and even the radicals among the champions of our acquisitive culture, may fall on their knees before the leaders of the people and beseech them not to commit any follies. But in order to be re-elected, the leaders of the people, the demagogues, must have the masses on their side, and they in turn demand that something should always be

---

5 See, Gabriel Bonnet de Mably, 'De la législation ou principes des lois', III, 3 and 4, in *Collection complète des œuvres*, ed. G. Arnoux, vol. 9 (Paris 1794/95; reprinted Aalen 1977) 290-356.
6 See, Benjamin Constant, *Cours de politique constitutionelle ou collection des ouvrages publiés sur le gouvernement représentatif*, ed. E. Laboulaye, 2 vols (Paris 1872) II, 539-60. Cf. S. Holmes, *Benjamin Constant and the Making of Modern Liberalism* (New Haven/ London 1984) 182-87.
7 At that time, Burckhardt compiled the final version of the first two volumes of his *Griechische Kulturgeschichte*. For the wider historical context of Burckhardt's *Greek Cultural History*, see now S. Bauer, *Polisbild und Demokratieverständnis in Jacob Burckhardts 'Griechischer Kulturgeschichte'* (Basel 2001). Bauer's study does not touch upon my concerns.

happening, otherwise they do not believe that 'progress' is taking place. One cannot possibly escape from that *cercle vicieux* as long as there is universal suffrage. One thing after another will have to be sacrificed – positions, possessions, religion, civilized manners, higher learning – as long as the masses can put pressure on their *Meneurs*, and until some power shouts: 'Shut up!' There is not the slightest sign of that for the time being. But ... that power can really only emerge from the depth of evil, and its effect will be hair-raising.

Buckhardt apparently believed that delegates of necessity had to yield to the interests of those whom they represented; otherwise, the masses would vote them out of office. In other words, Burckhardt asserted that a state of political equality eliminated the possibility of representation. Succinctly put, he regarded representation as an illusion. This premise had drastic consequences for his perception of the status and significance of ancient democracy in modern times. The liberal supporters of Benjamin Constant were able to keep direct democracy as practised by the Athenian *polis* at a comfortable distance, together with its potentially radical lessons for contemporary politics. As long as representative democracy was held to offer a viable alternative, the disturbing fact of mass-rule in ancient Athens could safely be filed away in the archives of history, bearing little relevance to current affairs.

By denying the efficacy of representation in his own time, indeed by rejecting the very principle, Burckhardt, on the other hand, all but eliminated the distinction between the ancient type of democracy and alternative modern forms. As a result, for him, Greek democracy was suddenly no longer a thing of the past. The events in fifth-century Athens had gained a burning urgency. Rather than a closed chapter of history, they were frighteningly real. With one strategic stroke, Burckhardt staked out a distinct theoretical space for himself, in which the historiography of ancient Greece came to bear crucial lessons for Europe's political future. This stroke worked in two ways: if no fundamental differences existed between ancient and modern democracies, Greek democracy could be analyzed in terms of ideological schemes articulated in modern political thought; inversely, once these schemes had proved their validity in the analysis of the past, they would have acquired greater plausibility when deployed in arguments about the present and future.

I.ii Political equality and class conflict:
Burckhardt's political thought between Tocqueville and Fustel de Coulanges

Within this self-defined theatre of operations, Burckhardt brought into play an armoury of concepts that he freely purloined from a variety of historians and political theorists. Scholarship on Burckhardt has so far paid rather little attention to the extent to which he compiled his texts out of quotations. To discover the original source of an idea or argument is frequently a matter of chance. In the nineteenth century, historians were in the habit of citing much-read philosophers or intellectuals without necessarily indicating the texts on which they drew: thus Rousseau and Benjamin Constant are 'absent presences' in Mommsen, Hegel in Droysen, and Tocqueville and Fustel de Coulanges in Burckhardt. My point that Burckhardt made extensive use of quotations has little to do with traditional *Quellenforschung*; rather, I am interested in the *political agenda* that informs his intertextual choices. Burckhardt fashioned his philosophy of history by appropriating those explanatory schemes and analytic categories from earlier writers that suited his argument, at times in contradistinction to the way in which these schemes and categories functioned in the source-text.

Unlike Constant, Burckhardt criticized the form of direct democracy that was practised in the Athenian *polis* not by comparing it to the modern version of representative democracy – this was, as we have seen, not a viable alternative for him – but by drawing attention to the inability of ancient Athens to reconcile general civic equality with the distinctly political inequality between the leaders and the masses:

> Eines scheint in Athen ganz unmöglich gewesen zu sein, nämlich die Einführung eines Systems, das Regierung durch Wenige mit Freiheit für alle verband, einer die Gleichberechtigung der Regierten voraussetzenden Oligarchie ... Denn der Mißbrauch der Gewalt wäre zu unvermeidlich gewesen. Thukydides selber sagt: es bedürfe des demokratischen Regiments, damit die Armen eine Zuflucht und die Reichen einen Zügel hätten. Die Griechen haben nie bürgerliche Gleichheit mit politischer Ungleichheit zu verbinden gewußt. Der Arme mußte zu seinem Schutz gegen Unbill Mitstimmen, Richter und Magistrat sein können. ...
> *Griechische Kulturgeschichte* I (= *Gesammelte Werke* [*GW*] V) 205.

One thing appears to have been entirely impossible in Athens: the introduction of a system combining rule by the few with freedom for all, in other words, of an oligarchy that would take as its basic assumption the equality of those being ruled ... For it would have been impossible to avoid the abuse of power. Thucydides himself says that a democratic regime is necessary so that the poor may have a refuge and the rich a restraint. The Greeks were never able to combine civic equality with political inequality. The poor man had to be able to act as voter, judge and government official in order to protect himself against injustice. ...

This quotation is taken almost verbatim from Fustel de Coulanges' influential book *La Cité antique* of 1864, where the relevant passage reads:

> On aurait peut-être évité l'avènement de la démocratie, si l'on avait pu fonder ce que Thucydide appelle *oligarchia isonomos*, c'est-à-dire le gouvernement pour quelques-uns et la liberté pour tous ... Les Grecs n'ont jamais su concilier l'égalité civile avec l'inégalité politique. Pour que le pauvre ne fût pas lesé dans ses intérêts personnels, il leur a paru nécessaire qu'il eût un droit de suffrage, qu'il fût juge dans les tribunaux, et qu'il pût être magistrat.[8]

Perhaps the coming of democracy could have been avoided if it had been possible to establish what Thucydides calls *oligarchia isonomos*, that is to say sovereignty for some and liberty for all ... The Greeks were never able to reconcile civic equality with political inequality. In order to protect the poor man from being abused in his personal affairs, they

---

8 Fustel de Coulanges, *La Cité antique. Étude sur le culte, le droit, les institutions de la Grèce et de Rome*, 27th edn (Paris 1922) 387. Burckhardt indicates in his text that he is following Fustel here (*Griechische Kulturgeschichte* I, 206), but he does not say to what extent he echoes Fustel's formulations. Right after the quotation given above, Fustel argues that it is precisely the enormous control of the *polis* over human life in its entirety that makes everyone want to participate in its power. Burckhardt makes this thought his own.

deemed it necessary that he have the right to vote, that he be judge in the tribunals and that he have the possibility to act as magistrate.

This all but direct quotation is by no means exceptional. In fact, the entire conceptual architecture that Burckhardt employed to explain the socio-political processes he deemed responsible for the disintegration of the Greek *polis*, he derived from Fustel's masterpiece, changing hardly anything at all in what he took over. We shall see the reason for this in due course.

For Fustel, the desire of the masses for political participation and, after its fulfilment, for political equality, was not a sign of moral decay, but had its engine in a defining feature of Greek politics: the absence of a moral code that would keep the strong from abusing their power. This point of view was diametrically opposed to a conservative article of faith, namely that the masses, rather than the rulers, were the true sources of evil in modern times: witness the repeated exhortations of the counter-revolutionary Catholic Donoso Cortés. Fustel, in contrast, rejected this verdict of guilt in his historiographical analysis of the Greek *polis*: evil, he held, did not emanate from the subjects, but from the lack of moral restraints on the part of the rulers.

In his *Griechische Kulturgeschichte*, Burckhardt explained the decline of the Greek *polis* with the help of an axiom formulated by Tocqueville, namely that political equality would inevitably entail ongoing efforts to attain social equality as well. In a speech he delivered as a delegate in October 1847, Tocqueville stated:

> La Révolution française, qui a aboli tous les privilèges et détruit tous les droits exclusifs, en a pourtant laissé subsister un, celui de la propriété. ... Aujourd'hui que le droit de propriété n'apparaît plus que comme le dernier reste d'un monde aristocratique détruit ... c'est à lui seul maintenant à soutenir chaque jour le choc direct et incessant des opinions démocratiques ....[9]

> The French Revolution which abolished all privileges and destroyed all special rights left one of them intact, the right of property ... In our time, when the right of property appears only as the last remnant of a destroyed aristocratic world ... it alone must bear every day the direct and unceasing assault of democratic opinions ...

Tocqueville thus set up an antagonistic relation between political equality and economic inequality. This alleged antagonism was to become crucial both for the so-called liberal and for the so-called conservative thinkers in their endeavours to play off 'liberty' against 'equality' – a move that was only plausible if one radically depoliticized the notion of 'liberty'. Burckhardt even went a step further in suggesting that political equality would eventually result in the breakdown of social stability. Let us take a closer look at how he endowed this tenet with historical plausibility.

Without ever substantiating his claim empirically, Burckhardt posited that 'reflection' was the mortal enemy of 'tradition'. In so doing, he joined a controversy that dated back to Burke's critique of the French Revolution. Whenever reflection prevailed over customs (put

---

[9] Alexis de Tocqueville, *Œuvres, papiers et correspondance*, ed. J. P. Mayer (Paris 1952-) (hereafter *OC*), XII, 36-37.

differently: tradition), so the argument went, it sooner or later gave rise to political equality, which in turn served as a catalyst for the levelling of social and economic hierarchies as well:

> Alle Herrschaft der Reflexion im Staatswesen drängt über kurz oder lang auf Gleichheit der Bürger im weitesten Umfange; auf wie viele Lebensbeziehungen sich diese Gleichheit ausdehnen werde, hängt von den Umständen ab... Nun wird man sich umzusehen haben nach solchen griechischen Staaten, bei deren Gründung bereits die Reflexion nicht nur tätig, sondern unvermeidlich das Bestimmende gewesen ist. Dies waren die Kolonien.[10]
> *Griechische Kulturgeschichte* I [= *GW,* V] 202.

The dominating presence of reflection within a state sooner or later drives towards the equality of citizens conceived in the widest possible terms; how many social relations this equality affects depends on the circumstances. Now one has to look around for those Greek states at the founding of which reflection was not only active, but even unavoidably the defining factor. Those were the colonies.

Fustel de Coulanges had argued that in the *polis,* 'public interest' and hence 'utility' replaced adherence to tradition and religious commitment.[11] This was the beginning of man's self-determination, but also of intense controversies over the meaning of 'utility'. For the social norms, which had hitherto constituted the unquestioned basis of communal life became the subject of deliberation and change. Despite appearances, Fustel did not align himself with the outlook of the Catholic counter-revolutionaries. Quite the contrary: he assessed the process of reflection that was set in motion at the time in positive terms. For instance, he highlighted the enormous amount of civic discipline required of the Athenian citizens to make their democracy work.[12]

In contrast, Burckhardt, from the outset, dismisses the very notion of 'public interest' as an illusion. Once political reflection has weakened tradition, the various social groups that make up a civic community will assert their own particular interests on strictly utilitarian grounds:

> Als Regierungsprinzip galt jetzt nirgends mehr das Altüberlieferte oder gar die Religion, welche dasselbe hatte befestigen helfen, sondern der sogenannte öffentliche Nutzen, welcher notwendig wandelbar ist oder so aufgefaßt wird; dieser öffentliche Nutzen und die Gleichheit aber sind jetzt Wechselbegriffe. Das große Regierungsmittel aber, die Quelle nicht bloß der einzelnen Maßregeln, sondern des Rechts, der eigentliche Souverän ist die allgemeine Abstimmung, tatsächlich am Gängelbande von Demagogen ...
> *Griechische Kulturgeschichte* I [= *GW,* V] 242.

At that time, tradition – to say nothing of religion – with its stabilizing effects was no longer acknowledged as a principle of government anywhere. It had been replaced by 'public utility', which is by definition subject to change and is regarded as such. Public utility and equality are now interchangeable terms. The great means of government, the

---

10 That this view is no longer tenable today hardly needs to be pointed out. That political reflection leads to political equality is a pure idealist assumption.
11 *La Cité antique* 387.
12 *Ibid.*, 393. Fustel's scheme of emancipation seems to be indebted to Donoso Cortés's famous 'Speech on Dictatorship' (January 1849), although these ideas had become something of a common-place in the new wave of counter-revolutionary thought after the events of 1848. Fustel's evaluation of the events was, however, the exact opposite of Donoso's.

source not only of individual measures, but of law itself, the true sovereign is the general vote, whose reins are held by demagogues ...

As emerges from this and other passages, Burckhardt considered 'public interest' as an illusion, and 'utility' only as a slogan used by different social groups to legitimize their own interests. In his eyes, the establishment of political equality had two fateful consequences: the creation of a new desire to take the next step towards economic equality; and the provision of a new instrument to bring this about – political decision-making by majority vote. Burckhardt described the origins of this fateful nexus thus:

> In der alten Zeit der Geschlechterherrschaft nämlich hatte man die Misere kaum gekannt. Erst die Gleichheit der Rechte machte die Ungleichheit der Lage recht fühlbar. Ein Ausgleich durch Arbeit aber (welche der Reiche bedurft und der Arme gegen Lohn geleistet hätte) war unmöglich wegen der allgemeinen Antibanausie.
> *Griechische Kulturgeschichte* I [= *GW*, V] 243.

In the old times when aristocratic families ruled, people hardly noticed their wretched conditions of existence. Only equality of rights made inequality of position truly noticeable. Compensation through labour (which the rich needed and the poor would have provided for a wage) was impossible owing to the general disdain for manual work.

Burckhardt took this line of argument almost directly from Fustel who had taken it, in his turn, from Tocqueville and other commentators on the 1848 revolution in France.[13]

> La démocratie ne supprima pas la misère; elle la rendit, au contraire, plus sensible. L'égalité des droits politiques fit ressortir encore davantage l'inégalité des conditions.
> *La Cité antique* 397.

Democracy did not eradicate misery; on the contrary, it made it even more keenly felt. The equality of political rights brought the inequality of social conditions even more to the fore.

Here we have the origins of Burckhardt's notion that the equality of political rights rendered long-standing socio-economic inequalities glaringly obvious. This very axiom formed the centre of Tocqueville's theory of the revolution. In Burckhardt, it became the motor that kept the internal struggles within the Greek city-states going until the final breakdown of their civic communities. Burckhardt argued that the poor citizens, once empowered politically, would begin to pursue material interests in their desire to abolish economic inequality as well. In Burckhardt's scenario, this was the moment when class struggles dramatically erupted in the political sphere. Being in the majority, the poor employed the popular vote to change the existing distribution of property:

> Jetzt wurde der Arme inne, daß er als Herr der Stimmen auch Herr des Besitzes werden könne.
> *Griechische Kulturgeschichte* I [= *GW*, V] 243.

Now the poor man realized that as master of the votes, he could also become master of property.

---

13 See Tocqueville's notes for February 1848 (revised in 1850), *OC* (n. 9, above), XII, 96-97.

This sentence, too, was taken all but verbatim from Fustel's *La Cité antique*:

> Le pauvre avait l'égalité des droits. Mais assurément ses souffrances journalières lui faisaient penser que l'égalité des fortunes eût été bien préférable. Or il ne fut pas longtemps sans s'apercevoir que l'égalité qu'il avait pouvait lui servir à acquérir celle qu'il n'avait pas, et que, maître des suffrages, il pouvait devenir maître de la richesse.
> *La Cité antique* 398.

> The poor man had equality of rights. But naturally his daily sufferings made him think that equality of property would have been much preferable. Now, it did not take him long to realize that the equality he had could help him acquire the one he did not have. As master of the votes he could become master of wealth.

For Burckhardt, this thought was absolutely pivotal, the crucial factor in the entire political process of Greek civilization. It was also the core of his conception of social order in the modern age. Let us take a closer look at the reasons he gave for the outbreak of the struggle between rich and poor:

> In Griechenland aber begann, als die Gleichheit da war und man nicht mehr um Prinzipien und Rechte zu kämpfen hatte, der Krieg zwischen Reich und Arm, in manchen Städten schon sogleich mit Eintritt der Demokratie, anderswo nach einer längern oder kürzern Zwischenzeit der Mäßigung. *Griechische Kulturgeschichte* I [= *GW,* V] 242.

> In Greece, the war between rich and poor began when equality had been achieved and it was no longer necessary to fight over principles and rights. In many cities, this happened as soon as democracy had been established, elsewhere after a longer or shorter interval of restraint.

Burckhardt, again, was drawing on Fustel here, who had argued:

> Lorsque la série des révolutions eut amené l'égalité entre les hommes et qu' il n'y eut plus lieu de se combattre pour des principes et des droits, les hommes se firent la guerre pour des intérêts.
> *La Cité antique* 397.

> Once the succession of revolutions had led to equality among men, and there was no longer any need to fight with one another over principles and rights, people went to war with one another over interests.

Fustel took this thought to its logical conclusion when he observed (*La Cité antique* 399) that: 'Il (the poor man) organisa une guerre en règle contre la richesse'. 'The poor man organized a regular war against wealth.'

Burckhardt's explanation of the change and decline of the Greek city-states can be summed up as follows. Since the *polis* exercized quasi-total power over its citizens, it could enforce arbitrary expropriations. The masses could not resist the temptation to abuse their majority in the assembly and thus to transform political equality into social equality. Naturally, the oligarchs defended themselves as much as they could. The class war that resulted from this socio-political dynamic ruined the Hellenic *polis*.

I.iii Majority vote and the de-legitimization of the social order

The establishment of political equality had two significant consequences: it turned the assembly of the people into the decisive political institution, and the vote of the majority into the primary instrument of politics. According to Burckhardt, this entailed, first, that in Greek democracy, the purview of outright political authority in society constantly increased; and second, that an unstoppable merry-go-round of decreeing was set in motion which re-arranged the order of things over and over again. Again, French political thought had anticipated these ideas. Thus the Abbé Sieyès ceded a quasi-divine omnipotence to the sovereign people, refusing to subject their will to any restraint:

> La volonté nationale ... n'a besoin que de sa réalité pour être toujours légale, elle est l'origine de toute l'égalité. Non seulement la nation n'est pas soumise à une constitution, mais elle ne peut pas l'être, mais elle ne doit pas l'être, ce qui équivaut encore à dire qu'elle ne l'est pas.[14]

> The national will ... does not need anything but its own existence to be legal. It is the source of all legality. Not only is the nation not subject to a constitution, but it *cannot* be and it *must not* be; which is tantamount to saying that it is not.

According to this conception, a nation forever remains in a state of nature; it has only rights, no obligations. This renders the sovereign undefinable since it may change its outlook at any time. Rousseau, for one, would not have gone so far. He would have granted to critics of democracy that a political community in charge of sovereign power could exist only as long as the stability of its will was guaranteed.[15] But then, Rousseau deemed democracy fully capable of maintaining such stability. Here Burckhardt begged to differ – and in differing, he eliminated the claim of democracy to be a legitimate form of government. In other words, he drew anti-democractic consequences from the fact that the *pouvoir constituant* as conceived by the Abbé Sieyès could not really be defined. If no stable will stood behind the voting that goes on in the assembly, no subject existed that could exercize sovereignty; rather, the procedure of voting itself in its constant repetition became, quite literally, the sovereign. Let us recall Burckhardt's assessment of majority vote as a form of government:

> Das große Regierungsmittel aber, die Quelle nicht bloß der einzelnen Maßregeln, sondern des Rechts, der eigentliche Souverän ist die allgemeine Abstimmung ...
> *Griechische Kulturgeschichte* I [= *GW,* V] 242; cf. pp. 14-15, above.

> The great means of government, the source not only of the individual measures, but of law itself, the true sovereign is the general vote ...

Burckhardt's formulation contains a deliberate paradox: it is not the people that are 'sovereign', but the procedures of decision-making. This is the reason why, for Burckhardt, modern as well as ancient Greek democracy was 'programmed' to expand constantly the sphere of politics:

---

14 *Qu'est-ce que le tiers état?*, ed. R. Zapperi (Geneva 1970) 182.
15 As is illustrated by his treatment of government (*Contrat Social* III, 1) and, in particular, the legality of suspension of laws in a case of crisis (*Contrat Social* IV, 6 'De la Dictature').

Von unten herauf wird kein besonderes Recht des Staates mehr anerkannt; Alles ist discutabel; ja im Grunde verlangt die Reflexion vom Staat beständige Wandelbarkeit der Form nach ihren Launen; zugleich aber verlangt sie eine stets größere und umfangreichere Zwangsmacht, damit der Staat ihr ganzes sublimes Programm, das sie periodisch für ihn aufsetzt, verwirklichen könne (Zusatz: Der Staat soll alles Mögliche können, aber nichts mehr dürfen). So die Staatsform immer discutabler und der Machtumfang immer größer...
Über das Studium der Geschichte 324.[16]

The common people no longer recognize a special right of the state; everything is open to discussion; indeed, the state is required to change form constantly according to the whims of current ideas; at the same time, however, current ideas demand an ever greater and more comprehensive power of coercion so that the state may realize the entire sublime programme that they periodically decree. (Addition: the state should be capable of doing all sorts of things, but no longer be permitted to do anything.) The more the form of state becomes the subject of discussion, the greater the scope of power.

The unspoken assumption of Burckhardt's argument is that if all decide, everything is up for decision – the entire social order can be put on the agenda of political decision-making. At least in principle, in a democracy, the institutions of the state are incapable of arresting their absorption by society. Burckhardt saw worrying symptoms of this condition in the states of the nineteenth century. Saddled with solving every conceivable ill of society, they became both totalitarian and completely fragile at the same time. This process went hand in hand with their democratization:

... die sogenannte Democratie, d.h. eine aus tausend verschiedenen Quellen zusammengeströmte, nach Schichten ihrer Bekenner höchst verschiedene Weltanschauung, welche aber in Einem consequent ist: insofern ihr nämlich die Macht des Staates über den Einzelnen nie groß genug sein kann, sodaß sie die Grenzen zwischen Staat und Gesellschaft verwischt, dem Staat Alles das zumuthet was die Gesellschaft voraussichtlich nicht thun wird, <zugleich> aber Alles beständig discutabel <und beweglich> erhalten will und zugleich einzelnen Kasten ein specielles Recht auf Arbeit und Subsistenz vindiciert.
Über das Studium der Geschichte 370-71.[17]

... so-called democracy, i.e. an ideology put together from a thousand different sources, varying according to the strata of its apostles, but consistent in one respect: namely that the power of the state over the individual can never be great enough for it, so that it blurs the boundaries between state and society, burdens the state with everything that society is unlikely to do, but at the same time wants to maintain everything as permanently up for discussion and open to change, while providing individual castes with a special entitlement to work and subsistence.

---

16 *Über das Studium der Geschichte. Der Text der 'Weltgeschichtlichen Betrachtungen' nach den Handschriften*, ed. P. Ganz (Munich 1982).
17 It seems to have been Tocqueville who first formulated this thought: 'Le pouvoir social accroît sans cesse ses prérogatives... Ainsi donc, deux révolutions semblent s'opérer de nos jours, en sens contraire: l'une affaiblit continuellement le pouvoir, et l'autre le renforce sans cesse: à aucune époque de notre histoire il n' a paru si faible ni si fort', *De la Démocratie en Amérique*, in *OC* (n. 9, above), I.2, 319-20.

Burckhardt thus projects the threatening spectre of a state at the mercy of fluctuating majorities and their shifting opinions. Such a state no longer has a will of its own; in fact, it has completely lost its 'political' qualities. This alarming vision served Burckhardt as a heuristic model to account for the dissolution of the *polis*:

> Überall war durch die beständigen Volksversammlungen alles *momentan* und willkürlich geworden; ihre Beschlüsse banden sich an keine frühern Beschlüsse desselben Volkes und durchlöcherten die Gesetzgebungen ...
> *Griechische Kulturgeschichte* I [= *GW*, V] 250 (my italics).

Everywhere, the constant national assemblies rendered everything evanescent and arbitrary; their decisions were not tied to any prior decisions of the same people and so eroded the process of legislation ...

This progressive loss of legitimacy would not have taken place if the citizens had decreed the order only once. Such a single foundational act could then have served as the basis and point of reference for all future political transactions. In a democracy, however, such foundational acts were bound to recur over and over again. The constant reshuffling of the social order ruined the rule of law since, inasmuch as the assembly incessantly changed individual laws, it turned their *overall* validity into an object of discussion.

With this chain of arguments Burckhardt put forward the first comprehensive attack on 'decisionism' under the veneer of a historiographical work on classical antiquity. A government based on this principle, he believed, generated two related antinomies. First, there was an inherent contradiction between the particularity of competing interests and the normative force of the law. Whenever the defenders of the traditional order opposed a new law passed by majority vote, two different interests were at variance with each other. As a result, even though the interest of the majority could win the day in the assembly, it remained a *particular* interest. Burckhardt underscored the paradoxical fact that an *ephemeral* majority was thus in charge of setting up legal norms that claimed universal validity.[18]

Second, Burckhardt drew attention to what he saw as a stark contradiction inherent in all democratic forms of government: insofar as any act of establishing a social order implied a sovereign autonomy, and insofar as the establishing will was the only source of authority on which an established order could rest, it was of crucial importance that this establishing will remained constant and binding. This, however, was precisely not the case in a democracy: the establishing will simply could not retain these requisite qualities since it articulated itself in the vote of a randomly constituted popular assembly, whose vote on any given issue could change at any time. It followed, for Burckhardt, that in a democracy whatever had been established utterly lacked authority.

The only way to resolve these contradictions was to remove the constitutional law, as soon as it had been established, from being subject to further changes; only then could it acquire universal acceptance and authority. But that was precisely what Greek democracy had been unable to achieve. Burckhardt construed the consequences of this constituent flaw of Greek democracy as a fateful maelstrom: the *polis* could not endow its law with plausible validity since validity presupposed an element of obligation and continuity; the assembly, however,

---

18 See *Griechische Kulturgeschichte* I [= *GW*, V] 243.

had the power to revoke any law at any time. In other words, Burckhardt identified a paradoxical historical constellation, in which every decision could be overturned and put into a state of limbo, an imaginary dustbin of history for previously binding obligations that had been put out of commission. Such a state produced a distinct lawlessness. Democracy created a historical situation in which society lacked a normative order by constantly under-mining the value of its own decisions.

I.iv Material interests and the dissolution of society in civil war

In his early work *The Age of Constantine* (1854), Burckhardt followed an 'organic' theory of decline resembling that of Ernst von Lassaulx. In contrast, Fustel explained the decline of the Greek *polis* in terms of class struggle – a thoroughly social way of accounting for historical change. The two conceptions are mutually exclusive. Why, then, did Burckhardt's later work on Greek cultural history contain such a remarkable number of quotations from Fustel's *La Cité antique*? To gauge the full significance of Burckhardt's borrowings from *La Cité antique*, it is essential to realize that Fustel operated with theories that to a great extent ran counter to those prevailing in German historicism.

First of all, in Fustel's view of ancient history, social factors were of prime importance. For him, tensions and contradictions in the fabric of society represented an intrinsic source of unrest and historical change. Second, he utterly marginalized the 'state' as an historical agent and downplayed the whole area of foreign policy. Third, he stressed those factors in historical processes that operated at a more general level than human intentionality and subjectivity. Fourth, with his emphasis on social processes he sidelined the 'world-historical individuals' so cherished by German historicists. Finally, Fustel analyzed dynamic socio-political configurations with the categories of modern political philosophy in the tradition of Auguste Comte and, above all, Tocqueville. This 'sociological' approach made him unpalatable to most German-speaking historians, who indeed ignored his work until well into the 1990s. But it was also the reason why Fustel acquired such outstanding significance for Burckhardt. For by recourse to *La Cité antique*, Burckhardt was able to put into practice a conception of 'cultural history' that, while in many respects diametrically opposed to German historicism, perfectly suited his political agenda.

In his *Griechische Kulturgeschichte*, Burckhardt broke with his earlier interpretation of cultural decline as a consequence of 'biological' laws or the 'natural' exhaustion of vital energies. Instead, he adopted Fustel's explanatory schemes. Rather than undergoing a natural process of growing, flowering, and withering, political communities fell apart because of class struggle. He thereby placed himself in the tradition of Catholic counter-revolutionaries like Donoso Cortés – and in opposition to the organic views that were so in vogue at the time. To put it more succinctly: by appropriating the analytic categories of Fustel's *La Cité antique*, Burckhardt appropriated a 'French' mode of historical analysis which related cultural phenomena strictly to social factors. Let us consider the practical consequences of this new departure, by which Burckhardt distanced himself from the organic metaphors which continued to prevail in the work of his German colleagues for years to come.

First of all, Fustel's explanatory schemes enabled Burckhardt to transform the decline of the ancient Greek *polis* into a historiographical narrative that yielded political lessons for the present. Second, and more important, it provided him with a theoretical model that allowed him to explain why Greek art was able to maintain its extraordinarily high standards despite the dissolution of the *polis*. It is true that in his lectures *On the Study of History* Burckhardt had already formulated the idea of three different powers (*Potenzen*) – state, religion, culture – which underwent an independent evolution. For art in particular, he had posited a high degree of autonomy vis-à-vis political and social processes.[19] But as long as he stuck to the notion of culture as a quasi-organic entity, he was unable to account for this autonomy in theoretical terms. For as an organic entity, high culture, once it had exhausted its material base, had to fade away fast.[20]

Now Burckhardt, following the *communis opinio* of the nineteenth century, considered it entirely self-evident that Greek culture manifested an enormous and impressive creativity in several spheres, despite the fact that the *polis* declined. Already in his early work, *The Age of Constantine*, he faced the difficulty of having to exempt the production of art from his biologically conceived notion of an 'aging' ancient world – and he was unable to make sense of this exception.[21] In his *Griechische Kulturgeschichte*, on the other hand, he had little difficulty in showing that the political and social processes unfolded quite independently of artistic production. The destructive struggles between the classes might have constricted the material scope of that production; but they hardly, if ever, affected the intrinsic laws that regulated artistic creativity.[22]

Furthermore, Fustel's categories allowed Burckhardt to address more directly than before one of his foremost concerns: the fate of the culture of Old Europe (*Alteuropa*) in the face of the social catastrophes that he considered imminent. Fustel's model of historical analysis afforded a flicker of hope: for if a determined group of educated individuals, willing to make personal sacrifices, managed to maintain an autonomous sphere for art, then there was the possibility that neither capitalism ('trade' and 'business') nor revolution nor the fickleness of state-power could fully extinguish the flame of 'higher' culture. These considerations most plausibly explain the changes Burckhardt introduced in his theory of history.

This conceptual switch has further ramifications for Burckhardt's philosophy of culture. When he began to direct his attention to the 'class struggles' in the Greek city-state, the theme of 'material interests' quickly took centre-stage in his thoughts on the history of Western civilization. Fustel, too, pointed out that an interest no longer checked by bounds of religion and custom, triggered a dynamic that endangered the social order:

> On ne voit plus le principe supérieur qui consacre le droit de propriété; chacun ne sent que son propre besoin et mesure sur lui son droit. *La Cité antique* 400.

---

19 See *Über das Studium der Geschichte* (n. 16, above) 107, 158, 182-83 and passim.
20 Cf. Ernst v. Lassaulx, *Neuer Versuch einer alten, auf die Wahrheit gegründeten Philosophie der Geschichte*, ed., with intro., by E. Thurner (Vienna 1952) 78, 142, and 159-60.
21 See E. Flaig, 'Der Begriff der "Alterung" in J. Burckhardt's "Zeit Konstantins des Großen"', in *Archiv für Begriffsgeschichte* 28 (1987) 201-13.
22 Cf. Burckhardt's late treatise 'Die Kunst des Altertums', in J. Burckhardt, *Gesamtausgabe*, 14 vols, (Basel, Stuttgart, Berlin, Leipzig 1929-1934), XIII. Jörn Rüsen, by contrast, sees an 'organic' pattern underlying Burckhardt's interpretation of Greek history, see J. Rüsen, 'Die Uhr, der die Stunde schlägt. Geschichte als Prozeß der Kultur bei Jacob Burckhardt', in *Historische Prozesse*, ed. K.-G. Faber and Chr. Meier (Munich 1978) 186-217.

The higher principle which consecrates the right of property is no longer discernible; everybody feels only his own needs and tailors his rights accordingly.

If what counts as right is determined by individual needs, a legal order cannot be sustained. Burckhardt illustrated this point in his *Griechische Kulturgeschichte* as follows:

Von der späteren Zeit der demokratischen Polis, seit der Schlacht von Chäronea, wendet sich der Blick bekanntlich gerne ab, es ist aber alles Eine Kette von Ursachen und Wirkungen bis zur gegenseitigen Ausrottung, bis zur Verödung desjenigen Griechenlands wie es die Römer übernahmen, und dieser Krankheitsgeschichte wird sich die Darstellung, sobald sie objektiv verfahren soll, nie entziehen können. ... Das Hauptübel war, daß sich die Demokratie mit der starken antibanausischen Gesinnung gekreuzt hatte, daß die Gleichheit der Rechte mit der Abneigung gegen die Arbeit zusammengetroffen war, worauf die Nichtstuer die Mittel des Stimmrechts und des Gerichtswesens auf permanente Bedrohung der Besitzenden wandten. Es ist wahnsinniger Mißbrauch der Majorität in einer Sache, welche unvermeidlich auch diese wieder in eine Majorität und Minorität spalten muß... *Griechische Kulturgeschichte* I [= *GW*, V] 254.

It is well known that the later periods of the democratic *polis*, after the battle of Chaironeia, are usually ignored; but one single chain of causes and effects leads up to the mutual annihilation of the Greek states, and the destruction of the Greece that was taken over by the Romans. A historical narrative that strives to be objective can never ignore this case history ... The main evil was the synthesis of democracy and a strong anti-banausic ethos, and the combination of equality of rights with low esteem of labour. This resulted in a situation where the idlers exploited the franchise and the judicial system as a permanent threat to the propertied classes. It is an insane abuse of the majority in matters that will inevitably split the latter again into a majority and a minority ...

In other words, civil wars – conceived as wars between the poor and the rich – accelerated the self-destruction of the political sphere. This process was tantamount to an erosion of social cohesion, with a slow, yet comprehensive disintegration of society as such. Once the state itself has degenerated to the point of being a mere instrument for the promotion of special interests, no instance is left to counterbalance the collision of diametrically opposed desires. Since these desires are material in nature, a compromise is out of the question, for the simple reason that material desires are insatiable. We shall return to this axiom below.

At this point, Fustel de Coulanges and Jacob Buckhardt part company. When Fustel pondered in what way the emergence of 'interest' led to a utilitarian disposition under the banner of (economic) 'utility' and in what way popular needs started to condition the judiciary, he did so exclusively as a historian analyzing a distinct historical phenomenon, that is, the ancient city-state. Fustel saw an effective caesura between antiquity and modernity, believing that Christianity, with its emphasis on individual liberty, introduced a principle into history which forever prevented a return to the oppressive ancient state. For him, the troubles of the Greek city-states had nothing to do with the political circumstances of his own age. Fustel used the analytical models and theories that Tocqueville had derived from his study of contemporary conflicts and applied strategically in public affairs only as heuristic instruments in order to analyze processes of social disintegration in antiquity. In other words, he defused their political explosiveness. At the same time, it did not occur to him to invoke events of ancient history as timeless *exempla* for debates about the political and social order.

Not so Burckhardt, who used the schemes and categories of *La Cité antique* in a way unintended by its author. Burckhardt appropriated Fustel's 'antiquarian' point of view for his own purposes and recharged ancient democracy with the kind of presentist 'menace' that it possessed in the texts of Tocqueville. In so doing, he endowed the pursuit of 'material interests' with the capacity to unleash those impetuous energies that he regarded as the cause of historical changes in ancient as well as modern times. Burckhardt thus contributed to a wide-spread discourse that had become increasingly virulent after the workers' strikes and rebellions of the 1830s and concentrated on the political consequences of demands for material advantages. Donoso Cortés, for instance, regarded these events as the main source of the evils of contemporary society. In his 'Speech on Dictatorship', delivered on 4 January 1849, which acquired a pan-European notoriety, Cortés proclaimed:

[E]l germen de las revoluciones está en los deseos sobreexcitados de la muchedumbre por los tribunos que la explotan y benefician.[23]

The germ of revolutions lies in the desires of the crowd, stirred up by the tribunes, who exploit them to their own advantage.

Cortés, the harshest proponent of counter-revolutionary Catholicism, was by no means the only one who held this opinion. 'Liberal' politicians and publicists chimed in. Before the revolution of 1848, these had already started to adopt the concepts of counter-revolutionary Catholic thinkers. Burckhardt turned their central axiom into the cornerstone of his reflections on culture. The decline of the Greek *polis*, for him, taught a more general lesson:

Die Wünsche aber sind weit überwiegend materieller Art, so ideal sie sich auch gebärden, denn die Weitmeisten verstehen unter Glück nichts anderes; materielle Wünsche aber sind in sich und absolut unstillbar, selbst wenn sie unaufhörlich erfüllt würden, und dann erst recht. *Historische Fragmente*, in *Gesamtausgabe* (n. 22, above), III, 432.

Desires, however, are overwhelmingly of a material nature, even if they are dressed in an idealistic garb, for most people take happiness to mean nothing else. Material desires, however, are in and of themselves absolutely insatiable, even if they are continuously satisfied – or rather – especially when they are continuously satisfied.

In his *Griechische Kulturgeschichte*, Burckhardt expressed the same idea:

Die Gier der dotierten Masse hinwiederum war aus innern Gründen unerfüllbar und mußte stets zu neuen Änderungen drängen. VIII, 204

The greed of the remunerated masses, on the other hand, was inherently unfulfillable and had to bring about constant new changes.

---

23 Juan Donoso Cortés, *Obras Completas*, vol. II (Madrid 1970) 311.

These passages reveal that Burckhardt employed the concept of material interests in the same radical sense in which Donoso had used it[24] – as a means systematically to associate such concepts as 'the masses' and 'the sovereignty of the people' with political catastrophe. He thus openly expounded a philosophy of history according to which naked material interests undermined the cultural determinants that should ideally shape our habitual dispositions.

Burckhardt regarded this development as nothing short of disastrous. Once they had gained the upper hand, material interests set in motion a fateful causal chain: human beings ceased to follow their intellect and higher ideas; their readiness for self-sacrifice broke down, and they were no longer concerned with promoting culture, since they had less and less motivation to do so. Once material drives triumphed and social interaction within a culture was predominantly oriented towards mercenary gain, the power (*Potenz*) 'State' declined. Quickly, all struggles turned into struggles over the distribution of wealth. This process, Burckhardt believed, would not come to a halt by itself since all material desires were inherently insatiable. In the end, they would induce the masses to tear one another to pieces.

According to Burckhardt, democracy was the political order in which these naked material interests could best be articulated. Consequently, in all democracies, a war of the poor against the rich was bound to arise sooner or later:

> Jetzt wurde der Arme inne, daß er als Herr der Stimmen auch Herr des Besitzes werden könne. In Athen und wohl auch sonst ließ er sich zunächst honorieren für seine Anwesenheit in Volksversammlung und Gericht, dann verkaufte er seine Stimme, besonders als Richter, lud den Reichen alle Arten von Leiturgien auf und verfügte Konfiskationen (samt Exil) ohne alles Recht – außerhalb Athens dann erfolgte Annullierung der Schulden und allgemeiner Umsturz. Denn bei den ersten Mitteln war das Gefühl der Misere, nämlich das Gelüste, immer nur weiter gewachsen. Der Besitz hatte alle Weihe verloren, und jeder maß sein Recht nur nach seinem sogenannten Bedürfnis (d.h. Gelüste). Und für all dies genügte eine momentane Stimmenmehrheit. Überall sieht man nur Revolution und Gegenrevolution, nur Faktionen am Ruder, alle Fügsamkeit ist nur erzwungen und voll Hintergedanken an Umschwung.
>
> *Griechische Kulturgeschichte* I [= *GW*, V] 243.

Now the poor man realized that, as master of the ballots, he could also become master of property. In Athens and arguably elsewhere as well, he first received remuneration for his presence in the popular assembly and the courts, then he sold his vote, in particular in his capacity as judge, imposed every sort of special tribute upon the rich and decreed confiscation of property (in addition to exile) without any legal basis. Outside Athens, annulment of debt and general revolution ensued. For the first measures had increased the feeling of wretchedness, that is, the intensity of desire. Property had entirely lost its sacred quality, and everybody determined his right according to his own needs (i.e. desires). And in order to enact all these measures a momentary majority vote sufficed. Wherever one looks, there is nothing but revolution and counter-revolution; factions only are at the helm; all obedience is but enforced and fraught with ulterior motives of change ...

---

24 See Donoso's letter to cardinal Fornari, 19 June 1852, in Juan Donoso Cortés, *Der Abfall vom Abendland*, ed. P. Viator (1849) 95.

This protracted state of war led to the gradual destruction of the political as well as the social sphere. No institution was able to provide a counterweight to the opposing factions since the state itself had degenerated into a mere instrument of competing particular interests. The result was a relapse into a state of nature somewhat reminiscent of Hobbes. But whereas for Hobbes everybody was at war with everybody else (*bellum omnium contra omnes*), Burckhardt projected a succession of conflicts between different social groups.

For Burckhardt, then, the notion of 'material interests' was not merely an analytical tool. It was a concept that had political relevance in contemporary discussions about the stability of the social and political order in general. Burckhardt was not merely concerned with the analysis of the fall of the Greek *polis*. Rather, he used his historiographical narrative to define a stance in political controversies of the day. As contemporary France showed, the lessons of history were crucial ones:

> Erbärmlich und hilflos ist die Lage überall, wo von unten herauf und durch die Presse regiert wird, aber so elend wie in Frankreich geht es doch nirgends. Selbst Boulanger ist nur *pétulance* und *contrefaçon* und gar alles ist *réclame* ... Frankreich ... wird von Strebern bis aufs Mark aufgefressen. So kann' s aber noch lange gehen! Die Griechenstaaten haben über zweihundert Jahre so geserbelt, bis die Bevölkerung sich allmählich aufgerieben hatte und die Verödung eintrat, d.h. zwei Drittel der Städte nur noch menschenleere Trümmer waren. Wo Streber gewaltet haben, erhebt sich die Tyrannis nur noch momentan und lokal, und das Strebertum wird immer wieder Meister. Wenn nicht die Römer drüber gekommen wären, hätte auch der Rest der Nation sich aufgezehrt. Also Geduld! Und richte man sich aufs dauernde Elend ein. JBB (n. 3, above), IX, 125-26.

Wherever the government is run from below and by the press, the situation is miserable and hopeless, but nowhere are matters more desolate than in France. Even Boulanger is only *pétulance* and *contrefaçon* and everything is *réclame* ... France is being devoured to the bone by opportunists. But this can go on for years to come! The Greek states kept warring until the population gradually wiped itself out and desolation ensued, that is, when two-thirds of the cities were depopulated ghost-towns. Where opportunists had ruled, tyranny arose only temporarily and locally, and opportunism always reasserted itself. If the Romans had not arrived, the rest of the nation would have destroyed itself as well. Therefore, patience! We must prepare for a protracted period of misery.

According to Fustel, too, Greek history ended in a long period of agony that began with the Peloponnesian War and lasted until the Roman conquest. For him, this agony continued in incessant struggles over the redistribution of wealth even in the Roman Empire, though with diminished force. Yet he found a great many apologetic, even respectful words, in particular for Athenian democracy.[25] Burckhardt, in contrast, depicted a social process of disintegration in his *Griechische Kulturgeschichte* that picked up speed after the Peloponnesian War.

His prediction about the outcome of the crisis in contemporary France, however, did not fully converge with his historiographical staging of decline in ancient Greece. There was, according to Burckhardt, one essential difference between modern Europe and Greek

---

25 *La Cité antique*, 399ff.

antiquity. The Greeks could not find a way out of democracy and thus succumbed to ruinous civil wars:

> Welches aber auch die Leiden und Wirren sein mochten, tatsächlich behauptet sich immer die Demokratie als das jetzt einzig Mögliche, und auch wenn sie gelegentlich in jene Tyrannis der spätern Art umschlägt, so stellt sie sich stets wieder irgendwie her. Als Timoleon in Sizilien auftrat, schauderten die Sikelioten vor allem, was Rednerbühne und Agora hieß, weil von daher alle Tyrannien über sie gekommen waren, aber auch Timoleon konnte nichts als überall Demokratien herstellen. Auf diesem Boden wächst nichts anderes mehr, bis die großen Monarchien kommen.
>
> *Griechische Kulturgeschichte* I [= *GW,* V] 253.

Whatever its trials and tribulations, democracy actually always asserts itself as the only possibility left. Even when it occasionally turns into a tyranny of the later type, it always reconstitutes itself somehow. When Timoleon appeared in Sicily, the Sicilians were horrified by everything that went by the name of rostrum and assembly place since from those all tyrants had descended upon them. But even Timoleon was unable to do anything but restore democracies everywhere. On this soil nothing else will grow any more until the great monarchies arrive.

Modern nation states, however, maintained large standing armies. That was why they did not succumb to the anarchy of civil war that was the necessary fate of democracies. After a succession of serious social upheavals, Burckhardt predicted, these modern nation states would turn into ruthless military dictatorships. Here, too, the much-lauded Basel prophet erred. Let me conclude this first part by suggesting that the more Burckhardt ostensibly detached himself from the content of his narrative and insisted on an apolitical stance, the more fiercely he effectively engaged in contemporary political controversy and polemic.

II Culture and war – the enhancement of existence and the aestheticization of history

In Burckhardt's eyes, the trend towards democracy threatened to destroy Western civilization since it diminished man's capacity to create and maintain 'high culture'. He thought that democratic forms of government inevitably lowered human motivation to a level so base that it could not sustain cultural production in the higher sense. The fall of society into a state of lawlessness was always an imminent possibility for him. This does not imply that Burckhardt considered any other form of political constitution as inherently conducive to cultural creativity. Rather, he thought that the greatness of an age, that is, above all its cultural productivity, depended on the quota of individuals willing and able to make personal sacrifices. The willingness to make sacrifices thus acquired cardinal importance in Burckhardt's philosophy of history. What does he mean by this notion? And how does it play itself out in his *Griechische Kulturgeschichte*?

II.i Heroism versus utilitarianism

Claude Lévi-Strauss observed that every form of humanism strove in the end 'to separate human beings from each other and to claim for an ever more exclusive minority the privilege of a humanism that was corrupted from the start'.[26] Those who endorse the image of an ideal human existence, according to Lévi-Strauss, were easily tempted to monopolize this ideal for themselves. Ultimately, this amounted to 'denying others a comparable degree of humanity'.[27] With this in mind, let us return to Burckhardt and his *Griechische Kulturgeschichte*.

In this text, Burckhardt drew a fundamental distinction between two forms of existence along a dividing-line that appears in Homer and Hesiod: that of the *heros* (that is, the warrior-hero) and that of the *banausos* (that is, the utilitarian trader and craftsman). The upshot of his comparison, illustrated with reference to the *Odyssey*, reads as follows:

... ein stärkerer Gegensatz läßt sich allerdings nicht denken als der zwischen dem Banausen und derjenigen Denkweise, die es darauf ankommen läßt, ob man sterbend dem Feinde Siegesruhm verschafft oder siegend von ihm solchen gewinnt.
Griechische Kulturgeschichte IV [= *GW*, VIII] 42.

It is hard to imagine a starker contrast than that between the *banausos* and the mentality of those men who put their life at risk in battle in order that in death they may hand the glory of victory to the enemy or, as victors, win glory for themselves.

For Burckhardt, the willingness to risk a violent death characterized a special form of existence. Untainted by any base utilitarian considerations, the hero distinguished himself by his ability to develop and sustain a truly aesthetic outlook on life. Burckhardt regarded this aesthetic disposition as a defining feature of Western culture and a reason for its superiority over all others. In other words, he granted the attribute 'fully human' only to those who accomplished something special by raising themselves above the level of 'mere existence', that is, far above utilitarian ends and material interests. In the light of Lévi-Strauss's reflections, we are evidently dealing with a special type of humanism here – one that not only deprives those who belong to foreign cultures of a comparable degree of humanity, but, in addition, draws such a distinction within Western culture itself.

Again, Burckhardt was not alone in endorsing this point of view. In the eighteenth century, the leading distinction in philosophical reflections on culture involved public versus private interests. The ideologues of the nineteenth century saw the crucial fault-line as running between idealistic and material interests, between human activity directed towards cultural ends and those drives and instincts that were determined by nature. Belief in the validity of this distinction easily generated paranoia about the state of culture. What would happen if material interests increasingly gained the upper hand? For Burckhardt (as for Tocqueville), there was little doubt that men would first lose the capacity for great cultural achievements, then the ability to wage war; politics would gradually degenerate into a mere struggle over the distribution of wealth; and finally society as a whole would stagger from one civil war to the next.

It evidently did not occur to them to question whether it made sense to speak of 'material interests' and 'motivations determined by nature' in the context of society. For a growing portion of intellectuals, who conceived of themselves as apostles of 'high culture' while at the same time affecting a deep pessimism about the future of Western culture, the humanity of their

---

26 Quoted in W. Lepenies and H. H. Ritter (eds), *Orte des Wilden Denkens. Zur Anthropologie von Claude Lévi-Strauss* (Frankfurt 1970) 137.
27 C. Lévi-Strauss, *Die traurigen Tropen* (Cologne 1960) 141.

fellow Europeans was not a full humanity at all if it remained below a certain threshold of 'idealistic' commitment. Many a cultural critic at the time was obsessed with averting the threat of cultural decline and thereby rescuing Western civilization from suffocating in the quagmire of materialism. Let us consider the solution Burckhardt had to offer.

II.ii *War as a means of enhancing existence*

Book One of *Griechische Kulturgeschichte* contains a brief but revealing discussion of the causes of the defeat of Athens in the Peloponnesian War. Despite the protracted nature of the conflict, Burckhardt considered the city's collapse as regrettably swift:

> Athen nach seiner bisherigen Geschichte und seinem Hochgefühl hätte im Grunde etwas mehr verzweifelten Widerstand (ἀπόνοια) leisten können.
> *Griechische Kulturgeschichte* I [= *GW*, V] 213.

Considering its previous history and elation, one could have expected Athens to put up a somewhat more desperate resistance (ἀπόνοια).

In his view, Athenian democracy had been thriving on an extraordinary *pathos*, which he regarded as a source of great moral strength to the citizenry. This *pathos* should have enabled it to resist the Spartans longer. The key phrase to note here is 'desperate resistance': a seemingly innocuous formulation at the time, but politically incriminated for us to-day. Burckhardt continued:

> Die (wohlbemerkt äußerst zahlreichen) Oligarchen aber, indem sie (405 v. Chr.) den letzten Widerstand ... brechen halfen, beförderten aus allen Kräften die Niederlage der Vaterstadt, weil jeder Sieg derselben doch nur ein Sieg des Demos gewesen wäre...

But the (indeed, very numerous) oligarchs promoted the defeat of their city to the best of their ability by helping to break the last resistance in 405 BC, because every victory of their city would only have been a victory for the *demos* ...

The oligarchs, in other words, thwarted that 'desperate resistance', that final heroic effort, to which Burckhardt attached so much importance. It failed to happen not because of a lack of energy but because of internal strife: the class struggle between rich and poor, which was ultimately fuelled by material interests. Athens failed in its world-historical duty because material interests had already begun to dominate politics. Insofar as it failed to play its part, Athens deprived European history of a wonderful example of desperate heroism. The question arises: why was this kind of heroism so important to Burckhardt?

The answer to this question can be found in the lectures *On the Study of History*, where Burckhardt articulated his theory of the moral dimension of war. For future reference, it is important to note that Nietzsche attended some of these lectures, and knew either the manuscript or the main ideas:

> Ein Volk lernt wirklich seine volle Nationalkraft nur im Kriege <, im vergleichenden Kampf gegen andere Völker > kennen, weil sie nur dann vorhanden ist; auf diesem Punct wird es dann suchen müssen, sie festzuhalten; allgemeine Vergrößerung des Maßstabes.
> *Über das Studium der Geschichte* 344.

Only in war, only in its competitive struggle with other nations, does a people really become aware of its full national energy, for this energy manifests itself only in war. The people will then strive to maintain its energy at this level. [The result is a] general enhancement of the standard.

Burckhardt thus advances the following two arguments. First, war was the ideal medium to raise human existence above the basic impulses of nature. If life had an inherent tendency to strive towards a vital summit, then athletic competition in the sense of the Greek *agon* did not suffice. War mobilized energies in a much more intensive fashion. Secondly, war raised the standard of all. The experience of war created new yardsticks of intensive communication and devotion to a common cause, both in the individual and even more so in the community. If a people managed to preserve this newly acquired standard of existential intensity, then their ability to muster resources and strive tenaciously for higher goals would result in cultural achievements. Burckhardt's philosophy of history posited a systematic correlation between the cohesiveness of a civic community and its cultural productivity.[28]

Why should this be the case? Burckhardt offered the following explanation:

Der lange Friede bringt nicht nur Entnervung hervor, sondern er läßt das Entstehen einer Menge jämmerlicher, angstvoller Nothexistenzen zu, welche ohne ihn nicht entständen und sich dann doch mit lautem Geschrei um 'Recht' irgendwie an das Dasein klammern, und den wahren Kräften den Platz vorwegnehmen und die Luft verdicken, im Ganzen auch das Geblüt der Nation verunedlen. Der Krieg bringt wieder die wahren Kräfte zu Ehren. <Jene jämmerlichen Nothexistenzen bringt er wenigstens zum Schweigen? – >[29]

Über das Studium der Geschichte 344-45.

Long periods of peace not only cause enervation, they also allow the emergence of a host of wretched characters [Nothexistenzen] whose despicable, fearful lives would not otherwise be possible. Then these characters try to preserve their existence somehow by making a great fuss about 'rights' and thus deprive the true forces of their space. They thicken the air and also generally debase the national stock. War restores the glory of the true forces. <At least it silences these wretched characters?>

Thus Burckhardt described the evolutionary profits (in the Darwinian sense of the 'survival of the fittest') that accrued to a community in and through war. The balance of power among

---

[28] He used this idea to explain the astonishing vibrancy of Athenian cultural activities after the Persian Wars: see *Griechische Kulturgeschichte* I [= *GW*, V] 208-11.

[29] In this context, Burckhardt explicitly referred to the following plea by Heinrich Leo, published in the *Volksblatt* of June 1853: 'Gott erlöse uns von der europäischen Völkerfäulnis und schenke uns einen frischen, fröhlichen Krieg, der Europa durchtobt, die Bevölkerung sichtet und das skrophulose Gesindel zertritt, was jetzt den Raum zu eng macht, um noch ein ordentliches Menschenleben in der Stickluft führen zu können.' ('May God redeem us from the corruption of the European peoples and grant us a fresh, merry war that will rage through Europe, weed out the population and crush the scrofulous rabble which spreads out so much these days that it is no longer possible to lead a proper human life in this stifling air.') It is important to note that the conception of war as beneficial for the hygiene of a people had nothing to do with official military doctrine. Burckhardt compiled his theory of history from a number of diverse sources.

the various social 'types' of a nation underwent drastic shifts. Since war involved great efforts and high risks, those types would gain in importance who were able to meet the demands of war and willingly subject themselves to the highest exertions and dangers. Types lacking in this ability would lose in rank and prestige. As a result, extreme talents, whether in the area of instrumental skills or the moral aptitude to make personal sacrifices, would quickly start to flourish.

Burckhardt made no secret of his antipathy to 'rights' and 'securities'. The existence of 'rights', he believed, produced a moral disposition towards the material interests of everyday life; as a result, men became incapable of taking risks and making sacrifices. His theory of war and his demonization of material interests were intimately connected. He summarized this connection thus:

> Sodann enorme sittliche Superiorität des Krieges über den bloßen gewaltsamen Egoismus des Einzelnen: er entwickelt die Kräfte im Dienst eines Allgemeinen und zwar des höchsten Allgemeinen (Der Krieg allein gewährt den Menschen den großartigen Anblick der allgemeinen Unterordnung unter ein Allgemeines), und innerhalb einer Disciplin, welche zugleich die höchste heroische Tugend sich ent <falten> läßt.
>
> *Über das Studium der Geschichte* 345.

War, then, possesses an enormous ethical superiority vis-à-vis the sheer brutal egotism of the individual: war develops forces in the service of a general good (war alone grants men the great spectacle of a collective's complete subordination to a general goal) and that within a discipline that allows the blossoming of the highest heroic virtue.

War, for Burckhardt, was superior to a duel or the Greek *agon*, because it taught the individual to overcome his egoism and to subordinate himself to a common goal. The passage above suffices to show that Burckhardt cannot justifiably be called a 'liberal', not even an *Altliberaler* ('liberal of the old school') for he evidently regarded the subordination of the individual to a collective goal as 'ethically superior' to the pursuit of private goals. War and aristocratic competition (*agon*) surpass the utilitarian outlook on life as well as the main elements of liberal-bourgeois society, that is, the exchange of goods, which Burckhardt contemptuously called 'trade'.

As goes without saying, individual self-sacrifice, in Burckhardt's eyes, was a moral phenomenon. Human beings raised themselves above the level of everyday life and their mundane interests in order to work together in the service of an idea and a common cause that demanded complete devotion. But this moral phenomenon, for him, was simultaneously an aesthetic event; or, put the other way, this moral event contained an aesthetic dimension. For it was a 'great spectacle', as Burckhardt called it in one of the marginal comments quoted above. The aestheticization of war will be on the agenda shortly. But before we turn to this problem, we need to discuss Burckhardt's conception of total war.

II.iii The invention of total war and the anxiety about the survival of culture

For Burckhardt, war signified more than the brief military engagement of two opposing armies. Ideally, the entire existence of a people was to be at stake. This was most likely to happen in a defensive war:

Nur müßte es womöglich ein gerechter und ehrenvoller Krieg sein, etwa ein Vertheidigungskrieg wie der Perserkrieg war, welcher die Kräfte der Hellenen in allen Richtungen glorreich entwickelte. Ferner ein wirklicher Krieg um das gesammte Dasein.

Über das Studium der Geschichte 345.

But probably it would have to be a just and honourable war, for instance, a defensive war like the Persian War, which gloriously developed the forces of the Hellenes in every respect. Furthermore, it would have to be a true war, in which the entire existence [of a nation] is at stake.

It is important to realize that with these observations Burckhardt here diverged from the theorists of war who were in vogue in the middle of the nineteenth century. Carl von Clausewitz, for one, the great Prussian theorist of war, maintained the exact opposite. Like Carl Schmitt later on, Clausewitz considered it a twofold triumph of European modernity that wars had become limited and no longer affected the existence of entire peoples and that, moreover, warring nations began to distinguish sharply between combatants and non-combatants. Burckhardt, on the other hand, sketched the basis for a theory of 'total war' that stood in sharp contrast to the official military doctrines endorsed in Prussia and elsewhere at the time.

This point merits further elaboration. In Book 7 of *On War*, which appeared in its second edition in 1853, Clausewitz discussed the difference between 'absolute' and 'real' war. 'Absolute' war came closest to realizing an ideal type of war since it aimed at the total annihilation of the hostile forces. 'Real' war, on the other hand, for a multitude of reasons did not quite reach this Platonic ideal of warfare. Clausewitz showed how in modern times, in particular in the course of the eighteenth century, wars had become increasingly demilitarized: risks and dangers diminished, the population no longer took part in battle, engagements turned into mere skirmishes for diplomatic reasons, in which the existential tension and intensity of warfare could no longer be felt. This, however, changed once again with the French Revolutionary Wars and especially the Napoleonic Wars, which Clausewitz described as the great caesura in modern military conflict:[30]

Der Krieg war urplötzlich wieder eine Sache des Volkes geworden, und zwar eines Volkes von 30 Mio, die sich alle als Staatsbürger betrachteten. ... Seit Bonaparte also hat der Krieg, indem er zuerst auf der einen Seite, dann auf der anderen wieder Sache des ganzen Volkes wurde, eine ganz andere Natur angenommen, oder vielmehr, er hat sich seiner wahren Natur, seiner absoluten Vollkommenheit sehr genähert.

All of a sudden, war was again a matter of the people, and a people of 30 million at that, who all deemed themselves citizens. ... Since the days of Napoleon, war, by becoming a matter of the people again first on one side, then on the other, has taken on a completely different nature, or rather, it has come very close to its true nature, its absolute perfection.

It is important to note, however, that what Clausewitz called 'absolute war' was different from the 'total war' that Spengler and Ludendorff propagated in the 1920s and 1930s, although, at

---

30 Carl von Clausewitz, *Vom Kriege. Vollständige Ausgabe im Urtext*, ed. W. Hahlweg, 17th edn (Bonn 1966) 868 and 870.

first sight, it appears as if he anticipated their notion. First of all, the aim of Clausewitz's 'absolute war' was the annihilation of the enemy forces. This was precisely what Clausewitz deemed praiseworthy about Carnot and especially Napoleon. These generals heightened the importance of victory on the battlefield and decisively changed the logic of warfare. The unconditional attack on the main enemy forces became the main strategic operation and the quick decision on the battlefield the primary aim of war. Accordingly, the Prussian theorist distinguished sharply between combatants and non-combatants. Secondly, war, for him, always remained subordinated to politics.

In contrast, total war mobilized an entire nation in its service, and erased the distinction between combatants and non-combatants. Hence Ludendorff, in his book on 'total war', published in 1935, explicitly rejected Clausewitz's view of war:

> Das Wesen des Krieges hat sich geändert, das Wesen der Politik hat sich geändert, so muß sich auch das Verhältnis der Politik zur Kriegführung ändern. Alle Theorien von Clausewitz sind über den Haufen zu werfen. Krieg und Politik dienen der Lebenserhaltung des Volkes, der Krieg aber ist die höchste Äußerung völkischen Lebenswillens. Darum hat die Politik der Kriegführung zu dienen.   E. Ludendorff, *Der totale Krieg* (Munich 1935) 10.

The character of war has changed, the character of politics has changed and therefore the relation between politics and warfare must change as well. All of Clausewitz's theories are to be discarded. War and politics both serve the preservation of a nation's life, but war is the highest expression of a people's will to life. That is why politics needs to be subservient to warfare.

According to Ludendorff, war represented the greatest exertion a people could undertake to guarantee their continued existence. Therefore, as he remarked on the same page, 'total politics' had to 'take measures even in periods of peace to prepare a people's struggle for survival in war'.

Ludendorff thus radicalized the problem: if wars were struggles that always implicated the existence of an entire people, then peace was nothing but a brief truce, an interval to be used to prepare for the next round of combat. Ludendorff's take on war was not so much military as political. And it was so in a new sense: all considerations now revolved around the perpetual struggle of a people for their continued existence.

II.iv Cultural and hygienic consequences of a radicalized war

It turns out that the first widely-read German-speaking author to formulate a concept of 'total war' was Jacob Burckhardt. This is a little embarrassing for the Burckhardt hagiographers, not least because, ever since the end of World War II, they have held up his historiography as a positive alternative to Ranke's statism and the militant nationalism of the Prussian School. To be sure, Burckhardt can hardly be made responsible for the theories of total war proffered by Spengler and Ludendorff, which differed quite dramatically, in many ways, from the relevant observations in *On the Study of History* and the *Griechische Kulturgeschichte*. Still, Spengler's remark that 'war is the eternal form of higher human existence; the purpose of states is war; their very existence signifies a readiness for war',[31] if it partly surpassed Burckhardt, also partly alluded to his definition of the Greek *polis* as a semi-totalitarian organization meant to ensure survival.[32]

The concept of total war was significant for Burckhardt because he posited that a civic community could carry over the existential intensity reached during war into times of peace. On the basis of this presupposition Burckhardt developed several claims with a strong exhortatory character: war was to be a means by which to reach a more intense form of being; but the ultimate purpose of this intensity was not future warfare, but cultural achievements. In other words, war set a standard, but it was not to be the permanent condition of human civilization. Burckhardt's judgements of Sparta illustrate this train of thought: they tend to be very respectful, but betray little sympathy (*Griechische Kulturgeschichte* I [= *GW,* V] 102-10).

The authors of the Conservative Revolution and the ideologues of war in the 1920s were able to use this chain of arguments for their own ends. They only needed to intensify Burckhardt's claims concerning the suffocation of culture in material interests. In their polemics against this threat, they resorted to the following hypothesis: only in permanent armed conflict could man retain his cultural dimension and rise above material interests; once this struggle abated, society was unable to sustain the level of spiritual intensity attained in war; as soon as peace set in, this intensity degenerated completely. Permanent war was therefore vital for the preservation of culture since it was the only means by which the willingness of the entire community to make the necessary sacrifices could be kept at a consistently high level. Authors of the so-called 'war-generation' – Spengler, Jünger, Heidegger – fomented to the point of paranoia this fear of cultural decline, of sinking into the morass of material interests or a state of inauthenticity. But hardly anybody articulated this fear as vehemently as Burckhardt: his thoughts on war and culture were available, in written form, from 1905, when Jacob Oeri published his lectures *On the Study of History* under the title *Weltgeschichtliche Betrachtungen*. True, Nietzsche provided more radical and earlier formulations of this topic, but these were inspired, to a considerable extent, by Burckhardt's lectures, which Nietzsche attended in 1870/71. I shall return to this point.

To be sure, Burckhardt, in some respects, only configured a new pattern of thought out of discursive positions readily available at the time. Yet the way in which he formulated the problem of cultural decline was more radical – and so were his solutions. As we have seen, he did not derive his radicalized notion of war from contemporary military theorists like Clausewitz. It seems that he drew it from his study of ancient warfare. In his eyes, wars in antiquity differed fundamentally from modern wars:

Ganz besonders aber sind die heutigen Kriege zwar wohl Theile Einer großen allgemeinen Crisis, aber einzeln für sich ohne die Bedeutung und Wirkung echter Crisen; das bürgerliche Leben bleibt dabei in seinem Geleise (und grade die jämmerlichen Nothexistenzen bleiben alle am Leben), sie hinterlassen aber enorme Schulden, d.h. sie sparen die Hauptcrisis für die Zukunft zusammen. Auch ihre kurze Dauer nimmt ihnen den Werth als Crisen; die vollen

---

[31] 'Krieg ist die ewige Form höheren menschlichen Daseins, und Staaten sind um des Krieges willen da; sie sind Ausdruck der Bereitschaft zum Kriege.' O. Spengler, *Preussentum und Sozialismus* (Munich 1920) 52.
[32] Cf. *Griechische Kulturgeschichte* I [= *GW,* V] 57-79.

> Kräfte der Verzweiflung werden nicht angespannt, bleiben aber auch nachher nicht siegreich auf dem Schlachtfeld stehen; – und doch könnte nur durch sie die wahre Erneuerung des Lebens erfolgen, d.h. die versöhnende Abschaffung des Alten durch ein wirklich lebendiges Neues. *Über das Studium der Geschichte* 345.

> In particular, the wars of today may well be parts of a great general crisis, but in themselves, they lack the significance and the effect of true crises. Bourgeois life continues more or less as before (and precisely the wretched characters all remain alive). At the same time, these wars accumulate enormous debts, that is to say, they save the main crisis for the future. Their short duration, too, prevents them from becoming a true crisis. The full forces of desperation are not exerted and hence cannot emerge victorious on the battlefield. Only they, however, could bring about a real renewal of life: the conciliatory abolition of the old by a genuinely vital new.

Burckhardt makes three interesting points here, all of which were to have repercussions in the discourses of the New Right and the fascists.

First, there is the idea of a renewal of life through war, of abolishing the old through something vital and new. The Futurists only had to replace the expression 'conciliatory abolition' with 'violent abolition' and Burckhardt's observation could be used as a blueprint for the glorification of modern war.

Second, Burckhardt regretted the brevity of modern wars. Clausewitz, as we have seen, evaluated this issue rather differently. One question that arises is what wars Burckhardt had in mind when he referred to 'the wars of today'. This is not easy to determine. It seems safe to exclude the American Civil War: Burckhardt systematically ignored it. In fact, Burckhardt simply failed to make clear his point of comparison, presumably because he evaluated 'the wars of today' on the basis of an 'ideal type' of warfare he thought he could locate in antiquity. If Burckhardt had been interested in validating this notion empirically, he would have been faced with insurmountable problems: the length of the Peloponnesian War and the first two Punic Wars were the exception in antiquity. But Burckhardt seems little concerned with facts. What mattered to him was the construction of a model – and its message that if wars were short, then they would not permeate all of society.

The idea that all available social resources had to be mobilized in a civic community's struggle for survival was a central element of the rhetoric of total war. The inevitable consequence, or implicit premise, of this postulate was the subordination of all social activities to the necessities of war. If war did not affect all areas of social life, then those 'jämmerliche Nothexistenzen' would remain alive – in Burckhardt's view a clearly undesirable outcome – and only a few members of society would develop the capacity for self-sacrifice. Unmoved, Burckhardt drew the chilling conclusions from his premises: war not only served as a moral 'purification' insofar as it forced men to raise themselves above their everyday lives and material interests; it also served to cleanse a people in social terms insofar as it eliminated the part of the population that was unable to raise itself to the level of high moral exertion. As we shall see, this 'social cleansing' contained aspects of 'racial hygiene'.

Third, there was Burckhardt's concern with the mobilization of the 'full forces of desperation'. This expression became a key term in the militant rhetoric of the German war-generation during the 1920s, and hence a fixture in the repertory of that ideology which prepared the ground for the National Socialists. That generation regarded it as axiomatic that only 'desperate heroism' could bring about both victory and a genuine renewal of the German people.

II.v The aestheticization of war

Alongside its moral and social components, war, for Burckhardt, also possessed an aesthetic dimension. War could become a 'great spectacle' of the 'subordination of the entire community under a common goal'. What was Burckhardt's rationale for aestheticizing war? War as an aesthetic experience became possible only when the different moral reasons for individual and collective sacrifice had ceased to be of any great importance. It comes as no surprise that Burckhardt ultimately downgraded the significance of moral aspects and turned the beautiful into the sole point of reference:

> Das Wahre und Gute mannigfach zeitlich gefärbt und bedingt; aber die Hingebung <zumal die mit Gefahr und Opfern verbundene> an das zeitlich bedingte Wahre und Gute ist etwas unbedingt Herrliches. Das Schöne freilich könnte über die Zeiten und ihren Wechsel erhaben sein, bildet überhaupt eine Welt für sich.
>
> *Über das Studium der Geschichte* 230.

The True and the Good are historically coloured and conditioned in many different ways; but devotion <in particular, devotion involving danger and sacrifice> to the historically contingent True and Good is something unconditionally magnificent. The Beautiful indeed might transcend the times and their changes altogether. It represents a world of its own.

For Burckhardt, the self-sacrifice of individuals, larger groups or entire political communities for an idea represented 'something unconditionally magnificent'. This should be taken quite literally: when Burckhardt says 'unconditional', he means 'absolute', that is, regardless of the ends pursued and regardless of the moral significance of the actions involved. Self-sacrifice in war, for him, represented the ultimate indicator of a nation's ability to act out of spiritual and cultural motives.

Let us consider the implications of Burckhardt's point of view. Imagine the 'spectacle' of German SS units on the Eastern Front in the winter of 1944/45, taking a last heroic stand against the superior forces of the Red Army and thus allowing the continuation of industrial mass slaughter in Auschwitz. In purely aesthetic terms, there is no difference between their self-sacrifice and that of the three hundred Spartans at Thermopylae. From an *aesthetic* point of view, both events have the same quality.[33]

---

[33] Burckhardt insisted repeatedly on defending the disposition towards self-sacrifice against moral objections: 'Die Größe einer Zeitepoche hängt an der Quote der Aufopferungsfähigen, nach welcher Seite es auch sei ... Hingebung an eine Sache, welche es auch sei, mit gänzlichem Absterben der persönlichen Eitelkeit.' ('The greatness of an age depends on the proportion of those willing to sacrifice themselves, regardless for what cause ... Devotion to a cause, whatever it is, with complete disregard for personal vanity.') Jacob Burckhardt Archiv, PA 207, 131 recto, quoted in J. Große, *Typus und Geschichte. Eine Jacob-Burckhardt-Interpretation* (Cologne, Weimar, Vienna 1997) 436 n.76. This definition of greatness fits the case of the warrior much better than that of the artist. Jörn Rüsen offers a very precise discussion of Burckhardt's 'aestheticization of history': cf. 'Jacob Burckhardt', in

In other words, Burckhardt discussed the moral phenomena of war and self-sacrifice within an amoral framework. He had no other choice. In order to emphasize the significance of war and sacrifice for 'high culture', he had to remain neutral towards the moral dimension of warfare. At the beginning of the twenty-first century, this moral indifference has become deeply problematic. But even in the context of nineteenth-century historiography, Burckhardt's posture represented something of an anomaly. Most of his colleagues believed in progress and the inherent value of the nation, and for those very reasons could not grant the same kind of moral dispensation upon which Burckhardt insisted. For Theodor Mommsen, for example, history implied not just political but also moral progress.

In stark contrast to 'liberal' historians, Burckhardt had nothing but contempt for human rights – as for rights in general. It is quite impossible to recognize human rights and show moral indifference towards violent social processes. Burckhardt tore asunder the traditional triad of the good, the beautiful, and the true. He historicized (and thereby relativized) the good and the true, while exalting the beautiful as a transhistorical absolute. Historiographically speaking, this meant that the most disastrous catastrophes could offer magnificent spectacles of desperate heroism and total devotion:

> Ganz anders stellen sich zu unserm Gefühl diejenigen Bevölkerungen, von deren letzten Kämpfen und Untergang Kunde erhalten ist: die lycischen Städte gegen Harpagus, Carthago, Numantia, Jerusalem gegen Titus. Solche scheinen uns aufgenommen in die Reihe von Lehrern und Vorbildern der Menschheit in der Einen großen Sache: daß man an das Gemeinsame Alles setze und daß das Einzelleben der Güter höchstes nicht sei. Sodaß aus ihrem Unglück ein herbes, aber erhabenes Glück für das Ganze ensteht.
>
> *Über das Studium der Geschichte* 242.

Those nations whose last struggles and fall are documented elicit a completely different reaction in us: the Lycian cities against Harpagus, Carthage, Numantia, Jerusalem against Titus. These seem to belong to the ranks of models for humankind in that they teach us the greatest of all lessons: that one has to devote everything to the common cause and that individual existence is not the highest of goods. Thus from their misfortune there arises a bitter, but sublime happiness for the whole.

This passage makes clear why Burckhardt was not satisfied with the Athenian surrender in 405 BC. His was an aesthetic dissatisfaction. The fall of the Athenians was not a magnificent spectacle. With their swift surrender, the Athenians deprived later generations of a beautiful scene of struggle and destruction. According to Burckhardt's philosophy of history, catastrophes had to be incorporated into an ideal image, an image of eternal beauty that occidental humanity could hand down from generation to generation through its poets and historians, who were to disregard moral considerations and focus exclusively on the sublime and the consolation of the beautiful.

It would be possible to trace many of the thoughts that Burckhardt brought into a systematic correlation in the works of other nineteenth-century authors. An intertextual analysis could

---

Deutsche Historiker, ed. H.-U. Wehler (Göttingen 1972), III, 3-28; see also his 'Die Uhr der die Stunde schlägt' (n. 22, above).

A COMMENT ON EGON FLAIG'S ESSAY

LIONEL GOSSMAN

The history of our century has made younger German scholars – to their immense credit – particularly sensitive to elements in Burckhardt's work that were overlooked in traditional interpretations. Johannes Wenzel, Hannelore and Heinz Schlaffer, and more recently Professor Flaig,[1] both in his book on the *Griechische Kulturgeschichte* and in the brilliant paper he presented at the Princeton conference, have underlined what I myself have long tended to think of as a dangerous intellectual dandyism in Burckhardt, an anti-bourgeois, anti-utilitarian aestheticism that reminds one more of Tocqueville's friend Gobineau than of the liberal Tocqueville himself, with whom Burckhardt had otherwise much in common.[2]

Curiously enough, the same twentieth-century history, at the very time that it was being lived, led other scholars – particularly the German refugee scholars who, in the early 1940s, expanded awareness of Burckhardt in the English-speaking world beyond the familiar *Civilization of the Renaissance in Italy* – to underscore quite different aspects of Burckhardt: his scepticism with respect to philosophies of history, his rejection of the '*terribles simplificateurs*', his anti-statism and anti-nationalism, his horror of fanaticism, violence, and cruelty. In Germany itself, this was the Burckhardt promoted courageously – in opposition to the nihilist heroics and theatricality of the National Socialists – just before and even during the Second World War by Alfred von Martin, the Munich sociologist who resigned his teaching position shortly after the National Socialists came to power in 1933.[3]

Support for both readings – that of Wenzel and the Schlaffers and that of von Martin – can be found in Burckhardt. There are many strands in his work and they do not always come together harmoniously. It is unlikely that Burckhardt himself would have been much troubled by that. He preferred plurality to unity, inclusiveness to coherence, and he valued liberty far more highly than equality (which he tended not to distinguish from identity). He was considerably – and willingly – less systematic than some of his interpreters.

Professor Flaig has presented a disturbingly prefascist Burckhardt, a forerunner of Ernst Jünger or Henry de Montherlant. The Burckhardt I will present is the traditionally '*altliberal*' sceptical humanist, the Burckhardt denounced by the young Nazi historian Christoph Steding, a protégé of Carl Schmitt, in the shrill 800-page diatribe against Dutch and Swiss neutralism and liberalism that he published on the eve of World War II and that was twice reissued in the course of the War.[4] I would insist that Burckhardt's liberalism is part of his published record and not

---

1 J. Wenzel, *Jacob Burckhardt in der Krise seiner Zeit* (Berlin 1967); H. Schlaffer and H. Schlaffer, *Studien zum ästhetischen Historismus* (Frankfurt am Main 1975); E. Flaig, *Angeschaute Geschichte: zu Jacob Burckhardts 'Griechische Kulturgeschichte'* (Rheinfelden 1987).
2 See A. S. Kahan, *Aristocratic Liberalism in the Social and Political Thought of Jacob Burckhardt, John Stuart Mill, and Alexis de Tocqueville* (New York 1992).
3 Notably in *Nietzsche und Burckhardt* (Munich 1941). The Gestapo intervened to limit circulation of a second edition (1942). See also his *Die Religion Jacob Burckhardts* (Munich 1942).
4 *Das Reich und die Krankheit der europäischen Kultur* (Hamburg 1938).

simply, as Professor Flaig suggested, a private matter, evidence for which lies chiefly in personal statements to friends. To begin with, the correspondence is no less a 'text' than anything else Burckhardt wrote, especially since many of his 'texts' were published from the manuscripts of lectures intended for a limited Basel audience. Only the rhetorical situation of the letters is somewhat different from that of other texts in the Burckhardt canon. One could even argue that the correspondence is Burckhardt's greatest literary achievement. His decision to have as little as possible to do with the regular channels of commercial and scholarly publication in his time – which he saw as hostage to the demands of the market – virtually ensured that a great deal of literary energy and imagination would be expended not only on his lectures, but on the letters he wrote to his close friends. In addition, Burckhardt's liberalism is inscribed in the main texts – in the art historical writings as well as in the more familiar works of cultural history or the general reflections on history. His *writing* itself, with its kaleidoscopic perspectives, its brusque transitions, its sly ironies, its composition by accretion (it reminds me in some ways of Montesquieu), could be seen as quintessentially liberal.

To me, the interesting question raised by Professor Flaig is: What are the connections between fascism and a certain current of 'liberalism' that seems to have been more concerned with the individual as personality or individuality than with the individual as a bearer of rights and subject of moral decisions, the principle underlying which presents itself to that subject in terms of a universal law valid for all moral subjects? The idea of the individual as personality, I suspect, is close to the 'cultural' tradition of Herder and Goethe. An individual, in this sense, is always part of a larger culture but aims constantly to expand itself to embrace the thoughts, experiences, and points of view of other individuals and other cultures within the totality of human culture. The individual as bearer of rights, in contrast, belongs to the rationalist tradition and is arrived at by a process of abstraction and analysis. At the extreme limit, as Benjamin Constant suggested, this individual is emptied of content and falls victim to *anomie*. One strand of liberalism thus appears to emphasize the distinctiveness of each individual, another the equality of all individuals. Liberals of the first kind – and Burckhardt was probably one – seem most fearful of the encroachments of the state and the mediocrity allegedly induced by mass education, mass culture, and the mass media. What they apprehend is not so much injustice or a trampling of individual rights as the destruction of individuality and creativity.

But in what conditions does opposition to democracy, apprehended as the breeding ground of dictatorships, become – paradoxically – complicity with demagogic and despotic political movements? In what conditions do suspicion of the power of the state and fear of the 'mass' lead to acceptance of right-wing totalitarian or authoritarian regimes? One thinks of the notorious fracas over the significance of the work of Burckhardt's French contemporary, Fustel de Coulanges, the author of *La Cité antique* – the so-called '*bagarre Fustel*'. Fustel himself managed to avoid taking sides clearly between Left and Right (he died a few years before the Dreyfus Affair made that virtually impossible), but the tensions in his work were brought noisily to the fore in 1905, when a plan to mark the twenty-fifth anniversary of his death precipitated a bitter dispute between two factions both of which laid claim to his legacy. On one side, Charles Maurras and *Action française* with their emphasis on the historian's fear of democracy and the masses and on the importance he attributed to myth and religion as the foundation of social cohesion; on the other, his more liberally inclined, strongly republican students, Emile Durkheim and Gabriel Monod (a Jew and a Protestant), who, while certainly not repudiating the social theories of their teacher (Durkheim's sociology in particular is obviously marked by Fustel's reflections on myth and religion), emphasised his republicanism, his horror of dictatorship and tyranny, his commitment to liberty and individuality. Like Fustel, Burckhardt himself was lucky enough never to have been confronted with really hard choices. Later generations with views close to his did not escape so easily, however, and their responses were varied: from Thomas Mann's rejection of fascism and conversion to democracy, by way of the ambivalent acquiescence in authoritarian regimes of Paul Valéry or Ortega y Gasset, to the admittedly always somewhat diffident and ironical collaboration with fascism of Thierry Maulnier and Montherlant.[5] Fustel had already recognized the difficulty of occupying a detached neutral or liberal position. 'Il a toujours cherché à se détacher des factions', he wrote in his 1858 thesis on Polybius, in whom he appears to have seen a mirror image of himself, 'il a voulu rester neutre entre l'aristocratie et la démocratie. Mais les circonstances ne permettaient pas cette impartialité; et au moment décisif, il a dû agir exactement comme s'il appartenait à une faction ... Ainsi les sages eux-mêmes sont dominés par ces luttes qui remplissent la vie des cités; ils ne peuvent échapper aux factions.'[6]

***

The above comments, written in April 1999, were a response to the stimulating talk that Professor Flaig gave to a Princeton University audience on April 9, 1999. The version of that talk, which I was asked to review from the point of view of the English translation two years later, and which appears in this volume, is at least twice as long as the original paper and would require a different, fuller response. This is not the place for such a response. A couple of additional remarks do seem justified, however, since Professor Flaig has not been satisfied to mount an attack on Burckhardt as an enemy of democracy and the promoter of a dangerous

---

5 This question was the essential subject of a recent PhD thesis at Princeton University by Christine Foureau on a right-wing French periodical of the interwar period, *La Revue Universelle (1920-1940): Aux Origines du Pétainisme*. Foureau cites (p. 55) a telling passage by one contributor to the journal (Saint-Brice) in which fascism and 'bolshevism' are compared: 'Les deux systèmes partent de la faillite du libéralisme parlementaire pour chercher une formule de restauration de l'autorité dans la démocratie. Ainsi tous deux ont été amenés à concevoir la nécessité de l'unité politique et de la discipline rigoureuse. Ici s'arrêtent les rapprochements. Dans le système bolchévik la prétendue dictature du prolétariat aboutit à la mainmise de l'Etat sur les rouages de la vie économique, à la stérilisation des initiatives individuelles, à la stagnation et à l'exploitation des masses par quelques dirigeants. C'est exactement l'opposé des directives mussoliniennes. Dans la forme fasciste, l'Etat n'intervient que pour diriger, discipliner et contrôler. On réduit au minimum les interventions de l'Etat .... On stimule les initiatives individuelles. On les exalte en leur montrant comme but de la concentration des efforts la grandeur de la patrie. L'appel au travail est un appel à l'expansion nationale.' (15.5.1927) The individual as understood and defended by Burckhardt may well emerge from a different tradition from that of the Anglo-French Enlightenment. The individual as envisaged by Locke or Rousseau is the notional product of a process of rigorous abstraction; the individual, as Burckhardt conceives of him, is both an autonomous personality and at the same time part of a concrete historical and cultural whole from which he cannot be dissociated. The chief concern in the Anglo-French tradition is with individual rights; the chief concern in the alternative tradition is with the full and free cultural development of the individual human personality. Saint-Brice's article indicates that fascism was seen as compatible with the latter concern, whereas 'bolshevism' was hostile to it.
6 *Polybe, ou la Grèce conquise par les Romains*, ed. B. Hemmerdinger (Naples 1984 [Amiens 1859]) 28, 29.

tendency to aestheticize war and politics, but has challenged even the common view of him as an old-style liberal. At times it seems as if the apparently sceptical and liberal Swiss patrician was a greater source of political evil, albeit insidious and masked, than the statist and nationalist historians of the Second German Empire.

By focusing attention on Burckhardt's denial of the feasibility of *representative* government, Professor Flaig greatly enhances our understanding of the historian's political ideas. This section of the essay, as well as the close examination of the relation between Fustel and Burckhardt, is thoroughly convincing and illuminating – even if I would question Flaig's claim that Fustel was a pure academic who lacked Burckhardt's anti-democratic animus. Fustel in fact shared Bachofen's belief that religion and myth were the foundation of social cohesion and property. They were replaced in this role by law, but Fustel's work provided no clear answer to the question whether tradition or law provided a more secure foundation for property. Despite his assertion that historical comparisons of antiquity and modern times were misleading and anachronistic, and despite his sober, dispassionate writing style – the political implications of which have been well examined by Charles-Olivier Carbonell – *La Cité antique* was easily read as a cautionary tale of woe, the relevance of which to contemporary political and social developments no one in the France of the Second Empire and the early days of the Third Republic failed to perceive.[7]

Much of Professor Flaig's essay, however, seems at least as 'fraught with political agendas' as he claims Burckhardt's work was. He wishes to present a certain image of Burckhardt and quotes selectively in accordance with that aim. That there is an objective basis in Burckhardt's work for the kind of reading Professor Flaig offers is certain, but there is equally an objective basis for the kind of reading offered by Karl Löwith or Ernst Cassirer or Peter Gay. I have myself drawn attention to Burckhardt's deep hostility to democracy and to the particular use made of him during the years of the Cold War.[8] But the relation of liberalism and democracy has long been problematical and most liberals, including those who hoped to reconcile the two, have been fully aware of this.[9]

Professor Flaig considers that the term 'liberal' has become a 'political catchword' that lacks 'the analytical exactitude necessary to bring out with precision the pertinent differences between the diverse political stances and discourses that shape a period'. But 'liberal' seems no worse in this respect than many other terms of political discourse, including 'fascist' and 'democratic' (or, for that matter, most words in everyday language), and it is the task of political scientists and

---

7 C.-O. Carbonell, *Histoire et historiens: une mutation idéologique des historiens français 1865-1885* (Toulouse 1970). On Fustel's disclaimer of the contemporary relevance of his work, see B. Hemmerdinger, 'Fustel de Coulanges et la lutte des classes à Athènes et à Paris', *Belfagor* 34 (1979) 555 '... sous le Second Empire, un historien ne manque jamais de protester que son livre n'est pas un pamphlet contre le pouvoir'.

8 In a paper on 'Burckhardt in der angloamerikanischen Geisteswelt' presented at the Jacob-Burckhardt-Kolloquium in Basel, 30-31 May 1997, to appear in *Beiträge zu Jacob Burckhardt*; in 'Burckhardt in the Twentieth Century: Sketch of a *Rezeptionsgeschichte*' (originally given as a talk at the *Kunsthistorisches Institut*, Florence, 1999) in *Jacob Burckhardt: Storia della cultura, storia dell'arte*, ed. M. Ghelardi and M. Seidel (Venice 2002) 17-40; and in 'Burckhardt: Cold War Liberal?' (originally given as a talk at the *Internationales Forschungszentrum Kulturwissenschaften* Vienna, 2000) in *Journal of Modern History* 74 (2002) 538-72.

9 For a wonderfully clear, succinct account, see N. Bobbio, *Liberalism and Democracy* (London 1990).

historians constantly to define and redefine its shifting meanings in relation to the other terms of political discourse at any given time and in particular historical cases. Professor Flaig himself makes frequent use of the term, if only to deny that it can properly be applied to Burckhardt. Burckhardt's praise of war, for instance, and the accompanying claim that 'the subordination of the individual to a collective goal is "ethically superior" to the pursuit of private goals' are said to disqualify him as a liberal or even an *Altliberaler*. But the view that, in antiquity at least, war promoted human qualities of courage, dedication, self-sacrifice, etc., which inevitably languished in societies occupied with '*doux commerce*', was held by a fair number of the founding thinkers of modern liberalism. Montesquieu, Humboldt, and Constant immediately come to mind. Constant especially was deeply concerned with the question of ensuring a passionate devotion to liberty (by which he meant the liberty of all, not simply one's own) among citizens who are accustomed to act not out of passion but out of calculated self-interest. Even his literary masterpiece, *Adolphe*, is about the drying up of the capacity for passionate engagement in modern, educated, reflective men. Stendhal and Tocqueville had similar concerns, as did Mill and Arnold.

Like others, Burckhardt did sometimes see virtue in war, but does this mean that he was unequivocally in favour of total war (that is, war involving all the citizens, not just the military) as in antiquity or 'since Bonaparte' (hardly one of his heroes) in our modern, nationalist and democratic times? And does it not require some sleight of hand to slip from Burckhardt's belief that the dedication required by war sets a new standard in peace by raising men out of routine and mediocrity and making them capable of great things to the later claim of various spokesmen for the 'Conservative Revolution' that, as the intensity generated by war degenerates in peace, a state of permanent war is necessary to maintain culture?

I am therefore not sure how to take Professor Flaig's disclaimer, at the end of his essay, of any intention of 'arguing that Burckhardt was a proto-fascist or that he paved the way for National Socialism' or that his 'aestheticization of violence and war led directly to the militant ideologies of the 1920s and 1930s.' He himself asserts immediately after making that disclaimer that 'it was only a small step from aestheticization to justification'. What to me is at issue is not Burckhardt's reputation, but respect for the complexity – and sometimes contradictoriness – of texts and ideas.

Princeton University

PER ME SI VA NELLA CITTÀ DOLENTE: BURCKHARDT AND THE *POLIS*

LIONEL GOSSMAN

It will be useful to open this brief account of Burckhardt's rather bleak view of the ancient *polis* with some contextualization, however rudimentary, of his reflections on the topic.

The political and social context of those reflections, to my mind, is first, the gradual erosion, during Burckhardt's lifetime, of the sovereignty of the city-republic of Basel, of which he was a citizen, as the Swiss Confederation transformed itself from a *Staatenbund* or confederation of independent states into a *Bundestaat* or federal state; and second, the corresponding erosion, within Basel, of the traditional political dominance of the ruling merchant elite, in which the Burckhardt family was prominent. Among the high points of these twin developments were the uprising of the subject country districts against the city of Basel in 1830, the so-called *Basler Wirren* or 'Troubles', and the *Sonderbundkrieg* or Swiss Civil War of 1847.

After three years of violent hostilities, the *Basler Wirren* were brought to an end by a federally imposed settlement that divided the state into two separate, independent half-cantons: Basel-Stadt and Basel-Landschaft. Burckhardt was just entering adolescence at this time, but the painful memory of these events and the humiliation of the federal mediation remained keen in Basel for many decades. During the period of the 'Troubles', moreover, Basel, disaffected and distrustful of the federal authorities, had sought an informal alliance with five other cantons that were also opposed to the liberal thrust toward greater centralization of power in the Confederation. This *Sarnerbund*, as it was called, after the town of Sarnen, where the first meeting of representatives from the participating cantons took place, never amounted to much and soon broke up. Basel, Protestant and commercial, had not much in common with backward, rural, and predominantly Catholic cantons like Schwyz and Uri. But fifteen years later these same cantons of Lucerne, Uri, Schwyz, Zug, and Unterwalden, united with Fribourg and Valais in armed struggle (the *Sonderbundkrieg*) to preserve their autonomy against the centralizing ambitions and policies of the more economically advanced, liberal, and chiefly Protestant cantons. The military victory of the progressive cantons was crowned by the Federal Constitution of 1848 which abolished many of the barriers of trade and settlement among the cantons and established a National Assembly with authority to legislate in certain areas for all Switzerland, as well as a permanent federal administration in the new capital at Bern. Basel remained loyal to the Confederation during the war, but there was a good deal of sympathy for the Catholic cantons in the city's governing class. Burckhardt himself reported on the conflict in the *Basler Zeitung* with great even-handedness.

The process of centralization and democratization begun in 1848 was continued by a major revision of the Constitution in 1874, as a result of which – one Basel *Ratsherr* or Senator is reported to have said – a centuries-old history finally came to an end, as Basel ceased to be a republic and became a mere municipality.[1]

Finally, it is important to mention the Austro-Prussian and Franco-Prussian Wars of 1866 and 1870 and the founding, after the Prussian victory in 1871, of the Second German Empire. As Burckhardt's learned biographer, Werner Kaegi, reminds us, the planning and the earliest redactions of both the *Griechische Kulturgeschichte* and the *On the Study of History* (published posthumously as *Weltgeschichtliche Betrachtungen*) date to the time of those two wars, which Burckhardt saw as harbingers of catastrophes to come. 'I am dying of grief', Flaubert wrote to George Sand at this time. 'What breaks my heart is (1) human ferocity; (2) the conviction that we are about to enter an era of stupidity. We will be utilitarian, militaristic, American, and Catholic, very Catholic! You'll see! ...What wretchedness! Is it possible to believe in progress and civilization in the face of everything now taking place? What good is science? Prussia, full of scientists, is committing abominations worthy of the Huns – worse, because they are systematic, cold-blooded, deliberate, without excuse of passion or hunger.'[2]

Burckhardt's response was not unlike Flaubert's and it is worth bearing that in mind as we consider his reflections on the Greek *poleis*. For some of the central themes of the *Griechische Kulturgeschichte* appear to have had quite a lot to do with the issues Burckhardt believed were important to him as a citizen of Basel, a Swiss, and an educated European in the second half of the nineteenth century: the relative merits of confederations of small states and of larger, centralized states; the relation of individual freedom and state power and, in particular, of liberty and democracy; the effect on culture of unlimited power struggles among rival states and of democratic resentment of elites within them; and democracy as a breeding-ground of demagogy, chauvinism, and war.

Let us take a quick glance now at the literary context of Burckhardt's reflections on the *polis*. Comparison of the Swiss cantons with the Greek *poleis* had been for some time a topos both of the historiography of Switzerland (in the work of Johannes von Müller, for instance[3]) and of the historiography of ancient Greece. In late 1847, for instance, in the immediate aftermath of the *Sonderbundkrieg*, the latest British historian of ancient Greece, George Grote, published *Seven Letters on the Recent Politics of Switzerland*. As the twenty-two cantons present 'a miniature of all Europe', Grote declared in the Preface, being 'extremely various with respect to race, language, religion, civilization, wealth, habits, etc.' and 'exhibiting the fifteenth century in immediate juxtaposition with the nineteenth', they are 'interesting, on every ground, to the general intelligent public of Europe.' To him in particular, however, they presented 'an additional ground of interest, from a certain political analogy (nowhere else to be found in Europe) with those who preeminently occupy my thoughts, and on the history of whom I am still engaged – the ancient Greeks.'[4] Grote here sets

---

1 See W. Kaegi, *Jacob Burckhardt: eine Biographie* (Basel 1947-82), VII, 124.
2 Gustave Flaubert to George Sand, 30 October 1870, *Selected Letters of Gustave Flaubert*, trans. F. Steegmuller (London 1954) 217.
3 See W. Kaegi, *Jacob Burckhard* (n. 1, above), VII, 21, and W. Rihm, *Das Bildungserlebnis der Antike bei Johannes von Müller* (Basel 1959).
4 G. Grote, *Seven Letters on the Recent Politics of Switzerland* (London 1847) iii-iv.

three situations in parallel: the Greek *poleis* of antiquity, the Swiss cantons, and the modern European states. Grote's *Letters* went through several editions and were well known in Basel, as was his monumental *History of Greece* (1846-56).

Fifteen years later, in 1863, just before Burckhardt got down to thinking seriously about a course or book on *Griechische Kulturgeschichte*, another eminent English historian, Edward Freeman, brought out the first volume of a *History of Federal Government*, which was to have spanned the entire period from the Achaean League to the Civil War in the United States. In fact, only the first volume, on ancient Greece, was ever published, but it did not pass unnoticed in Basel by any means. It was reviewed sympathetically and in detail in the *Schweizerisches Museum* by Wilhelm Vischer-Bilfinger, Burckhardt's colleague in the chair of Greek at the University and his former teacher. (This was the Wilhelm Vischer who later brought Nietzsche to Basel.) Vischer noted that Freeman had recently visited Switzerland to study those cantons where direct democracy was still practised and that his next volume was expected to cover the Swiss Confederation and the various German Leagues of the late Middle Ages. The first volume of the British historian's work, Vischer wrote, 'takes a decidedly contradictory stand in relation to a number of recent German publications, in which the unification movement of the German peoples has too often clouded clear and unprejudiced historical vision by making the unique goal of the state appear to be the development of its external power and by overlooking the infinitely rich cultural life that small states, and in the first instance the small city-states of Greece, have been able to promote'.[5] Vischer made no secret of the German scholars he had in mind: he named specifically Mommsen with his 'idolatry of pure power' and Droysen with his excessive partiality for Macedonia – the Prussia of antiquity, according to Droysen himself. Immediately after the publication of his *History of Hellenism* in 1843, Droysen had in fact turned his attention to the history of Prussia, and by the time Vischer wrote his review had established himself as an authority on the subject. There was little disagreement about the drift of Droysen's historical argument: in the summary of a contemporary German historian, 'Macedonia was Prussia, Greece Germany, Asia Europe'.[6]

Vischer's review of Freeman reminds us, if we needed reminding, that there was a wider German as well as a specifically Swiss context for reflection on the relative merits of small states and large states, confederations and centralized states, and for historical analogies between antiquity and the modern world, such as that between Prussia and Macedonia. Napoleon's defeat of Prussia and Austria had sparked a good deal of discussion, among German thinkers and writers, on the relation between the enduring German *Kulturvolk*, as defined by the Romantics, and its shifting political organization. It was argued, even by many who started out from Herder's vision of the nation as a cultural entity rather than a political one, that in order to protect itself against conquerors like Napoleon and to develop its full

---

5 Quoted by Kaegi, *Jacob Burckhardt* (n. 1, above), VII, 31. By adopting the generic term 'Kleinstaaterei' – which the upholders of the *Machtstaat* used to convey their contempt for the 'anachronistic' remnants of a weak and flawed political order – in order to designate the source of 'unendlich reiches Geistesleben', Vischer underlined what to him, and no doubt many of his fellow-Basel citizens, was the deeply questionable character of the preoccupation of German historians such as Droysen and Mommsen with power and political success.

6 H. Schulze, *Staat und Nation in der europäischen Geschichte* (Munich 1994) 180.

potential, the German *Kulturvolk* needed a strong political state – a 'centre', as Michelet said when he contrasted France, which had one, with Germany and Italy which did not – a state far stronger than the old Empire (to which Napoleon had administered the *coup de grâce*) had ever been.[7] The political state was the fulfilment, from this perspective, of the cultural nation. It marked the transformation of a natural community into a moral one, according to Burckhardt's fellow citizen of Basel, Johann Jacob Bachofen – who, like Burckhardt, had been a student of Ranke in Berlin.[8] Burckhardt himself had not been averse in his youth to the search for a new political form for Germany, though it is doubtful that he ever envisaged anything resembling what the later national historians were to defend. At any rate, he had become convinced by the late 1840s that nationalism was a revolutionary force more likely to destroy the extremely varied yet closely interrelated cultures of 'old Europe' (*Alteuropa*) than to preserve them, as his teacher Ranke believed.

Freeman's *History of Federal Government* thus addressed questions that were of interest to all Germans, of particular interest to German-speaking Swiss as members of the German *Kulturvolk*, and of still more immediate interest to Baselrs as citizens of an old city-republic within a Confederation evolving relentlessly, under liberal influence, into a unified federal state. It is not at all surprising that it was reviewed attentively by Vischer-Bilfinger.

The professor of Greek had in any case been meditating on its central topic at least since the time of the Swiss Civil War. In 1849, for instance, when it fell to him to give the public lecture to the students and their parents that was a regular feature of the opening exercises at the Basel *Pädagogium*, he had chosen as his topic the question of centralization and confederation in the construction of the ancient state or *polis* – a topic that, only two years after the Swiss Civil War and a year after the new federal constitution, was obviously of more than antiquarian interest to a Basel audience.[9] Equally, the relation between *Stadt* and *Land* in the state or *polis* – the core of the lecture concerned the relation of the Greek *polis* to the simpler communities or *demoi* out of which it had been forged – must have struck a chord in an audience of Basel parents, many of whom could well have participated in the painful events of 1830-33.

Vischer distinguished in his talk between two models of the ancient state: on the one hand, a centralized model, characterized in the case of Athens, by the complete identification of the state and the erstwhile inhabitants of the communities or *demoi*, and in the case of Sparta, by the dominion of a conquering and invading core group (in Sparta's case, the Dorians) over the erstwhile indigenous communities; and, on the other hand, a confederate model, characterized by a fairly loose association of the relatively autonomous communities, as in the Aetolian and Achaean Leagues. As even-handedly as possible he evaluated the advantages and disadvantages of the various political structures he had described – a centralized state,

---

7 *Ibid.,* 182-85. The editors of the *Archiv für deutsche Kulturgeschichte* announced in their Prospectus that 'cultural history follows with intense interest every struggle of the *Volksgeist* to incarnate itself in the form of a state' ([1858] 1:23). Cf. J. Hutchinson, *The Dynamics of Cultural Nationalism* (London 1987) 41: 'In terms of its own communitarian goals, cultural nationalism is a failure, and it regularly shifts into a state politics to institutionalize its programme in the social order. In doing so, it paves the way for its suppression by political nationalism.'
8 See my *Basel in the Age of Burckhardt* (Chicago 2000) 191-92.
9 *Über die Bildung von Staaten und Bünden, oder Centralisation und Föderation im alten Griechenland* (Basel, Schweighauser'sche Universitaets-Buchdruckerei, 1849), Bib. Univ. Basel, E.bb.I.36.

tending toward democracy, in which all citizens were equal; a centralized state, tending toward aristocracy, with a hierarchy of full citizens, *perioikoi*, and helots; and a confederation constituted by the free banding together of independent communities. While acknowledging that the centralized states had proved incapable of uniting to form a single national state and that the Greeks had also failed to develop a viable and lasting constitution for a confederate state, Vischer nevertheless closed his lecture with words of praise for small states as bearers of culture – words that were still being echoed by Max Weber in 1916 in a talk on 'Germany among the European World Powers'. I quote Vischer: 'If, on the one hand, the particularism of the Greek people presents a sorry picture, we ought not to forget, on the other, that out of that very particularist spirit grew the infinitely varied life which flowered in glorious achievements of art and thought that will be objects of admiration for all ages and that fully make up for the political shortcomings of the state.'[10] Burckhardt almost certainly knew of this lecture by his colleague and former teacher. As he was living and teaching in Basel at the time, he could well have heard it, but even if he did not, it was published immediately and he would have been almost morally obliged to read it. In any case, he could hardly have been ignorant of Vischer's ideas about the ancient *polis* or of their connection in his colleague's mind with the politics of Basel, Switzerland, and Germany.

Burckhardt's lectures on *Griechische Kulturgeschichte* are as deeply marked, in my view, as Vischer's lecture, by the author's experience and preoccupations as a citizen of Basel and by the characteristic Basel reflection on the relations of politics, power, and culture, the *Großstaat* or *Machtstaat* and the *Kleinstaat*. That is not to say, however, that Burckhardt accepted without qualification the analogy between the Greek *poleis* and the Swiss cantons. On the contrary, his work seems to have been intended in part as an examination and, ultimately, even a rejection of that analogy in any strict sense. In general, Burckhardt's aim seems to have been to provide a more sober and realistic evaluation of the *polis* than those who had represented it as a model of liberty or culture. He did not dispute its great cultural achievements, as we shall see – though he argued, in a strikingly Hegelian move for a professed anti-Hegelian, that the universalization of those achievements and their integration into the general cultural heritage of mankind could occur only as a consequence of the *political* ruin of the *polis* and the transformation of its citizens into *Bildungsmenschen* or men of culture[11] – but he persistently emphasized the price in terms of individual happiness that had had to be paid for those achievements. Similarly, like his fellow-Swiss Benjamin Constant a generation earlier, he drew a sharp distinction between ancient liberty and modern liberty. He had himself been deeply influenced as a schoolboy in Basel by the idealistic philhellenism of the German neohumanists – Wolf, Winckelmann, Schiller, and Goethe – but some time before he embarked on the *Griechische Kulturgeschichte*, he had already questioned both their vision of ancient Greece and the enthusiasm it had inspired in him himself as a young man. In 1859, for instance, when he delivered the memorial address on the centenary of

---

10 *Über die Bildung von Staaten und Bünden* (n. 9, above) 14. Cf. Max Weber, 'Deutschland unter den europäischen Weltmächten', in his *Gesammelte politische Schriften*, ed. J. Winckelmann (Tübingen 1958) 170-71.
11 Cf. J. Michelet, *Introduction à l'histoire universelle*, in his *Œuvres complètes*, ed. P. Viallaneix, 21 vols (Paris 1971-), II (1972) 233: 'la cité grecque est trop étroite pour que le rêve s'accomplisse; il faut un monde plus large.'

Schiller's birth in the great hall of the new Basel Museum in the Augustinergasse, he pronounced a surprising judgment on the celebrated 'Hymn to Joy' ('*An die Freude*'). Schiller's poem was 'an intoxication...unable to stand up to logical examination', he declared, maliciously reminding his listeners that with all his enthusiasm for the gods of Greece, in the well-known poem of that title, Schiller had remained primly monotheistic. The enthralling neohumanist picture of ancient Greece as a uniquely happy age of mankind, an age of beauty, harmony, and joy, he went on to argue in the *Griechische Kulturgeschichte*, was 'one of the greatest historical frauds ever perpetrated'.[12] In Burckhardt's mature view there are no perfect ages in history. Since the human condition does not change, all historical situations inevitably mix good and evil, suffering and fulfilment. The historian can only point to the relative advantages and disadvantages of different situations and to the complex ways in which good and evil are interwoven.

In revising the neohumanist image of antiquity, Burckhardt drew not only on his own reading of the literary sources and on the severe judgments of Christian theologians from Bossuet to De Wette, with whom he himself had studied at the University of Basel, but on ideas articulated by the neohumanists themselves. In the Introduction to the *Griechische Kulturgeschichte*, for instance, he quotes from a classic work of 1817, *Die Staatshaushaltung der Athener*, by August Böckh, who – like Ranke and Droysen – had been one of his teachers at the University of Berlin in the early 1840s: 'The Ancients', Böckh had written, 'were unhappier than most people believe'.[13] In the very first chapter of his work, Böckh had articulated a position with which Burckhardt could not but have sympathized. 'I took the Truth as my goal', Böckh declared, 'and if we must moderate our unconditional admiration for the Ancients because it turns out that where they touched gold, their hands also got dirty, I will not regret that. Or should our accounts of the past be written only to inspire and edify the young? Should the classical scholar conceal that then, as now, everything under the sun was not perfect?'[14] Burckhardt could also have read in F.W. Riemer's *Mitteilungen* a remark of Goethe's dating to the year 1813: 'The Greeks were lovers of freedom, to be sure! But each one of them only of his own. For that reason there was within every Greek a tyrant for whose development only the opportunity was wanting.' That comment would echo throughout Burckhardt's work, in one place almost word for word.[15]

Let me turn now directly to the image of the *polis* presented in the *Griechische Kulturgeschichte*.

---

12 *Griechische Kulturgeschichte*, in *Gesamtausgabe* (Stuttgart 1930-34), vols VII-XI, IX, 343. Subsequent references to this work are to this edition, and are given in parentheses in the text. Italicised numbers refer to the recent abridged translation by Sheila Stern, with Introduction by Oswyn Murray, *The Greeks and Greek Civilization* (London 1998). However, not all the passages referred to here were included in this abridgement.
13 'Die Hellenen waren im Glanze der Kunst und in der Blüte der Freiheit unglücklicher als die meisten glauben', in *Die Staatshaushaltung der Athener* (Berlin 1817), II, 159.
14 *Ibid.*, I, 2. Quoted in Kaegi, *Jacob Burckhardt* (n. 1, above), VII, 24-25, n. 70.
15 J. W. von Goethe, *Werke*, Artemis-Ausgabe, *Gespräche*, 20 November 1813, I, 703. Quoted in Kaegi (n. 1, above), VII, 25. Cf. Burckhardt's remark: 'Die Tyrannis ist eine der ganz unvermeidlichen Formen der griechischen Staatsidee und in jedem begabten und ehrgeizigen Griechen wohnte ein Tyrann und ein Demagog', in *Griechische Kulturgeschichte*, in *Gesamtausgabe* (n. 12, above), VIII, 169.

An epigraph from the inscription on the portal of Hell at the beginning of Book III of Dante's *Inferno – Per me si va nella città dolente –* stands as a warning at the entrance to the section of volume I of Burckhardt's book entitled 'The *Polis*', giving clear notice of the author's intention to avoid '*Schönfärberei*', as he put it – the whitewashing and prettying up of historical reality and the idealization of the ancient *polis* characteristic, in his view, in their different ways, of German neohumanists and English democrats, of Goethe and Grote. This will not, the reader is advised, be a celebratory account of the ancient *polis*: it will tell of the violence by which it came into existence as an organized state, of the violence it consistently – and increasingly – exercized both on its citizens and on its neighbours, and of the enormous sacrifice of human happiness and freedom it exacted, even in its heyday, as the price of its greatness and its achievements in art and literature. From the total picture will emerge a Schopenhauerian view of life as rarely happy, redeemed only by the seemingly inexhaustible creative energies of human beings and their realizations in art, and a dark, rather un-Rankean view of history itself as a vale of tears, in which every achievement of culture is paid for by untold suffering, and in which the conflicting values and claims of individual development and community cohesion, reflection and belief, personal freedom and state power, cosmopolitan humanism or universalism and intense national identification and patriotism, are seldom, if ever, reconciled.[16] Implicitly, Burckhardt's account of the Greek *poleis* in the *Griechische Kulturgeschichte* challenged Ranke's optimistic belief that the development of strong, unified national states as the repositories and champions of popular cultures ensured the enrichment and consolidation of all of them. War to the death, not the balance of power, was the norm for the *poleis* in Burckhardt's account of them. In general, Burckhardt's position recalls Isaiah Berlin's view that (in Noel Annan's paraphrase) 'you cannot always pursue one good end without setting another on one side. You cannot always exercise mercy without cheating justice. Equality and freedom are both good ends, but you can rarely have more of one without surrendering some part of the other.'[17]

The founding of the state, Burckhardt relates, is always represented by the Greeks as instantaneous, not the result of an evolution (VIII, 62 [*43*]). It is, in effect, a traumatic birth, 'the decisive experience in the entire existence of a population' (VIII, 69 [*49*]). The radical and painful transformation of traditional tillers of the soil into citizens marks the passage from a kind of pre-history to history.[18] By an act of will, loose, 'natural' or 'organic' communities are shaped into a single state which recreates its members as free and equal citizens, requires the identification of each individual will with that of the whole, and tolerates no deviation, no difference, no independence, within or without. It is at least arguable that the ancient *polis*, as described in the *Griechische Kulturgeschichte*, represents in many respects, for Burckhardt, the very essence of the state, the state in its perfect state, so to speak, and the focus, therefore,

---

16 In his quietly defiant *Nietzsche und Burckhardt*, 2nd edn (Munich 1942), the sociologist Alfred von Martin highlights Burckhardt's insistence on history as a domain of immense human suffering and victimization. See especially section XVI, 'Die Leidenden' (121-25).
17 I. Berlin, *Personal Impressions*, ed. H. Hardy, intro. by N. Annan (London 1980) xv.
18 See *Gesamtausgabe* (n. 12, above), VIII, 69 [*49*], 'Until then, people had been tillers of the soil, now, as all came to live together, they became part-icipants in politics.' ('Bisher waren es "Landwirte" gewesen, nun, als alles beisammen wohnte, wurden es "Politiker".').

of his meditations on the state[19] – just as, shockingly no doubt from the standpoint of modern idealizers of the *polis* (but not from that of the ancients themselves, Burckhardt claims), Sparta, where 'the people is an army and the state an armed camp' (VIII, 109), is represented as the essence or perfect model (*'die vollendetste Darstellung'*) of the *polis* (VIII, 94).[20]

It was not unusual in Burckhardt's day, as we saw, to compare the Greek *poleis* and the Swiss cantons or the city-states of modern Europe. Burckhardt insists, in contrast, that those seemingly similar political formations are fundamentally different. If anything, Burckhardt's *poleis* resemble the new nationalist states of Europe rather than the late medieval city-states or the Swiss cantons. Both in their origins and in their fundamental ideology the ancient *poleis* should be sharply distinguished, Burckhardt declared, from the city-republics of the Middle Ages, to which they bear only a superficial resemblance. The latter are 'essentially something different – namely particular, more or less emancipated parts of previously existing empires' (VIII, 76 [*55*]). They are individuated pieces broken off from larger wholes, whereas the *polis* was the culmination of a process of absorption, integration, and, where it encountered resistance, destruction of smaller units. Moreover, the Church, which hovered over all the European city-republics and empires, drawing them together like a cloak spread over them, has no equivalent in antiquity (VIII, 76 [*55*]). On the contrary: religion is not an autonomous force in the *polis*; it is an integral part of it. In fact, the only religion *in* each *polis* is the religion *of* the *polis*. In Burckhardt's own words: 'The *polis* was basically the Greek's religion' (VIII, 80 [*58*]). Similarly, there is no conception of a natural law claiming universal validity. 'There are no *human* rights in antiquity, not even in Aristotle' (VIII, 74 [*53*]). Law, like religion, is an integral part of each *polis* but it affects only the citizens of that *polis*, no one else – not members of other *poleis* and not those within the *polis* (such as slaves or residents) who are not citizens. '*Nomos*, which embraces both the laws and the constitution', is seen as 'a higher objective instance that is not satisfied – as in the modern world – merely to protect and tax the individual and sustain military service, but instead claims to govern all individual existence and will, and to be the very soul of the whole. In the most elevated statements, law and constitution are praised as the invention and gift of the gods, the very character of the city and the preserver of its virtue' (VIII, 82 [*59*]).

The laws of each *polis*, in sum, are viewed as part of the very being of that *polis*, and each one looks on others as an absolutely alien existence, a challenge and threat to itself. With neither a common religion, nor a notion of universal law, the Greek *poleis* are lined up more starkly and uncompromisingly against each other than the medieval city-republics ever were. It is virtually impossible for them to co-operate or confederate. 'Since the *polis* is the highest power and the true religion of the Hellenes, the struggles of the *poleis* to promote or defend

---

19 During a brief discussion of Burckhardt's *Griechische Kulturgeschichte* with P. Vidal-Naquet at Princeton on 11 October 1994, in the course of which I expressed the view that a good part of the interest of Burckhardt's work lies in the fact that his reflections on the *polis* are in truth reflections on the state as such: the great classical historian replied that Burckhardt would have done better not to treat the *polis* as a state. I continue to believe that Burckhardt's interpretation of the *polis* as the pure form of the state, whether historically accurate or not, produced some of his morally and politically most deeply engaging pages. Perhaps only the citizen of a small city-state could have presented such a concrete and sobering picture of Leviathan.

20 For a modern consideration of Sparta as the type of the *polis*, see P. H. Rahe, *Republics Ancient and Modern* (Chapel Hill and London 1992) 134-85.

themselves have all the frightful horror of religious wars' (VIII, 85 [*61*]).²¹ Finally, among the inhabitants of the European city-republics the individual precedes the state. It cannot be said of the citizen of one of the modern city-republics (such as Basel) that he 'realizes all his talents and finds occasion for the exercise of every virtue in and through the state' or that 'all spirit and all culture stand in the strongest possible relation to the *polis*, so that the highest productions by far of the poetry and art of the age of greatest cultural flowering belong not to the domain of private enjoyment but to the sphere of public life' (VIII, 77 [*55*]). Only of the citizen of the ancient *polis* could it be said without any reservation that 'his "*Vaterstadt*" (*patris*) is not simply the home-town where he is happiest and to which he is drawn by homesickness, not simply the city to which, despite its faults, he feels proud to belong, but a higher, divinely powerful being' (VIII, 77 [*56*]). Burckhardt subscribed explicitly to the radical distinction drawn by another great Swiss *Altliberaler*, Benjamin Constant, between the ancient and the modern worlds, ancient and modern liberty. I quote Burckhardt:

> In modern times, if we discount philosophical and other kinds of blueprints, it is essentially the individual who defines the state, and who demands that it be as he needs it to be. What he asks of it in fact is only security, so that he can develop his individual energies and capacities to the maximum. In order to achieve this goal, he is prepared to make well calculated sacrifices in return, but feels gratitude and loyalty to the state to the very degree that it leaves him alone to go about all his other business without interference. The Greek *polis*, in contrast, starts from the whole that is held to precede the part; that is, the whole is held to precede the individual human being and the individual family or clan. (VIII, 77 [*55*])²²

The most terrible birthpangs accompany the construction of this state that is to be the '*Eins und Alles*' (VIII, 60 [*42*], IX, 314 [*64*] *et passim*), the alpha and omega, of the lives of all its citizens, and that becomes 'a fearful threat to any citizen the moment he no longer identifies totally with it', since it wields without any constraint the various instruments of coercion at its disposal: dishonour and public stigmatization ('*Atimie*'), exile, and death (VIII, 80). Burckhardt describes the rise of political man as a fall from innocence, as well as a kind of fulfilment.

> The time when people lived according to country ways (*komedon*), sometimes in small districts (*Gauen*) of seven or eight villages, had been ... more innocent; it had been necessary to defend oneself by arms against brigands and pirates, but essentially people had lived a peaceful agricultural life. Now *polis* stood against *polis* as rivals for political power and for their very existence ... The whole of Greek life had been straining toward this final form, the *polis*, without which the highest achievements of Greek culture would be inconceivable. But examples from historical times about which we have clearer knowledge allow us to form an idea of the cost of this synoecism [welding together of different human groups into the *polis*]: namely the resettlement by violent means or the total elimination of all those who put up any resistance. What we can have but an inkling

---

21 According to Rahe, 'the *polis* was akin to a party of zealots', *ibid.*, 134.
22 On Burckhardt's awareness of the difference between the Italian cities of the Renaissance and the Greek *poleis*, see also Kaegi, *Jacob Burckhardt* (n. 1, above), VII, 78-79.

of, is the suffering of the many who went along with the new order but were forced to leave behind their old villages, settlements, and little towns. ... Having to abandon the gravesites of their ancestors must have been experienced by the Greeks as a terrible misfortune ... In the entire course of history there is scarcely another example of such an accumulation of bitter suffering as we find in this Greek *polis*. (VIII, 64-65 [*45-46*])[23]

As the *Eins und Alles* that brooks no rival and no otherness, the *polis* is engaged externally in bitter competition or open warfare with other *poleis*, the very existence of which is a threat to its absoluteness; internally, according to Burckhardt, it oppresses its citizens mercilessly, promising death or banishment to all who deviate from total dedication to its purposes. The competition among the ancient *poleis* was quite unlike that among modern European cities, Burckhardt explains. Animosities among the latter, largely based on commercial envy and rivalry, convey no idea of the sometimes hidden, sometimes open animosity that the Greeks harboured against each other. 'The exclusiveness of the *polis*, its hostility to all other *poleis*, especially those closest to it, is not just a dominant feeling but to all intents and purposes an aspect of civic virtue.' (VIII, 279). And this relation of hostility to those on the outside repeats the *polis*'s harshness to oppressed parties and groups within it, as well as its oppression of the ancient rural populations. As internal divisions developed apace in the course of the fifth century, according to Burckhardt, the *polis*'s external ventures became more frequent, the intervals of peace shorter, treaties less likely to be respected. 'Each individual state became more and more convinced that all other states were in a life or death struggle with it and behaved accordingly, so that the time of the highest flowering of culture was also that of the most horrific violence.' (VIII, 280). The motive for these struggles was not necessity or interest, no specific advantage, but 'pure political hatred' (VIII, 281). As no one can accept submission to a rival, or trust that a rival who has submitted will continue in submission, all enemies are potentially fatal threats and must be eliminated. The rules of war are of unexampled harshness: the victor kills off all the males and sells the women and children into

---

[23] Burckhardt's account of the birth of the *polis* is considerably more pessimistic than Droysen's. Momigliano refers to a paper of 1847 on 'Die attische Communalverfassung', in which Droysen argued that Solon and Cleisthenes 'allowed freedom in religious, patrimonial, and administrative matters to the villages of Attica. They created a characteristic balance between the Athenian *polis* and its individual components, which eliminated any rivalry "zwischen Staat und Commune"', 'J. G. Droysen between Greeks and Jews', in *Quinto contributo alla storia degli studi classici e del mondo antico* (Rome 1975) 118. 'No doubt Droysen had in mind contemporary problems of the Prussian state in speaking of the balance "zwischen Staat und Commune"', Momigliano adds, underlining the contemporary relevance of Droysen's optimistic view of the state. Cf. Burckhardt, *Reflections on History*, trans. M. Hottinger (London 1941) 35-36: 'We cannot share the optimistic view according to which society came into being first, and the State arose as its protector, its negative aspect, its warden and defender ... Human nature is not like that ... There are two probable theories: (a) Force always comes first ... In many cases, the State may have been nothing more than its reduction to a system. Or (b) we feel that an extremely violent process, particularly of fusion, must have taken place. A flash of lightning fuses several elements into one new alloy ... In this way, the three Dorian races and the three Gothic tribes may have fused for the purpose or on the occasion of a conquest ... An echo of the terrible convulsions which accompanied the birth of the State, of what it *cost*, can be heard in the enormous and absolute primacy it has at all times enjoyed. We see this primacy as an established indisputable fact, while it is assuredly to some extent veiled history.'

slavery (VIII, 284).[24] Burckhardt's judgment is unequivocal: 'From time immemorial, worldly power has admitted of few restrictions on its actions whenever its interests were involved' (VIII, 282). In large heterogeneous empires it is nonetheless held in check in some measure by competing interests and forces, and it aims in general at achieving external peace. That, however, was not the case with the Greek *poleis*. On the contrary, from the fifth century on, internal unrest propelled them into external adventures and as soon as war broke out, they believed no holds were barred and everything was permitted (VIII, 282). The cruelty of the Spartans (VIII, 97-98, 102) was not exceptional but typical.

Internally, the *polis* subordinated every aspect of individual life to its ends. Burckhardt is again close to Constant: Man in the *polis* is a citizen, never an individual. Though it does not itself run schools, the *polis* does favour traditional education: gymnastics to exercise the body and encourage boldness and effort; music to instil a sense of order and law. The *polis* forms and educates citizens, in short, through the theatre, public architecture, and above all through the activities of daily life, such as participation in assemblies or the magistracy. In this way it created 'a unique product in world history – a general will that is immensely active and effective' ('*von höchster Tätigkeit und Tatfähigkeit*') (VIII, 79 [57]). But the corollary of the all-powerful state is 'the lack of individual freedom in every respect. Religious rites, the festival calendar, myth, all are indigenous; in this way the state is at the same time a church em-powered to hear and decide charges of impiety. To this combined power, temporal and spiritual, the individual is completely subordinate.' He must provide military service through-out his life, and his property is entirely subject to the control of the state. 'The *polis* exacted a high price for the modicum of security that it provided' and there was 'absolutely no way of protecting life or property from the inroads of the state' (VIII, 80 [57-58]). This servitude of the individual to the state is characteristic, Burckhardt argues, of all the constitutions of the *polis*, but it is at its worst, he insists, under democracy. In Burckhardt's history, the democratic *polis*, the ideal model of modern radicals, is the most oppressively illiberal of all.

The *Griechische Kulturgeschichte* is full of references to the harassment of the rich and talented by democratic regimes in which 'popular assemblies have usurped the functions of the Senate (*Rat*) and essentially taken over government' (VIII, 227). The voice of the nineteenth-century Basel *Altbürger* and *Altliberaler* is nowhere more audible. The equality of rights introduced by democracy, we are told, makes people keenly aware of inequalities they had hitherto accepted as part of the order of things. Inequality of wealth, in particular, becomes intolerable. But the contempt for most forms of labour (the so-called 'banausic' occupations), which the Greek democracies inherited from their aristocratic predecessors, left few opportunities for remedying this situation through work (VIII, 260-61). As a result, the poorer citizens first allow themselves to be rewarded for attending the assemblies and the courts, then they deliberately sell their votes, and begin to threaten the well-to-do, through the courts, with confiscations of property. The cancellation of debts is the next step. 'Property ceases to be sacred and everyone measures his rights according to his so-called needs (that

---

24 Could Burckhardt have had in mind the custom of the Swiss soldiers of the heroic days of the Confederation to take no prisoners? In his *Imagined Battles: Reflections of War in European Art* (Chapel Hill 1997), Peter Paret cites in a note the War Orders of the Confederation of 1476 and the Lucerne Decree of March 1499, 'which states: "Every community should have its men swear not to take prisoners when we have a battle ... but to kill everyone as our pious ancestors always did".' (11, n. 1).

is, desires). And for all that a momentary majority of votes was all that was required.' Respect for the continuity of tradition, law, and culture is destroyed. 'Everywhere we observe only revolution and counter-revolution' (VIII, 248-49).

The process of corruption was already advanced by the fifth century, when 'political organization had become predominantly democratic, individuality had been awakened and developed and was already in conflict everywhere with the state, and reasoning and argument were more and more the rule rather than simple fulfilment of one's duties' (XI, 264 [*273*]). A century later, the general character of Athenian life was that 'every one was more concerned with his rights than his duties, with enjoying pleasures than with making contributions' (XI, 329-30 [*301*]).

The state had ceased to be the *Eins und Alles*, the 'higher self' of every citizen, and become a common property to be exploited by individuals bent on their own pleasure and interest. Burckhardt takes the rhetor or demagogue and the sycophant or informer as typical products of democratic regimes. The man who has learned to speak well gets himself elected to lucrative positions in the state; the informer or investigator is necessary because too many elected officers have their hands in the till. Corruption is normal, not exceptional. The sycophant threatens everybody, however, the innocent as well as the guilty. No doubt with certain periods of the French Revolution in mind – twentieth-century readers could supply more recent instances – Burckhardt speaks of 'public terrorism' (VIII, 231-33). Fifth-century Athens, which neohumanist scholars had taught generations of students to admire as a Golden Age, presents a bleak picture in the political chapters of Burckhardt's *Griechische Kulturgeschichte*.

> The sycophants and the rhetors, the constant threat of legal prosecution by the state, especially on charges of venality and insufficient performance, along with the ever present danger of an accusation of impiety (*asebeia*), all of this taken together constituted an enduring state of terror. (IX, 326 [*73*])

By the fourth century the situation had become unbearable:

> The public assembly and the court of justice, with all their official forms and procedures, had become the theatre and the instrument of the worst forms of chicanery and persecution. When we envisage for ourselves the venal orators, the mass of resolutions and decrees that were never executed, the scandalmongers and slanderers,[25] the sycophants and false witnesses, the deliberate implicating of innocent people in criminal lawsuits, the silencing by means of murder of any one who is by right superior, we are taken aback by the enormous shamelessness with which evil exhibits itself publicly here. (X, 333)[26]

Finally Burckhardt comes out with it: 'This situation has its equivalent in the French *Terreur* of 1793/94' (XI, 333 [*303*]).

---

25 *Auspocher*, literally 'beaters', that is, those who drive the animals out of their habitat and force them within range of the huntsmen.
26 See also XI, 187 [*228-29*], 484-85.

Had modern Europeans not been so brainwashed about the glory of ancient Greece (XI, 189 [*230*]), Burckhardt concludes, they would have been forced to acknowledge that 'no political power [*Potenz*] in the whole of world history ever paid such a frightful price for existence as the Greek *poleis*.' It is childish, he insists, perhaps with Grote in mind, to imagine that it was the wicked Macedonians who came along one day and deprived the Greeks of their freedom and of every superior value. Firstly, the Greeks never enjoyed freedom as we moderns understand it. And secondly, the *polis* was undermined by its own internal contradictions. The negative aspects of the *polis* 'were old', as Burckhardt put it, and had been there in germ from the start. 'From the very time it demanded of all citizens [that they must strive to excel on its behalf], the *polis* developed, along with great dedication to the common good in many cases, situations in which attack and defence among the citizens themselves aroused the most power-ful passions and were excused' (IX, 314 [*64*]). The state's promotion of individual capacities for its own purposes, in short, inevitably produced personalities and desires that were less and less easily subordinated to those purposes, and as these desires gradually invested the state, the state itself lost the objective, almost divine character that had justified the sacrifices it required, as well as the authority and credibility on which it depended to obtain them.[27] The desires and satisfactions of the highly developed individual came to replace the earlier communal ones, until under democracy the will of the *polis* as the highest value known to the citizen, the value to which he was required to subordinate his own will, was replaced by the whims of the popular mass, which 'no longer represented a higher general will but only its own desires' (VIII, 275-76).

Adverting to the original theme of the Princeton conference, we might well now ask whether Burckhardt's account of the Greek *polis* was motivated by liberal or illiberal impulses? It was certainly not pro-democratic, and it is not hard to see how it could be construed as part of a conservative defence of privilege. But it is also, in some respects, a powerful restatement, in the age of Blood and Iron, of a classic liberal, anti-Machiavellian view of the state found in Benjamin Constant and, before him, in Montesquieu.

Princeton University

---

27 As he developed this point, Burckhardt could well have had in mind an address given by Wilhelm Vischer-Bilfinger at the graduation ceremony from the *Pädagogium* in 1836. 'At an early stage, the striving of the individual for prestige and distinction entered into conflict with the old customs and beliefs [i.e. 'that the individual is to be regarded only as a part of the state, that he can exist only in and through the state']. That striving was unusually intense among the people of Hellas and found expression both in the relations among states and in each individual community. This is the source of the infinitely rich abundance of life of that people and at the same time the obstacle to any lasting union of the various individual states and the origin of the jealous ambition which led the Hellenes to consume their noblest energies in mutual struggles ... Within each state, we find the same phenomenon as among the states. Each citizen seeks to win respect for his own individual character; when that cannot be done by legal means, illegal means are not disdained. The principle that the individual exists only in and through the state is indeed maintained, but inverted. So that instead of the individual will subordinating itself to the general will and losing itself in it, the state becomes the instrument by which the individual will achieves power and prestige. In the original way of looking at things, the community was the end; now it becomes the means. The Greek can win recognition only through the state; for that reason he continues to be attached to it, even after it has become simply a means of fulfilling his own ambitions. He remains ready to make great sacrifices for it and he considers exile the most frightful of punishments ...', W. Vischer, *Die oligarchische Partei und die Hetairien in Athen von Kleisthenes bis ans Ende des peloponnesischen Krieges* (Basel, August Wieland, 1836) 3-4.

designed the title vignette of Wagner's book.¹³ Like a picture puzzle, the unbound Prometheus on the cover of *The Birth of Tragedy*, seen from this different angle, reveals the lineaments of another famous Greek myth: the liberation of culture that Nietzsche envisioned in 1871 also entailed the emancipation from his own *Über*father Wagner – and the revolutionary, democratic ideals of the 1848 generation that the latter still represented.

The iconological ambiguities discernible in the title vignette emblematize the larger ideological contradictions and conflicts going on beneath the seemingly a-political surface of *The Birth of Tragedy*, with its Schopenhauerian metaphysics¹⁴ and eulogies on Wagner. These contradictions will be explored below in close examination of what one might call the political 'subtext' of Nietzsche's first book: the little essay on 'The Greek State' mentioned above. A careful, contextualized reading of this essay provides three new interpretative angles not just on *The Birth of Tragedy*, but on Nietzsche's overall intellectual formation in the early 1870s. First of all, 'The Greek State' marks an early – and hitherto unnoticed – rupture in Nietzsche's relation to Wagner. Already during his 'Tribschen idyll' (1869-1872)¹⁵ with the composer, as we shall see, Nietzsche called into question the neo-humanist, emancipatory image of the Greek *polis* that formed a central reference-point in Wagner's anti-capitalist aesthetics. This qualifies the chronology of Nietzsche's alienation from Wagner and, at the same time, emphasizes the ideological aspects of their eventual falling-out, which have hitherto been largely neglected, even by authorities in the field like Dieter Borchmeyer and Jörg Salaquarda.¹⁶ Nietzsche's estrangement from Wagner has traditionally been explained in the context of his disillusionment with Bayreuth at the *Ring* rehearsals in 1876; his distaste of Wagner's 'genuflection before the Cross' in Parsifal; and his rapidly decreasing acceptance, in the mid-1870s, of Wagner's intellectual tutelage. A little less traditional perhaps is Martin Gregor-Dellin's recent claim that the rift between the two men was, ultimately, the consequence of Wagner's 'mortally insulting' suggestion in 1877 that Nietzsche's physical frailty, especially his bad eyesight, was due to excessive onanism.¹⁷ What an analysis of 'The Greek State' shows is that beyond the biographical and the boudoir, Nietzsche's break with Wagner had an important political component.

Second, the ideas – about the *polis* and its agonistic ethos as well as the more general connections between politics and culture – that Nietzsche formulated in 'The Greek State' betray the emergence of a new father figure in his intellectual orbit, one whose influence soon came to rival Wagner's: Jacob Burckhardt. Nietzsche scholars, so far, have either neglected

---

13 See Ross, *Der ängstliche Adler* (n. 3, above) 259. In *The Case of Wagner* (1888), Nietzsche remarked that Wagner's father was an actor named Geyer, adding, mockingly, 'ein Geyer ist beinahe schon ein Adler': *KSA*, VI, 40.
14 See H. Lloyd-Jones, 'Nietzsche', in H. Lloyd-Jones, *Blood for the Ghosts: Classical Influences in the 19th and 20th Centuries* (London 1982) 165-81 (173).
15 A small town near Lucerne, Tribschen was Wagner's Swiss exile, where he and Cosima received the young Nietzsche on many occasions before the two moved to Bayreuth in 1872. See D. Borchmeyer, *Das Tribschener Idyll: Nietzsche-Cosima-Wagner. Eine Textcollage* (Frankfurt a. M. 1998).
16 See D. Borchmeyer and J. Salaquarda (eds), *Nietzsche und Wagner: Stationen einer epochalen Begegnung*, 2 vols (Frankfurt a. M. and Leipzig 1994), II, 1273-1386.
17 See M. Gregor-Dellin, *Richard Wagner. Sein Leben, sein Werk, sein Jahrhundert* (Munich 1980) 748-59.

or prettified Burckhardt's impact on Nietzsche's political thought.[18] When he is mentioned at all in the secondary literature, Burckhardt is usually credited with bringing about Nietzsche's critical re-assessment, after 1870, of the new German *Machtstaat*, indeed of the state as such,[19] and his transformation into a largely anti-political cosmopolitan freespirit – 'the good European'.[20] This role assigned to Burckhardt as the guardian angel saving Nietzsche's soul from the nationalist fiends of Tribschen and Bayreuth needs to be re-considered.[21] 'The Greek State' suggests that Burckhardt's impact on Nietzsche's thinking was deeply ambiguous and in many ways radicalized his anti-democratic, anti-modern views.

Third, there are important continuities between the political ideas Nietzsche expounded in 'The Greek State' and those of his later writings. These continuities call into doubt the image of Nietzsche as an essentially a-political thinker, concerned primarily with 'self-fashioning' – an image projected by, *inter alia*, Walter Kaufmann, Alexander Nehamas and Martha Nussbaum.[22] They also question the 'indeterminate', endlessly malleable Nietzsche, the ironic Proteus and playful debunker of meta-narratives, presented by post-modernist critics like Jacques Derrida and Gilles Deleuze.[23] As will be shown below, Nietzsche, in the different phases of his philosophical development, consistently upheld a number of deeply anti-egalitarian, illiberal views – views that he first voiced in 'The Greek State'. These anti-egalitarian continuities in his thought also make it very difficult to appropriate him – as political theorists like David Owen and Bonnie Honig have recently done[24] – as the prophet of a new '*agon*istic' form of democracy.

I

Even though it contains the clearest and most elaborate statement of Nietzsche's political thinking in the early 1870s, the essay on 'The Greek State' remains a little known text[25] so that

---

18 Neither K. Ansell-Pearson, *An Introduction to Nietzsche as a Political Thinker* (Cambridge 1994), nor B. Detwiler, *Nietzsche and the Politics of Aristocratic Radicalism* (Chicago 1990), contains a single reference to Burckhardt. The failure to explore Burckhardt's impact on Nietzsche's anti-democratic conception of ancient Greece is also one of the few lacunae in the otherwise excellent book by H. Cancik, *Nietzsches Antike. Vorlesung* (Stuttgart and Weimar 1995).
19 See, for instance, C. Pletsch, *Young Nietzsche: Becoming a Genius* (New York 1991) 111-12, and W. Kaufmann, *Nietzsche: Philosopher, Psychologist, Antichrist*, 4th edn (Princeton 1974) 180.
20 This was the label Nietzsche used to fashion a new cosmopolitan, francophile persona – and to indicate his detachment from Wagner's cultural nationalism. See *Human, All Too Human* II, 2 (The Wanderer and his Shadow): *KSA*, II, 593.
21 See Ross, *Der ängstliche Adler* (n. 3, above) 313.
22 See Kaufmann, *Nietzsche* (n. 19, above); A. Nehamas, *Nietzsche: Life as Literature* (Cambridge MA 1985); M. Nussbaum, 'Pity and Mercy: Nietzsche's Stoicism', in *Nietzsche, Genealogy, Morality: Essays on Nietzsche's 'On the Genealogy of Morals'*, ed. R. Schacht (Berkeley 1994) 139-67.
23 See J. Derrida, *Spurs: Nietzsche's Styles*, transl. B. Harlow, Chicago 1979, and G. Deleuze, *Nietzsche and Philosophy*, trans. H. Tomlinson, New York 1983.
24 D. Owen, *Nietzsche, Politics and Modernity* (London 1995) and B. Honig, *Political Theory and the Displacement of Politics* (Ithaca 1993). See also W. E. Connolly, *Identity/Difference: Democratic Negotiations of Political Paradox* (Ithaca 1991). These democratic readings of Nietzsche are subjected to a cogent critique in F. Appel, *Nietzsche contra Democracy* (Ithaca 1999) 1-16
25 An English translation is now available in F. Nietzsche, *On the Genealogy of Morality*, ed. K. Ansell-Pearson (Cambridge 1994) 176-86. So far, B. v. Reibnitz, 'Nietzsche's "Griechischer Staat" und das deutsche Kaiserreich', *Der altsprachliche Unterricht* III (1987) 76-89, provides the only detailed

a brief summary of its central arguments seems in order. Drawing on Plato's *Republic*,[26] Nietzsche glorifies the ancient Greek *polis* as an anti-socialist, anti-liberal archetype: a hierarchically structured, cruelly oppressive society, whose cultural excellence rested on the relentless exploitation of slave labour. Nietzsche leaves little doubt that he considers similar forms of oppression and exploitation as necessary preconditions for the cultural regeneration of contemporary Europe: 'In order for there to be a broad, deep fertile soil for the development of art,' he writes, 'the overwhelming majority has to be slavishly subjected to life's necessity in the service of the minority.'[27] Nietzsche identifies this minority as a tiny elite of great individuals endowed with artistic genius. To produce and protect such individuals in a caste-like society is the task of the state. It is the state, according to Nietzsche, which overcomes the natural *bellum omnium contra omnes*[28] and 'forces huge masses into such a strong cohesion that the chemical separation of society, with its pyramidal structure, has to take place'.[29] The state, with its 'iron clamps' both restrains and externalizes the violent instincts of its subjects, thereby establishing domestic peace, while perpetuating military conflict with other states. The latter, in Nietzsche's eyes, is no less important for cultural production than the former, for only out of a 'war-like society' will 'the radiant blossoms of genius sprout forth'.[30] Nietzsche concludes his essay by paying homage to Plato,[31] who 'through poetic intuition' grasped the 'actual aim of the state' in his *Republic*: 'the Olympian existence and constantly renewed creation and preparation of genius'.[32] He explains the fact that Plato actually conceived this genius not in terms of artistic excellence, but of wisdom and knowledge, by ascribing these judgments to Socrates, whose rejection of art Plato, 'struggling against himself', adopted as his own.[33]

discussion of the text, its context and reception. But see L. Alfieri, *Apollo tra gli schiavi: La filosofia sociale e politica di Nietzsche, 1869-1876* (Milan 1984) 137-65, and the astute comments in R. Safranski, *Nietzsche: Biographie seines Denkens* (Munich 2000) 61-70. The interpretation of 'The Greek State' in K. Ansell-Pearson, *An Introduction to Nietzsche as a Political Thinker* (Cambridge 1994) 71-78, overemphasizes the parallels to Rousseau and Hegel.

[26] On the similarities between Nietzsche's and Plato's ideal *polis* see H. Ottmann, *Philosophie und Politik bei Nietzsche*, 2nd edn (Berlin and New York 1999) 44-48.

[27] *KSA*, I, 767. Nehamas's discussion of suffering ignores the crucial cultural justification of physical and psychological pain that Nietzsche offers here: Nehamas, *Nietzsche* (n. 22, above) 121-23.

[28] Nietzsche actually employs the Hobbesian phrase here, though he seems to have taken it from Schopenhauer's *World as Will and Representation I*, see A. Schopenhauer, *Werke*, 5 vols (Zurich 1988), I, 432 and 448.

[29] *KSA*, I, 769.

[30] *KSA*, I, 772.

[31] Nietzsche's assessment of Plato in the early 1870s is still predominantly positive. In his 'Introductory Lectures on the Platonic Dialogues' (1871/72), he portrays him as the epitome of a Greek sage and 'als agitatorischen Politiker, der die ganze Welt aus den Angeln heben will und unter anderem auch zu diesem Zwecke Schriftsteller ist': *Nietzsche Werke: Kritische Gesamtausgabe*, ed. G. Colli and M. Montinari (Berlin and New York 1967-), II/4, 8-9. Nietzsche's references Plato in this period reveal a particular sympathy for his political philosophy. See F. Ghedini, *Il Platone di Nietzsche* (Naples 1999) and Ottmann, *Philosophie* (n. 26, above) 146-51, 260-66, 276-81.

[32] *KSA*, I, 776.

[33] *KSA*, I, 776-77. Cf. Nietzsche's later attempt to dissociate Plato and Socrates in *Beyond Good and Evil* (1886): '... ja man darf, als Arzt, fragen: "woher eine solche Krankheit am schönsten Gewächse des Alterthums, an Plato? hat ihn doch der böse Sokrates verdorben? wäre Sokrates doch der Verderber der Jugend gewesen? und hätte seinen Schierling verdient?"', *KSA*, V, 12.

These idiosyncratic reflections on the Greek *polis*[34] belonged to an early draft version, about a hundred and twenty pages long, of *The Birth of Tragedy*, entitled 'The Origin and Aim of Tragedy' ('Ursprung und Ziel der Tragödie').[35] On his return from a long vacation in Lugano (12 February-2 April 1871), Nietzsche stopped at Tribschen (3-8 April 1871), where 'The Origin and Aim of Tragedy' was read and discussed with Cosima and Richard. Nothing is known about the content of these discussions and their impact on Nietzsche's subsequent revisions of the manuscript. But when he re-worked 'The Origin and Aim' for publication in April/May of that year, Nietzsche excluded the sections on the sociopolitical background to Greek tragedy in their entirety. This purged version of the manuscript was subsequently incorporated into *The Birth of Tragedy*,[36] where political context, as we have seen, played but a marginal role.

We can only speculate why Nietzsche excluded these 'political' sections from the manuscript, but it seems highly likely that he did so at the request of Wagner. The Master (as Wagner liked to be called) was the only figure in Nietzsche's intellectual vicinity at the time powerful enough to override his authorial intentions in such a way. That Nietzsche had intended the sociopolitical sphere to be an integral part of his analysis of Greek tragedy is evidenced by a number of notes in his unpublished manuscripts, fragments and plans (the so-called *Nachlaß*). Between the winter of 1869 and the spring of 1871, Nietzsche jotted down dozens of outlines for what would eventually become *The Birth of Tragedy*, most of which included chapter headings on slavery and the state.[37] The importance he attached to this part of the book is further underlined by the fact that he carefully excerpted the relevant passages from 'The Origin and Aim' in April 1871, labelling the new excerpt a 'Fragment of an extended version of *The Birth of Tragedy*'.[38] This fragment was almost identical with the essay on 'The Greek State' that Nietzsche offered as a birthday present to Cosima Wagner in

---

34 Of course, classical scholars before Nietzsche had depicted slavery and the violence of political life in the small city-states as necessary ingredients of the cultural excellence of ancient Greece. Nietzsche himself singled out F. A. Wolf in this context. 'Wenn Friedrich August Wolf die Nothwendigkeit der Sklaven im Interesse einer Kultur behauptet hat, so ist dies eine der kräftigen Erkenntnisse meines großen Vorgängers, zu deren Erfassung die Anderen zu weichlich sind': *KSA*, VII, 156. On the role of slavery see M. Finley, 'Ancient Slavery and Modern Ideology', in his *Ancient Slavery and Modern Ideology* (New York 1980) 11-66, and G. Cambiano, *Polis: Un modello per la cultura europea* (Rome 2000). On political strife, see G. Billeter, *Die Anschauungen vom Wesen des Griechentums* (Leipzig and Berlin 1911) 212-15, 422-30. Still, Nietzsche's reflections on the *polis* contrasted sharply with the classicizing image of Hellenic society that continued to inform the work of most nineteenth-century German *Philologen*.

35 See *Nietzsche Werke: Kritische Gesamtausgabe* (n. 31, above), III/5 142-55.

36 See B. v. Reibnitz, *Ein Kommentar zu Friedrich Nietzsche, 'Die Geburt der Tragödie aus dem Geiste der Musik (Kap. 1-12)* (Stuttgart and Weimar 1992) 43-46.

37 See, for example, *KSA*, VII, 79-80, 103-04, 119, 158. In his lectures on the 'History of Greek Literature' (1874/75), Nietzsche, similarly, presented a contextualized reading of the ancient authors, paying particular attention to their 'social status' (*sociale Stellung*): see H. Cancik and H. Cancik-Lindemaier, *Philolog und Kultfigur: Friedrich Nietzsche und seine Antike in Deutschland* (Stuttgart and Weimar 1999) 126-27. V. Pöschl, 'Nietzsche und die klassische Philologie', in *Philologie und Hermeneutik im 19. Jahrhundert: Zur Geschichte und Methodologie der Geisteswissenschaften*, ed. H. Flashar, *et al.* (Göttingen 1979) 141-55 (151), calls Nietzsche a 'Vorläufer der soziologischen Kulturbetrachtung'.

38 See *KSA*, VII, 333-49.

December 1872, as the third of the 'Five Prefaces to Five Unwritten Books': a luxurious, leatherbound manuscript in Nietzsche's best hand-writing.[39]

Nicely packaged though it was, Nietzsche's gift did not go down well in Tribschen. On 1 January 1873, an irritated Cosima noted in her diary that Nietzsche's manuscript was 'not amusing at all' and revealed a 'clumsy abrasiveness' (*ungeschickte Schroffheit*).[40] There followed a three-week hiatus in the correspondence between the Master and his self-proclaimed disciple – something quite unusual during the Halcyon days of their friendship in the early 1870s. Though notoriously narcissistic and easily irritated, Wagner was not unjustified in feeling abraded by Nietzsche's essay. 'The Greek State' drew the composer's attention to the fundamental differences between his own conception of the *polis* and that of his supposed devotee and prophet. Despite his turn to Schopenhauerian pessimism in the 1850s, Wagner never abandoned the idealized image of classical Greece projected by Winckelmann, Schiller and Humboldt.[41] Like these earlier neo-humanists, Wagner regarded the republican city-state of the fifth century BC as the necessary background to the moral and cultural perfection of Greek antiquity:[42] a model of complete, harmonious social integration, a 'free

---

39 The manuscript is preserved in the Goethe-Schiller-Archiv (Stiftung Weimarer Klassik), Weimar. It was first published in Maximilian Harden's political weekly *Die Zukunft*, which steered a radically *realpolitisch*, pro-Bismarckian course in the 1890s: F. Nietzsche, 'Der griechische Staat', *Die Zukunft* 3 (1895) 599-608. For Harden's debt to Nietzsche see B. V. Weller, *Maximilian Harden und die 'Zukunft'* (Bremen 1970) 105-06: 'Bei Nietzsche fand [Harden] den Begriff der Macht formuliert. [...] Politik wurde – durch die Nietzsche-Rezeption – von Harden nicht als der Bereich erklärt, in dem Individualsittlichkeit herrschte, sondern als der, in dem "Macht sich das Recht hämmert".' Three years after 'The Greek State', interestingly, Harden published the notes on slavery from Burckhardt's lecture manuscripts on Greek cultural history: see J. Burckhardt, 'Sklaverei in Griechenland', *Die Zukunft* 25 (1898) 17-31. A facsimile edition of 'The Greek State' was published by Keiper during the Second World War in the series *Dokumente zur Morphologie, Symbolik und Geschichte*: F. Nietzsche, *Fünf Vorreden zu fünf ungeschriebenen Büchern* (Berlin 1943).

40 C. Wagner, *Die Tagebücher*, 2 vols, ed. M. Gregor-Dellin and D. Mack (Munich and Zurich 1976) I, 623. Wagner's reaction to Nietzsche's second public lecture in Basel, 'Socrates and Tragedy' (1 February 1870), already revealed a certain degree of scepticism: even though he agreed with Nietzsche's (thoroughly Wagnerian) musings on the Greek tragedians, Wagner confessed his 'terror' (*Schreck*) in face of the 'boldness' (*Kühnheit*) with which Nietzsche had presented his 'new ideas': R. Wagner to F. Nietzsche, 4 February 1870, in Borchmeyer/Salaquarda, *Nietzsche und Wagner* (n. 16, above), I, 49-50. Borchmeyer rightly remarks that 1872, a year that in many ways marked the apex of their friendship, also saw a considerable number of subtle rifts (*untergründige Differenzen*) between Nietzsche and Wagner: D. Borchmeyer, 'Richard Wagner und Nietzsche', in Müller/Wapnewski, *Wagner Handbuch* (n. 4, above) 125-26.

41 See, e.g., his impassioned exclamation in a letter to Nietzsche: 'O Freund! Wo die hymnischen Worte hernehmen, wenn wir aus unsrer Welt auf jene unbegreiflich harmonischen Wesen [i.e. the Greeks] blicken!': R. Wagner to F. Nietzsche, 4 February 1870, in Borchmeyer/Salaquarda, *Nietzsche und Wagner* (n. 16, above), I, 50. This is *echt* Winckelmann. In his Zurich Writings, Wagner consistently labelled the Greeks 'harmonisch', 'heiter', 'naiv', 'unreflektiert' 'schön, stark und frei'. Schadewaldt, 'Richard Wagner und die Griechen' (1962) (n. 4, above) 9, argues that Wagner rejected the 'epigonenhaften Klassizismus' of the nineteenth-century German Graecophiles, but remained indebted to the ideas 'der damaligen klassischen Altertumswissenschaft historisch-romantischen Gepräges', that is, to the thought of Droysen, Welcker, Boeckh, and, especially, K. O. Müller.

42 For the civic humanist ideas informing early German philhellenism see Winckelmann's programmatic statement in his *Geschichte der Kunst der Alterthums* (Dresden 1764) 130: 'In Absicht der Verfassung und Regierung von Griechenland ist die Freyheit die vornehmste Ursache des Vorzugs der Kunst. Die

association of artistic individuals', as he called it in his 1849 essay on 'The Artwork of the Future'.[43] Even more emphatically than Schiller and Humboldt, Wagner associated this cultural and moral perfection with the system of direct democracy practised, as he saw it, in Periclean Athens.[44] In 'Art and Revolution', he described the public performance of an Aeschylean play as a communitarian event: 'The Athenians came together from the state assembly, from the courts of law, from the countryside, from the ships, from the camps of war...and filled the amphitheatre with thirty thousand men, to watch the performance of the most profound tragedy, the *Prometheus*, to gather before this mightiest artwork, to comprehend themselves and their own activity, to form the closest unity with their own essence, their corporation, their god'.[45] Like the young Hegel in the early 1790s,[46] Wagner conceived Greek tragedy as a popular festival and an essentially democratic institution. With the Bayreuth *Festspiele*, he sought to revive this notion of a 'public art' (*öffentliche Kunst*). The auditorium of the *Festspielhaus* was to be modelled on an 'ancient amphitheatre', so that the audience would sit in complete equality, not divided by estates as in the feudal-hierarchical 'system of boxes and galleries [Logenränge]'.[47] In all of these respects, then, Greek civilization represented an ideal for Wagner and a potential remedy for the fragmented, alienated and oppressed people of contemporary Europe. It only had one flaw in his eyes: the institution of slavery. The division between free man and slave, according to Wagner, was the reason for the decline of Athens and – as he put it in decidedly Left Hegelian fashion – 'the fateful hinge of world history'.[48]

As we have seen, Nietzsche begged to differ. Greek civilization, for him, was anything but 'ideal', and hardly compatible with the canonical philhellenist labels 'serenity', 'moderation', and 'humanity'.[49] In many respects, 'The Greek State' represented Nietzsche's first

---

Freyheit hat in Griechenland allezeit den Sitz gehabt ...'. F. Meinecke, *Die Entstehung des Historismus*, in his, *Werke*, 9 vols (Munich 1957-79), III, 292, comments: 'Ein kausaler Hauptgedanke Winckelmanns nun war, daß ... die politische Freiheit es sei, von der die Kunst "gleichsam" das Leben erhalte und mit deren Verlust sie "notwendig" sinken und fallen müsse. Wir kennen diesen durch das ganze 18. Jahrhundert gehenden Gedanken von der belebenden Wirkung der Freiheit und der lähmenden Wirkung des Despotismus, der zu dem ... Gemeingut der Aufklärung gehörte.'
43 *GSD*, III, 198: 'die freie künstlerische Genossenschaft'.
44 For Wagner's admiration of Athenian democracy see U. Bermbach, *Der Wahn des Gesamtkunstwerks: Richard Wagners politisch-ästhetische Utopie* (Frankfurt a. M. 1994) 148-52.
45 *GSD*, III, 15. See also *ibid.*, 23.
46 For Hegel's views on Greek politics see J. T. Roberts, *Athens on Trial: The Antidemocratic Tradition in Western Thought* (Princeton 1994) 214-20, and P. Kain, *Schiller, Hegel, and Marx* (Kingston and Montreal 1982) 34-74.
47 R. Wagner, 'Das Bühnenfestspielhaus in Bayreuth' (1873), quoted in Müller/Wapnewski, *Wagner Handbuch* (n. 4, above) 11.
48 *GSD*, III, 33. On the design of the Festspielhaus see F. Spotts, *Bayreuth: A History of the Wagner Festival* (New Haven 1994) 30-54.
49 See his comment in the notes to the (unpublished) fifth Untimely Meditation 'Wir Philologen' (1875): 'Das Menschliche, das uns das Alterthum zeigt, ist nicht zu verwechseln mit dem Humanen', *KSA*, VIII, 17.

concentrated effort[50] to deconstruct the classicized Greece of German neo-humanism[51] and to project a dark, violent, 'tragic' Greece as an anti-humanist counter-ideal. This deconstructive effort entailed the dissection of the old Winckelmannian connection between 'liberty and letters', which formed a cornerstone of Wagner's panegyrics on the ancients in his Zurich Writings. In fact, Nietzsche's conception of Greek politics in 'The Greek State' was diametrically opposed to Wagner's, as the following, slightly schematized, juxtaposition shows. Wagner's ideal Greek city-state was Athens; Nietzsche, by contrast, praised Sparta and the military ethos expressed in its Lycurgian constitution.[52] For Wagner, the *polis* functioned according to Aristotle's model republic, where citizens rule and are being ruled in turn; for Nietzsche, the model was Plato's aristocratic, coercive state.[53] The cultural activities within the *polis*, according to Wagner, aimed at social integration and the creation of harmonious, ethical (*sittlich*) citizens; according to Nietzsche, the marvel of Greek culture depended on strict social segregation and the preservation of aggressive, competitive instincts within the population. Wagner considered slavery as a profoundly disturbing, but ultimately contingent aspect of Athenian culture; Nietzsche regarded slavery as an essential feature of Greek civilization: the clearest expression of its inhuman, oppressive character and the *sine qua non* of its artistic achievements.

'The Greek State', however, called into question not just Wagner's conception of the *polis*, but his politics as such. Nietzsche's eulogy on ancient slavery was interlarded with polemical attacks on the modern ideologies of liberalism and socialism and their – in his eyes – preposterous insistence on the 'dignity of man' and the 'dignity of work', respectively. Such 'conceptual hallucinations' had destroyed the 'prelapsarian innocence of the slaves' by handing them the 'fruit of the tree of knowledge'.[54] The rights of man, democratization, pacifism – these were all expressions of a shallow 'optimistic worldview' that had 'its roots in the teachings of the French Enlightenment' and that now threatened to undermine state power and corrode culture. The reactionary solutions to the social question, the statism and the cultural elitism expounded in 'The Greek State' were deeply at odds with Wagner's worldview. In the eyes of his friend Heinrich Köselitz (alias Peter Gast), it was precisely Nietzsche's 'anti-revolutionary, anti-democratic taste [Kultur]' that 'forever separated him from Wagner's cause'.[55]

---

50 Later attempts include 'Homers Wettkampf '(1872), 'Wir Philologen' (1875) and 'Wissenschaft und Weisheit im Kampfe' (1875).
51 See V. Pöschl, 'Nietzsche und die klassische Philologie' (n. 37, above) 148: '[Nietzsche] war leidenschaftlich bemüht, die von der deutschen Klassik, von Winckelmann und Goethe begründete Idealisierung des Griechenbildes...abzubauen und ein anderes, volleres und, wie er glaubte, realeres Bild des alten Griechentums an seine Stelle zu setzen.' Cancik, *Nietzsches Antike* (n. 18, above) 35-49, provides an excellent analysis of Nietzsche's revaluation of the philhellenist *Griechenbild*.
52 Neo-humanist Graecophiles like Schiller vehemently rejected the institutions of Lycurgus because they reduced the Spartan subjects to mere means: see Roberts, *Athens on Trial* (n. 46, above) 212. For Nietzsche, by contrast, the large majority of people in the *polis* were just that: means to the higher end of artistic genius.
53 B. Yack, *The Longing for Total Revolution: Philosophical Sources of Social Discontent from Rousseau to Marx and Nietzsche* (Princeton 1986) 360, rightly remarks: 'The participatory republicanism of the *polis* inspires in [Nietzsche], even in his youth, none of the enthusiasm it inspires in Rousseau and the young Hegel.'
54 *KSA*, I, 765-66.
55 Quoted in Borchmeyer/Salaquarda, *Nietzsche und Wagner* (n. 16, above), II, 1253.

As proof-reader of Wagner's memoirs and copyist of the 1848-Urtext of *Siegfried*,[56] Nietzsche was well aware of the composer's early anarcho-socialist leanings, his indebtedness, since the Paris years (1839-1842), to the thought of Saint-Simon, Fourier, and especially Proudhon,[57] his participation in the Dresden riots of 1849, his lasting friendship with the radical democrat and revolutionary August Röckel.[58] In this respect, too, Wagner's thinking was characterized by a much higher degree of continuity than some of his biographers have allowed.[59] Despite various official retractions, especially for the sake of his royal patron Ludwig II, Wagner remained faithful to the basics of his early revolutionary thought, especially the ideal of a non-oppressive, non-exploitative society.[60] In *German Art and German Politics* (1867), he again lashed out against the state and the commodification of culture in capitalist society. The essays in *Art and Religion* (1880) reiterated many of his Feuerbachian ideas from 1849. The Rousseauean notion, first expressed in 'The Artwork of the Future', that 'we are all human beings and therefore equal',[61] still permeated the so-called 'Regenerational Writings' of the early 1880s.[62] The *Ring*, begun in 1848 and completed in 1874, stands as a powerful testimony to his continuing anti-capitalist stance. Though the exorbitant ticket prices eventually undermined the original plan, Wagner had conceived the *Festspiele* as 'Volksfeste' (popular festivals) – and the 'Volk', for him, were 'all those who experience hardship [Noth]'.[63] The proletariat evidently belonged to the alienated modern masses that were to be redeemed by his *Gesamtkunstwerk*. Nietzsche's 'Greek State', by contrast, explicitly denounced the egalitarian

---

56 See C. Wagner, *Tagebücher* (n. 40, above), I, 401. That Nietzsche regarded Wagner's *Siegfried* as a revolutionary work is evident in *The Case of Wagner* (1888): '"Woher stammt alles Unheil in der Welt?" fragte sich Wagner. Von "alten Verträgen": antwortete er, gleich allen Revolutionsideologen. [...] "Wie schafft man das Unheil aus der Welt? Wie schafft man die alte Gesellschaft ab?" Nur dadurch, daß man den Verträgen ... den Krieg erklärt. Das thut Siegfried.': *KSA*, VI, 19-20.
57 See Nietzsche's disdainful comment, in *The Case of Wagner*, that 'Wagner hat, sein halbes Leben lang, an die Revolution geglaubt, wie nur irgendein Franzose an sie geglaubt hat': *KSA*, VI, 19.
58 See J. Heyne, 'Über die Beziehung zwischen Richard Wagner und August Röckel', *Katalog des Richard-Wagner-Museums Graupa b. Dresden* (Dresden 1989).
59 See, e.g., C. v. Westernhagen, *Wagner* (Zurich and Freiburg 1979) and H. Mayer, 'Richard Wagners geistige Entwicklung' in *idem*, *Richard Wagner* (Frankfurt a. M. 1998) 11-69. Even Mayer (64) concedes, however, 'daß Wagner in allen Wandlungen doch niemals völlig mit seinen früheren fortschrittlichen Anschauungen zu brechen vermag; daß immer wieder auch der Revolutionär Wagner auflebt und an einzelnen Stellen siegreich durchbricht'.
60 For these continuities in Wagner's political thinking see Bermbach, *Der Wahn des Gesamtkunstwerks* (n. 44, above) 307-12. On the 'Bakunist' elements in his writings see Mayer, 'Richard Wagners geistige Entwicklung' (n. 59, above) 48-49, 53-56.
61 R. Wagner, *Gesammelte Schriften und Dichtungen* (Leipzig 1907), III, 41.
62 See his qualification, in 'Heldentum und Christentum' (1881), of Gobineau's racial theories, which, as Wagner remarks, overlook the fact that 'beim Überblick aller Racen die Einheit der menschlichen Gattung unmöglich zu verkennen [ist]'. For Wagner, the human species as such possesses 'die Anlage zur höchsten moralischen Entwicklung': *GSD*, X, 276-77. Nietzsche never embraced such a universalist, egalitarian conception of humanity, as the following comment in *The Gay Science* (1882) reveals: 'Wir sind keine Humanitarier; wir würden uns nie zu erlauben wagen, von unsrer "Liebe zur Menschheit" zu reden – dazu ist Unsereins nicht Schauspieler genug! Oder nicht Saint-Simonist genug, nicht Franzose genug.' *KSA*, III 630. With the label 'Schauspieler', Nietzsche was alluding to Wagner whose 'Schauspieler-Natur' he had emphasized as early as 1874, see *KSA*, VII, 756.
63 *GSD*, III, 59.

rhetoric of the French Revolution as 'completely un-Germanic' and 'Romanistically flat'.[64] Instead, it called for a radicalized form of capitalist exploitation, a capitalism without the comforting ideology of human rights. This was its 'tragic' message to the new industrial slaves: to bear the chain without caprice or consolation and to renounce all 'optimistic' attempts to change their social being.[65] For the 'Olympean' group of masters and artists, on the other hand, the tragic worldview recommended by Nietzsche implied the 'heroic' determination not to succumb to compassion and weakness in face of the 'terrifying' facts of an exploitative society. Anything else would court disaster. 'If culture were left to the discretion of the people', Nietzsche mused, the result would be 'iconoclastic destruction' – 'the cry of pity' of the oppressed masses would 'tear down the walls of culture'.[66]

With this last image, Nietzsche was probably alluding to the Paris Commune,[67] an event that strikingly brought to the fore the political differences between himself and Wagner.[68] At the end of May 1871, as Thiers's government troops were quelling the uprising in a 'Week of Blood', bourgeois newspapers in Germany and Switzerland published greatly exaggerated reports about acts of vandalism and arson attacks by the *fédérés*.[69] The (as it turned out, spurious) news that the retreating Communards had set the Louvre on fire and thus destroyed its precious artworks threw Nietzsche into an almost existential crisis.[70] In a letter to his

---

64 *KSA*, I, 773. For Nietzsche's critique of Rousseau and the French Revolution see K. Ansell-Pearson, *Nietzsche contra Rousseau: A Study of Nietzsche's Moral and Political Thought* (Cambridge 1991) 19-102, G. Goedert, 'Fortschritt durch "Freiheit, Gleichheit, Brüderlichkeit"? Zu Nietzsches Kritik der Französischen Revolution', in *Fortschritt im geschichtlichen Wandel*. Schriftenreihe der freien Akademie 18, ed. J. Albertz (Berlin 1998), and U. Marti, *'Der große Pöbel und Sklavenaufstand'*: *Nietzsches Auseinandersetzung mit Revolution und Demokratie* (Stuttgart 1993).
65 See L. Gossman, *Basel in the Age of Burckhardt: A Study in Unseasonable Ideas* (Chicago 2000) 426: 'The pessmistic and tragic view of life has the obvious advantage, from the point of view of the ruling class, of providing no justification whatsoever for the slaves to feel that they should be recognized as the equals of their masters.'
66 *KSA*, I, 768.
67 Marc Sautet, Hubert Cancik, and Rüdiger Safranski argue that the original version of 'The Greek State' was written under the impact of the Paris Commune: see Sautet, *Nietzsche et la Commune* (Paris 1981) 92-93; Cancik, *Nietzsches Antike* (n. 18, above) 61; and Safranski, *Nietzsche* (n. 25, above) 65. Reibnitz, 'Nietzsches "Griechischer Staat"' (n. 25, above) 79, n. 13, is more cautious in her dating of the text.
68 Note that Nietzsche completed 'The Origin and Aim of Tragedy', which contained the original version of 'The Greek State', in the last week of March 1871, that is, after the Commune had been established on 18 March 1871. On Nietzsche's reception of the Commune see Sautet, *Nietzsche et la Commune* (n. 67, above) and Alfieri, *Apollo* (n. 25, above) 125-30.
69 On the German reception of the Commune see G. Grützner, *Die Pariser Kommune: Macht und Karriere einer politischen Legende. Die Auswirkungen auf das politische Denken in Deutschland* (Cologne 1963). In his much-publicized Reichstag speech of 25 May, the leader of the Social Democrats, August Bebel, declared that the battle cry of the Parisian workers – 'War to the palaces, peace to the huts, death to hardship [Noth] and idleness!' – would soon be the battle cry 'of the entire European proletariat': *Stenographische Berichte über die Verhandlungen des Deutschen Reichstags* (I. Leg. Periode, I. Session 1871, 2. vol. 921), quoted in Grützner, *Pariser Kommune* (*op. cit.*) 36-37. Note that in 'The Greek State', Nietzsche had singled out idleness as a necessary precondition for the development of culture: *KSA*, I, 767. For the nineteenth-century debates on idleness and industry see A. Rabinbach, *The Human Motor: Energy, Fatigue, and the Origins of Modernity* (Berkeley 1990) 19-45.
70 E. Nolte, *Three Faces of Fascism: Action Française, Italian Fascism, National Socialism* (New York 1963) 61, shows that the young Charles Maurras reacted to the Week of Blood very similarly: 'only the

academic superior in Basel, Wilhelm Vischer-Bilfinger, dated 27 May 1871, he explained why he had had to cancel his lectures at the university the previous day: 'The news of the past few days', he wrote, 'were so terrible that I was in an unbearable mood. What is one's significance as a scholar in face of such earthquakes of culture! ... This is the worst day of my life.'[71] Arriving in Tribschen on the following day, he told Wagner, in similar terms, that his entire existence as a student of classical culture had been rendered worthless by this act of proletarian iconoclasm.[72] Wagner listened with dry eyes: an old associate of Bakunin[73] (who was rumoured to be amongst the arsonists), he made it quite clear to his youthful friend that his own sympathies lay with the Communards. As for the preservation of Europe's great cultural legacy: 'If you are unable to paint pictures again', Wagner declared, 'you do not deserve to possess them'.[74] A few weeks later, he re-emphasized his positive assessment of the Parisian incendiaries. 'The Communists' attempt to set all of Paris on fire', he told Cosima, was 'the only magnificent aspect' (*der einzige grandiose Zug*) of the uprising. That the renewal of culture could only take place after a work of destruction was something that he, Wagner, had already prophesied in *The Artwork of the Future*.[75]

Read against the backdrop of Wagner's comments on the Paris Commune, the anarcho-socialist ideas of his Zurich Writings and his republican, philhellenist conception of the *polis*, Nietzsche's 'Greek State' emerges as a poisonous gift to Bayreuth, a veiled declaration of independence from the Master – at a moment that is generally regarded as the highpoint of their friendship.[76] A contextualized reading of Nietzsche's essay thus qualifies the traditional chronologies of his relationship with Wagner, which posit the first rifts between both men

---

thought that the Louvre had been in danger agitated [Maurras] ... he disregarded the mass shootings, the terrible repression'. Nietzsche, likewise, took no notice of the thousands of Communards killed by the Versailles government in the last week of May – unlike the Wagners: see C. Wagner, *Tagebücher* (n. 40, above), I, 395.

71 See F. Nietzsche to W. Vischer-Bilfinger, 27 May 1871: *KSB*, III, 195. It seems that this was not rhetorical hyperbole. During an introspective moment in the summer of 1879, Nietzsche jotted down a list of occasions on which he had cried – the first was the Paris Commune: *KSA*, VIII, 583. The Commune had a very similar effect on Nietzsche's friend Rohde: see E. Rohde to F. Nietzsche, 28 May 1871, in *Nietzsche Briefwechsel: Kritische Gesamtausgabe*, ed. G. Colli and M. Montinari, II/2 (Berlin and New York 1977) 376-77.

72 See C. Wagner, *Tagebücher* (n. 40, above), I, 392.

73 See Wagner, *Mein Leben* (n. 3, above) 397-402.

74 C. Wagner, *Tagebücher* (n. 40, above), I, 392. For Wagner's sympathy with the Communards see also C. Wagner to F. Nietzsche, 2 June 1871, in *Nietzsche Briefwechsel* (n. 71, above) 382. As late as September 1878, Wagner declared that 'die Kraft dieser Bewegung [i.e. socialism] nur in der Zerstörung liegen könne; alles Konstruktive sei kindisch ... er [i.e. Wagner] wolle schon froh sein, wenn in unserer Gesellschaft noch so viel Kraft läge, das Bestehende zu vernichten, man habe aber an der Commune in Paris gesehen, wie kläglich mühsam dies Vernichten vor sich gehe': C. Wagner, *Tagebücher* (n. 40, above), II, 181. These observations echo the 1849 manifesto 'Die Revolution' in which Wagner lets the 'sublime goddess Revolution' say: 'Ich vernichte, was besteht, und wohin ich wandle, da entquillt neues Leben dem todten Gestein.' One of the main targets of the goddess's destructive energies is capitalist exploitation: 'Zerstören will ich die Ordnung der Dinge, die Millionen zu Sclaven von Wenigen, und diese Wenigen zu Sclaven ... ihres eignen Reichthumes macht': R. Wagner, 'Die Revolution', in R. Wagner, *Sämtliche Schriften und Dichtungen*, 16 vols (Leipzig 1911-16), XII, 249-51.

75 C. Wagner, *Tagebücher* (n. 40, above), I, 401.

76 See Müller/Wapnewski, *Wagner Handbuch* (n. 4, above) 125.

around 1874/75. It also draws attention to the important ideological aspects of their estrangement. In most of the critical literature on the break, these ideological aspects are reduced to Wagner's anti-semitism and nationalism. Nietzsche's critique of Wagner in the mid-1870s, accordingly, appears as that of a progressivist, cosmopolitan free-spirit overcoming the neo-Romantic, *völkisch* ideas of his former idol.[77] The above analysis of 'The Greek State', however, suggests that Nietszsche's separation from Wagner also contained a decidedly anti-modern, reactionary element. Finally, 'The Greek State' provides an important new interpretive perspective on *The Birth of Tragedy*, by highlighting the political implications of Nietzsche's Schopenhauerian terms, most notably his call for a rebirth of the tragic, pessimistic worldview of the Greeks. In the new foreword to the 1886 re-edition of the book, Nietzsche defined the central argument of *The Birth of Tragedy* as a repudiation of 'all the known prejudices of our democratic age', an attack on 'the great optimistic-rationalist-utilitarian victory' and on 'democracy, its political contemporary'.[78] Nietzsche's retrospective self-interpretations are generally to be taken with a grain of salt, but 'The Greek State' reveals that there was indeed a profoundly anti-democratic message inscribed in *The Birth of Tragedy*, a message that was quite at odds with the panegyrics to Wagner's cultural revolution at the end of the book. While officially propagating the Wagnerian cause, Nietzsche had in fact already begun to tread new paths that would soon lead him away from Bayreuth and the artwork of the future.

II

Initially at least, he was accompanied on these paths by the Swiss cultural historian Jacob Burckhardt. Nietzsche met Burckhardt in the spring of 1869 and was immediately fascinated by the 'inspiring loner' (*geistvoller Sonderling*), as he described the solitary *Altbasler* to his friend Erwin Rohde.[79] Over the next few years, the two men, who were colleagues at the University of Basel as well as the *Pädagogium*,[80] established a closer bond. This probably never amounted to a friendship (as Nietzsche liked to think), but it led to a frequent and, it seems, candid exchange of ideas in the early 1870s[81] that shaped Nietzsche's anti-classical revaluation

---

77 See, e.g., Kaufmann, *Nietzsche* (n. 19, above) 30-41.
78 *KSA*, I, 16.
79 F. Nietzsche to E. Rohde, 29 May 1869: *KSB*, III, 13: 'Nähere Beziehungen habe ich von vornherein zu dem geistvollen Sonderling Jakob Burkhardt [sic] bekommen; worüber ich mich aufrichtig freue...' The two best accounts of Nietzsche's relation to Burckhardt are E. Salin, *Jacob Burckhardt und Nietzsche* (Basel 1938) and A. v. Martin, *Nietzsche und Burckhardt. Zwei geistige Welten im Dialog*, 4th edn (Munich 1947). See also C. Andler, *Nietzsche und Burckhardt* (Basel 1926) and W. Kaegi, *Jacob Burckhardt: Eine Biographie*, 7 vols (Basel 1947-82), VII, 36-71.
80 The *Pädagogium* was primarily a preparatory college for the University, which also offered a general education to the sons of Basel's mercantile elite.
81 See F. Nietzsche to E. Rohde, 21 December 1871: 'Mit Jakob Burkhardt [sic] habe ich einige schöne Tage verlebt, und unter uns wird viel über das Hellenische conferirt.' Further evidence of his exchanges with Burckhardt can be found in the letters to C. v. Gersdorff, 7 November 1870 (*vertraute Spaziergänge*); C. v. Gersdorff, 18 November 1871 ('Dämonenweihe'); E. Rohde, mid-February 1872 (extended discussions on the *Birth of Tragedy*); E. Rohde, 19 March 1874 (Burckhardt's positive response to the second *Untimely Meditation*); F. Overbeck, 21 May 1875 ('Heute war ich mit Jacob Burckhardt zusammen'); E. Nietzsche, 8 July 1875 ('nachher spazierte ich mit Jakob Burckhardt ¾ Stunde im Münster-Kreuzgang'); C. v. Gersdorff, 26 September 1875 ('mit Jacob Burckhardt geht es immer gut'): in *KSB*, III, 257, 155, 244, 293/94; *KSB*, IV, 211; and *KSB*, V, 54, 71, 113.

of Hellenic civilization and his gradual ideological detachment from Wagner. At that time, Burckhardt, who rejected Wagner's musical as well as his political radicalism,[82] embodied a kind of surrogate father[83] for the young Nietzsche and an antidote to the Master's spell.[84] The effects of this antidote made themselves felt for the first time in 'The Greek State'.

To be sure, there is some evidence, both in the *Nachlaß* and in the early philological writings, that Nietzsche had developed the basic notions expressed in 'The Greek State' before his peripatetic discussions with Burckhardt in and around Basel.[85] His fascination with the pre-classical age of Greek history, for instance, dates back to his valedictorian essay at Schulpforta in 1864, which depicted the elegiac poetry of Theognis of Megara as a manifestation of the proud military ethos of the Dorian aristocracy. In this essay, the twenty-year old graduand interpreted sixth-century Megara as a rigidly stratified caste society threatened by a 'class war' (*certamen inter has classes*)[86] between the old landed elite and new democratic forces represented by the maritime merchants. Nietzsche's reflections on the cultural significance of the *polis* and *agon*, similarly, seem to predate his conversations with Burckhardt. As early as the winter of 1869, he remarked in his notebook that Greek civilization 'had to perish' after the Persian Wars, because its 'basic element', the 'ardently beloved small city-state',[87] engaged in a perpetual 'wrestling match' (*Ringkampf*) with other city-states, was replaced by the more centralized political structures of the Athenian and Spartan empires.[88]

---

82 See C. P. Janz, *Friedrich Nietzsche: Biographie*, 3 vols, 2nd edn (Munich 1993), I, 325; Salin, *Nietzsche und Burckhardt* (n. 79, above) 54, and Kaegi, *Jacob Burckhardt* (n. 79, above), VII, 40, 52, 53. While teaching at Zurich in the mid-1850s, Burckhardt was anxious to keep his distance from German revolutionaries like Gottfried Semper and Wagner, who had, as he remarked in a letter to a friend, 'imbibed too much poison': J. Burckhardt to J. H. Frey, 29 November 1855, in J. Burckhardt, *Briefe. Vollständige und kritisch bearbeitete Ausgabe*, ed. M. Burckhardt, 10 vols (Basel 1949-86), III, 213, see J. Wenzel, *Jakob Burckhardt in der Krise seiner Zeit* (East Berlin 1967) 32. See also H. Trog, 'Jacob Burckhardt', *Basler Jahrbuch* (1898) 97. The antipathy was reciprocal: see C. Wagner, *Tagebücher* (n. 40, above) II, 589, 837. Wagner's comments suggest that he – rightly – suspected Burckhardt of having influenced Nietzsche's apostasy from Bayreuth.

83 See A. Bollinger and F. Trenkle, *Nietzsche in Basel* (Basel 2000) 25: 'Nietzsche, der immer nach älteren, bedeutenden Lehrern, Mentoren, Vorbildern suchte ..., erkannte Burckhardts Bedeutung sofort, besuchte wenn möglich dessen Vorlesungen oder liess sich von Studenten Vorlesungsnachschriften anfertigen.'

84 For Burckhardt as an antidote to Nietzsche's Wagnerism, see Ross, *Der ängstliche Adler* (n. 3, above) 312-19.

85 In light of this evidence, Cancik, *Nietzsches Antike* (n. 18, above) 41, argues that Nietzsche developed his *Griechenbild* independently from Burckhardt. He underestimates the extent to which the exchange with Burckhardt confirmed and radicalized Nietzsche's initial findings. See F. Stähelin's Introduction to J. Burckhardt, *Griechische Kulturgeschichte*, I, ed. F. Stähelin (Berlin and Leipzig 1930) xxiii-xxix.

86 See F. Nietzsche, *Werke und Briefe. Historisch-Kritische Gesamtausgabe*, 5 vols, ed. H.-J. Mette *et al.* (Munich 1933-42), III, 56.

87 Note that Nietzsche used the word 'Kleinstaat' in this context and not '*polis*'. The latter appeared for the first time in his notes from 1874/75, that is, after he had read the transcripts of Burckhardt's lectures on Greek cultural history. It was largely thanks to Burckhardt that the term '*polis*' became common currency in German classical scholarship.

88 *KSA*, VII, 46. Cf. Nietzsche's notes to the essay 'Wissenschaft und Weisheit im Kampfe' (1875), *KSA*, VIII, 110: 'Die centralisierenden Tendenzen, durch die Perserkriege entstanden: ihrer haben sich Sparta und Athen bemächtigt. Dagegen war 776-560 davon nichts da: die Cultur der *Polis* blühte.'

The decisive impulses, however, seem to have come from Burckhardt.[89] In 1870, the year of his 'intimate walks' with Nietzsche, Burckhardt was busy preparing his lectures on the history of Greek civilization.[90] Presented, for the first time, in the summer semester of 1872, these lectures were a large-scale critique of the idealized Winckelmannian image of antiquity, which he regarded as a historiographical 'fraud' (*Fälschung*).[91] A convinced Schopenhauerian, Burckhardt emphasized the sombre, pessimistic *Weltanschauung* of the ancients and the violent political forces that formed the backdrop to their cultural flowering. Nietzsche immediately realized the parallels – he himself spoke of a 'wonderful congruence'[92] – between his own views on antiquity and those of Burckhardt. He also realized that the latter had gone further in his explorations of the dark sides of Hellas.[93] There can be little doubt indeed that Burckhardt, who had been gathering material for his lectures on Greek antiquity since 1867,[94] played the more prominent speaking role in this discursive community – and that Nietzsche was ready to listen. He acknowledged as much in his letters to Rohde, a fellow classicist, who sometimes accompanied the two men on their walks. Looking back on his conversations with Burckhardt, he told Rohde in December 1871 that one could now 'learn quite a few things about Hellenic civilization [*das Hellenische*] in Basel'.[95] In February 1872, he announced, in similar terms, that he would have 'much! to learn' from Burckhardt's lectures on Greek cultural history in the summer.[96]

In 'The Greek State', Nietzsche indicated this debt somewhat more obliquely, by dint of two concealed references to Burckhardt's lectures 'On the Study of History' and his book on the *Civilization of the Renaissance in Italy*, respectively. The first appears in the text as a paraphrase of Burckhardt's dictum that 'power is in itself evil';[97] the second in form of a positive comparison between the agonistic urges of the Greeks and the political instincts of the

---

[89] See Kaegi, *Jacob Burckhardt* (n. 79, above), VII, 46-50, 72-73, and S. Bauer, *Polisbild und Demokratieverständnis in Jacob Burckhardts 'Griechischer Kulturgeschichte'* (Basel 2001) 73-86.

[90] See J. Oeri, 'Vorwort des Herausgebers', in J. Burckhardt, *Griechische Kulturgeschichte*, 4 vols, ed. J. Oeri (Berlin and Stuttgart 1898-1902), I, vi.

[91] J. Burckhardt, *Griechische Kulturgeschichte* = vols V-VIII of J. Burckhardt, *Gesammelte Werke*, 10 vols (Basel and Stuttgart 1955-59), VI, 348. For Burckhardt's anti-classical reinterpretation of ancient Greece see K. Christ, *Hellas: Griechische Geschichte und deutsche Geschichtswissenschaft* (Munich 1999) 69-80; L. A. Burckhard, 'Das Bild der Griechen in Jacob Burckhardts "Griechischer Kulturgeschichte"', in *'Mehr Dionysos als Apoll': Antiklassizistische Antike-Rezeption um 1900*, ed. A. Aurnhammer and T. Pittrof (Frankfurt a. M. 2002), 113-34; and Lionel Gossman's article in this volume (47-59).

[92] See F. Nietzsche to E. Rohde, 29 May 1869, *KSB*, III, 13.

[93] See C. Andler, *Nietzsche und Burckhardt* (n. 79, above) 45: 'Nietzsche wußte, daß ihm Burckhardt in diesem Studium [of Greek culture] weit voraus war.'

[94] See Gossman, *Basel in the Age of Burckhardt* (n. 65, above) 297-98.

[95] F. Nietzsche to E. Rohde 21 December 1871: *KSB*, III, 257. See also O. Crusius, *Erwin Rohde: ein biographischer Versuch* (Tübingen and Leipzig 1902) 268.

[96] *KSB*, III, 294. That Nietzsche was willing to accept Burckhardt as his teacher is illustrated by his – unusual – decision to sit in on his colleague's historiographical lectures in 1870 and 1871. In one of his last 'mad epistles' from Turin, significantly, Nietzsche addressed Burckhardt (for the first time, in the informal 'Du') as 'our greatest teacher'. F. Nietzsche to J. Burckhardt, 4 January 1889, *KSB*, VIII, 574: 'Nun sind Sie – bist Du – unser grosser grösster Lehrer ...'.

[97] *KSA*, I, 768. This was a reference to J. Burckhardt, *Über das Studium der Geschichte. Der Text der 'Weltgeschichtlichen Betrachtungen' auf Grund der Vorarbeiten von Ernst Ziegler nach den Handschriften*, ed. P. Ganz (Munich 1982) 260.

'men of the Renaissance'.⁹⁸ With these two allusions, Nietzsche obviously intended to pay homage to his new mentor and inspiration. In fact, Burckhardt's influence is evident throughout the essay. The set of concepts around which Nietzsche constructed his anti-humanist ideal type of the *polis* – oppression, stratification, contest, war – were essentially Burckhardtian concepts. While Burckhardt never glorified these aspects of antiquity as Nietzsche did, he nevertheless regarded them as an integral part of its great cultural achievements. His claim that 'without the *polis*, higher Greek culture would be unthinkable'⁹⁹ forms a cornerstone of Nietzsche's argumentation in 'The Greek State'. Nietzsche's description of the *agon* as a 'bloody jealousy of one town for another, one party for another, the murderous greed of ... petty wars'¹⁰⁰ closely resembles certain passages in Burckhardt's portrait of the 'colonial age'. Like Burckhardt, Nietzsche regarded the *agon* as an essentially aristocratic notion that belonged to a pre-democratic age.¹⁰¹ Both Burckhardt and Nietzsche stylized this agonistic-aristocratic society of the seventh and sixth centuries BC as an anti-modern ideal.¹⁰² Their portrait of ancient Greece, though progressive in the context of contemporary classical scholarship, was also conditioned by deep-seated reactionary anxieties about the political developments in the nineteenth century, which Burckhardt liked to call 'the revolutionary age'.¹⁰³ 'The Greek State' suggests that Nietzsche adopted not just Burckhardt's views on the ancient city-state, but also his preoccupations with the revolutionary threat to the culture of modern Europe.

As a student in Leipzig (1865-1867), Nietzsche had observed the emergence of the German workers' movement with critical interest.¹⁰⁴ Once he moved to Basel, however, this critical interest turned into outright rejection, an almost paranoid fear of an imminent 'rabble and slave rebellion'.¹⁰⁵ Basel was a city rife with social conflict. Throughout 1869 and 1870, there were massive strikes in the local textile factories and the small ruling elite of the city felt increasingly

---

98 *KSA*, I, 771. This second reference to Burckhardt seems particularly significant in terms of Nietzsche's dissociation from Wagner, because the latter rejected the Renaissance as an age of shallow, artificial cultural achievements and immoral politics: see C. Wagner, *Tagebücher* (n. 40, above), I, 1002-04 and II, 763, 836-37, 864, 955, 1041.
99 Burckhardt, *Griechische Kulturgeschichte* (n. 91, above), V, 62. Cf. Nietzsche's very Burckhardtian reflections in the notes to 'Wir Philologen' (1875), *KSA*, VIII, 60: 'Die Kulturbedeutung der *Polis* instinktiv erkannt; Centrum und Peripherie [of the *polis*] für den großen Menschen günstig ... Das Individuum zur höchsten Kraft durch die *Polis* gesteigert. Neid, Eifersucht wie bei genialen Leuten.'
100 *KSA*, I, 771.
101 Neither Burckhardt nor Nietzsche actually used the term 'archaic' in this context: see G. W. Most, 'Zur Archäologie der Archaik', *Antike und Abendland* 35 (1989) 1-23 (11).
102 See A. D. Momigliano, 'Introduction to the *Griechische Kulturgeschichte* by Jacob Burckhardt', in A. D. Momigliano, *Studies on Modern Scholarship*, ed. G. W. Bowersock and T. J. Cornell (Berkeley 1994) 44-53 (50): 'Burckhardt's antipathy to democracy explodes in the famous chapter in which the paradoxical thesis is expounded that the Greek culture of the fifth century was the product not of a golden age, but of the resistance of the spirit to an age of iron. On the other hand, admiration for Greek aristocracies led him to the definition of the *agon*istic individualistic phase of Greek culture which, even if exaggerated by later scholars, is one of Burckhardt's genuine discoveries.'
103 See J. Burckhardt, *Historische Fragmente*, ed. E. Dürr (Nördlingen 1988) 288-89. See also Roberts, *Athens on Trial* (n. 46, above) 270: 'For Burckhardt...the degeneration of Athenian government into the rule of a petulant, impudent mob evoked more recent developments in France. What had been lost in the Athenians' move into democracy, Burckhardt believed, was nobility.'
104 See Ross, *Der ängstliche Adler* (n. 3, above) 145-49.
105 *KSA*, IV, 335.

besieged by a rapidly growing and more and more politicized working population.[106] In September 1869, four months after Nietzsche had given his inaugural lecture, the First International held its Fourth Congress in Basel. One of the attendants was Mikhail Bakunin.[107] Nietzsche came to see these events through the eyes of the Basel patricians, with whom he liked to associate: Wilhelm Vischer-Bilfinger, Johann Jacob Bachofen, and especially Jacob Burckhardt. He soon embraced Burckhardt's near-apocalyptic visions of an impending proletarian revolution and his concerns about massification as a permanent threat to *Bildung* and *Kultur*.[108] His responses to the social question as it posed itself in Basel in the early 1870s and his views on the politics of the day were remarkably similar to Burckhardt's. Like Burckhardt, Nietzsche rejected universal suffrage, the shortening of working hours – in Basel from twelve to eleven hours per day – the abolition of child labour and the broadening of humanistic education, in particular the establishment of 'educational associations' (*Bildungs-vereine*) for workers.[109] As he put it in the notes for his lectures *On the Future of Our Educational Institutions*, given in 1872, 'universal education is the stage prior to communism ... the condition for communism.'[110] Pauperization he regarded as a problem only insofar as it would prevent the worker 'and his descendants' from continuing to work 'for our descendants'.[111]

More important than these specific political issues, perhaps, were the larger concerns about 'culture and anarchy' which Nietzsche gradually took over from Burckhardt and which appear as a *leitmotiv*, for the first time, in 'The Greek State'. The Paris Commune again appears to have played a role in this process. The (supposed) arson attack on the Louvre filled Burckhardt with the same apocalyptic fears as Nietzsche and, like Nietzsche, he regarded it as an attack on his own existence. His one-time pupil Arnold von Salis reports that in May 1871, Burckhardt remarked with 'choking voice' and 'tear filled eyes': 'A piece of me has perished with the Louvre'.[112] The experience of the Commune, which highlighted the ideological chasm between himself and Wagner, brought Nietzsche closer to Burckhardt. Elisabeth Förster-Nietzsche recalls that on 27 May, 1871, when the news of the Louvre's destruction reached Basel, Nietzsche immediately went to visit Burckhardt at his home in St Alban Vorstadt, to share his grief with the older colleague. Burckhardt, however, had already left for Nietzsche's apartment in Schützengraben to do the same. Eventually both met in Nietzsche's house where they

---

106 See M. Burckhardt, 'Politische, soziale und kirchliche Spannungen in Basel um 1870', in *Franz Overbecks unerledigte Anfragen an das Christentum*, ed. R. Brändle and E. W. Stegemann (Munich 1988) 47-66 and Gossman, *Basel in the Age of Burckhardt* (n. 65, above) 13-105.
107 On Nietzsche and the Congress see Sautet, *Nietzsche et la Commune* (n. 67, above) 113-86.
108 For Burckhardt's political views, see J. Wenzel, *Jakob Burckhardt* (n. 82, above) 13-105; J. R. Hinde, *Jacob Burckhardt and the Crisis of Modernity* (Montreal 2000) 29-136; Gossman, *Basel in the Age of Burckhardt* (n. 65, above) 203-51; and Bauer, *Polisbild* (n. 89, above) 26-44, 87-102.
109 See F. Naake, *Friedrich Nietzsches Verhältnis zu wichtigen sozialen und politischen Bewegungen seiner Zeit* (Diss. Jena 1986) 61, 86, 89.
110 *KSA*, VII, 243.
111 *KSA*, II, 681.
112 A. v. Salis, 'Zum hundertsten Geburtstag von Jacob Burckhardt: Erinnerungen eines alten Schülers', *Basler Jahrbuch* (1918) 270-306 (294). For Burckhardt's response to the Commune see Wenzel, *Jacob Burckhardt* (n. 82, above) 39-40, 42, and especially Kaegi, *Jacob Burckhardt* (n. 79, above), V, 569-74.

discussed the fate of European culture, as Elisabeth tells us, for about an hour, pausing from time to time to heave deep sighs.[113]

Elisabeth's accounts of her brother's life are notoriously unreliable, but it seems entirely plausible that both men were united in their reaction to the Commune and that Nietzsche followed Burckhardt in interpreting this event as an onslaught on the cultural continuity of *Alteuropa*, another manifestation of the destructive energies first unleashed by the French Revolution. In a letter of 2 July, 1871, Burckhardt reflected on 'the terrible days…a month behind us…Yes, petroleum in the cellars of the Louvre and the flames in other palaces are an expression of what the Philosopher [i.e. Schopenhauer] calls "the will to live"; it is the last will and testament of mad fiends desiring to make a great impression on the world … The great harm was begun in the last century, mainly through Rousseau, with his doctrine of the goodness of human nature.'[114] In his lectures 'On the Study of History', Burckhardt had already singled out Rousseau for promoting the 'great optimistic will' that had suffused European society 'since the middle of the eighteenth century' with the hope for progress and change.[115] Nietzsche attended these lectures in the winter semester of 1870/71 – and was deeply impressed by them.[116] The association of Rousseau with the revolutionary movements of the nineteenth century and its shallow 'optimism' became crucial for Nietzsche's later discussions of socialism and anarchism. It was in 'The Greek State' that he made the connection for the first time.

In 'The Greek State', it will be remembered, Nietzsche also proposed a radical solution to this revolutionary threat of Rousseauean optimism: a massive increase in the coercive power of the state. In this respect, too, he drew on Burckhardt. At first sight, Burckhardt, the famous critic of state power in general and the Second German Empire in particular,[117] seems to be a rather unlikely inspiration for this idea. The views on the state that Burckhardt expressed in his lectures 'On the Study of History', however, were hardly as negative as the oft-quoted dictum on the 'evil' essence of power suggests. Burckhardt did not reject political authority as such,[118] but the Hegelian notion of the state as an embodiment of *Sittlichkeit* or morality. For Burckhardt, the origins of the state did not lie in any contractual agreement. 'As far as we can see', he observed in characteristically laconic fashion, 'violence always comes first'.[119] There was but one relative justification for state power in Burckhardt's eyes – 'the necessity of achieving great objectives in foreign affairs, the preservation and protection of cultures which would otherwise perish and the promotion of certain sections of the people, themselves given

---

113 In F. Nietzsche, *Gesammelte Briefe*, ed. E. Förster-Nietzsche and C. Wachsmuth, 5 vols (Berlin and Leipzig 1900-09), III (1904) 167.
114 Burckhardt, *Briefe* (n. 82, above), V, 129-30.
115 See Burckhardt, *Über das Studium* (n. 97, above) 283, 322, 353, 363.
116 See F. Nietzsche to C. v. Gersdorff, 7 November 1870: *KSB*, III, 155.
117 See Hinde, *Jacob Burckhardt* (n. 108, above) 120-28. See also, H. Hofmann, 'Jacob Burckhardt und Friedrich Nietzsche als Kritiker des Bismarckreiches', *Der Staat* 10 (1971) 433-53.
118 Political authority became one his central concerns in the years after the Commune: see Kaegi, *Jacob Burckhardt* (n. 79, above), V, 574. Von Martin, *Nietzsche und Burckhardt* (n. 79, above) 69-70, observes that Burckhardt 'der konservative Patrizier, muß für "Autorität" sein … Doch kann – und sollte – die Macht … eine höhere Funktion haben: als Wegbereiterin der Kultur und als Garant wenigstens irgendeiner Art von "Autorität"'.
119 Burckhardt, *Über das Studium* (n. 97, above) 257. Cf. Nietzsche's claim, in 'The Greek State', that 'Power gives the first right and there is no right which is not fundamentally presumption, usurpation and violence': *KSA*, I, p. 770.

to passivity'.[120] Burckhardt conceived this passive section of the people as a tiny elite of scholars and artists whose cultural productivity depended on their elevated, privileged status *vis-à-vis* the lower classes. Such a hierarchical structure of society could only be upheld by state authority. Hence Burckhardt's claim that 'under a durable tyranny, the arts and sciences thrive as well as or even better than in a republic; Greek culture would hardly have reached its full height without such ... institutions; even Athens needed its Peisistratean age'.[121]

The causal nexus between cultural excellence and political domination[122] was a central thought in the essay on 'The Greek State', where Nietzsche glorified, as we have seen, the 'iron clamps' of the archaic *polis* as the necessary precondition for the work of great artists like Archilochus. Like Burckhardt, Nietzsche repudiated all contractual or utilitarian interpretations of the state as 'false radiance' (*erlogener Glanz*).[123] The role of the state, for Nietzsche, was not to protect the individual rights of its citizens,[124] but to enforce the complete stratification of society, which alone would make possible the blossoming of the arts. His subsequent critique of the new German *Machtstaat* notwithstanding,[125] Nietzsche continued to ponder the ways in which particular social and political structures could enhance a nation's cultural production.[126] The tyrant, for him, remained an important source of patronage for the arts. In his (never completed) fifth *Untimely Meditation*, entitled 'We Philologists' (1875), he repeated almost

---

120 Burckhardt, *Über das Studium* (n. 97, above) 259. Burckhardt's impact on Nietzsche's political thought, thus, was much more complex than Pletsch, *Young Nietzsche* (n. 19, above) 112, allows: 'Sitting in on the lecture of Jacob Burkhardt, [Nietzsche] was exposed for the first time to a careful critique of the modern state ... From that point on, throughout his life, Nietzsche remained a severe critic of Prussian militarism, and statism in general.' In fact, Nietzsche developed the ultra-statist ideas of 'The Greek State' *after* he had attended Burckhardt's lectures 'On the Study of History' in 1870 and 1871.
121 Burckhardt, *Über das Studium* (n. 97, above) 297. Cf. Burckhardt's partial justification of the dictatorship of the Thirty Tyrants in Burckhardt, *Griechische Kulturgeschichte* (n. 91, above), V, 220: Insofar as they had staved off the social chaos of democracy, Burckhardt thought, there was a 'Schimmer of Rechtfertigung' for their rule.
122 This idea of a relation between a strong state and a flourishing culture became a commonplace of conservative *Kulturkritik* at the fin de siècle. In a letter to his brother Heinrich of 1904, Thomas Mann confessed that as an artist he was 'not at all interested in political freedom': 'Die gewaltige russische Literatur ist doch unter einem ungeheuren Druck entstanden? Wäre vielleicht ohne diesen Druck gar nicht entstanden?': T. Mann to H. Mann, 27 February 1904, in *Thomas Mann – Heinrich Mann: Briefwechsel 1900-1949*, ed. H. Wysling, 2nd edn (Frankfurt a. M. 1975) 25. In a later essay on Richard Wagner, Mann coined the phrase 'machtgeschützte Innerlichkeit' (inwardness protected by power) to critically express this notion of the state as a bulwark of culture: T. Mann, *Gesammelte Werke*, 13 vols, 2nd edn (Frankfurt a. M. 1974), IX, 419.
123 *KSA*, I, 769.
124 *KSA*, I, 774: '... daß der Staat ... nicht als Schutzanstalt egoistischer Einzelner gegründet ist'.
125 This critique was also indebted to Burckhardt's reflections on the fate of culture in the great centralized state. See Nietzsche's famous warning in the first *Untimely Meditation* to the effect that the establishment of the German Empire could lead 'to the defeat, even the death [Exstirpation] of German culture': *KSA*, I, 159. For Burckhardt as a critic of the Second Empire see P. Ganz, 'Einleitung', in Burckhardt, *Über das Studium* (n. 97, above) 73-74.
126 See Cancik, *Nietzsches Antike* (n. 18, above) 30-31, 42-49, 61-63. Cf. Kaufmann, *Nietzsche* (n. 19, above) 400-01, who contends that Nietzsche's 'antiracism, his appreciation of the Enlightenment and his admiration for Socrates' were 'as persistent' as his 'anti-statism'. 'The Greek State', in fact, shows that none of these labels can be applied in such absolute terms to the 'early' Nietzsche.

verbatim Burckhardt's comment on Athens' cultural debt to its tyrannical ruler: 'Without the tyrant Peisistratos, the Athenians would have never had tragedies'.[127]

Burckhardt's impact on Nietzsche's political thinking is also evidenced by his praise of war in 'The Greek State'. In his lectures 'On the Study of History' (1870/71), Burckhardt approvingly cited Heraclitus's saying that war was 'the father of all and the king of all' and ascribed to war an aesthetic quality as well as a certain vitalizing effect.[128] Ten years earlier, in his *Civilization of the Renaissance in Italy* (1860), he had described the violent struggles between the North Italian city-states as one of the catalysts for the cultural flowering of the Quattrocento. Raffael's *Stanza d'Eliodoro*, he argued, was inspired by the bloody streetfighting between two warring aristocratic factions in Perugia in 1497.[129] The great Renaissance individuals, who lived heroic, dangerous lives under the constant threat of death in battle, were the exact opposite, in Burckhardt's eyes, of the nineteenth-century bourgeois with his utilitarian mindset and petty commercial desire for 'security' (*Sekurität*).[130] Nietzsche studied – and partly plagiarized – Burckhardt's book on the Renaissance[131] early in 1871, that is, just at the time that he was writing the first draft of 'The Greek State'. In the 'paean on war'[132] that made up the last third of the essay, Nietzsche justified even the most brutal forms of military conflict in terms of their immense political, social and cultural benefits. War was an absolute 'necessity for the state', because it separated the 'chaotic mass' of people in 'military castes', forced the individual to overcome his 'egoistic' instincts, purified society and inspired great artists, just as the Trojan War had inspired Homer.[133] Like Burckhardt, Nietzsche posited a 'mysterious connection' between the agonistic instincts of the Greeks and their cultural creations, between 'battlefield and work of art' (*Schlachtfeld und Kunstwerk*).[134] Like Burckhardt, he juxtaposed the heroic warrior ethos of the ancients and the utilitarian worldview of the modern bourgeois, who merely sought to 'further his own selfish interests'. Reiterating an antisemitic commonplace of the late nineteenth century, he identified modern pacifism with an international 'stateless financial aristocracy'.[135]

---

127 *KSA*, VIII, 109.
128 Burckhardt, *Über das Studium* (n. 97, above) 344-46. See Egon Flaig's comments on Burckhardt's aestheticization of war in this volume (35-38). Cf., however, Ganz, 'Einleitung', in Burckhardt, *Über das Studium* (n. 97, above) 64-68.
129 J. Burckhardt, *Die Kultur der Renaissance in Italien: Ein Versuch*, ed. K. Hoffmann (Stuttgart 1988) 23-24.
130 For Burckhardt's critique of this bourgeois longing for 'Sekurität' see Burckhardt, *Über das Studium* (n. 97, above) 236.
131 See his lecture notes for the 'Encyclopaedie der klass.[ischen] Philologie', held in the summer term of 1871: *Nietzsche Werke: Kritische Gesamtausgabe* (n. 31, above), II/3, 347-53, which contains numerous unidentified excerpts from Burckhardt's *Kultur der Renaissance* (n. 129, above) 138-49.
132 *KSA*, I, 774: 'Päan auf den Krieg'.
133 *KSA*, I, 772-75.
134 *KSA*, I, 772. Julius Langbehn, one of the founding fathers of *völkisch* ideology, regarded this catalytic relation between war and art as characteristic of both Greek and German civilization: 'Krieg und Kunst ist eine griechische, eine deutsche, eine arische Losung': J. Langbehn, *Rembrandt als Erzieher*, 46th edn (Leipzig 1903) 217-18.
135 *KSA*, I, 774. There are a few other, barely concealed, attacks on 'Jewish finance' in the essay: 'Menschen, die durch Geburt gleichsam außerhalb der Volks- und Staatsinstinkte gestellt sind (772), 'jene wahrhaft internationalen heimatlosen Geldeinsiedler' (774) and '[die] in sonderbare Hände geratene moderne Geldwirtschaft (774). For Nietzsche's 'Aryan' (and implicitly antisemitic) inter-

Finally, Nietzsche's discursive community with Burckhardt is visible in the positive revaluation of the individual in 'The Greek State', which contrasts with his glorification, in *The Birth of Tragedy*, of the orgiastic loss of self-hood under the spell of the Dionysian principle. Burckhardt's lectures 'On the Study of History'[136] and the *Civilization of the Renaissance*, again, provided a crucial historiographical reference-point in this respect. For Burckhardt, the emergence of the individual in Renaissance Italy took place primarily in the context of tyrannical violence and immoral despotism.[137] The second section of Burckhardt's *Civilization of the Renaissance in Italy*, entitled 'The Development of the Individual', detailed this antihumanist process of self-fashioning. It is the most heavily marked section in Nietzsche's copy of the book.[138] If *The Birth of Tragedy* seemed predominantly concerned with the communitarian aspects of the Dionysian and depicted the individualizing force of the Apollonian as a mere illusion, 'The Greek State' eulogized the great individual, both as artistic and as military genius. In this respect, Nietzsche's essay points to his 'monumentalizing' representations of great historical figures such as Goethe, Napoleon, and Frederick II in the later writings. Concepts such as 'the great man' or 'the great historical individual' quickly replaced the metaphysical notions of will and representation, which lay at the heart of *The Birth of Tragedy*. It seems no exaggeration, therefore, to say that it was Burckhardt who awoke Nietzsche from his Schopenhauerian slumber.

What this little exploration of Burckhardtian traces in 'The Greek State' suggests is that Nietzsche's 'intimate' exchange with his older colleague had a powerful impact on his thinking in the early 1870s. At the same time, it shows that this impact was deeply ambivalent. On the one hand, Burckhardt helped Nietzsche to develop a new, innovative perspective not just on ancient Greece, but on history in general. He also contributed to Nietzsche's critical reassessment of Schopenhauer's philosophy and Wagner's neo-Romantic, nationalist mythologies. Sceptical, rationalistic, and cosmopolitan, Burckhardt played a pivotal role in paving the way for Nietzsche's philosophical emancipation in the mid-1870s, which ushered in the so-called free-spirit phase. On the other hand, Burckhardt, more than anyone else, it seems, led the young German classicist away from the *altliberal*, emancipatory legacy of

---

pretation of the Prometheus myth in *The Birth of Tragedy* see Cancik, *Nietzsches Antike* (n. 18, above) 62-63. Nietzsche's antisemitic remarks in the early 1870s are sometimes explained as a kind of youthful aberration, inspired partly by a desire to pander to Wagner: see, e.g., W. Santaniello, 'A Post-Holocaust Re-Examination of Nietzsche and the Jews', in *Nietzsche and Jewish Culture*, ed. J. Golomb (London and New York 1997) 21-55 (37). However, the allusions to a Jewish 'financial aristocracy' in 'The Greek State' might just as well be read as a tribute Burckhardt, who was a more conventional, but nevertheless convinced antisemite. See Gossman, *Basel in the Age of Burckhardt* (n. 65, above) 244: 'Burckhardt often associated the new middle-class culture with Jews, who served for so many critics of liberalism and democracy at the time as emblems of modernity – the quintessential *nuova gente* in their alleged rootlessness, intellectualism, commercialism, and parasitism.' See also A. Mattioli, *Jacob Burckhardt und die Grenzen der Humanität* (Munich 2001).

136 Cf. Burckhardt's phrase 'Entfesselung des Individuellen' in Burckhardt, *Über das Studium* (n. 97, above) 127, and Nietzsche's reference to the 'Entfesselung des politischen Triebes' by the 'men of the Renaissance' in 'The Greek State (*KSA*, I, 771) as well as his eulogy, in *Human All Too Human*, I (1878), on the 'Entfesselung des Individuums' in the Renaissance (*KSA*, II, 199).

137 See D. Norbrook, 'The Life and Death of Renaissance Man', *Raritan* 8,4 (1989) 89-110.

138 Nietzsche possessed two copies of Burckhardt's book: both are now at the Anna Amalia Bibliothek, Stiftung Weimarer Klassik, Weimar. For Nietzsche's markings see Sign. C482a, esp. 106-10.

German philhellenism and towards a new, radically anti-democratic conception of politics and culture, paired with an 'aesthetic immoralism'. Those critics who want to credit Burckhardt with handing Nietzsche-Hercules the bow and arrow to slay the Wagner-Vulture should acknowledge that these weapons were essentially double-edged.[139]

III

Insofar as it marks a crucial moment in Nietzsche's intellectual re-alignment in the 1870s, 'The Greek State' represents a transitional text. It is also a seminal text. The belief in the necessity of slavery for culture, the notion of the creative genius as the product of a hierarchically structured society, the glorification of war and the warrior ethos – these were ideas, first formulated in 'The Greek State', which Nietzsche would continue to uphold in his later writings. A brief overview must suffice here to point up these continuities.

In one of the most easily remembered passages of *The Birth of Tragedy*, Nietzsche described the effects of the Dionysian in terms of the 'Ode to Joy' from the last movement of Beethoven's Ninth Symphony: 'Now the slave is a free man, now all the rigid, hostile barriers set up between men by necessity [and] arbitrary power ... break apart. Now, under the gospel of world harmony, every man feels himself not only united [and] reconciled ... with his neighbour, but one ...'[140] There was not a trace of such emancipatory, egalitarian utopias in 'The Greek State', which posited an insurmountable, quasi ontological difference between that small group of 'Olympian' artists and the mass of slaves, the 'blind moles of culture'.[141] That Nietzsche's praise of ancient slavery (and his implicit call for its re-introduction in modern Europe) in the essay was not just a case of *épater le bourgeois* is demonstrated by the startling consistency with which he reiterates this point in the rest of his œuvre.[142] Even when he made a temporary – and, it would seem, superficial – truce with socialism in *Human, All Too Human* (1878), Nietzsche continued to envision a form of slavery, contemplating a 'massive import of barbarian people from Asia and Africa' so that, as he put it, 'the uncivilized world continually serves the civilized world'.[143] In *Daybreak*, he singled out China as a particularly well-suited source of immigrant workers for the West, because of its great supply of 'industrious ants'.[144] He bewailed the end of slavery in the United States after the Civil War and depicted the author of *Uncle Tom's Cabin* as a misguided disciple of Rousseau.[145] In *Beyond Good and Evil* (1886),

---

139 Burckhardt, incidentally, liked the Promethean symbolism of the title vignette: see *KSB*, III, 270.
140 *KSA*, I, 29. See M. S. Silk and J. P. Stern, *Nietzsche on Tragedy* (Cambridge 1983) 181: 'Dionysiac worship ... is essentially communal. It presupposes a *mass* of worshippers "whose civic past and social status have been totally forgotten"'.
141 *KSA*, I, 770. Cf. 'Wir Philologen' (1875), *KSA*, VIII, 60: 'Wie kann man die Alten nur human finden! Gegensatz des Genie's gegen den Broderwerber, das halbe Zug- und Lastthier. Die Griechen glaubten an eine Verschiedenheit der Rasse: Schopenhauer wundert sich, daß es der Natur nicht beliebt habe, zwei getrennte Species zu erfinden.'
142 See I. Christians, 'Die Notwendigkeit der Sklaverei. Eine Provokation in Nietzsches Philosophie', *Nietzscheforschung* 4 (1998) 51-83, and K. Brose, *Sklavenmoral. Nietzsches Sozialphilosophie* (Bonn 1990). See also O. Schutte, *Beyond Nihilism: Nietzsche without masks* (Chicago 1984) 160-69, 185-88.
143 *KSA*, VIII, 481-82.
144 *KSA*, III, 185.
145 *KSA*, XI, 61.

he argued that exploitation belonged to the essence of every society: as an 'original element' (*Ur-Faktum*) of history and 'a basic organic function' (*organische Grundfunktion*).[146]

In order to create and preserve such a system of continued exploitation, Nietzsche argued in 'The Greek State', society had to be rigidly stratified. The 'iron clamps' of the state were necessary to bring about the 'chemical separation' of the masses and to press them into a 'pyramidal structure'. Following the example of Plato's *Republic*, he projected a new 'configuration of society'[147] that was strictly hierarchical. The notion of 'hierarchy' (*Rangordnung*), which first appeared in 'The Greek State', became a recurrent theme in the next twenty odd years of Nietzsche's philosophizing. It informed his radically inegalitarian plans for educational reform in 1872, laid out in the lectures *On the Future of Our Educational Institutions*,[148] and his belief, expressed in the second and third *Untimely Meditation*, that 'the goal of humanity lies in its highest specimen'.[149] To achieve this goal, society had to be hierarchically structured, like the caste-society described in the Laws of Manu, which Nietzsche held up as an example for European civilization in *The Antichrist*. 'A high culture', he remarked there, 'is a pyramid'[150] – the exact image he had used in 'The Greek State'. The notion of rank-ordering also permeated Nietzsche's ethical doctrines, for instance, the claim, proffered in *Beyond Good and Evil* that there be different moralities for different types of human beings.[151] In a fragment of 1888, Nietzsche even went so far as to identify his entire philosophical project with the notion of rank-ordering: 'My philosophy aims at an ordering of rank, not at an individualistic morality'.[152]

The great individuals at the top of the new social order projected in 'The Greek State' comprised the artistic as well as the military genius. The violent struggles between the city-states were part and parcel of the ethical as well as the aesthetic excellence of ancient Greece. Nietzsche frequently reiterated this early 'paean on war' in his subsequent publications.[153] In *The Gay Science* (1882), for instance, he invoked Heraclitus's saying that 'war is the father of all',[154] and lamented that in contemporary Europe 'the esteem for war and the pleasure in war diminish, while the comforts of life are now desired just as ardently as warlike and athletic honours were formerly'.[155] The warrior ethos was a defining characteristic of the 'noble men' described in the *Genealogy of Morality*,[156] whose ruthless exploits provided 'the poets' with 'something to sing about'. In the *Genealogy*, Nietzsche also interpreted the birth of the state as

---

146 *KSA*, V, 208.
147 *KSA*, I, 769.
148 See *KSA*, I, 698-99.
149 *KSA*, I, 383-84.
150 *KSA*, VI, 241. T. Brobjer, 'The Absence of Political Ideals in Nietzsche's Writings: the Case of the Laws of Manu and the Associated Caste-Society', *Nietzsche-Studien* 27 (1998) 300-18, argues against a political reading of *The Antichrist*, but cf. D. Dombowsky, 'A Response to Thomas Brobjer's "The Absence of Political Ideals in Nietzsche's Writings"', *Nietzsche-Studien* 30 (2001) 387-96.
151 *KSA*, V, 156.
152 *KSA*, XII, 273. For the notion of *Rangordnung* in Nietzsche's philosophy, see Detwiler, *Nietzsche* (n. 18, above) 175-78, and Appel, *Nietzsche* (n. 24, above) 23-30.
153 For Nietzsche's glorification of war, see T. L. Pangle, 'The "Warrior Spirit" as an inlet to the political philosophy of Nietzsche's *Zarathustra*', *Nietzsche-Studien* 15 (1986) 140-79, and C. Nolte, *Nietzsche und der Nietzscheanismus* (Munich 2000) 212-19.
154 *KSA*, III, 448. Cf. Burckhardt, *Über das Studium* (n. 97, above) 344.
155 *KSA*, III, 395-96.
156 *KSA*, V, 262.

an act of violent conquest – in terms strongly reminiscent of the relevant passage in 'The Greek State'. The 'blonde beasts of prey', invoked, notoriously, in chapter 17 of the book,[157] seem to be descendants of the 'tiger-like warriors' in the earlier essay.

Read in conjunction with his later writings, 'The Greek State' not only shows Nietzsche at an important ideological crossroads, but also highlights considerable continuities in his thought. It draws attention to a normative base underlying his ethico-political ideas which qualifies his 'post-modernist' image as a ludic, protean relativist. It also calls into question recent attempts to interpret his notion of the *agon* as the blueprint of a new, radical form of democracy.[158] 'The Greek State' is an important text not least because it reminds us that in political terms, Nietzsche's revolutionary philosophy had a decidedly counter-revolutionary dimension.

IV

In 'The Greek State', Nietzsche addressed the same question that Wagner had posed, twenty-two years earlier, in *Art and Revolution*: what were the social and political conditions that had brought about the cultural excellence of ancient Greece? For both men, this question was closely related to another one: what were the social and political conditions that prevented a renaissance of Greek culture in contemporary Europe? Wagner's answer to the second question singled out political oppression and an all-encompassing market economy that enslaved a large section of the people, commodified art and alienated the artist from his public. The rebirth of Greek culture in the nineteenth century, accordingly, hinged on a 'great revolution of human society' (*große Menschheitsrevolution*) that would do away with capitalism and the state. Political authority, Wagner believed, would no longer be necessary in a post-revolutionary future, where every man, in one form or another, would be an artist himself. Nietzsche, by contrast, regarded Wagner's solution as part of the problem. The liberal ideals of the 1848 generation, their rhetoric of rights and humanism, in his view, perpetuated a false revolutionary optimism that made a modern revival of tragic Greek art all but impossible. The 'harsh truth' (*grausame Wahrheit*)[159] that Nietzsche communicated to the Wagners in 1872 was that a renaissance of the Hellenic cultural ideal necessitated a renaissance of the oppressive, exploitative structures of the Greek state and a recantation of precisely those 'conceptual hallucinations' that imbued Wagner's Zurich Writings.

In his autobiography *My Life*, Wagner recalled his state of elation and liberation when, at the height of the Dresden riots, on 8 May 1849, a revolutionary guardsman informed him of the destruction of the old opera house with an allusion to Schiller's 'Ode to Joy': 'Herr Kapellmeister, the divine spark of joy has ignited, the ramshackle building has burnt down to the ground.'[160] Nietzsche was proof-reading *My Life* in the final months of 1870. When he invoked Schiller's credo of universal fraternity in *The Birth of Tragedy*, he sent out a most Wagnerian message. With 'The Greek State', he took it back.

Queens' College, Cambridge

---

157 *KSA*, V, 275.
158 See Honig, *Political Theory*, and Owen, *Nietzsche* (both n. 24, above)
159 *KSA*, I, 767.
160 Wagner, *Mein Leben* (n. 5, above) 414. Wagner had previously conducted a performance of Beethoven's Ninth Symphony in the opera house. For the political uses of the 'Ode to Joy', see E. Buch, *Beethoven's Ninth: a Political History* (Chicago 2003).

ON THE GENEALOGY OF THE GENEALOGICAL METHOD:
OVERBECK, NIETZSCHE, AND THE SEARCH FOR ORIGINS*

ANDREAS URS SOMMER

'In religion and related areas more than anywhere else, the new is burdened with the prejudice that it has come into being arbitrarily. The old has value in and of itself.'[1] Thus Franz Overbeck (1837-1905), recently appointed professor of New Testament Studies and Ancient Church History at the University of Basel, described the contemporary tendency to consider only the original, embryonic stages of a religion as authentic and free of degeneration.[2] A critical reading of Friedrich Nietzsche's *Birth of Tragedy* (1872), published two years after Overbeck's inaugural lecture, reveals an obsession with origins surprisingly similar to the one which Overbeck identified in the Christian (or rather Protestant) milieu.[3] It takes quite a few tricks of the deconstructive trade to interpret Nietzsche's first philosophical book as a text whose 'claims ... can [all] be undermined by means of statements provided by the text itself'. A notion that leads Paul de Man to conclude, 'the entire system of valorization at work in *The Birth of Tragedy* can be reversed at will'.[4]

I am not altogether convinced that de Man's conclusion is valid – or that his premises are correct. Reading Nietzsche's early texts – that is, the ones he actually published and not the oft-quoted 1873 fragment 'On Truth and Lies in an Extra-Moral Sense' – one can hardly ignore their authoritative and political-reformatory character. Despite his own retrospective self-interpretations, the young Nietzsche did not attempt a deconstructive subversion of all

---

* I would like to thank the *Swiss National Foundation for Science* and the *Freiwillige Akademische Gesellschaft Basel* for supporting this and many other projects of mine.
1 F. Overbeck, *Über Entstehung und Recht einer rein historischen Betrachtung der Neutestamentlichen Schriften in der Theologie* (Basel 1871) 3; repr. in F. Overbeck, *Werke und Nachlass*, ed. E. Stegemann *et al.* (hereafter *OWN*) (Stuttgart and Weimar 1994-), I, 83.
2 On Overbeck's intellectual development up to his meeting with Nietzsche see N. Peter, *Im Schatten der Modernität. Franz Overbecks Weg zur 'Christlichkeit unserer heutigen Theologie'* (Stuttgart and Weimar 1992) 42-118. On his inaugural lecture in Basel see A. U. Sommer, *Der Geist der Historie und das Ende des Christentums. Zur 'Waffengenossenschaft' von Friedrich Nietzsche und Franz Overbeck* (Berlin 1997) 29-43.
3 See B. v. Reibnitz, *Ein Kommentar zu Friedrich Nietzsche, 'Die Geburt der Tragödie aus dem Geiste der Musik' (Kap. 1-12)* (Stuttgart and Weimar 1992).
4 P. de Man, *Allegories of reading: Figural language in Rousseau, Nietzsche, Rilke, and Proust* (New Haven 1979) 117-18. Cf. M. Foucault, 'Nietzsche, Genealogy, History', in M. Foucault, *The Foucault Reader*, ed. P. Rabinov (New York 1984) 76-100, which shows a similar tendency to construct wholly un-genealogical continuities between Nietzsche's later concept of genealogy and his earlier understanding of history.

that which we believe to know about ourselves and the world – at least not in his published writings. Instead, he engaged in a radical and radically reactionary form of cultural criticism which at times resembles that of thinkers like Paul de Lagarde.[5]

To legitimise these radically new ideas in his early works, Nietzsche frequently had recourse to a normative early period, which he identified with the pre-classical and pre-Socratic, in other words, the archaic age of ancient Greece.[6] Nietzsche's friend Overbeck, who later gratefully acknowledged 'the lesson learnt from the *Birth of Tragedy*' in his own 1873 polemic *On the Christian Character of our Present-Day Theology*,[7] also measured modern manifestations of the Christian faith against the archetype of early Christianity, or what he called 'ur-Christianity' ('*das Urchristentum*').[8] At the same time, though, he did not hypostatize early Christianity as a timeless norm, as so many Protestants had done since the days of Pietism, if not before. Instead, he confined himself to pointing up the inherent contradictions between the primitive Church, with its otherworldliness and its expectations of an imminent apocalypse, and the manifold forms of its subsequent secularization. Unlike Nietzsche, Overbeck did not argue for a renewal of the archaic age. For him, there was no path leading back to a more authentic Christianity, with the exception of Pascal's path of renunciation. Overbeck, who did not take this path himself, threw the theologians of his time into a deep crisis of legitimation by questioning their claim to identify their own creed with that of early Christianity.

Nietzsche's *Birth of Tragedy* and his contemporaneous fragments have received more scholarly attention in the German and Anglo-American world than is warranted by their philosophical significance or content. Overbeck's thought, by contrast, has been virtually ignored outside Germany and Switzerland, where new interest in him was sparked not least by the recent publication of the *Werk- und Nachlassausgabe*. In Great Britain and North America, however, he is still known predominantly as 'Nietzsche's friend'.[9]

This paper focuses not on Nietzsche's and Overbeck's early works, but on those later writings that reveal a certain critical distance from their initial fascination with origins. There are precious few signs in Nietzsche's so-called 'free-spirit phase' (*c.* 1876-83) of an excessive veneration of the gods of Greece or even of Dionysos. At about the same time, Overbeck, who never cared much for the Greek gods in the first place, turned to examine how the origins of Christianity (which he had once held up to his fellow theologians as a mirror of their supposed '*Christlichkeit*' in his 1873 polemic), through processes that could roughly be described as

---

[5] See A. U. Sommer, 'Zwischen Agitation, Religionsstiftung und "Hoher Politik". Friedrich Nietzsche und Paul de Lagarde', *Nietzscheforschung. Ein Jahrbuch*, IV (1998) 169-94.

[6] See H. Cancik, *Nietzsches Antike. Vorlesung* (Stuttgart and Weimar 1995).

[7] F. Overbeck, *Über die Christlichkeit unserer heutigen Theologie*, 2nd edn (Leipzig 1903) 15; repr. in *OWN*, I, 269.

[8] See F. W. Graf, 'Theolog und Antitheolog. Die Neuentdeckung Franz Overbecks', *Evangelische Kommentare. Monatsschrift zum Zeitgeschehen in Kirche und Gesellschaft*, XXVII (1994) 678-81.

[9] None of his works have been translated into English. The only English monograph known to me appeared in a Swiss-German publishing house: M. Henry, *Franz Overbeck: Theologian? Religion and History in the Thought of Franz Overbeck* (Frankfurt a. M., Berlin, and Bern 1995). See the review of this book in *Theologische Zeitschrift* LII (1996) 183-84. There is now also a very lucid chapter on Overbeck in L. Gossman, *Basel in the age of Burckhardt: A study in unseasonable ideas* (Chicago 2000).

the Hellenization of a Jewish sect, had become an *arcanum*, a no longer accessible field of primitive history. In Nietzsche's and Overbeck's early works, which indirectly inspired each other, the origins of Hellenism and of Christianity, respectively, functioned as an absolute measure for their critique of contemporary Western civilization. The period of their work that will be explored here – which began with the dissolution of Nietzsche's and Overbeck's shared household, and Nietzsche's departure from Basel – sees their emancipation from such a hypostatised notion of origins. The aim of this paper is threefold: it first investigates the new yardsticks of cultural criticism that Nietzsche and Overbeck employed after they abandoned their idealization of the archaic; it then examines whether their dissociation from the archaic as a norm implied an embrace of modernity; and, finally, it situates their rather untimely notion of modernity in the context of their critical projects. The focus of this paper will be on Nietzsche's and Overbeck's different revaluations of the archaic as they manifested themselves in their *opera magna*: the *Genealogy of Morality*, and the *Kirchenlexikon* (Church Lexicon) respectively.

II

At first sight, Overbeck's few publications give the impression of a scholar who became afraid of his own initial boldness in 1873 and henceforth confined himself to learned shop-talk. Apart from New Testament and Patristic specialists, few will be tempted to take a closer look at his *Studies in the history of the Old Church* (1875), *On the Church Fathers' Interpretation of the Dispute between Paul and Peter at Antioch* (1877), *On the History of the Canon* (1880), or *On the Beginnings of Patristic Literature* (1882). Overbeck seems to have failed to achieve what Nietzsche won by turning his back on the academic community: a wide philosophical reception and universal literary fame. This failure could be explained by reference to Overbeck's autobiographical writings which repeatedly stress his lack of ambition.[10]

Overbeck's literary remains, however, cast doubt on this image of a learned one-track specialist who only sought to cultivate his tiny scholarly garden, negligent of where its fruit would fall. The weightiest part of these remains is the so-called *Church Lexicon*, a convoluted work of more than 20,000 octavo pages, comprising excerpts, notes and personal reflections that are alphabetically lematized and connected by cross-references. Even before he took up his chair in Basel, Overbeck used the *Church Lexicon* as a reservoir for his lectures and research projects. He did not conceive it as a literary work, but as a kind of foundation for a projected 'secular history of the Church', which was not only to include religious themes. In 1919, Overbeck's former student Carl Albrecht Bernoulli published a carefully compiled selection from the *Church Lexicon*, entitled *Christianity and Culture*, which immediately attracted widespread public interest and, among other things, provided Karl Barth with decisive stimuli in the conception of his dialectical theology.

---

10 See F. Overbeck, *Selbstbekenntnisse. Mit einer Einleitung von Jacob Taubes* (Frankfurt a. M. 1966) as well as the new critical edition of Overbeck's notes in *OWN*, VII.1.

The recent critical edition of the most substantial parts of the *Church Lexicon* gives us insight into its author's peculiar mode of research and thought.[11] Overbeck, it seems, was never content with a particular finding and continually revised, or cross-referenced it to other findings, only to return to it again later, thus opening up new and often revealing contexts. This was a method of working that he carefully restrained in the writings published during his lifetime, but one which he indulged all the more in the privacy of the *Church Lexicon*. It was a method that never reached an irrevocable opinion or final certainty. Even though he did not aim at an aphoristic style, Overbeck's work is full of aphoristic deftness and polish. His lexicographic enterprise opposed all forms of dogmatism – religious as well as ideological – simply because its ramifications did not allow any form of completion or closure. With its innumerable cross-references and revisions, the *Church Lexicon* all but nullified the normative power of origins.

Having sketched some of the complexities of Overbeck's unpublished work, let us consider a published one, the seemingly polished, specialized tract *On the Beginnings of Patristic Literature*.[12] The latter offered a peculiar literary-historical account of the Old Church that ignored all dogmatic issues and concentrated, instead, on the *form* of the works it examined. Even though it was greeted with surprising enthusiasm by Overbeck's later arch-enemy Adolf von Harnack[13] and other members of the theological guild, this approach failed to set a precedent in patristic studies[14] – however much recent commentators emphasize its seminal character.[15]

What is the topic of Overbeck's essay and what does it have to do with the search for origins? At first sight, Overbeck's attempt to re-evaluate patristics as a literary historical (rather than a dogmatic) discipline seems to have been an intervention in a very specific scholarly debate in the field of Church History, without any further implications. However, a closer look quickly reveals that there was much more at stake than merely learned methodological discussions. Overbeck emphasized that the literature of the Church Fathers, whose rudimentary beginnings he saw in the works of the apologists of the second century, was crucially different from the kind of Christian literature that was written until about 150. The demarcation line Overbeck drew between Patristic literature and early Christian literature (or what he called '*Urliteratur*') was not just a chronological one. It denoted a fundamental

---

11 See *OWN*, IV and V.

12 First published in *Historische Zeitschrift* 48 (1882) 417-72. I am quoting from the orthographically modernized book edition: F. Overbeck, *Über die Anfänge der patristischen Literatur* (Basel 1954). A new critical edition will soon appear in *OWN*, III.

13 See A. Harnack's article in *Zeitschrift für Kirchengeschichte* 6 (1884) 120-21, and *idem*, *Lehrbuch der Dogmengeschichte*, 4th edn (Tübingen 1909), I, 266, n. 1.

14 See Bernoulli's critical comments in his introduction to Titus Klemens von Alexandria, *Die Teppiche (Stromateis). Deutscher Text nach der Übersetzung von Franz Overbeck*, eds. C. A. Bernoulli and L. Früchtel (Basel 1936) 28. The now canonical book on patrology by Berthold Altaner and Alfred Stuiber lists Overbeck's tract in its bibliography, but largely overlooks his critical analysis of the relation between content and form in the literature of the Church Fathers: see B. Altaner and A. Stuiber, *Patrologie. Leben, Schriften und Lehre der Kirchenväter* (Freiburg i. B., Basel, and Vienna 1993) 6.

15 See M. Tetz, 'Über Formengeschichte in der Kirchengeschichte', *Theologische Zeitschrift* 17 (1961) 413-31, and *idem*, 'Altchristliche Literaturgeschichte – Patrologie', *Theologische Rundschau* 32 (1967) 1-42, as well as W. Nigg, *Franz Overbeck. Versuch einer Würdigung* (Munich 1931) 85-110.

formal distinction between the early textual sources of Christendom – to which he apportioned the canonical texts of the New Testament and the letters of the so-called Apostolic Fathers – and the Patristic works: 'This [i.e. the *Urliteratur*] is a literature that Christianity created out of its own means, insofar as it grew on the ground and out of the proper interests of the Christian community before it blended with the world around it ... It keeps a safe distance to the existing forms of profane world literature.'[16] According to Overbeck, the earliest testimonies of Christianity were created in a kind of literary vacuum. Though drawing on Jewish traditions,[17] they showed no tendency to grow into or fuse with the surrounding Roman-Hellenic culture. Christian *Urliteratur* was destined for the immediate consumption within a community still largely indebted to Judaism, not for a wider external public. Its individual elements – particularly the *Epistles* – were conceived as answers to very concrete questions in very concrete circumstances, rather than as universal statements of the one true faith. The process of canonization occluded the real contexts and themes of *Urliteratur* for the sake of trans-historical dignity and universal applicability. As Overbeck puts it in his 1880 treatise *On the history of the Canon*: 'It is in the nature of all canonization to render its objects unrecognisable and one might say with some justification that all the writings in the New Testament ceased to be understood the moment they were canonized.'[18]

Overbeck did not consider Christian *Urliteratur* as a preform of Patristic literature. 'If one separates Christian *Urliteratur* from Patristic literature', he remarked, 'then it is no longer difficult to identify the latter as Graeco-Roman literature imbued with Christian faith and Christian interest'.[19] This sounds innocent enough at first – just like the remark that 'Christianity was able to produce a viable literature only in connection with the existing world literature'.[20] This longing for 'connection' initially grew out of an acute threat to Christianity from a hostile world, which Christianized 'heathens' like Justin Martyr confronted with their apologies in order to soften the fear as well as the aversion of the non-Christian public vis-à-vis the new religion.[21]

Overbeck, however, was not willing to accept the idyllic interpretations of this process that were offered by the Patristic scholars of his time. In contrast to them, he did not see the difference between Christian *Urliteratur* and Christian 'world literature' merely in the fact that the latter clothed the old Christian faith in the new garb of Graeco-Roman worldliness. Overbeck keenly sensed the profound scruples of the early Church Fathers of the second half of the second and the first third of the third century, that is: the apologists, the fighters against heretics, Ireneus of Lyons and, most of all, Clement of Alexandria, who wrote for a 'pagan' public and employed the forms of profane literature for the sake of the outer and inner self-preservation of Christianity. 'The Church Fathers', Overbeck wrote, were 'writers against their own will: despite themselves'.[22] In contrast to their modern exegetes, they realized more

---

16 Overbeck, *Anfänge der patristischen Literatur* (n. 12, above) 36.
17 The 'evangelical form', Overbeck wrote, 'was the only original form ... with which Christianity enriched world literature'.
18 *OWN*, II, 393.
19 Overbeck, *Anfänge der patristischen Literatur* (n. 12, above) 37.
20 *Ibid.*, 38.
21 See *ibid.*, 43-45.
22 *Ibid.*, 41.

or less clearly that the self-preservation of Christianity in the Graeco-Roman world could not be achieved without a loss of religious substance. Hence their scruples. Even when they believed themselves to be transposing what they considered to be the essence of Christianity into the literary forms of Hellenism, the forms – particularly those of philosophical discourse – did not leave the essence untouched. Like few other scholars of his time, Overbeck had a clear understanding of the mutual interdependence of content and form. He refused to do what many of his fellow theologians practice to this day: to consider the content as something that can easily be separated from the form and to assume that only the form, but not the content, was subject to historical contingency. Overbeck's subtle analysis of Clement's work in the last third of his treatise shows how much such formal matters reflected a fundamental caesura, namely the irrevocable end of Christian *Urliteratur* and hence of Christian '*Urgeschichte*' ('early history').[23]

Unable to find a satisfactory answer to the question 'whether a form of expressing one's thought as easily misunderstood as the literary one could be an appropriate and worthy way to proclaim the truth of Christianity',[24] Clement escaped to the clandestine formlessness of the *Stromateis*, a seemingly unstructured collection of thoughts. But the formlessness of the *Stromateis*, Overbeck believed, was their 'intended and characteristic form'.[25] Clement's work was without a true beginning and a true end, a rhetorical game of hide-and-seek, in which truth was 'not immediately made known', but 'partially hidden' and the initiated were allowed access 'only with some difficulty'.[26] Critics have rightly pointed to the parallels between what Overbeck called the form of formlessness in Clement's work and Overbeck's own writings.[27] With its many 'self-references' and its mixture of gathered data and 'general reflection',[28] the *Church Lexicon* indeed shows a number of similarities to Clement's last work.

But let us return to *On the Beginnings of Patristic Literature* and the question of origins. According to Overbeck, Clement, like his contemporary Christian authors, had to resort to seemingly oblique means in order to make the teachings of Christianity accessible to the faithful as well as to the outsiders. Especially among the former, Overbeck argues, there was considerable distrust of the written word, particularly when it showed literary ambitions, and a strong preference for oral instruction. This postulated phonocentrism[29] (to use a fashionable term of post-structuralism) reflects less a general tendency of Western rationality than a very specific crisis originating in the disappearance of the primitive Christian world, its literature, and its audience. The very limited public of *Urliteratur*, that is, the members of the early Christian community, was gradually replaced by a more cosmopolitan audience. Consisting largely of Christianized 'pagans', on the one hand, and 'pagans' who had remained 'pagans', on the other, this new audience made the emergence of a fresh universal kind of literature

---

23 *OWN*, V, 616-25.
24 Overbeck, *Anfänge der patristischen Literatur* (n.12, above) 62.
25 *Ibid.*, 63.
26 *Ibid.*, 61, quoting *Stromateis* VI, 1, 2.
27 See Bernoulli's introduction to *Die Teppiche* (n. 14, above) 60, and esp. Tetz, *Formengeschichte* (n. 15, above) 425-26. But cf. the critical comments of A. Pfeiffer, *Franz Overbecks Kritik des Christentums* (Göttingen 1975) 74, n. 234.
28 B. v. Reibnitz in her introduction to *OWN*, IV, xiii.
29 See, for instance, Overbeck, *Anfänge der patristischen Literatur* (n. 12, above) 41.

inevitable. 'Every work of literature', Overbeck comments, is 'a symptom of its audience.'[30] The canon of New Testament writings, whose origins were more or less obscure apart from their time of composition (after 150), enabled the Church Fathers to stave off the 'danger ... of losing themselves in the foreign world of profane literature':[31] 'When Clement wrote his *magnum opus*, a selection had already been made from Christian *Urliteratur* according to the principle of apostolic descent. This new selection [of writings] had already attained the status of a unique and eternally valid document of Christian revelation and a norm for all things Christian that was henceforth applied to all forms of literature dealing with the Christian church and that allowed the Church Fathers to take the momentous step beyond the apologetic and the polemic.'[32]

Even though he sounds quite matter-of-fact here, Overbeck evidently perceived this process as a decline of the authentically Christian, simply because the new exegetes of the canon concealed the original intentions of the *Urliteratur* for the sake of dogmatic generalization: hence his judgment to the effect that 'the canon of New Testament writings is the death certificate of early Christian literature.'[33] The genesis of patristic literature, thus, was not the glorious induction of Christianity into the Graeco-Roman world, but the tragedy of an irrevocable, catastrophic loss. The death of the Apostles and their immediate disciples had gradually weakened the connection to the beginnings of Christianity, but as long as its original structure and following was preserved, this weakening was not yet tragic. The tragedy began when the representatives of the Church gave in to the pressure of the outside world and allowed Christianity's adaptation to Graeco-Roman civilization.

Thus, in Overbeck's writings Hellenism features neither as a classical ideal (as it did for Winckelmann and the German neo-humanists) nor as a pre-classical norm (as it did for Nietzsche), but in its late 'Alexandrian'[34] guise: as the *causa formalis* of the fall of the early Christian world. Overbeck, however, refrained from condemning post-classical or even classical Greece like Nietzsche. Far from turning Greek antiquity into an ideal (or an anti-ideal) type, he focused – despite a number of general comments on the Greeks in the *Church Lexicon*[35] – on the very concrete impact of Graeco-Roman civilization on a religious

---

30 *Ibid.*, 66.
31 *Ibid.*, 68.
32 *Ibid.*, 68.
33 *Ibid.*, 29.
34 See *Anfänge der patristischen Literatur* (n. 12, above) 50, and *OWN*, IV, 4.
35 See for instance the lemma 'Greeks (Religion) Various', where he compares Erwin Rohde's and Ulrich von Wilamowitz-Moellendorf's reconstruction of Greek religion: 'Rohde treats them [i.e. the Greek religious concepts] like a free spirit – as ancient, classical and naïve; Wilamowitz treats them like a trickster: in an unpleasantly modern, that is, biased, way – romantically, sentimentally': *OWN*, IV, 431. 'I am of the opinion that Rohde's judgment on Burckhardt's *Griechische Kulturgeschichte* (whose publication he [i.e. Rohde] did not witness) would never have been as grotesquely impolite as that of Wilamowitz (*Griechische Tragödien*, vol. II, 2nd edn (Berlin 1899), p. 7)': *OWN*, IV, 432; cf. *OWN*, V, 652. On the whole, Overbeck does not have many good things to say about Wilamowitz. Under the lemma bearing his (Wilamowitz's) name, he writes: 'Sometimes Wilamowitz speaks of a "classically calibrated, schoolmasterly conception" of Hellenism (*Griechische Tragödien*, vol. II, p. 150). His *own* conception of Hellenism might be called a "modern Germanically calibrated" one, however – and strikes me as more "schoolmasterly" than anybody else's': *OWN*, V, 651. None the less, Overbeck himself sometimes acknowledges that antiquity 'for us ... represents a model, for it has lived a life

formation that had grown up entirely out of Jewish roots. *On the Beginnings of Patristic Literature* suggests that Graeco-Roman civilization, in Overbeck's eyes, embodied 'the world' from which the early Christians tried to keep away.[36] In order to 'signify something in this world', however, Christianity had to adapt to the forms of 'world literature' (*Weltliteratur*).[37] The establishment of the Church, therefore, was intimately related to antiquity:[38] 'Christianity is the phosphorescent glow of the decomposing ancients.'[39] As much as Christianity was a product of the ancient world, as much as it belonged to this world and carried many of its elements into modernity, there could be no doubt, for Overbeck, that the Christian participation in Hellenistic culture was not just a threat to the new faith, but the beginning of its dissolution.

To be sure, he acknowledged the many ways in which Christianity transformed classical antiquity while adopting and preserving it. In the *Church Lexicon*, he quoted a passage from Jakob Philipp Fallmerayer (1790-1861), who conceived Christianity as a 'social revolution' that turned everything that existed in the *orbis romanus* upside down: 'Is it not true that [Christianity], which began as an inconspicuous, contemptible little group of "artisans, women, beggars, and slaves", gathering in a few back alleys of Rome, slowly but with frightening patience, undermined the civil law, the *rostra* on the *Forum Romanum*, the gods on the Capitoline Hill, the public cults, the imperial administration, the diadem, the army, the social hierarchy, the customs and the assets of Romulus' descendants and that, after the irreparable bankruptcy of all ethical and political forces, it sketched the plan of a new universal order on the ruins?'[40]

Yet Overbeck refrained from endorsing Fallmerayer's suspicion, so reminiscent of Gibbon, that Christianity was responsible for the decline of the ancient world. Only three pages later, however, and under the same lemma ('Christianity and Antiquity: General Observations'), he quoted Bruno Bauer, who viewed Christianity as a 'revolutionary modification of antiquity' which had become, precisely for that reason, 'a thing of the past'.[41] In his own reflections, however, Overbeck tended to place more emphasis on continuities than on the apparently so abrupt and 'revolutionary' caesurae between antiquity and Christianity.[42] He had no doubt that

---

which the more recent nations are living again; and in all fields, they [the ancients] have made experiences that we are just making again': *OWN,* IV, 12-13. But this remark, ultimately, amounts to little more than the old *historia magistra vitae* motto.

36 *Anfänge der patristischen Literatur* (n. 12, above) 42.

37 *Ibid.,* 39.

38 For him – as for Nietzsche – modern Christianity was a relic of classical antiquity: 'Christianity belongs to antiquity. It is the continuation of antiquity. Only if we make a totally arbitrary cut through antiquity can we consider Christianity as something separated from it.' *OWN,* IV, 159.

39 *Ibid.,* 157.

40 *Ibid.,* 159-60. Overbeck is quoting from J. P. Fallmerayer, *Gesammelte Werke*, vol. III (Kritische Versuche), ed. G. M. Thomas (Leipzig 1861) 486-87 – an excerpt from a review of Johannes Joseph Ignaz von Döllingers *Heidenthum und Judenthum* (1858). Overbeck probably wrote this passage down in the 1870s or 1880s.

41 *OWN,* IV, 161. See B. Bauer, *Kritik der Evangelien und Geschichte ihres Ursprungs*, 2nd edn (Berlin 1851), I, xvi.

42 At least in his later years, Nietzsche, by contrast, subscribed to the theory that Christianity bore the sole responsibility for the decline of the ancient world: see A. U. Sommer, *Friedrich Nietzsche: Der Antichrist. Ein philosophisch-historischer Kommentar* (Basel 2000).

in its relation with the outside world, the Christian Church, long before it became a state church in the fourth century, knew very well how to adapt itself to the social conditions of the Roman Empire. In his *Studies on the History of the Old Church* (1875), he re-examined the commonplace that Christianity had fought for the abolition of slavery. In contrast to most previous scholars, Overbeck argued that the members of the early Church had viewed slavery with disinterest and sometimes actually stressed its social utility. There was little evidence that they showed any humanitarian commitment or humanitarian attitude, however much modern theology liked to claim that they had. Monasticism, of course, rejected slavery along with the notion of personal property, but insofar as it represented an isolated phenomenon within the Church, this only showed 'how far the early Church was from accepting the right to "individual self-determination" which led to the political abolition of slavery'.[43] Instead, the early Church was 'fundamentally unconcerned about the political emancipation of men'.[44] According to Overbeck, it protected 'all the institutions [of the Roman Empire] and showed no interest in shaking or even questioning these, since it considered them as bulwarks of its own power.'[45]

Since the Middle Ages, reforming Christians have tried to interpret Christianity as a revolutionary force, invoking its origins as a normative counter-balance to the later readiness of the Church to identify itself with the interests of the state and its institutions. So, with diametrically opposed intentions, did the late Nietzsche, whose *Antichrist* denounced the (in his eyes) anarchistic desires of the early Christians. Such reformatory aims, however, seem to be totally absent from Overbeck's portrait of early Christendom which sees the only emancipatory force of the first Christians in their decided withdrawal from the 'world' into the pious inwardness of an isolated community. Early Christianity's hope for change, according to Overbeck, resided in its eschatology, which he considered as its principal driving force.[46] Because of their apocalyptic expectations, the early Christians did not give much thought to the world, let alone their own earthly future, and felt little desire actively to change it. To read social emancipatory ideals into their thinking, consequently, was absurd. Christianity's otherworldliness implied not the transformation, but the rejection of the world, contrary to the subsequent claims of liberal and progressive historians of the Church.

Even though he believed that the transformations which Christianity underwent at the end of the second century tainted the old contents of its faith forever, Overbeck, unlike Nietzsche, never called for a renaissance of its origins. Instead he sought to highlight the fundamental discontinuities in Church history. This history he conceived not as a process of organic growth, but as a series of palimpsestic over-writings of an original text that was no longer understood. His studies on the primitive Church dwelled on the origins of Christianity to measure subsequent developments, but only in order to show that the later Church, despite the

---

43 *OWN*, II, 189. As E. Flaig, 'Sklaverei', *Historisches Wörterbuch der Philosophie*, ed. J. Ritter and K. Gründer, IX (Basel 1995) cols 976-985 (978-79), shows, Overbeck's assessment has been supported by recent scholarship.
44 *OWN*, II.
45 *Ibid.*, 200.
46 See E. W. Stegemann, 'Ende der Zeit – Zeit des Endes. Overbeck und die Apokalyptik', in *Franz Overbecks unerledigte Anfragen an das Christentum*, ed. R. Brändle and E. W. Stegemann (Munich 1988) 167-81. Cf. N. Peter, 'Unerledigte Anfragen und befragte Erledigungen: Eine erste Rezeption und Diskussion dreier Beiträge', *ibid.*,196-207, esp. 204-06.

strenuous efforts of a Clement, soon became an institution substantially different from the early one. At any rate, if Overbeck assessed the claims of contemporary Christianity with reference to its beginnings, he only employed the standards of the Church itself which had set up these beginnings as normative by canonizing the New Testament.

The Church Fathers, Overbeck believed, no longer understood the true meaning of the early Church. Consequently, they created, by way of their exegetical artistry, all kinds of possible parallel words and artificial paradises, but failed to re-discover the authentic, that is, the original. Modern scholarship, according to Overbeck, could widen and deepen our understanding of the *mentalité* of the early Christians, but it also forced us to acknowledge that it had become impossible to live according to their doctrines. The development of the Christian faith is contingent upon historical conditions, whose recreation, for Overbeck, was neither desirable nor feasible in the nineteenth century.[47]

III

Hildegard and Hubert Cancik have rightly asked whether Nietzsche may have 'influenced Overbeck's conception of *Urliteratur* ... and his work on the beginnings of Church historiography and patristic literature'.[48] Examining Nietzsche's lecture notes, they conclude that during his work as a professor at the University of Basel, he was concerned with scholarly topics – 'original literature', the formation of canons, discontinuities, 'the relation between "literature and society"' – quite similar to Overbeck's.[49] It would be an interesting exercise to compare these lecture notes with Overbeck's (very few of which, unfortunately, have been edited so far) as well as the philological works of their mutual friend Erwin Rohde. The result of such a comparative analysis would probably be that Nietzsche, far from being the inspiration and driving force behind Overbeck's forays into the history of origins, merely partook in what Overbeck frequently called a 'discursive community'. As his studies on *The Acts of the Apostles* reveal, Overbeck had already begun critically to examine Christian *Urliteratur* before he came to Basel and encountered Nietzsche.[50] In terms of the question we posed at the beginning, the most conspicuous difference between Overbeck's and Nietzsche's conception of the original existed in the first half of the 1870s, when Nietzsche, as we have already pointed out, attempted to resuscitate the civilization of archaic Greece, while Overbeck felt neither the calling nor the necessity to do so.

---

47 H.-P. Eberlein, *Theologie als Scheitern? Franz Overbecks Geschichte mit der Geschichte* (Essen 1989) 120, views Overbeck's project as inherently flawed, 'The historical-formalistic approach develops its own proper dynamic which prevents Overbeck from analysing this text's [i.e. the Gospel according to John] content, its more or less universal way of coming to terms with the world, which its author wanted to express, as the quite well-developed, literary form of the gospel demonstrates'. In fact, the search for such a 'content' is irrelevant, because we, or at least Overbeck, can no longer partake in the kerygmatic and living conditions of the evangelists.
48 H. Cancik and H. Cancik-Lindemaier, *Philolog und Kultfigur. Friedrich Nietzsche und seine Antike in Deutschland* (Stuttgart and Weimar 1999) 124. See also *ibid.*,72.
49 *Ibid.*, 126-27.
50 See the excellent analysis in J.-C. Emmelius, *Tendenzkritik und Formgeschichte. Der Beitrag Franz Overbecks zur Auslegung der Apostelgeschichte im 19. Jahrhundert* (Göttingen 1975), which also pays close attention to Overbeck's lectures.

In the mid-1870s, however, Nietzsche began to distance himself from the idea, first stated in *The Birth of Tragedy*, that the original possessed a practical normativity. The first clear evidence of this is his second *Untimely Meditation* (*On the Use and Disadvantage of History*), whose functional conception of history called into question the normative values of the original. To be sure, neither 'antiquarian' nor 'monumental' historiography, as sketched by Nietzsche, can do without recourse to the original (and even 'critical' historiography remains fixated, *ex negativo*, on it), but the philosophical meta-perspective of the second *Untimely Meditation* makes it quite clear that 'origins' are retrospective projections for the 'enhancement of life', not real, given facts.[51]

Human, All Too Human I (1878) provides further proof for its author's emancipation from the mythologies of the origin. Nietzsche here all but abandoned his former attempts to restore an 'original' state. The book also marks Nietzsche's formal emancipation from the treatise-like style of his earlier works. With its aphoristic reduction of supposedly great ideas – in particular metaphysics and religion – to the human, all-too human conditions of their creation, however, it silently skirts the question about the standards of this criticism. Nietzsche undertakes a 'psychologization' of the great problems of mankind, in order to reveal them in all their triviality. One might consider Nietzsche's approach – not to *solve* the old problems, but to present them as mere illusions or utopias – as an essential characteristic of the Enlightenment, to which he, in fact, professed allegiance with the dedication to Voltaire. All too often, however, the neat bourgeois witticisms of *Human, All Too Human* seem to overshadow the ideal- and idol-shattering gestures of the book.[52] Even though the two volumes of *Human, All Too Human* together constitute Nietzsche's most extensive work, it would almost seem as if Nietzsche had conceived this *mélange* as a 'little' text caricaturing the 'big words' – of the metaphysician, the priest, the politician, and Wagner. Only in the *Gay Science* do the 'little words', that is, the aphorisms, become truly great literature. What matters here, however, is that Nietzsche's former obsession with origins as trans-historical ideals has all but disappeared. In abandoning the ideas and ideals of metaphysics, he abandoned the normative conception of origins.

Yet Nietzsche continued to reflect on the significance of the original even in his 'free-spirit' period. His argumentative strategy as a cultural reformer now, however, was not to idealize a particular stage or culture that once was: 'the old civilizations have lost their greatness ... and historical education forces us to admit that they will never come to live again; it would take unbearable stupidity and equally unbearable zealotry to deny this. But men can consciously choose to develop into a new culture'.[53] Nietzsche is no longer interested in the origin (*Ursprung*) of a phenomenon, but in its provenance or descent (*Herkunft*).

With this shift of focus, Nietzsche adopted the principles of 'critical history', as laid out in the second *Untimely Meditation*. There he demanded that the critical historian 'must have the power and must use this power from time to time, to break up a past and dissolve it in order

---

51 See Sommer, *Der Geist der Historie* (n. 2, above) 44-72.
52 This begs the question whether in *Human, All Too Human*, Nietzsche, despite his ostentatiously aristocratic attitude, was not perhaps involuntarily paying homage to Voltaire as the much-maligned 'philosopher of the bourgeoisie'. Of course, this would be doing injustice to Voltaire.
53 *Menschliches, Allzumenschliches* I, 24, in F. Nietzsche, *Sämtliche Werke: Kritische Studienausgabe*, ed. G. Colli and M. Montinari, 15 vols (Munich, Berlin, and New York 1980) (hereafter *KSA*), II, 45.

to be able to live: this he achieves by taking the past to court, subjecting it to torture and, finally, condemning it; and every past deserves to be condemned.'[54] Origins, for Nietzsche, are no longer normative reference-points, thus, according to which man should orient his actions, but the dubious 'causes' of those institutions that presently claim authority: 'As soon as the emergence of religion, art, and morality has been described in a way that these phenomena can be fully explained, without having to resort to the assumption of *metaphysical interventions* at the beginning and in the course of their development, the strongest interest in the purely theoretical problem of the "thing in itself" and the "phenomenon" ceases to exist'.[55]

This implies that origins still provide a central analytical tool, but that they need to be actively divested of the supernatural aura with which 'religion, art, and morality' seek to endow them. For Nietzsche, these are institutions that emerged from purely secular causes. He who strips away the mythologies woven around them understands the nature of things. Not just the beginnings, but also the development, the further history of a thing *after* its beginning determines its essence. What Nietzsche provides in *Human, All Too Human I*, therefore, is not a secularised metaphysics of origins that deduces the 'essence' of a historical phenomenon (and all things are historical phenomena) from its beginning. In fact, he denies the very possibility of metaphysical speculations about 'essences': 'with religion, art and morality, we do not touch on the "essence of the world itself"; we are in the realm of representation, beyond which no "intuition" can carry us.'[56]

On the one hand, Nietzsche, like the French *philosophes*, seems to consider scientific methodology as a quasi-omnipotent tool and rejects everything supra- and irrational. On the other hand, he does not seem to think that it could provide any metaphysical insight into the 'thing-in-itself' (however that may be constituted), simply because the 'thing-in-itself', just like the 'essence of the world', lies beyond all human perception, if it lies anywhere at all. Nietzsche's rejection of 'religion, art, and morality' as means to comprehending the world is implicitly directed against Schopenhauer, especially against his revaluation of Buddhism and ascetic Christianity as a metaphysics for the people. Insofar as they are worldly conditioned, 'religion, art, and morality', in Nietzsche's opinion, are of no use when it comes to defining the 'essence of the world'.

Nietzsche's argumentation is not entirely convincing. For even if 'religion, art, and morality' have thoroughly secular origins, this does not mean that they cannot teach or contain any truths. Nietzsche confuses genesis and significance here. The 'harmlessness of metaphysics in the future' (to quote the title of the aphorism in question) does not reside in its historicity. Nietzsche's euphoric embracement of science seems to overlook the metaphysical premises underlying those disciplines – physiology and genealogy – with which he wants to answer the question 'why our worldview is so different from the essence of the

---

54 *Unzeitgemäße Betrachtungen. Zweites Stück: Vom Nutzen und Nachteil der Historie für das Leben* (1874) 3, in *KSA*, I, 269. Even the critical historian, however, Nietzsche adds, must try 'to provide himself, quasi *a posteriori*, with a past, from which he would like to descend, as opposed to the one from which he descended. This is invariably a dangerous attempt, because it is so difficult to find a borderline in the negation of the past', *ibid.*, 270.
55 *Menschliches, Allzumenschliches* I, 10, in *KSA*, II, 30.
56 *Ibid.*

world as we know it'. Still, what Nietzsche formulates here is a sketch of the program of the genealogical method, which he will put into action in the *Genealogy of Morality*.

Far from being an antiquarian exercise, this genealogical programme is a 'school of suspicion',[57] which undermines the legitimacy of existing institutions, especially morality. Genealogy explores the origins of a phenomenon in order to question (and to undermine) its present validity. In the preface to the *Genealogy*, Nietzsche claims that he always harboured a suspicion of everything 'that has hitherto been celebrated on earth as morality'.[58] 'My curiosity as well as my suspicion', he writes, 'brought me to the question about the origins of our notions of Good and Bad.'[59] Nietzsche's declared aim in his later writings is not only to destroy 'our moral prejudices'[60] (and all forms of contemporary morality are prejudices for him), but also to give birth to a new morality, that will be radically different from the basic assumptions of 'slave morality'. He does not give us many clues, however, as to who is to enact his new master and individual morality.

A superficial reading of these passages in *The Antichrist* that glorify the Hindu Laws of Manu and recommend the model of a rigorous caste system, for instance, could easily overlook the fact that these laws function predominantly as a contrast to Christianity, but hardly as a blueprint for a new, utopian society.[61] The later Nietzsche's authoritative stance as law-giver – for instance, in the 'Law Against Christianity' – is contradictory insofar as his principal recommendation for the redemption of culture is the creation of a society of great individuals establishing and living by their own laws.

Nietzsche's genealogical project resorts to the 'origins', broadly speaking, in order to demonstrate the total contingency of all that which is commonly regarded as steadfast, sanctioned by natural law and eternally valid. According to Nietzsche's diagnosis, our moral concepts have not come into being by the help of practical reason or the discovery of the true 'human nature'. On the contrary, they rest on the gradual self-empowerment of the large masses, which prevailed over the values of the few 'naturally' strong. The origins of morality that Nietzsche wants to expose, therefore, lie in power interests and power struggles. The origins of 'guilt' and the 'guilty conscience' (subjects that Nietzsche discusses in the second section of the *Genealogy*) also reside in the devious prehistoric dynamics of cruelty and their internalisation in the absence of an outlet for them. In contrast to *Human, All Too Human*, the *Genealogy* no longer refers to the origins in order to explain the essence of a phenomenon; rather, it investigates the dislocations and 'overwritings' that have buried the origins almost completely.

Nietzsche's larger philosophical development in this period could be described as an abandonment of the origins as a normative force, a development that should be seen in terms of what he calls his 'anti-Romantic self-treatment'.[62] His later work focuses on the difference

---

57 *Menschliches, Allzumenschliches* I, 'Vorrede' 1, in *KSA*, II, 13.
58 *Zur Genealogie der Moral. Eine Streitschrift* (1887), 'Vorrede' 3, in *KSA*, V, 249.
59 *Ibid.*
60 *Ibid.*, 248.
61 See T. Brobjer, 'The Absence of Political Ideals in Nietzsche's Writings. The Case of the Laws of Manu and the Associated Caste-Society', *Nietzsche-Studien* 27 (1998) 300-18, which takes issue with Cancik, *Nietzsches Antike* (n. 6, above) 147-49. See also A. U. Sommer, 'Ex oriente lux? Zur vermeintlichen "Ostorientierung" in Nietzsches *Antichrist*', *Nietzsche-Studien* 28 (1999) 194-214.
62 *Menschliches, Allzumenschliches* II, 'Vorrede' 2, in *KSA*, V, 371.

between the original and the originated, which frequently occludes the original almost entirely. Nietzsche's emphasis on the fundamental difference between descent and descendant, however, is no longer accompanied by a call for the restoration of origins. Yet it still condemns that which eventually became of the original. This condemnation, at first sight, merely points to the non-identity of institutions present and past, and, consequently, to the contingency of the present ones. However, it also implies an injustice: Nietzsche's recapitulation of moral history seems to argue that that which has become should not exist at all. This Mephistophelean wisdom, it seems, defies the weapons of the custodians of morality and moral philosophy who often succumb to the naturalist fallacy.

IV

What are the relations between Nietzsche's genealogical project and the learned treatises of his friend Overbeck? Nietzsche's concern for the (much delayed) completion of *On the Beginnings of Patristic Literature*, evidenced in his letters, is not enough to postulate close systematic ties.[63] Our parallel examination of Nietzsche's and Overbeck's writings of the late 1870s and the 1880s, none the less, suggests that the 'discursive community' of both men went beyond the exchange of niceties and health reports, untiring good turns (on Overbeck's part) and untiring complaints (on Nietzsche's part). The anti-Romantic relativization of the original as a normative force, as we have seen, became an essential aspect of their thinking in this period. Overbeck initiated this move insofar as he evaluated the present forms of Christianity with reference to its origins, without, however, invoking these origins as an orientation for life in the present. In *On the Beginnings of Patristic Literature* Overbeck's formalist analysis of early Christian literature emphasized the unbridgeable gap between the original and the derived.

Nietzsche, for his part, first relativized the power of origins in the second *Untimely Meditation*, by presenting them as fictional (if regulative) notions. He thus revised his own idealizations of them in *The Birth of Tragedy*, where he presented the culture of archaic Greece as normative. *Human, All Too Human* marked the first real suspension of such original norms, whose allegedly divine dimension Nietzsche interrogated by help of a hermeneutics of suspicion. He developed this interrogation further in the *Genealogy of Morality* which focused precisely on the all-too human power struggles behind contemporary institutions in order to question their apparently eternally valid status. The psychologizing method of *Human, All Too Human* thus gave way to an examination of origins centred on the question of power. This examination emphasized not only the relativity of the descendant, but also that of the descent itself. Origins are always – this is a central tenet of both Nietzsche and Overbeck – relative to that which became of them. Neither of the two men, at this stage, believed in absolute origins anymore, from which everything else could be derived. Most

---

63 As early as 14 November 1879 Nietzsche wrote to Overbeck to express his wish that Overbeck's 'treatise on the emergence of Christian literature be completed this winter', Friedrich Nietzsche, *Sämtliche Briefe: Kritische Studienausgabe*, ed. G. Colli and M. Montinari, 8 vols (Berlin and New York 1986) (hereafter *KSB*), V, 463. See also the letters of 8 July 1881 (*KSB*, VI, 101) and 29 January 1882 (*KSB*, VI, 163). But in contrast to other writings by Overbeck, we do not have any written comment by Nietzsche on *The Beginnings of Patristic Literature*. The papers in his *Nachlaß* do not contain any direct reference to it either.

importantly, they now considered origins without any specific value – neither for themselves, nor for that which they originated.

While it seemed, initially, that Overbeck was a latecomer and imitator of Nietzsche, assimilating the former's formalist approach in his own theological studies, we have seen that he actually anticipated Nietzsche's suspension of normative origins. His exploration of origins, particularly in *On the Beginnings of Patristic Literature*, opens vistas that are still absent in *Human, All Too Human* I, but that permeate the *Genealogy of Morality*: for instance, the notion of the discontinuity between the origin of a phenomenon and its subsequent development. If *On the Christian Character of our Present-day Theology*, like the *Birth of Tragedy*, decried the deviation from the origins as decay and betrayal, *On the Beginnings of Patristic Literature* soberly reported an unbridgeable difference. This profound distinction between origins and that which they originated was one of the principal postulates of the *Genealogy of Morality*.

If one tried to analyse the genesis of Nietzsche's genealogical method in a genealogical way and read it as a palimpsest,[64] one would find the traces of Overbeck's exploration of origins. Overbeck's 'palaeontology'[65] belongs to the history of the genealogical project – and not just as a footnote. However, apportioning Overbeck's 'palaeontology' of Christianity to the genesis of Nietzsche's genealogical project does not mean that it represents its origin as such. Nietzschean genealogy precludes any direct causalities or seamless dependences.

V

Genealogy also implies the realization of differences. And these must not be glossed over in the case of Nietzsche and Overbeck. The two men gradually grew apart and their former brotherhood-in-arms began to crumble. Overbeck's desire to have an impact on the fate of modern Christianity, let alone 'the world', declined proportionally to Nietzsche's increasing demand for a universal audience. This demand was only barely concealed beneath his stereotypical rhetorical addresses to the select few. Overbeck, who never liked to pose as a cultural reformer in the first place, had nonetheless called for a fundamental self-reflection of Christian theology in *On the Christian Character of our Present-day Theology*. Subsequently, however, he seemed to resign himself to pure scholarly activity. We may assume that someone who studied the reception of literary works as carefully as Overbeck did not part from the 'big public' without some premeditation.[66]

As the extensive appendices to the second edition of *On the Christian Character of our Present-day Theology* show, Overbeck came to realize that he had failed to shake up his theologising contemporaries. So he continued to exercise his anti-fideistic pyrrhonism in a

---

64 See the remarks in the *Nachlaß* papers from 1887-88, *KSA*, XIII, 128 (fragment 11 [302]).
65 Overbeck, *Anfänge der patristischen Literatur* (n. 12, above) 36.
66 In view of his private writings, Overbeck is currently being re-discovered as a 'great literary figure, a master of nuances': K. Flasch, "'Ich darf wohl sagen, dass mich das Christentum mein Leben gekostet hat'", *Frankfurter Allgemeine Zeitung*, no. 238, Supplement 'Literatur' (14 October 1997), L45.

kind of scholarly underground.⁶⁷ Though not a belligerent atheist, Overbeck none the less considered Christianity, perhaps even religion as such,⁶⁸ as an historically obsolete phenomenon, whose death certificate he issued with his Church historical studies. But he refused to engage in a frontal attack *à la* Nietzsche, something he probably considered as a senseless act of body-stripping. The most authentic element of the Christian faith, in his eyes – the undaunted readiness for and the wise defiance of death – had come to naught in contemporary Christendom. On the other hand, Overbeck continued to search, beyond the boundaries of the Church, for a '*memento mori* which would serve our human life here on earth ... Instead of consoling ourselves on death, let us try to accept it in the most honest way possible, by paying more attention to what it means in *our sphere*'.⁶⁹ In a cross-reference to this entry on 'death (and other things)', Overbeck continued: 'E.g. as an incentive for all our actions.'⁷⁰

In his lifetime, Overbeck was evidently unwilling to share such philosophical reflections with the public. Furthermore, he was sceptical about the scope of his own abilities – in contrast to Nietzsche, who merely coquetted with self-restraint. Methodologically, Overbeck, the scholar, limited himself to purely scientific historical work. Just as he refused Nietzsche's later techniques of psychologization and physiologization, Overbeck refrained from all 'transvaluative' aspirations. With unshakeable perseverance, he pointed to the unrepeatability of origins and the impossibility of extracting any timeless substance from them. He probably would not have dreamed of posing as the originator of a new world.

This, however, was the declared goal of Nietzsche, whose genealogical project aimed at the subversion of all those powers and institutions that demanded acceptance and subjection. Nietzsche gradually realized that in order to achieve this goal, he would have to employ more than just historical methods – even though he believed that the latter had a high potential for the exposure of allegedly timeless traditions.⁷¹ Eventually, he began to use a broad range of strategies from scientific medical arguments to pure polemic. The real end of Nietzsche's exercise was to turn himself into the originator of a new order, to become the law-giver of a new age. If Nietzsche had achieved this end – whose political implications seem hardly compatible with the liberal-democratic ideals of our contemporary theorists⁷² – he would probably have experienced the same fate that he ascribed to the origins: misunderstandings, re-writings, and distortions. This, indeed, is what happened to his work. And therein lies the

---

67 See *OWN*, IV, 402, 'Precisely because historiography is such a problematic science with regard to its results and because it does not provide any certain knowledge, scepticism is the only philosophical attitude compatible with it.'
68 See *OWN*, V, 318, 'All that religion can be reproached for could be summarized in the reproach of inhumanity.'
69 *OWN*, V, 604-05.
70 *Ibid.*, 605, n. 1.
71 See, e.g., *Menschliches, Allzumenschliches* II, *Vermischte Meinungen* 17, in *KSA*, II, 386.
72 See the authoritative study of Nietzsche's political thought by H. Ottmann, *Philosophie und Politik bei Nietzsche* (Berlin and New York 1987, 2nd edn 1999) and, more recently, G. Goedert, 'Fortschritt durch "Freiheit, Gleichheit, Brüderlichkeit"? Zu Nietzsches Kritik der Französischen Revolution', in, *Fortschritt im geschichtlichen Wandel*, ed. J. Albertz, Schriftenreihe der Freien Akademie XVIII (1998) 151-70. One can hardly describe the late Nietzsche solely as a philosopher of self-creation, as A. Nehamas tends to do in his *The Art of Living: Socratic Reflections from Plato to Foucault* (Berkeley and Los Angeles 1998).

tragedy of all teachings that are or claim to be origins: they have a considerable potential for self-destruction.

University of Greifswald

TOWARDS 'RASSENHYGIENE': WILAMOWITZ AND THE GERMAN NEW RIGHT[1]

EGON FLAIG

I Introduction

> In the first third of the twentieth century, the history of ideas took a special turn in Germany. Roughly speaking, this development had affiliations with, and was conditioned by, expressionism, phenomenology, the youth movement, and the circle around Stefan George. It was aloof to the Christian tradition, anti-bourgeois, anti-rational; it was elitist and latently 'prone to fascism' [*latent 'faschistoid'*]. The shock of the Great War decisively defined, yet did not trigger, this special development: the rational world of the nineteenth century seemed broken, elemental depths [*'Urgründe'*] appeared.[2]

This is how Walter Burkert characterised the constellation in the history of ideas that gave rise to the so-called 'Third Humanism' with its mission to infuse classical antiquity with new, contemporary relevance – in personal as well as political affairs. It is customary to attribute this agenda to a younger generation particularly receptive to right-wing extremism. What I should like to demonstrate in this essay is that this heightened receptivity within classics for the ideas and values of the *völkisch* movement, which was increasingly gaining in momentum during these years, was by no means limited to the younger generation. A leading German scholar, Ulrich von Wilamowitz-Moellendorff, started to endorse and propagate crucial principles of *völkisch* ideology towards the end of his life.

In setting out my argument, I shall neither comment on the public pronouncements of German classicists during and after World War I nor discuss the minutiae of the personal and intellectual relationships that existed between Wilamowitz and other scholars. My chosen method of approach is the close textual analysis of key concepts and semantic figures that Wilamowitz employed in his scholarly writings. More specifically, I want to compare and contrast certain arguments about race and culture that Wilamowitz presented in a text published in 1910 with his treatment of similar issues in his monumental *Der Glaube der Hellenen* ('The Faith of the Hellenes') – published in 1931, the year he died. Few historians know the passages that I want to focus on in this book, telling as they are; and even those interested in the history of classical scholarship tend to pass them over in silence.

---

[1] I would like to thank Ingo Gildenhard for his critical yet sympathetic comments on the manuscript.
[2] W. Burkert, 'Griechische Mythologie und die Geistesgeschichte der Moderne', in *Les Études Classiques aux XIXe et XXe Siècles: Leur place dans l'histoire des idées*, Fondation Hardt Entretiens XXVI (Geneva 1980) 187.

II 'Staat und Gesellschaft der Griechen' or 'what is the category of "race" doing in an argument about "culture"?'

In 1910, Wilamowitz contributed a chapter to a book about state and society in classical antiquity. His contribution was entitled 'Staat und Gesellschaft der Griechen' ('State and Society of the Greeks').[3] In the second edition (published in 1923), Wilamowitz made some changes in the text: they were mostly minor and do not affect my argument. In 1994, Jürgen von Ungern-Sternberg, an ancient historian from the University of Basel, published a reprint of the second edition. His aim was to re-introduce certain thoughts of Wilamowitz into the scholarly debate. Wilamowitz's book, so Ungern-Sternberg argued, had not received the attention that it deserved among classicists in the years before and after World War I: now was the time to return to Wilamowitz's text, as a document that opposed racism and promulgated the insight that Greek culture was to a certain degree dependent on oriental influences.[4] Let me state right away that I have grave doubts about the merits of this agenda.

In the nineteenth and early twentieth centuries, the origins of the Greek city-state and its relationship to its Phoenician equivalent were two of the most hotly debated topics in historical research, inextricably bound up with questions of how to specify and explain differences and similarities between Eastern and Western cultures and their respective status and prestige in world history.[5] Unlike many other scholars (such as Jacob Burckhardt), Wilamowitz was by and large uninterested in the question of priority when he discussed this subject.[6] What captured his attention in 'State and Society of the Greeks' were the structural analogies he perceived between the archaic culture of the Greeks and that of the Phoenicians. In his endeavour to explain why these cultures shared a particular 'vivacity' (*Regsamkeit*), the category of 'race' made a decisive appearance:

> Palästina heißt ja nach dem übers Meer während der Völkerwanderung aus Kreta eingesprengten Stamme der Philister, der sich freilich so weit semitisiert hat, daß seine Eigenart sich nicht mehr fassen läßt. So wird sich die ungemeine Regsamkeit der syrischen Küstenbevölkerung, der Phönikier, wohl durch Rassenmischung erklären, ganz ebenso wie bei den Griechen, und so werden die vielen Ähnlichkeiten verständlich, die diese Semiten mit diesen Indogermanen haben, im Gegensatze zu ihren Sprachverwandten.
>
> *Staat und Gesellschaft* 24.

The name 'Palestine', of course, derives from the interspersed tribe of the Philistines, which, during the migration of the peoples, crossed the sea from Crete. This tribe, however, has since turned Semitic to such an extent that its original characteristics can no

---

3 U. v. Wilamowitz-Moellendorff, 'Staat und Gesellschaft der Griechen', in *Die Kultur der Gegenwart. Ihre Entwicklung und ihre Ziele. Teil II, Abteilung IV, i: Staat und Gesellschaft der Griechen und Römer bis zum Ausgang des Mittelalters*, ed. P. Hinneberg (Leipzig and Berlin 1923) 1-214.
4 See U. v. Wilamowitz-Moellendorff, *Staat und Gesellschaft der Griechen*, with intro. by J. von Ungern-Sternberg (reprint of the 2nd edn [1923]) (Stuttgart and Leipzig 1994).
5 See M. Bernal, *Black Athena. The Afroasiatic Roots of Classical Civilization. Volume 1: The Fabrication of Ancient Greece 1785-1985* (New Brunswick 1987), and cf. S. Marchand and A. Grafton, 'Martin Bernal and his critics', *Arion* 3rd series 5.2 (1997) 1-35.
6 Burckhardt conceded chronological priority to the Phoenicians, see his *Griechische Kulturgeschichte* I (*Gesammelte Werke*), V, 57.

longer be distinguished. Hence the extraordinary vivacity of the coastal inhabitants of Syria – the Phoenicians – may be explained by the mixing of races, in the same way as that of the Greeks. And hence the many similarities that these Semites – in contrast to their linguistic kin – have in common with these particular Indo-Europeans, become intelligible.

Wilamowitz here argues that south of the Syrian coast the invasion of Indo-European peoples had led to 'a mixture of races' (*Rassenmischung*), similar to the one the Greeks underwent in becoming Greeks. This mixing of races was responsible for setting these two peoples apart within their respective linguistic group: the Phoenicians were something special among the Semites, the Greeks unique among the Indo-Europeans. What are we to make of Wilamowitz's concept of *Rassenmischung*? How does it fit into the intellectual milieu of his age? At first glance, the type of argument we find here seems to be sharply opposed to racism. Indeed, von Ungern-Sternberg interprets the passage above in precisely this way.[7] But a note of caution is in order. A few basic reflections reveal the problems of such a position and suggest that Wilamowitz's own fight against the notion of racial superiority was doomed to failure through the very concepts he employed.

In the historical and political debates of the nineteenth century, arguments for 'race' as a determining factor in human history were omnipresent. Yet it is crucial to realise that scholars conceived of this category in different ways. This range of possibilities needs to be borne in mind – not least since Wilamowitz's use of the term gains its distinct semantic profile against the spectrum of other available conceptions. Some historians, like Mommsen or Droysen, would not have used 'race' to explain a cultural phenomenon in the first place. (In other words, Wilamowitz, had he wanted to explain cultural phenomena without resorting to a notion of race could have done so.) Others, like Burckhardt and Taine, regarded racial differences as the result of environmental factors. Yet another position, widespread and very influential, endorsed a strictly *biological* definition of 'race' – and this is precisely the one Wilamowitz employs in the passage above.

Wilamowitz expressed an opinion well-known within a specific current of Darwinist evolutionary biology, namely that racial mixture was a positive phenomenon conducive to the evolution of a culture.[8] His notion of '*Rassenmischung*', that is, miscegenation, presupposed that particular peoples possessed particular natural properties. When these were mixed they generated new natural dispositions, such as 'extraordinary vivacity'. Wilamowitz credited these 'natural' features with advancing further historical developments. It should be obvious that a conception of 'race' such as Taine's does not fit into this kind of argument.

In short, Wilamowitz conceived of 'race' in a biological sense, and as an operative factor in cultural evolution. It is true that the potentially racist implications of this position do not appear as long as one tries to explain, as Wilamowitz does here, cultural similarities rather than differences. Yet in the end, to argue that it was racial mixture that produced certain special features in the Greeks and Phoenicians does not eschew racist implications. First of all, if a mixture of races can produce new races that are 'biologically' equipped with unique

---

7 See his introduction to Wilamowitz, *Staat und Gesellschaft* (n. 4, above) vi: '... So fegt er ein weiteres Mal alle Rassenideologie beiseite.'

8 See, for example, W. Schallmeyer, *Über die drohende Entartung der Kulturmenschheit* (Berlin-Neuwied 1891), and cf. H.-G. Marten, *Sozialbiologismus* (Frankfurt a. M. and New York 1983).

cultural features, we are dealing by definition with 'superior races'. Secondly, once such superior races have come into being, how does their existence square with the notion that initially it was the *mixture* of races that generated cultural superiority? According to this line of thought, it is almost inevitable that the very concept of a 'superior race' (with all its theoretical – and political – consequences) enters into conflict with the supposedly positive aspects of miscegenation. In this context, it is worth noting that Wilamowitz never spoke out in favour of the *equality* of races.

This raises the question how Wilamowitz would employ the notion of race to explain cultural differences, rather than similarities. For the moment, however, I simply want to note that, in this particular passage, he regards 'race' in an overtly biological sense as a valid concept for the analysis and explanation of cultural phenomena. Let us move on to the next passage, where Wilamowitz argues that Greek and Phoenician culture evolved in similar ways:

> Wir sehen also die Griechen und die Phönikier eine analoge Entwicklung durchmachen und ziemlich zur selben Zeit eine gewaltige Expansion über die See beginnen, als Händler und als Kolonisten in friedlichem und feindlichem Wettbewerb. Davon erzählt uns die griechische Tradition z. B. für Sizilien: phönikische Spuren sind gleichwohl unter der griechischen Schicht dort nicht zutage getreten. Dagegen haben die Griechen in Nordafrika westlich von Kyrene, wie es scheint, nicht versucht, den Phönikiern ihr Kolonialland streitig zu machen: Karthago ist eine Macht geworden, die erst mit Massalia, dann mit Rom um die Herrschaft in dem westlichen Meere gerungen hat.
>
> *Staat und Gesellschaft* 25.

So we see Greeks and Phoenicians undergoing an analogous development. Almost simultaneously, they began a tremendous expansion across the Mediterranean, as traders and colonists in peaceful as well as hostile competition. This is revealed to us by the Greek tradition, for instance in the case of Sicily. However, no Phoenician traces have appeared on this island below the Greek layer. In contrast, it seems that the Greeks did not attempt to contend with the Phoenicians for their colonial land in North Africa west of Cyrene. Carthage became a power that struggled for supremacy in the Western Mediterranean, first with Massalia, then with Rome.

In terms of economic expansion, Wilamowitz was prepared to put the Phoenician city-state on an equal footing with the Greek *polis*. As is shown by the next passage, he also subscribed to Aristotle's opinion that Carthage was well governed since it was founded on the freedom of its citizens and the rule of law. For Wilamowitz, these two aspects were the necessary as well as the sufficient conditions for ancient communities to develop their political affairs in the best possible way:

> Karthagos Verfassung hat Aristoteles nicht nur neben den hellenischen beschrieben, sondern sogar unter die besten gerechnet; das Reich Philipps war für ihn ebensowenig ein Staat wie das des Dareios. Darin liegt, daß diese semitische Stadt ganz wie die der Griechen auf Bürgerfreiheit und Gesetz gegründet war (allerdings war es eine Plutokratie), in scharfem Gegensatze zu der Staatlosigkeit der semitischen Wüstenstämme und der orientalischen Despotie. Man kann dann kaum umhin, Ähnliches für die Städte der

phönikischen Küste anzunehmen, und so zeigen sich in einem der wichtigsten Stücke diese Arier und diese Semiten gleichermaßen vielen ihrer Sprachverwandten überlegen.

Staat und Gesellschaft 25-26.

Aristotle not only described Carthage's constitution as on a par with the Greek ones, but even counted it among the best. The kingdom of Philip, in contrast, was no more of a state for him than that of Dareios. The reason for this is that this Semitic city was founded, just like those of the Greeks, on civic liberty and the rule of law – although it was a plutocracy – in sharp opposition to the statelessness of Semitic desert-tribes and oriental despotism. It is thus hard not to assume that the cities of the Phoenician coast showed similar features. Hence these Arians and these Semites prove to be equally superior to many of their linguistic kin in one of the most important traits.

Wilamowitz, to be sure, immediately qualified his praise of Carthage by adding in brackets that it was a plutocracy ('*allerdings* war es eine Plutokratie'), thereby marking the Punic city as a community under the rule of Mammon. In so doing, he relied on a perceived difference between Greeks and Phoenicians that had already been of crucial importance to Jacob Burckhardt in his historiographical construction of the uniqueness of the ancient Greeks. In Burckhardt's view, the Phoenician cities were driven by mercantile utilitarianism, the Greek ones were not.[9] In other words, Wilamowitz here delineates a hierarchy of cultures, using the criteria of freedom, law, and type of government. In a first step, he sets apart the Greeks and the Phoenician coastal cities from 'stateless' Semitic tribes and Oriental despotism; then he proceeds to draw a further distinction within the superior nations, namely between the Phoenicians, who handed over their political affairs to their wealthiest citizens, and the Greeks, who did not. The result of this analysis is obvious: the Greeks are singled out as the supreme people.

The perceived supremacy of the Greeks is also the keynote of the next passage from 'State and Society of the Greeks'. It deserves to be quoted at length since Wilamowitz here vigorously argues that this supremacy has nothing to do with 'racial purity':

Das Erbe der älteren Kulturen ist unschätzbar, und man versteht auch die Griechen um so besser, je mehr erkannt wird, wieviel sie übernommen haben. Denn was sie auch übernehmen, der Geist, der es steigernd und adelnd durchdringt, der Geist der Freiheit, ist rein hellenisch; die Herrschaft des unübersetzbaren hellenischen Logos ist es auch. In Platons Schule hat man auch dieses Verhältnis vollkommen treffend beurteilt. So halten die beiden entgegengesetzten Modemeinungen vor den Tatsachen der Geschichte nicht stand. Der Fanatismus der reinen Rasse kann sich mit einigem Scheine auf die Griechen berufen, deren Sprache und Kultur auf ihrer Höhe eine unvergleichliche Einheit und Reinheit zeigt. Aber das ist das letzte Ergebnis einer langen Entwicklung, und zugrunde liegt gerade hier eine unübersehbare Mischung der Völker und der Kulturen, und selbst das arische Blut ist keineswegs rein. Ja man muß sagen, daß die griechische Kultur nur so lange wächst, als sie die Kraft hat, Fremdes in sich aufzunehmen. Als sie so fertig ist wie

---

[9] 'Man wollte nicht von oben gelenkt werden und verübelte es wohl den Tyrannen ganz besonders, wenn sie die nützliche Tätigkeit zu befördern suchten. Griechenland hatte eine andere Bestimmung, als in Gestalt von lauter kleinen Karthagos auszuleben ...' (*Griechische Kulturgeschichte* I, 175).

ihre künstliche Literatursprache und sich ebenso hochmütig dem Fremden und dem Neuen verschließt, wird sie innerlich hohl und zeugungsunfähig, wenn auch von einer unüberwindlichen passiven Widerstandskraft. Also um den Glauben an die Autochthonie des Hellenentums ist es ebenso geschehen wie um seine vorbildliche rein naturgemäße Entwicklung in Staat und Literatur und Kunst. Aber nicht geringer ist der Wahn, die Griechen für abgesetzt oder bedroht durch die Babylonier zu halten, gerade wie es ein Wahn ist, die religiöse Bedeutung der Juden damit abzutun, daß Jahweh von Haus aus nichts Besseres war als Marduk oder Kamos. In Wahrheit wurzeln diese Verkehrtheiten einerseits in dem Rassenhochmut, der Arier sowohl wie der Semiten, anderseits in den Vorurteilen der jüdisch-christlichen Tradition und der antijüdischen und antichristlichen Polemik. Diese giftigen Dünste dürfen das reine Licht der Wissenschaft nicht trüben, und gerade die Beschäftigung mit den Hellenen ist geeignet, sie zu verscheuchen.

Staat und Gesellschaft 26-27.

The heritage of the older cultures is invaluable. It is true of the Greeks, too, that the more we recognise how much they adopted, the better we understand them. For whatever they adopt, the spirit that permeates, enhances, and ennobles it, the spirit of freedom, is purely Greek. The same applies to the rule of the untranslatable Greek Logos. In Plato's academy, this relation, too, was assessed in perfectly appropriate fashion. Hence neither of the two conflicting views that are currently fashionable stands up to the facts of history. The fanaticism of racial purity may invoke the Greeks with a certain semblance of truth insofar as their language and culture, at their best, show an incomparable unity and purity. But this is the final result of a long development that involves an indeterminable mixture of peoples and cultures; even the Arian blood is by no means pure. Indeed, it has to be said that Greek civilization only grew as long as it had the strength to assimilate foreign elements. When it was as complete as its artificial literary language and, with the same arrogance, closed itself off to the foreign and the new, it became internally hollow and sterile, even though it showed an insuperable passive power of resistance. Thus, the belief in the autochthony of Hellenic culture and its exemplary, purely natural development in state, literature, and art is done for. But to regard the Greeks as aloof from, or threatened by, the Babylonians is no less of a delusion, just as it is delusory to dismiss the religious significance of the Jews by saying that Yahweh was originally nothing other than Marduk or Kamos. In reality, these follies are rooted, on the one hand, in the racial arrogance of both Arians and Semites, and, on the other, in the prejudices of the Judeo-Christian tradition and the anti-Jewish and anti-Christian polemics. These poisonous vapours must not dim the pure light of science, and the study of the Greeks in particular is apt to dispel them.

The ability to appropriate other cultures thus allowed the Greeks to strengthen their own. What set the Greeks apart was their 'spirit'. Wilamowitz ascribes a unique spirit to the Greeks – a 'Geist der Freiheit' or 'spirit of liberty'. It should be stressed that in this context 'liberty' does not mean political liberty, but carries idealistic connotations: the term refers to the existence of a special creativity among the Greeks that enabled them to transform everything they adopted from other cultures into organic features of their own. The transformative labour of the Greek *Geist* ensured that all foreign elements underwent a process of assimilation and sublimation during which they became genuinely 'Greek'. As a result, Greek culture, despite incorporating a large amount of foreign material, was able to retain its internal coherence and purity (*eine unvergleichliche Einheit und Reinheit*). It is this unique quality of Greek culture, according to Wilamowitz, that makes its driving force, the 'Logos', untranslatable.

This represented an important contribution to existing theories of culture and acculturation. In contrast to many adherents of German historicism, Wilamowitz did not conceive of culture as a 'natural' entity that grew like a flower according to its own internal laws of development. Quite the contrary: Greek culture, for him, was creative only so long as it was able to assimilate foreign elements. Taken to its extreme, this theory redefines culture as permanent acculturation.[10] Wilamowitz thus rejected the notion of 'autochthony' as well as the idea of a culture's 'pure natural development' (*rein naturgemässe Entwicklung*).[11]

He did, however, insist on the uniqueness of the Greeks. Yet at this point in 'State and Society of the Greeks', he explains this uniqueness not with reference to 'race' (or a 'mixture of races') but ascribes it to a genuine Greek 'spirit'. In the passage above, it is not entirely clear what Wilamowitz means by this or how this spirit manifests itself in history. Later in the work, it becomes apparent that Wilamowitz by and large accepts a Burckhardtian view of Greek culture: the Greeks were able to think about the world without being handicapped by the existence of a powerful priestly caste or a centre that exercised strong political control.[12]

In the extract under discussion, Wilamowitz, after introducing the notion of a unique Greek spirit, takes issue with two opposing points of view. On the one hand, he rejects those who insist on the racial purity of the Greeks, charging them with a demented 'Rassenhochmut' – a colourful German word for 'racism'. On the other, he dismisses the so-called 'Panbabylonians', an intellectual movement at the turn of the century that liked to trace all of Western culture back to its alleged ancient Babylonian origins.[13] For Wilamowitz, the heated debate about 'cultural origins' was pointless to begin with, given that whatever the Greeks adopted (irrespective of the actual amount), they thoroughly 'Hellenized' it in the process and then developed it further as they saw fit. It was this ability for assimilation and improvement that set the Greeks apart as more dynamic than any of the cultures to which they might be indebted.

In short, Wilamowitz in this last passage argues that cultural phenomena cannot be explained at all by 'natural' factors such as 'race' or other biological categories. Rather, it was

---

10 Wilamowitz's endorsement of a certain kind of 'diffusionism' is all the more striking in light of Marchand's and Grafton's findings that its opposite – independent evolution – 'had always been the hegemonic conviction inside the classicists' charmed circle', 'Martin Bernal and his Critics' (n. 5, above) 10.

11 The tradition of thought that Wilamowitz attacks here includes Herder, who argued that each culture was an organic entity that, like a plant, simply needed to follow its intrinsic laws of growth, and Wilhelm von Humboldt, who put this cultural monadism on a systematic footing, see his 'Über die Gesetze der Entwicklung der menschlichen Kräfte' (1791), in *Werke*, vol. I, ed. A. Flitner and K. Giel (Darmstadt 1960) 43-55. L. v. Ranke used this notion to demonstrate that the importation of foreign, North-American ideas led to the French Revolution, see his 'Frankreich und Deutschland' [1832], in *Sämtliche Werke*, vols XLIX and L, ed. A. Dove (Leipzig 1887) 61-76.

12 See *Griechische Kulturgeschichte* II, 31-37, 125-35, and the theory of the forces set out in Burckhardt's *Über das Studium der Geschichte. Der Text der 'Weltgeschichtlichen Betrachtungen' nach den Handschriften*, ed. Peter Ganz (Munich 1982) 254-92.

13 See A. Jeremias, 'Die Panbabylonisten: Der alte Orient und die aegyptische Religion', *Im Kampf um den alten Orient* 1 (1907).

the free spirit permeating Hellenic culture and its ability to import and assimilate foreign elements that accounted for the incomparable greatness of the ancient Greeks. In this context, Wilamowitz summarily dismissed racial explanations of Greek cultural achievements.

If we compare the argument Wilamowitz endorses here with the one he sets forth in the passage we first looked at, a glaring contrast emerges. In the first passage, race was an operative factor, in the last, race seems completely bracketed. This shows that in 'State and Society of the Greeks' Wilamowitz used several different explanatory schemes that were at variance with each other. Evidently, he was unclear about the categories he employed. It is worth noting that Wilamowitz's thinking on the ancients in 1910 falls way short of the kind of conceptual rigour and systematic coherence one finds in Johann Gustav Droysen, say, or in Theodor Mommsen, or Jacob Burckhardt. This lack of coherence did not remain without consequences.

III 'Der Glaube der Hellenen' or the destruction of religion to make room for a politics of the sacred

Twenty-one years after 'State and Society of the Greeks', Wilamowitz published two long volumes on Greek religion. It was his final great achievement, 'the last great, infinitely precious work', as Hans Joachim Mette has called it.[14] I consider it his intellectual testament. The book was entitled *Der Glaube der Hellenen* (*The Faith of the Hellenes*). This is strange indeed, for Greek religion was not at all based on faith. While faith is an important element in Judaism and plays a crucial role in Christianity, it simply is not a useful category for capturing the characteristic features of the pagan religions of antiquity.[15]

As the sociology of religion since Max Weber has shown, a religion based on the principle of 'faith' implies certain intellectual and social prerequisites, in particular the existence of a clearly articulated creed or dogma, adherence to which is binding for all participants, as well as an organised priesthood that takes control of religious practices. In turn, once a powerful group of religious specialists is put in charge of the administration of the sacred, it tends to impose clear restrictions on what poets and philosophers may publicly proclaim about the nature of the divine. With Weber and Bourdieu, we may therefore draw an ideal-typical opposition between religions based primarily on faith and the civic religions of pagan antiquity.[16] We are dealing with two fundamentally incompatible and mutually exclusive forms of constructing human communication with the divine sphere.

Generally speaking, the Greeks placed the greatest emphasis on participation in the rituals and cults of the community, particularly the civic sacrifices. 'Faith', in the sense of an expressed belief in a body of dogma, did not enter into the picture. Indeed, Greek literature and philosophy as we know it would have been inconceivable if Greek religious beliefs had

---

14 H. J. Mette, 'Nekrolog einer Epoche: Hermann Usener und seine Schule. Ein wirkungsgeschichtlicher Rückblick auf die Jahre 1856-1979', *Lustrum* 22 (1979/80) 5-106 (90).
15 See R. Bultmann, art. 'πιστεύω', in *Theologisches Wörterbuch zum Neuen Testament* (Stuttgart 1959), VI, 174-82, and D. Lührmann, art. 'Glaube', *Reallexikon für Antike und Christentum*, XI (1981) col. 58-68.
16 See M. Weber, *Wirtschaft und Gesellschaft* (Tübingen 1980) 260-82, and P. Bourdieu, 'Genèse et structure du champs religieux', *Revue française de Sociologie*, 12 (1971) 295-334, esp. 302-06 and 318-21.

been organized around a concept of faith. As long as poets and intellectuals showed devotion to the rituals of the common cult, they were by and large allowed to say anything about the gods they wanted – from the depiction of divine immorality in Homer to the relegation of the gods to the *intermundia* in Epicurean philosophy.

Jacob Burckhardt had already stated in no uncertain terms that there was no literary evidence of any form of faith in the whole of Greek mythological poetry: the poets and their audiences did not 'believe' in the modern theological sense of the term.[17] Moreover, as Burckhardt saw as well, if a community were to switch from one form of religion to the other, this would entail radical changes in its social, cultural, and political make-up.[18] It is worth pointing out that Adolf von Harnack, a colleague and rival of Wilamowitz, elevated the opposition of a religion of faith (*Glaubensreligion*) and a religion of sacrifice (*Opferreligion*) to the main heuristic principle of his research.[19]

Hence what Wilamowitz set out to do – to construct Greek religion as a religion of faith – was not a viable project to begin with. Put differently, *Der Glaube der Hellenen* was one of the most awkward titles an author could possibly give to a book on ancient Greek religion. Wilamowitz must have been well aware of the fundamental objections that could be raised against his project, yet evidently this professor-turned-prophet did not care.

As it turns out, the oddity of the title is nothing compared to the introduction that follows. What we read here simply confounds the mind. Within the first fifty pages or so, Wilamowitz managed to dismiss the comparative study of religion advanced by Usener and others, opting instead to understand the ancient Greeks in their own language. He declared – several times over – that the Olympian deities actually exist (*à la* Walter F. Otto), and endorsed a pantheistic notion of revelation. Finally, he referred to philosophy and science in the tradition of Plato as 'a religion of the heart, more immortal than all divinities'.

Brief, breathless sentences abound. Wilamowitz's propositions are formulated like ultimate truths that preclude any form of disagreement. It seems that the limited time he had left at this stage of his life forced the author abruptly to pronounce verdicts that were meant to stand for a long time to come. For this very reason, personal confessions frequently intruded into Wilamowitz's argument, without making it any more coherent.

The generic character of the text – including the comprehensive nature, the structuring of the material, and the use of footnotes – leaves no doubt that Wilamowitz meant to produce a scholarly work. At the level of presentation, he already set himself apart from someone like Walter Otto. Nonetheless, entire paragraphs of this text are highly problematic, precisely since Wilamowitz's dogmatic pronouncements rule out proper discussion of their validity just like the hymnic intonations of Walter Otto, or the priestly gestures of Nietzsche.

On the level of politics, however, the text is coherent, indeed brutally explicit. To illustrate this point, I want to take a closer look at three crucial aspects of Wilamowitz's discourse: his re-definition of religion; his treatment of Judaism; and his use of a notion of race more reminiscent of Nazi rhetoric than classical scholarship, including his own earlier publications.

---

17 See J. Burckhardt, *Griechische Kulturgeschichte* II, 20, 31-32, 87-91, 125-34.
18 *Ibid.*, 196-98.
19 See A. v. Harnack, *Die Mission und Ausbreitung des Christentums in den ersten drei Jahrhunderten*, 4th edn (Leipzig 1924) 15-18.

III.i Redefining Religion

In redefining the concept of religion, Wilamowitz seemed to pursue two primary objectives. On the one hand, he introduced an elitist religion of 'experience', accessible only to the chosen few; on the other, he prepared the ground for stripping the specifically Judeo-Christian belief in a supreme Deity which had revealed itself to mankind, of its conceptual validity and world-historical significance. The following are the main semantic operations he carried out to achieve these goals:

First of all, he attacked the Judeo-Christian concept of revelation:

> Auch das ist überwunden, was ein berühmter 'liberaler' Theologe einmal gesagt hat, Religion beginne mit dem Glauben an eine Offenbarung – wenn man nicht sagen will, daß der Mensch erst Mensch ward, als ihm in der Seele die Ahnung des Göttlichen aufging. Das testimonium animae, über das Tertullian in einer glücklichen Stunde geschrieben hat, ist freilich eine Offenbarung, aber die kommt von innen, nicht aus einem Buche.
>
> *Glaube der Hellenen* I, 9.

That which a famous 'liberal' theologian once said, is antiquated, too, namely that religion begins with the belief in a revelation – unless one wants to say that man became human only when the intimation of the divine blossomed in his soul. To be sure, the testimony of the soul (*testimonium animae*), about which Tertullian wrote in a felicitous hour, is a revelation, but it comes from the inside, not out of a book.

By reducing revelation to an intensive emotional experience that may come as a sort of enlightenment, Wilamowitz invalidates the traditional Christian meaning of the concept. In keeping with this line of reasoning, Wilamowitz elsewhere calls nature 'God's uncreated revelation' (*die ungeschaffene Offenbarung Gottes*).[20] This is not a metaphor, but a pantheistic view that conceives of the experience of 'revelation' as an event potentially lacking in transcendence.

Second, he redefines the very concept of faith:

> Denn nicht ein Kultus oder ein Katechismus macht die Religion, sondern das gläubige Herz und das freie Handeln gemäß diesem Glauben. *Glaube der Hellenen*, 13.

For neither cult nor catechism define a religion, but the faithful heart and the free conduct of one's life according to this faith.

For more than seventeen centuries 'faith' could not be separated from catechism. To be sure, there have been minor intellectual currents since the seventeenth century, mainly of evangelical and pietist affiliations, that tried to formulate a genuinely individualistic concept of faith clearly distinct from all official theology. Yet Wilamowitz goes a step further. He opts for a notion of radically individualistic experience (*Erlebnis*) as the central essence of his faith, which he sets off against the 'faith of the masses':

---

20 *Glaube der Hellenen* I, 349. In this respect he seems to have been partly inspired by Goethe, see *Glaube der Hellenen* II, 530: 'Den Gott als Schöpfer haben wir aufgegeben. In der Natur haben wir die Offenbarung des Göttlichen (Goethe XLII 211: "Wer die Natur als göttliches Organ läugnen will, der läugne nur gleich alle Offenbarung."...).'

> Neben dieser individuellen Religion des Herzens, die dem einzelnen doppelt heilig ist, weil er sie sich selbst erworben hat, steht die Religion der Gemeinschaft mit ihrem Kultus und der Bindung ihrer Mitglieder. *Glaube der Hellenen* I, 13.

> Alongside this individual religion of the heart which is doubly sacred for each individual person since he acquired it for himself, stands the religion of the community with its cult and the bond among its members.

A fundamental polarity opens up between a belief, acquired by an individual through a radically individualistic insight, and the belief of the 'masses', which does not deserve this name since it is a mere heirloom handed down by tradition. For Wilamowitz, the two cultural phenomena are only loosely related.

Third, he uses this contrast between the 'religion' of the individual and that of the larger community to advance an elitist extremism:

> Die Masse der Menschen besteht immer aus Gattungswesen, ihr πιστεύειν ist ein πείθεσθαι, aber es erheben sich doch manche zu eigenem Denken und haben ihren Glauben, auch wenn sie um der Gemeinschaft willen sich nicht absondern und auch an den Formen des Kultus teilnehmen. *Glaube der Hellenen* I, 13.

> The majority of men always consists of generic beings; their belief is obedience. But some do rise to the level of individual thought and have their own belief, even if they do not withdraw themselves for the sake of the community and also participate in the various forms of cultic practice.

Here the differences in religious experience are overtly transformed into a social dichotomy between an elite endowed with superior intellectual abilities, and a large mass lacking them. This radical elitism has political implications. Wilamowitz divides human beings into different species. Indeed, he makes no secret of the fact that he regards certain subgroups within the masses as subhuman, namely those to whom he attributes a 'worship of the belly'. This, he thinks, 'ist die Religion des euripideischen Kyklopen, V. 335. Sie gehen uns nichts an, sie sind ja eigentlich Tiere wie der Kyklop'.[21]

As goes without saying, this line of 'reasoning' is utterly irreconcilable with universalist notions like the concept of human rights.[22] Indeed, once such essential distinctions between human beings are taken for granted, all forms of government based on political equality immediately lose their *raison d'être*. Wilamowitz here speaks out in favour of the dichotomy that the *völkish* movement needed. He legitimates the division of a people into those who lead (*Führer*) and those who must be led (*Geführte*).

Fourth, Wilamowitz claims that the Greek gods actually exist:

> Die Götter sind da. Daß wir dies als gegebene Tatsache mit den Griechen erkennen und anerkennen, ist die erste Bedingung für das Verständnis ihres Glaubens und ihres Kultus.

---

21 *Glaube der Hellenen* I, 14, 'It is the religion of the Euripidean Cyclops, v. 335: they do not concern us; in truth, they are animals just like the Cyclops'.
22 Droysen paved the way in this respect, see his quotation from the *Phaedo* in § 79 of his *Historik*, ed. v. P. Leyh (Stuttgart 1977) 443. If this is to be called 'liberalism', it follows that liberalism prefigured elements in the idiom of National Socialism.

> Daß wir wissen, sie sind da, beruht auf einer Wahrnehmung, sei sie innerlich oder
> äußerlich, mag der Gott selbst wahrgenommen sein oder etwas, in dem wir die Wirkung
> eines Gottes erkennen.   *Glaube der Hellenen* I, 17.

The gods exist. The first prerequisite for understanding the belief and the cult of the Greeks is that we realise and accept this as a given fact just as they did. Knowledge of their existence is based on a perception, be it internal or external, be it the perception of the godhead itself or of something in which we discern its effect.

A few years earlier, Walter F. Otto had argued for the real existence of the Greek gods.[23] What had been a shocking avowal of paganism in 1929 became a methodological precept for Wilamowitz: without this belief it is impossible to understand Greek religion. Wilamowitz outbid Otto and other neo-pagans of the 1920s by making a pseudo-mystical experience the very precondition for the scholarly apprehension of the Greek gods.

Finally, Wilamowitz deprived religion of its institutional and conceptual autonomy: 'wir sind berechtigt, von Religion zu reden, wo immer der Mensch sich einer Idee, einer Sache opfert, weil sie ihm heilig ist'.[24] 'Religion' here seems to refer to the ultimate commitment of a specific individual; this commitment may take the form of self-sacrifice, for the sake of one's family, one's city or country. Taken this way, religion ceases to be a specific domain of social life and turns into an existential moment, lived with the utmost degree of vital intensity.

Implying that an encounter in battle may result in a religious experience, Wilamowitz opposed Burckhardt's concept of religion as one of the three historic forces (the other two being 'state' and 'culture'). For if 'religion' consists in the special intensity of a charged moment in life, it has ceased to exist as an autonomous domain. By advancing this definition of religion, Wilamowitz aligned himself with those German intellectuals who opposed 'authenticity' to 'inauthenticity'. Religion becomes a litmus test for an individual's ability to enhance his existence. At the time Wilamowitz wrote these lines, the yearning for authenticity had changed from a mere intellectual current into an outright political slogan. Like many others of his generation, Wilamowitz thus spoke out in favour of endowing politics and war with 'sacral' significance.

Overall, Wilamowitz presents a much more radical argument than Otto. He also pursued his agenda more persistently and endowed it – in terminology and references – with all the trappings of seemingly solid scholarship. The peculiar, but evidently programmatic title of his book sets the tone for a representation of religion that is in line with certain right-wing currents in German intellectual life. Why should Wilamowitz have wished to do this?

---

23 W. F. Otto, *Die Götter Griechenlands. Das Bild des Göttlichen im Spiegel des griechischen Geistes* (Bonn 1929).
24 *Glaube der Hellenen* I, 13, 'We have the right to define as religion wherever a human being sacrifices himself for an idea or a cause because it is sacred to him'.

III.ii *Eliminating Judaism from European culture*

Ninety years earlier, Johann Gustav Droysen proposed that Christianity had been shaped more profoundly by Hellenism than by Judaism.[25] This opinion, radically opposed by Ernest Renan, became pervasive and dominant in Germany within the circles of certain Protestant theologians and classicists. These scholars, for example A. v. Harnack, fundamentally redefined Christianity. For them, Christian religion had more to do with Greece than with Israel – it was by and large an offspring of Hellenism.

This throws new light on the political agenda behind *Der Glaube der Hellenen*: it also points up the limits of harmless oddities by an emeritus professor of classical philology. Writing a book in the year 1928 with the explicit purpose of demonstrating that the Greeks possessed a religion of faith was not a politically neutral act. Far from it: it was a contribution to a long-standing German discourse that endeavoured to downplay the unique part played by Judaism in Western civilization. With *Der Glaube der Hellenen*, Wilamowitz joined the ranks of those German intellectuals who were fighting a continuous war against Judaism and its role in Western culture. He even handed them a new weapon. What did this weapon consist in?

Droysen, Harnack, and other philhellenic historians took it for granted that Christianity was very different from the Greek religion of the classical period. They considered Christianity a genuine product of late Hellenism, a culture which underwent profound changes because of new religious needs and did so under the impact of philosophy and oriental influences.[26] Wilamowitz, however, set out to show that the late Hellenistic conception of religion was a simple transformation of certain ideas in archaic Greek religion. In other words, he constructed an essential continuity between the religion of Homer and a special form of pantheistic Christianity. The category that linked the two periods was the very notion of 'faith' that he had re-defined in such a fundamentally new manner.

Thus Wilamowitz endorsed a radical version of the idea that Greek culture was the main source of Western culture. For Droysen, Burckhardt, and Harnack it was a central source, but not an exclusive one: these scholars minimized the part played by Judaism in its formation. For Wilamowitz, however, even the most central aspect of Western religion, monotheism – which is an essential Jewish element – derived from the Greeks: not from the late Hellenistic Greeks, but from the archaic Greeks. In this model, there is no room left in the Western tradition for any central contribution from Judaism.

As far as I know, Wilamowitz's book was the most radical elimination of Jewish culture from the origins and traditions of Western civilization that had been written so far in an academic setting, under the pretension of being addressed to a community of scholars. It was written ten years before the physical elimination of Judaism in Germany began. To buttress his argument, Wilamowitz had to drop some important axioms of his former notion of cultural history:

---

25 The main argument behind Droysen's history of the Hellenistic age can be gleaned from the Latin title of the thesis he submitted for his doctoral disputation, *A doctrina Christiana Graecorum quam Iudaeorum religio propius abest*, see A. Momigliano, 'J. G. Droysen between Greeks and Jews', in *History and Theory* 9 (1970) 139-53, and K. Christ, *Von Gibbon zu Rostovtzeff. Leben und Werk führender Althistoriker der Neuzeit* (Darmstadt 1972) 58.

26 R. Reitzenstein, *Die hellenistischen Mysterienreligionen. Nach ihren Grundgedanken und Wirkungen*, 3rd edn (Leipzig and Berlin 1927) 15-17 and 102-04.

> Überhaupt pflegt wichtiger zu sein, was ein Volk und auch ein Mensch Besonderes hat, als was allen gemeinsam ist, und es liegt eine tiefe Wahrheit in der Ansicht des Aristoteles von dem πρότερον φύσει, das ein anderes ist als das in der Erscheinung Frühere. Im ältesten Hellenentum lag der Keim der platonischen Gottheit.
>
> *Glaube der Hellenen* I, 11.

At any rate, the uniqueness of a people or a human being tends to be of greater importance than what they share with all others; and there is a profound truth in Aristotle's view on the *proteron phusei*, which is different from that which is prior in appearance. The most ancient layer of Hellenism contained the seed of the Platonic deity.

In this passage, Wilamowitz revoked his former idea that a culture evolves, and maintains its creative capacities, as long as it is able to take in alien elements and to assimilate them, that is, the idea that a culture is not an organic entity with a 'natural development' that unfolds in a strictly endogenous process. Now Wilamowitz asserted the exact opposite: he took it for granted that a religious belief can evolve from a seed-like essence in the manner of plants; and he deployed this organic metaphor as a crucial explanatory scheme.

Yet anyone only superficially familiar with Max Weber's *Sociology of Religion* knows that what Wilamowitz argued here is not possible: there is no link between the Homeric Zeus and the Platonic deity. The Platonic deity is totally absorbed by its duty to maintain justice, a concept which existed in Egypt more than twelve centuries before Plato shocked his contemporaries with it.[27] Wilamowitz endorsed an absurd opinion with the weakest arguments possible – and he defended it against assumptions he himself had formulated eighteen years earlier.

Such an aboutface hardly happens for academic reasons. The semantics of the text and its political context contain decisive hints of what lies behind Wilamowitz's new model of cultural development:

> Dieser Glaube an einen persönlichen Gott, der die Geschicke der Menschen bestimmt (μοῖρα Διός), sittliche Forderungen erhebt und ihre Verletzung ahndet, ist aus der Erhöhung des Zeus zum Vater der Götter und Menschen erwachsen, also in Fortbildung des homerischen Zeus. Er hat sich in Ionien gebildet. Hesiod hat das meiste dazu getan, daß er sich auch im Mutterlande verbreitete, große Dichter haben den Glauben vertieft. Damit waren die Götter, die unter ihm standen, nicht verdrängt, manche von ihnen wurden im Kultus und auch von den gläubigen Menschen stärker verehrt, weil sie ihnen näher standen und die alte Religionsübung sich erhielt; der höchste blieb er doch.
>
> *Glaube der Hellenen* I, 350.

This belief in a personal deity who determines the destiny of human beings (*moira Dios*), who establishes ethical maxims, and punishes their transgressions, grew out of the elevation of Zeus to the father of gods and humans, that is, in a further transformation of the Homeric Zeus. He took shape in Asia Minor. More than anyone else, Hesiod was responsible for his dissemination in the motherland, great poets deepened the belief in him. This did not mean that the gods beneath him were expelled; some of them were

---

27 On this topic, see the essays in *Gerechtigkeit. Richten und Retten in der abendländischen Tradition und ihren altorientalischen Ursprüngen*, ed. J. Assmann, B. Janowski, and M. Welker (Munich 1998).

worshipped more intensely in cultic practice, and also by religious men, because these gods were closer to them and the old religious observance survived. Yet Zeus remained the highest.

In this paragraph, Wilamowitz deprived Judaism of one of its main contributions to Christianity: the notion of a personal divinity, at the same time lord of destiny and guarantor of justice. His assertion presupposed that Greek poets invented and mastered novel theological problems and even succeeded in formulating a systematic monotheistic theology and disseminating its contents among the people. It is unnecessary to show that Wilamowitz's assertions are nonsense. What is important here is the realization that he was forced to write this nonsense in order to stick to his programme: to effect a radical and absolute marginalisation of Judaism. But how could Wilamowitz deny that the ancient Hebrews were the first to articulate the concept of monotheism?[28]

... Denn in Ionien ist der Fortschritt gemacht, das Göttliche, das in so verschiedener Richtung den Menschen band und zugleich schützte, mit dem einen Gottesnamen zu rufen. Und wenn sich die meisten auch nicht begrifflich klar machten, welche Folgerungen auf die Einheit der Gottheit in dieser Person zu ziehen wären, die Dichter, welche das taten und alles voll aussprachen, haben mit ihren Worten starken Widerhall gefunden. In den Kulten freilich blieb Zeus was er gewesen war, vielleicht der oberste, aber doch einer von vielen. Der Zeus, der nur durch den Eigennamen sich von θεός unterschied wie Jehova bei den Lutheranern, gehört einer anderen Religion an, als sie in dem Kulte der Staaten geübt ward. Der Jude meinte Jahve, wenn er Gott sagte, der Grieche Gott, auch wenn er Zeus sagt. So früh schon hat sich diese Kluft aufgetan, die nicht überbrückt werden sollte.
Glaube der Hellenen I, 348.

For in Asia Minor, the step forward was taken to call upon the divine that bound the human in so many ways and, at the same time, protected him, by the one name of god. Few people realised what conceptual conclusions were to be drawn from the unity of the divine in this person, but the poets, who did so and fully articulated everything, found strong resonances with their words. In the cults, to be sure, Zeus remained what he had been: perhaps the highest, but still one of many gods. Zeus, who differed from *theos* only on account of his name, just as Jehova does among the Lutherans, belongs to a religion different from the one practised in the cult of the states. The Jew meant Yahweh when he said 'God', the Greek means 'God', even when he says 'Zeus'. At such an early stage, this gulf opened up, which was not to be bridged.

Wilamowitz posited that henotheism – that is, the subsuming of all gods under one name – constituted historical progress, leading towards a monotheistic conception of the divine. As he well knew, however, the religious beliefs and practices of Greek culture do not betray the slightest hint of monotheistic cult. But monotheism is, of course, the defining feature of Judaism. How can the desired superiority of the Greeks be asserted nevertheless? Wilamowitz achieved this by dividing religion into two parallel phenomena: on the one hand, the civic religion practiced by the city-states in their public rituals; on the other, the religion of the

---

28 See J. Assmann, *Moses der Ägypter. Entzifferung einer Gedächtnisspur* (Munich 1998) 47-87.

poets – and philosophers. It is in the latter category, in the intellectual religion of the Greeks, that, according to Wilamowitz, the concept of a truly universal divinity was first discovered.

But what about Amos, and Joel, and Isaiah? After all, the prophets of ancient Israel preceded the Greek philosophers by more than two hundred and fifty years. For Wilamowitz, this did not matter. The true universal divinity cannot be Jewish, it has to be Greek, purely Greek. There are two monotheisms, Wilamowitz argued, a false (Jewish) one and a real (Greek) one. The Jews, he claimed, automatically think of their national God even though they appear to worship the Lord of all Being, whereas the Greeks automatically think of the Lord of all Being when they invoke Zeus.

Wilamowitz did not deign to give any reasons for these assertions that flew in the face of everything known about the history of religion. He never argued his case. When *Wilamowitz ipse* speaks, the need for sustained argumentation ceases. He writes *ex cathedra*, authorized as it were by a special type of knowledge immune to such mundane issues as historical veracity. Wilamowitz does not concern himself with totem and taboo, he prefers to converse in Greek with the Greeks. As a result, he simply 'knows' that the Jews could not conceive of a truly universal deity, whereas the Greeks could and did.

The implications of this position for Wilamowitz's conception of Western cultural history are drastic. According to Wilamowitz, the Christian God has his origins not in Israel, but in ancient Greece, for the Jewish notion of God is narrowly conceived, bound to a specific nation, and lacking in universal qualities. In other words, Wilamowitz argued that Christians have been deceiving themselves for centuries in believing that the God of the Old Testament had anything to do with their religion, and he did his best to liberate them from this 'delusion'. A gap existed, he claimed, which separates the universal religion of the Greeks from Judaism, and this gap 'was not to be bridged': it forever separates occidental Christian culture with its origins in ancient Greece from that alien culture of Judaism which has nothing to do with the West and to which the West owes nothing.

The last step in Wilamowitz's purification of occidental culture was to rid Christianity of remaining Jewish elements. To do so, he attacked the Biblical notion that God created the world by the mere power of his word:

> In der nicht so sehr sophistischen wie populären Mahnung zur εὐσέβεια redet Xenophon Memor. I 4 von dem weisen δημιουργός, der die Menschen gemacht hat. Daraus darf man keinen Zeus Schöpfer der Menschen oder der Erde ableiten, weder diesen Schöpfergott noch den Begriff der Erschaffung von Himmel und Erde. Selbst im Spiel haben die Hellenen so etwas selten gesagt. Die plumpe Vorstellung einer Schöpfung aus dem Nichts verstieß gegen ihre altüberkommene Frömmigkeit, die in der Natur die ungeschaffene Offenbarung Gottes, also das Göttliche in ihr, nie verkannt hat, so lange sie wirklich Hellenen blieben.
>
> *Glaube der Hellenen* I, 349.

In his admonition towards *eusebeia* at *Memorabilia* I.4, which is not so much sophistic as populist, Xenophon speaks of the wise *dêmiourgos* who created the humans. One must not derive an image of Zeus as the creator of man and the earth from this passage, or the idea of a divine creation of heaven and earth. Even in jest, the Greeks rarely said such a thing. The crude conception of a *creatio e nihilo* offended their traditional piety. The

Greeks never failed to realise the uncreated revelation of god in nature, that is, the divine in nature, as long as they remained truly Greek.

Why this aggressive, contemptuous tone? Wilamowitz was here trying to deepen that gap between Greeks and Jews which was 'not to be bridged'. In endowing 'Greek monotheism' with a strictly pantheistic outlook, he took sides. In the year 1929/1930, such a purified conception of Christianity – a Christianity rid of the Semitic notion of the Creation – resonated with the religious ideas of the *völkisch* movement. Christian faith as defined by Wilamowitz could easily be reconciled with the alleged 'monotheism' of ancient Greek civilization and its purported belief in a supreme god who did not create the world, but who is manifest within it. In a sense, Wilamowitz thus helped to reshape traditional Christianity in such a way that it approached the political theologies of the revolutionary German Right. For the idea of the eternity of the world was the basic link between the neo-paganist and atheistic currents within the *völkish* movement.

The paragraphs that I have singled out for discussion add up to an agenda of direct political relevance. In *Der Glaube der Hellenen*, Wilamowitz attempted to redefine the role of Judaism and Hellenism in Western culture. His main interlocutors are Harnack and Otto.

To conclude this section, let me summarise the main points that mark this engagement:

1. Both Wilamowitz and Otto regarded Judaism as an alien element in European culture which could not be assimilated.

2. Wilamowitz maintained against Harnack and Otto that monotheism was the result of an internal development within archaic Greek culture. In its consequences this hypothesis was opposed to Nietzsche's genealogical critique of Christianity. Whereas Nietzsche sought to radicalize the historical break with Christianity in order to re-valorise the pre-Socratic elements of Greek culture for modern times, Wilamowitz believed that a reaffirmation of the Greek foundations of Christianity would suffice for the necessary reorientation of modern European culture.

3. Otto considered Christianity as a foreign element, against which he invoked the help of the Greek gods. These would survive as long as 'the European spirit' was not 'entirely subdued by the Oriental spirit or by utilitarian prudence'.[29] Otto diagnosed a war-like situation, in which the European spirit was threatened by total defeat. Wilamowitz, on the other hand, endorsed a conciliatory position: for him, a pantheistic notion of monotheism had

---

29 Otto, *Die Götter Griechenlands* (n. 23, above) 14, 'und sie werden bleiben, solange der europäische Geist, der in ihnen sein bedeutendste Objektivierung gefunden hat, dem Geist des Orients oder der zweckhaften Verständigkeit nicht ganz unterliegt'. This is an indirect allusion to Jacob Burckhardt's preface to 'Kunst des Altertums', *Gesamtausgabe*, vol. XIII, 23: 'The hour, when our culture ceases to find the types of the great Greek gods (*die großen griechischen Göttertypen*) beautiful, will be the beginning of barbarism.' Burckhardt thus located the guarantee for the continuation of European culture in the aesthetic appreciation of the Greek gods. In this case, Burckhardt did not name the enemy, but used the vague 'barbarism' instead. It could refer to utilitarianism, the revolutionary masses, or the establishment of a counter-revolutionary dictatorship. In contrast, Otto named the enemy as oriental, utilitarian, and prudent. In the 1920s, the charge of intellectualism had anti-French as well as anti-Semitic connotations, but the reference to the Orient makes the anti-Semitic meaning clear. Publication of Otto's book in 1929 was not lost on Wilamowitz, see H. Cancik, 'Walter Otto als Religionswissenschaftler und Theologe am Ende der Weimarer Republik (I und II)', in *Antik-Modern. Beiträge zur römischen und deutschen Kulturgeschichte*, ed. H. Cancik (Stuttgart 1998) 139-63 and 165-86.

a rightful place within European culture. It was justified by its Greek roots as well as its neo-pagan affiliations. Reduced to this kind of monotheism, Christianity became Greek and, as such, acceptable.

4. Against a theistic conception of Christianity, Wilamowitz affirmed the position of Otto, who believed in the real existence of the Greek gods. He elevated actual belief in them to the status of a hermeneutic pre-condition for successful research on Greek religion. By enshrining a neo-pagan sentiment as the axiomatic premise for the scholarly investigation of Greek religion, Wilamowitz thus endowed neo-paganism with a more comprehensive legitimacy. But he also announced the beginning of a new age in which the gods would manifest their presence again – a new awakening, as it were, which was also heralded by the circle around Stefan George and other groups under the influence of Nietzsche. Ironically, by insisting on the existence of the Greek gods so emphatically, Wilamowitz promoted a return to early Greek culture, like his old enemy, Nietzsche.

Why did *Der Glaube der Hellenen* receive so little attention, while Otto's book had a second edition in 1934 and a third in 1947? I suspect that Wilamowitz's attempt to join the ranks of the *völkisch* movement was doomed to failure since the position that he could have assumed was already taken by a younger generation. Habitual dissonances might also have played a role: as a typical German professor, he would have appeared insufficiently visionary to the young.

IV Racism in its National Socialist form

At the beginning of *Der Glaube der Hellenen*, Wilamowitz attacked his colleague Hermann Usener for employing a comparative method in the study of Greek religion. Usener had used ethnographic data in his analysis of Greek and Roman phenomena. By 1931, philologists in Cambridge had been doing so for decades. Wilamowitz firmly denied that such an approach could yield valid insights. To buttress this point, he insisted on qualitative differences between East African tribes and Polynesian communities on the one hand, and his beloved Greeks on the other. If these cultures did indeed differ in essential ways, any attempt to compare their cultural features would necessarily be a preposterous undertaking. But on the basis of what category did Wilamowitz establish such fundamental differences? He found it without hesitation: race.

> Das Axiom, alle Menschen sind gleich, dürfte gerade von der Naturwissenschaft umgestoßen oder doch berichtigt sein. Die Vererbung und die körperliche und geistige Veredlung bewirken, daß von einer Gleichheit der Menschen selbst innerhalb desselben Volkes nicht die Rede sein dürfte, wenn nicht die lügnerische politische Phrase zurzeit herrschte, was die Wissenschaft nicht beirren darf. In einer Gesellschaftsordnung, einem Staate, der mit dem Axiom Ernst macht, wird nur eine andere Klassenherrschaft begründet, die der Masse, Ochlokratie, und es ist nur folgerichtig, wenn das eingestanden und durch die Vernichtung der höher gezüchteten Volksgenossen durchgeführt wird. Noch viel einleuchtender sollte es sein, daß für die verschiedenen Menschenrassen die Gleichheit des Geistes noch viel weniger denkbar ist wie notorisch für ihre Körper. Damit will ich prinzipiell gar nicht bestreiten, daß die Vorstellungen der Völker, die sich über die niedrigste Stufe des Menschentums nicht zu erheben vermocht haben, für die

Embryologie der griechischen Religion etwas ausgeben können; aber diese hatte ihre Kinderjahre, Jahrhunderte hinter sich, als sie sich von dem indogermanischen Urvolke absonderte, hatte vorher Jahrhunderte in diesem gelebt, und bis zu dem Zustande des Menschen der Eiszeit waren wohl Jahrtausende.   *Glaube der Hellenen* I, 10.

The axiom 'all men are equal' should have been overturned or at least corrected, by the natural sciences in particular. Hereditary transmission and physical as well as intellectual ennoblement would make it impossible to speak of human equality even within the same people if it were not for the false political phraseology prevailing today. This, however, must not disconcert science. A social order or a state that takes this axiom seriously, only establishes another form of class-based rule, namely that of the masses, ochlocracy. It is only logical if this is conceded and carried out by the extermination of the higher bred members of the people's community. It should be even more obvious that equality of intellectual abilities is even less conceivable for different human races than, as is common knowledge, physical equality. In saying this, I do not want to dispute in principle that the mentality of those peoples unable to raise themselves above the most primitive level of humanity might tell us something about the embryonic stages of Greek religion. But Greek religion had already outgrown its infant stage for centuries when it split off from the Indo-European Ur-people in which it had lived for centuries. Between that stage and the humanity of the Ice Age there probably lay millennia.

Wilamowitz here denies the fundamental equality of man.[30] For revolutionary movements and schools of thought ever since the sixteenth century, the equality of man meant that the natural differences among human beings were insignificant insofar as they could not be used to justify the domination of one man over another. 'The proposition that all men are created equal' – as Abraham Lincoln put it in his Gettysburg Address – was crucial for the modern concept of democracy and universal human rights. For Wilamowitz, who, as we have seen, had used race and racial difference as heuristic categories as early as 1910, the step towards endorsing an overt, and particularly offensive, form of racism was presumably a small one. The lengthy passage quoted above is fraught with key concepts and formulations that would merit a more detailed discussion within a larger study of the notions of race and racial inequality in German classics. Here I simply want to point out some particularly striking aspects:

1. Wilamowitz considered inequalities that are the product of culture (*körperliche und geistige Veredelung*, physical and intellectual ennoblement) and inequalities that are the product of nature (*Vererbung*, heredity), as interchangeable. The standard authors of the Enlightenment would have conceded that culture creates inequalities; but they would not have located these inequalities in the realm of nature. The combination of cultural and natural factors in the creation of human inequality is a central rhetorical strategy of ideologists opposed to the notion of political equality. By insisting on inequalities as an inevitable fact of nature, they justify the perpetuation of historical, that is contingent, social and cultural modes of domination.

---

30 By positing that human races are unequal, especially in terms of intellectual capacity, Wilamowitz dismissed comparative methods. Ethnology deals with cultures, as he saw it, that did not rise above the most primitive level of humanity. It is therefore absurd to compare these inferior races with the 'noble Greeks', as Usener did. Indeed, doing so represents an offence to the Greeks' racial superiority.

2. When Wilamowitz adduced research in the 'natural sciences' as evidence for his dismissal of the equality of men, the kind of science he drew upon is *Rassenforschung* (racial science) as undertaken by men like Wilhelm Schallmeyer, Alfred Ploetz, and Ernst Haeckel.[31] By the beginning of the twentieth century, their 'racial doctrine' (*Rassenlehre*) was coupled with eugenics and transformed into a theory of eugenics (*Rassenhygiene*). For a long time this 'science' suffered from a lack of respect within the scientific community, but it gradually managed to win a certain amount of support in the United States, Germany, Switzerland, Sweden, and Great Britain.[32] By the end of World War I, eugenic theorists began to clamour for state-sponsored programmes for the extermination of 'lives unworthy of life' (*lebensunwertes Leben*), and politicians started to put their ideas into practice.[33] In Germany, these ideas also became a major source of inspiration during the 1920s for the right-wing grouping 'Science Against Democracy'.

3. It is no coincidence that Wilamowitz spoke of 'ochlocracy' in this context – the word used by ancient Greek thinkers to denounce democracy. He rejected egalitarianism as a valid political principle, believing that it would lead to the 'extermination of the higher bred members of the people's community'. But Wilamowitz provided no empirical evidence to show why political equality would result in such a programme of extermination. The 'extermination' he feared was a key concept in the political debates of the 1920s and 1930s. It was the openly declared aim of left-wing revolutionaries to destroy the ruling class. But, for them, to destroy a class meant to deprive it of the economic resources which it used to exercise power: no one on the left called for the physical extermination of the bourgeoisie.

Not even the Russian Revolution brought about such an extermination. The murderous consequences of the Russian Revolution affected all classes indiscriminately. This, however, was an issue debated at the time. Just as Hans Günther interpreted World War I as a civil war within the 'Nordic' race, positing that in all armies the officers and military leaders were 'Nordic',[34] the American racial scientist Lothrop Stoddard tried to interpret the Russian Revolution as a racial struggle, in which the inferior race – the 'undermen' – tried to exterminate the superior race.[35] When Wilamowitz spoke of 'extermination' he evoked the possibility of a civil war between the different races of one nation, a widely disseminated notion at the time.[36]

4. Wilamowitz alerted his readers to a fatal threat to occidental civilization, by ascribing to the left-wing parties eliminationist intentions that were in fact absent from their programmes as well as their practices. This strategy, employed by many demagogues of the extreme

---

31 See W. Schallmeyer, *Vererbung und Auslese im Lebenslauf der Völker* (Jena 1903); A. Ploetz, *Die Tüchtigkeit unserer Rasse und der Schutz der Schwachen* (Berlin 1895); E. Haeckel, *Gemeinverständliche Werke*, vol. III (Leipzig 1924).
32 See *Rasse, Blut und Gene: Geschichte der Eugenik und Rassenhygiene in Deutschland*, ed. P. Weingart, J. Kroll, and K. Bayertz (Frankfurt a. M. 1988) 320-54.
33 See H.-W. Schmuhl, *Rassenhygiene, Nationalsozialismus, Euthanasie. Von der Verhütung zur Vernichtung 'lebensunwerten* Lebens', 1890-1945 (Göttingen 1987); H. Friedlander, *Der Weg zum NS-Genozid: Von der Euthanasie zur Endlösung* (Berlin 1997).
34 See E. Conte and C. Esser, *La quête de la race. Une anthropologie du nazisme* (Paris 1995) 80-81.
35 L. Stoddard, *The Revolt of Civilization. The Menace of the Undermen* (New York 1923).
36 A notion expressed by, e.g, E. Fischer and H. Günther, cf. Conte and Esser, *La quête* (n. 34, above) 67-73.

right in the 1920s and 1930s, was a ready-made formula for stirring up political fear and hatred. By insinuating that the Left was out to exterminate Europe's social and cultural elites, Wilamowitz called upon the latter to defend themselves.

In 1931, such rhetorical manœuvres helped create a mental disposition susceptible to the idea of extermination as an act of prevention. But the extermination at issue now is not an imaginary one perpetrated by the Left; it is an extermination discussed and prepared by right-wing groups of the Weimar era, which, like Wilamowitz, tried to justify such an extermination as self-defence.

5. Wilamowitz used the vocabulary of the new pseudo-science of eugenics. Binding and Hoche, for example, entitled their book of 1920 *Die Freigabe der Vernichtung lebensunwerten Lebens* (*The Permission for the Destruction of Lives unworthy of Life*).[37] The very specific German brand of science called '*Bevölkerungswissenschaft*' (Science of population and population movement)[38] – a science deeply involved in the organised genocide in Eastern Europe and in the Holocaust – used a similar, highly aggressive vocabulary.[39] Once people are split into inferior and superior races, their mixture becomes a genuine problem. That is why the National Socialists could always claim that they were acting in self-defence, against an attack on the racial substance of the German people. If they did not put a halt to miscegenation, the moral and cultural qualities of the Aryan stock would deteriorate. Wilamowitz thus endorsed the same point of view as the *völkisch* movement.

6. There are other terms in the paragraph quoted above which underscore Wilamowitz's new political affiliations. For instance, the word '*Volksgenossen*'. Why this term? Why not use the traditional '*Bürger*', 'citizens'? Since the middle of the 1920s, the word '*Bürger*' had acquired negative connotations for the extreme Right in Germany. Ernst Jünger was proud of the fact that Germans had never been good '*Bürger*'. In Jünger's eyes, '*Bürger*' stood for a despicable kind of political behaviour – the exact opposite of the warrior and the worker.[40] In 1910 Wilamowitz was not afraid to use the word '*Bürger*', in 1928 he avoided it, using '*Volksgenossen*' instead. At the beginning of the 1920s '*Volksgenosse*' had become a watchword of the extreme Right, which used it from the very beginning as an alternative to '*Staatsbürger*' (citizen). In 1929/30, the word had become a synonym for 'German'. Here, too, Wilamowitz employed the language of the *völkisch* movement, which was dominated by the Nazis.

7. Wilamowitz also used the expression '*höher gezüchtet*' ('higher bred'). That is no longer the sublime language of German idealistic philosophy and '*Bildung*'. On the one hand,

---

37 K. Binding and A. Hoche, *Die Freigabe der Vernichtung lebensunwerten Lebens, ihr Maß und ihre Form* (Leipzig 1920).
38 I. Pinn and M. Nebelung, *Vom 'klassischen' zum aktuellen Rassismus in Deutschland. Das Menschenbild der Bevölkerungstheorie und Bevölkerungspolitik* (Duisburg 1992).
39 See Weingart, Kroll, and Bayertz, *Rasse, Blut und Gene* (n. 32, above); B. Massin, 'Anthropologie raciale et national-socialisme: Heurs et malheurs du paradigme de la "race"', in *La science sous le Troisième Reich: Victime ou alliée du nazisme?*, ed. P. Ayçoberry and J. Olff-Nathan (Paris 1993) 197-262.
40 See E. Jünger, *Der Arbeiter. Herrschaft und Gestalt* (Hamburg 1932) 13, 'Auf über ein Jahrhundert deutscher Geschichte zurückblickend dürfen wir mit Stolz gestehen, daß wir schlechte Bürger gewesen sind'.

Wilamowitz continued to insist that 'pure' races do not exist.[41] On the other hand, he spoke of 'higher' and 'lower' races, even within a single people. This amalgamation of concepts and categories enabled Wilamowitz to emphasise assimilation and acculturation. (Though it should be noted that in *Der Glaube der Hellenen* – in contrast to the text of 1910 – Wilamowitz stressed that other nations become 'hellenized', whereas the Greeks hardly adopt anything at all; if they do, it tends to concern technical matters that are immediately incorporated into the Hellenic way of life.) At the same time, he asserted racial hierarchies whenever this was expedient. When heterogeneous racial elements are mixed, it follows logically, for Wilamowitz, that their relative proportion in the new species is the decisive factor in cultural history.[42]

This is classics in a new key. The internationally renowned German philologist speaks of race and 'breeding' in an overtly socio-biological sense. He takes a number of concepts directly from the eugenicist textbooks of his day, and employs them strategically in crucial topical debates.[43] The same eugenicist ideas were later taken up by the Nazis and implemented in their 'breeding' (*Züchtung*) programmes that were to produce a racially superior species.

Put into its historical context (that is, the years 1925 to 1935), almost every word of the last quotation from *Der Glaube der Hellenen* reveals strong affiliations with the political idiom of the German new Right. Traditional *Quellenforschung*, which tries to identify the original texts from which Wilamowitz took his ideas, does not lead to any deep insights here. However, once we read his book in conjunction with right-wing best-sellers of the time, for example, works by Oswald Spengler and Ernst Jünger, and once we compare his terms with the concepts of the extreme Right (concepts such as breeding, extermination, and eugenics), it becomes all too apparent that the renowned German classicist Ulrich von Wilamowitz-

---

41 See *Glaube der Hellenen* I, 50, 'So ist es ein offenkundiger Widersinn, wenn die Leute so anmaßlich von reiner Rasse reden, wo immer ein wenig Adelshochmut im Hintergrunde liegt. Rassenreinheit gibt es weder bei Menschen noch bei Göttern, aber die Hellenen haben es vermocht, recht viele Fremde zu hellenisieren, Menschen und Götter.' (Thus it is evident nonsense when people speak so presumptuously of pure race. A bit of aristocratic arrogance always lies at the heart of this. There is no racial purity among either humans or gods, but the Greeks were able to hellenize quite a few foreigners, humans and gods.')

42 While Wilamowitz refused to compare Greek cultural phenomena with similar ones in 'primitive' cultures, he endorsed comparisons between the high cultures of the ancient Mediterranean, see *Glaube der Hellenen* I, 11, 'Wenn ich eine Theologie brauchen soll, so liegt mir die der griechischen Philosophen am nächsten, von der die Religionshistoriker selten Notiz nehmen, und wenn ich andere Religionen vergleichen soll, so sehe ich lieber auf die Nachbarn der Griechen, Semiten und Ägypter und lerne bei Wellhausen und Erman.' (When I need a theology, the one closest to me is that of the Greek philosophers, which is rarely discussed by historians of religion. When I am supposed to compare other religions, I prefer to look at the neighbours of the Greeks, the Semites and Egyptians, and learn from Wellhausen and Erman.) Within these limits, Wilamowitz employed a comparative approach, in order to tear open radical, insurmountable cultural differences, which he charges with ideological significance. At times he bolstered these differences with reference to racial inequality: either by introducing the concept of natural inequality into debates about the best political organisation for racially mixed nations; or, by explaining differences in 'cultural potential' (*Kulturfähigkeit*) with reference to miscegenation. It is true that Wilamowitz made use of this approach only sporadically. Nevertheless, he helped to endow these ideas with scientific authority. The Nazi historians Vogt and Schachermeyer took the same path in the 1930s.

43 See P. Weindling, *L'hygiène de la race. Tome 1: hygiène médical et eugénisme en Allemagne 1870-1933* (Paris 1998) 42-66.

Moellendorff began, towards the end of his life, to speak the language of the *völkisch* movement. By endowing it with his own scholarly authority, he also helped disseminate this language.

To conclude. It was not only the 'younger generation' that made up the right-wing intellectual milieu in Germany and established the concepts of the *völkisch* movement in the years before Hitler came to power.[44] The emeritus chair of classical philology at the University of Berlin, Wilamowitz-Moellendorf, writing as a classicist, actively helped to shape the discourse of National Socialism. The keener cultural scientists are to produce scholarship that can be put to immediate or programmatic political use, the more they will be receptive to highly politicized 'sciences', or endorse the conceptual architecture of *political* movements.

University of Greifswald

---

[44] See J. Herf, *Reactionary modernism. Technology, culture and politics in Weimar and the Third Reich* (Cambridge 1987), esp. chapters 2 and 7.

FROM LIBERALISM TO NEOROMANTICISM:
ALBRECHT DIETERICH, RICHARD REITZENSTEIN, AND THE RELIGIOUS TURN IN *FIN-DE-SIÈCLE* GERMAN CLASSICAL STUDIES*

SUZANNE MARCHAND

German intellectual historians have long recognized the distinctness of 'the generation of the 1890s' – and its radical departures from its liberal forebears. Though historians of other countries have also noted a big generation shift among those who came of age between roughly 1885 and 1905, for German historians, this generational change seems particularly consequential, and is usually portrayed as a perilous one: a rising tide of irrationality, aggressiveness, and racial prejudice infiltrates a liberal culture world, setting the scene for Nazism.[1] Until recently, this literature was cordoned off from a much more positive set of discussions about the birth of modernism and the development of a new set of forward-looking, social-scientific disciplines, a story in which the Germans certainly play an important role.[2] But, inspired particularly by work in the history of science, the barriers between these two narratives, which we might call, on the one hand, 'the crisis of liberalism,' and on the other, 'the revolt against historicism', have been collapsing. In what follows, I will attempt to trace this double-edged modernization story for the great humanistic discipline of the nineteenth century, *Altertumswissenschaft*, and to illustrate here the ways in which generational and ideological conflict must be seen in the context of new interdisciplinary initiatives, evidentiary circumstances, and broad scale cultural changes.

The story of modernization, and that of the destruction of liberalism, belong together, perhaps nowhere more so than in the field sketched below, namely classical studies. Here, as will be suggested throughout this essay, modernization brought both positive benefits, in the form of new sources and wider perspectives, and new dangers, born of less exacting standards, far-flung comparisons, and an openness to new ideas, which included, *c.* 1900,

---

* The author is greatly indebted to Peter Brown, Susan Crane, Anthony Grafton, Susannah Heschel, David Lindenfeld, Glenn Penny, and Guy Strousma, as well as to the editors of this volume, for their comments on earlier drafts of this essay.

Abbreviations   BGStA   Berlin, Geheimes Staatsarchiv (Dahlem)
                  BSB   Berlin, Staatsbibliothek (Handschriftenabteilung)

1 See, for example, Fritz Stern's highly influential *The Politics of Cultural Despair* (Berkeley 1961), or, more recently, *Handbuch zur 'Völkischen Bewegung' 1871-1918*, ed. U. Puschner, W. Schmitz, and J. H. Ulbricht (Munich 1996).
2 See, for example, H. S. Hughes, in his classic work *Consciousness and Society: The Reorientation of European Social Thought, 1890-1930* (New York 1958); W. Everdell, *The First Moderns: Profiles in the Origins of Twentieth-Century Thought* (Chicago 1997).

racial anti-Semitism. It is this essay's purpose neither to idealize late nineteenth-century liberals nor to make excuses for their younger critics, but rather to describe the intellectual and institutional circumstances and consequences of their interaction. For what happened to German classical studies in the twentieth century, the liberals and the modernizing group I will call the neo-Romantics, probably deserve equal credit – and equal blame.

Certainly one of the aims of this essay is to analyze the clash between these generations of classicists, but I also want to show that these clashes were neither simply personal, nor exclusively ideological, but were also the product of the rapidly changing public sphere and scholarly scene of the 1880s to 1920s. Here we need to understand the ways in which specialization, political and social changes, and, especially, the accumulation of mounds of new evidence, particularly from 'the Orient', prepared the way for new perspectives – or, indeed, created both the necessity and desire to return to three sorts of inquiry eschewed by mid-century scholars, namely, the impact of 'the East' on 'Western' ideas; the erotic life of the ancients; and the role of religion in pagan antiquity. Certainly, the liberal generation had begun to feel some of these pressures by the time they achieved professorial status, but most were unable, and unwilling, to alter their research programmes to suit the new opportunities, and new demands. Often, their reaction to the next generation represented a reeling-in of lines of inquiry they feared were now drifting back into the pre-*wissenschaftlich* waters of their Romantic forbears. I think it can be shown, that is, that the 'irrational' urges of the 1890s generation were both a logical extension of late liberal work, and a reaction to liberal suppression of questions posed by their 'fathers', the Romantics. This is, in many ways, the story of three generations, not two, and of the attempted, but not entirely successful, return of the Romantic repressed in the brave new world of the *fin de siècle*.

A final aim of this essay is to go to the heart of what I believe constitutes the intellectual crisis of the *fin de siècle*: the final, full-scale collapse of Christian and neohumanist world-views. By discussing the collapse of world-views, I do not mean simply to adumbrate individual crises of faith, in either God, for Christians, or the beauty of Greek culture, for neohumanists. For individuals, faith continued, or failed (as it had for Ernest Renan and Jacob Burckhardt in the previous generation); now the problem was, rather, that the textual and historical props for a whole set of institutional arrangements and their sustaining ideas were subjected, on a grand scale, to ideological and evidentiary assault. The neohumanist belief in Greek uniqueness, upon which the *Gymnasien* and the whole culture of German philhellenism was built, faced collapse in the wake of Germanophile school reform movements, the specialization and diversification of classical scholarship, vitalist weariness with liberal conventions, and finally, what I will call the second Oriental Renaissance (see below). At the same time, confidence in Judeo-Christian uniqueness was shaken by increasingly historicist Biblical criticism at a time of massive church-leaving, the expansion of radical new free-thought movements, and greatly increased knowledge of other cultures and faiths. The two scholars scrutinized here, Albrecht Dieterich (1866-1908) and Richard Reitzenstein (1861-1931), both participated in the tearing down of these liberal institutions and convictions, and tried to envision new foundations for classical studies and for religious belief; neither, however, succeeded entirely in leaving behind the world of their fathers, or in bequeathing durable frameworks to the future.

One of the important claims of this paper is that these two worldviews fell, essentially, together, and did so, in large part, because the rather narrow sort of historicism upon which they were based could not withstand the opening up of new perspectives and new sources – particularly from the Near East – which accompanied the languishing of Humboldtian humanism's cultural dominance in the last quarter of the nineteenth century. These new sources pressed theologians and classicists, who had, since F. A. Wolf's declaration of philological independence, largely gone their own ways, to confront precisely the subjects I described above as anathema to 'liberal' *Wissenschaftler*, namely, the impact of the East, sex, and religion. Having shared, for most of the century, a common, perhaps Hegelian, conviction that Oriental mysticism (including Judaism) had been left behind by history, and that Greek rationalism and individualism should provide the foundations for modern German *Bildung* and modern German faith, liberal theologians and classicists found it very difficult to assimilate this new material, and the neo-Romantic types who found particular delight in promoting it. Nor did they approve of the interdisciplinary and comparative methods the younger generation employed to interpret it. The reactions of the 'liberal' fathers in both fields were remarkably similar, and tell us a great deal about why, again for both admirable and objectionable reasons, 'modern' ideas were so haltingly accepted in German academe. I have thus included a great deal of information, below, about both the second Oriental Renaissance and the *fin-de-siècle* crisis in theology. Neither of these phenomena are well-known to classicists, but as I hope the following will illustrate, both deserve to be more completely integrated into the history of the discipline.

In defining the late 'liberal' as against the 'neo-Romantic' generation, I divide, for the most part, those who came of age in the 1870s and 80s from those who published their first works in the 1890s and after. Of course there are some who do not fit this chronology, and drawing lines is complicated by the fact that several members of the 'liberal' generation, like Ulrich von Wilamowitz-Moellendorff (1848-1931) and Eduard Meyer (1855-1930), lived long into the postliberal era, whose opening I date to about 1900. I hasten to note that what makes these scholars 'liberals', for me, is certainly not their politics: Eduard Meyer, for example, was politically as far to the right as Walter F. Otto. Rather, those I describe as 'liberals' are those who, by and large, maintained the tradition of secular humanism and *Kulturprotestantismus*; though increasingly historicist in orientation, they betrayed, at significant moments, a residual attachment to aestheticizing Graecophilia, faith in the autonomy of Greek culture, belief in data collection (as opposed to intuition), and resistance to interdisciplinary or comparative endeavours. These men largely suppressed, or repressed, the 'irrational' passions of the Greeks, suggesting that the real Hellenes had been too sophisticated to really believe in their gods or act on their drives; though they usually acknowledged that the Greeks borrowed from their neighbours to the East. This admission was generally followed by the claim that upon arriving in Greece, gods, rituals, words, and pot styles immediately became authentically Greek – and the authentically Greek, not the authentically human, Western, or 'Aryan' – to invoke some of the other terms in circulation – was thought to be their only concern.

The 'neo-Romantics', on the other hand, took borrowing from the East more seriously, both for scholarly and for non-scholarly reasons. They benefited from the explosion of studies of India, Persia, and Egypt in the second half of the nineteenth century, while feeling alienated, too, from cheerful endorsements of Greece's ability to fight free of 'oriental', 'irrational', legacies. This generation both forced the question of religion to the forefront and began to kick the props out from under presumptions of Graeco-Christian uniqueness, destroying, in the process, the foundations upon which Humboltian humanism had been built. Reitzenstein, lecturing in the Kaiser's presence in 1907, summarized quite succinctly the palpable decline of neoclassical humanism occurring around him: 'We feel it', he wrote, referring both to his own era and to the world of Augustus, 'the era of humane culture [*Humanität*] is over, an era of religiosity [*Religiosität*] is opening again'.[3]

That this new religiosity had its own limitations is certain, and I want here to clarify one of the important intellectual consequences of the second Oriental Renaissance and the neo-Romantic revolt, and that is its failure to bridge a divide that had opened already in the Enlightenment between Greeks and Jews. Though the generation of Dieterich and Reitzenstein took very seriously the religious convictions of Mandaens, Zoroastrians, Babylonians, Mithraists, and devotees of the Eleusinian mysteries, the study of Judaism continued to be, as in the era of high liberalism, left to Jews outside the academy; and as Uriel Tal showed some time ago, attempts to adduce the 'essences' of the two religions drove them further apart.[4] Thus some effort is expended, here, in illustrating the peculiar, and ominous, tendency in the German interpretation of Hellenistic and ancient oriental texts to exclude the Jews from the new, much less Graeco-centric history of humankind that was being pioneered, and to erase them entirely as participants in the evolution of religious ideas.

To understand this reaction against liberal classicism and theology, then, we need to understand both internal and external forces, from the dynamics of specialization, which pushed younger scholars into less familiar Greek realms, to the new appeal of 'decadent' or primaeval eras and religious questions. We need to appreciate the effects of the new masses of material swamping European museums and libraries, as well as the impact of the rapid expansion of the middle class visual universe, which now included the work of Puvis de Chavannes and Arnold Böcklin, as well as Islamic, African, and Japanese forms. We need to recognize the importance of newly affordable travel to exotic locales, an opportunity not available, or not seized upon, by the liberal generation. All of these practical considerations – which asserted influence gradually, not suddenly – are as important as changes in ideology, politics, and philosophy, stemming from conventionally-adduced sources such as disillusionment with bourgeois conventions, the rise of mass politics and hyper-nationalism, and readings of Nietzsche and Schopenhauer. To be succinct: by about 1910, liberalism lost its dynamism in classical scholarship, as it did in European culture and politics more broadly, not only because it had been overturned by more radical sentiments, but also because it had reached the limits of its effectiveness and appeal.

Clearly, the aims of this paper are multiple. On the one hand, I want to describe a change of generations in classics, on the other, I want to hint at broader reasons for the emergence of a new, 'neo-Romantic' cultural world from the ashes of the liberal old regime. Thus the first half of the paper discusses, in general, the late liberal collapse of the Christian and neoclassical worldviews in the context of the second Oriental Renaissance; the second presents two case studies of classicists whose reactions to liberalism were framed by both practical and affective

---

3 R. Reitzenstein, *Werden und Wesen der Humanität im Altertum* (Straßburg 1907) 20.
4 U. Tal, *Christians and Jews in Germany: Religion, Politics and Ideology in the Second Reich, 1870-1914* (Ithaca/New York 1975).

considerations. I hope that by proceeding in this way, I can offer both a general narrative describing generational change in the disciplines that concern us here, classics and theology, and two clear examples of a new, postliberal worldview. The conclusion, too, should suggest both the fruitfulness and the dangers of this neo-Romantic revolt.

I The decline of neoclassicism and the fin-de-siècle Oriental Renaissance

I will leave aside, here, an extensive discussion of liberal, historicist classicism, in large part because I have already told my version of the story elsewhere.[5] Suffice it to say that into the 1870s and 80s, an aestheticizing Graecophilia still characterized this realm, even as scholars and museum officials began to accumulate detailed knowledge about, and material evidence of, everyday life. Convinced that the job of explaining the history of religion belonged to the theological faculty, and the task of understanding Egyptian, Persian, Mesopotamian and Iranian cultures belonged to the Orientalists, most mid-century classicists focused on national, or sub-national topics. Enormous effort was put into compiling and editing texts, inscriptions, and images, and often broad-brush interpretation deferred to some later time, at which scholars would have not simply 'individual crumbs from antiquity's table',[6] as Ernst Curtius said about the proceeds of the Olympia excavations (begun in 1875), but enough ingredients for a full and satisfying meal.

The mid-century aversion to studying religion was not, however, merely a product of positivist restraint, or even of the tradition of Kulturprotestantismus; it was motivated by fear that those who took up such 'irrational' subjects as Greek mystery religions would be tarred with the Creuzerian brush. In the post-Romantic chill of the 1820s, Friedrich Creuzer, author of a wide-ranging study of the migration of religious symbols and ideas (*Symbolik und Mythologie der alten Völker,* first edition 1810-12) had been accused of crypto-Catholicism and speculative flights of fancy. Though Creuzer did not have to give up his job, the polemics against him, especially those of August Lobeck and K. O. Müller, had left Creuzer isolated and demoralized, and his 'romantic' form of universal history discredited.[7] As Alfred Körte explained in 1915, after 1820, the scathing critiques of Creuzer's *Symbolik* had snuffed out this sort of research almost to the present day: '... the chilling shower of pitiless criticism and insipid rationalism destroyed not only the mischievous frauds and the extravagant fake-flowers of neoplatonic and Romantic speculation, but also many green stalks, that would have born good fruit ...' Lobeck's derogatory view of the mysteries made them insignificant and

---

5 Chiefly in *Down from Olympus. Archaeology and Philhellenism in Germany, 1750 - 1970* (Princeton 1996); but aspects of this world and its decline are also described in 'The Ancients and the Moderns in German Museums', in *Museums and Memory*, ed. S. Crane (Stanford 2000), 179-99, and in my essay on Adolf Furtwängler, forthcoming in *Olympia 1875-2000. 125 Jahre Deutsche Ausgrabungen,* ed. Judith Kerr (Mainz 2003).
6 E. Curtius, 'Die Ausgrabungen von Olympia', report no. 10, in *Archäologischer Anzeiger* 34 (1876) 216.
7 For a discussion of Friedrich Creuzer's work and the debates surrounding him, see J. Blok, 'Quest for a Scientific Mythology: F. Creuzer and K. O. Müller on History and Myth', *History and Theory*, suppl. 33 (1994) 26-52.

absurd: 'Small wonder, that for a long time no one who cared about his scholarly reputation would have anything to do with the Eleusinian mysteries ...'.[8]

But, Körte noted, by the *fin de siècle*, the Creuzer taboo had lost much of its power, and disciplinary boundaries were subjected to new pressures as the positivist collecting projects described above pushed particularly younger scholars into hitherto untilled fields of study. Here liberal 'mavericks' like Hermann Usener (1834-1905) were enormously influential in shaping the postliberal revolt. As the foremost classicist at the University of Bonn, Usener was instrumental in inducing numerous young philologists to tread on unfamiliar turf; in his 1882 Rektoratsrede (an important public occasion, on which scholars often summed up their aims), he declared: 'The true philologist must be a knight without fear', one willing, that is, to take on any text, no matter how arcane, unappealing, or intractable.[9] Usener's interests ran, in particular, to religious subjects, and his works ranged widely, from saints' lives and early Christian festivals (in which he noted pagan survivals) to astrology, etymology and comparative folkore and mythology – a set of studies he hoped would unite (through philological purification) the faiths and offer modern men a new, self-conscious, form of belief.[10] If his ecumenical message frequently failed to translate, Usener was, nonetheless, very important in ushering in, through historicist doors, the neo-Romantic revival described below.

Crucial in the making of the generation of Usener's students was the convergence of an emerging cultural pessimism (rampant amongst the humanistic elite, though not, for example, in the women's movement or among socialists) and what I will call the second Oriental Renaissance. (The first was identified long ago by Raymond Schwab, who gave it the rough dates of 1680-1880.[11]) The two – pessimism and 'Orientalism' – are much more closely linked than anyone, including Edward Said, has previously noted, and their consequences for European humanism profound.[12] The *fin-de-siècle* popularity of the Orient rode in on a tide of new scepticism about Europe's civilizing mission abroad and the deleterious effects of 'civilization' at home. From wild-eyed warnings about 'decadence' and 'neurasthenia' to debates about how to treat the colonized, waning confidence in Euro-centric liberal triumphalism was evident: how healthy was urban, industrial society for its members? How could 'civilization' be shared with others without exposing them to its evils, or Europeans to more and more miscegenation and violence? If the French were first to worry about degeneration, the northern Italians, disappointed by the results of the *Risorgimento*, soon followed. And, despite having won the Franco-Prussian war, the Germans too by the 1880s began to evince

---

8 A. Körte, 'Zu den eleusinischen Mysterien', *Archiv für Religionsgeschichte* 18 (1915) 116-17. Walter Burkert says that Lobeck's *Aglaophamus* 'reduced the speculations about Mysteries and Orphism to tangible but undeniably banal realities', see his *Greek Religion*, trans. J. Raffan (Cambridge MA 1985) 1.
9 See A. Momigliano, 'Hermann Usener', in his *New Paths of Classicism in the Nineteenth Century*, in *History and Theory* 21.4 (1982) 39.
10 H. Usener, 'Mythologie', in *Archiv für Religionswissenschaft* 7 (1904) 32.
11 R. Schwab, *The Oriental Renaissance: Europe's Discovery of India and the East, 1680-1880*, trans. G. Patterson-Black and V. Reinking (New York 1984); French original published in 1950.
12 I am referring here, of course, to Said's well-known *Orientalism* (New York 1978), a book which contains brilliant insights as well as perverse representations of the study of the East. For a more detailed evaluation, see Marchand, 'German Orientalism and the Decline of the West', *Proceedings of the American Philosophical Society* 145.4 (December 2001) 465-73.

decadence-anxiety, spawned by fear of failing to complete successfully the ascent to world-power status.

At first, the theme of decline and fall touched Roman history more powerfully than Greek. Already by 1876, Felix Dahn had published what would be the most popular boys' novel of the Wilhelmine era, *Ein Kampf um Rom*, set in Rome's twilight years. If Dahn's novel looked back to Tacitus's paean to the Germanic noble savages, however, other treatments implicitly warned the Germans against the fate of the Romans. In the 1880s, the historian Otto Seeck adopted quasi-racial Darwinism, attributing the Empire's collapse to miscegenation and unnatural selection ('*Ausrottung der Besten*').[13] Max Weber's subtle essay, 'The Social Causes of the Decline of Ancient Culture' (1896), suggested that Junker politics and the constriction of the East Elbian labour market threatened Bismarck's Caesarist Empire, just as labour shortages on the *Latifundia* had undermined Roman power.[14]

But Rome was not the only ancient civilization whose deterioration required scrutiny; J.J. Bachofen, Jacob Burckhardt, and Friedrich Nietzsche also offered poignant portrayals of the frailty of Socratic civilization, and by about 1900, it seems, a handful of young scholars had decided that the 'true' Greece was a much less rational and happy place than their forefathers (and schoolmasters) had claimed. This elegiacal, and elitist anxiety about degeneration was evident in Erwin Rohde's *Psyche: Seelencult und Unsterblichkeitsglaube der Griechen* (2 vols, 1890-94), which underscored the deep significance of sober, soil-rooted ancestor cults, and the longevity of Greek belief in the soul and immortality. In art, the lapsing of Winckelmannian normativity was even more pronounced. By invoking the classical world not through depictions of the deeds of Apollo and Athena, but by portraying the erotic and comical antics of satyrs and nymphs, the Swiss painter Arnold Böcklin earned wide praise; he had, one commentator argued, substituted the vital life-pulse of the real Greeks and Romans for 'the cold marmoreal statuary of official ancient classicism'.[15]

Of course, the 'Orient' had long been treated as the quintessential world of decay, the place where great civilizations had been frittered away by substitution of sensual indulgence for good, honest work. But, by the *fin de siècle*, sensual indulgence seemed not only less objectionable, but perhaps even the sign of a richer, wiser culture, which recognized the superficiality of industrial hustle and bustle. It is certainly possible to find signs of an emerging orientalist vitalism in this era, in Nietzsche's Zarathustra and Paul Deussen's work on Indian mysticism, in Sven Hedin's travelogues, and the rising popularity of Japanese and Chinese art. As religious quests replaced Grand Tours, the East replaced Rome as the mecca for travellers in search of experience. Before the war's outbreak, Hermann Hesse and Hermann Graf Keyserling – destined to be central Weimar-era cultural figures – went East, not South, to find

---

13 See Seeck's infamous chapter by this title in his *Geschichte des Untergangs der antiken Welt*, vol. I (originally published in 1895, reprint of 4th edn, Stuttgart 1966) 269-395. Karl Christ, however, rightly warns against seeing Seeck, who emphasized changes in social structure, as a proto-Nazi. See Christ, 'Der Untergang des Römischen Reiches in antiker und moderner Sicht', [1970] in *Römische Geschichte und Wissenschaftsgeschichte*, vol. II (*Geschichte und Geschichtsschreibung der Römischen Kaiserzeit*) (Darmstadt 1983) 188.
14 See W. J. Mommsen, *Max Weber and German Politics, 1890-1920*, trans. M. S. Steinberg (Chicago 1984) 21-22.
15 F. H. Meissner, *Arnold Böcklin,* 3rd edn (Berlin 1898) 48.

themselves;[16] but they were not the only young *Bildungsbürger* of their generation to look to the Orient for spiritual inspiration. In Germany as in America, England, and France, 'eastern wisdom' grew increasingly enthralling.[17] Buddha, Leopold von Schroeder argued in 1905, was beginning to replace Socrates as the idol of the intellectual elite.[18]

These atmospheric, affective changes were in part provoked by, and in part provoked, a second 'Renaissance' in the professional study of the Orient, one which increasingly impinged on the study of classical antiquity proper. Although Schwab's original 'Oriental Renaissance' ended about 1880, there is a strong case to be made that for most fields of 'oriental' study, the period between 1880 and 1920 was in fact much more productive and revolutionary. Not only were hieroglyphic and cuneiform decipherments cleaned up and standardized – allowing new, much larger generations of scholars to be trained in these fields – many new texts in previously unreadable languages (Pahlavi, Soghdian) flooded European libraries. Egyptian, Mesopotamian, and Sanskrit studies became recognized professional specialties, and well-trained philologists began to produce dissertations, new editions, collections of inscriptions, specialized journal articles, and grant proposals; institutes for the study of the modern Orient – like the Berlin *Orientalisches Seminar* (founded in 1885) – sprang into being. By 1905, there were more than 50 chairs for 'oriental' studies in Germany.[19]

Funded by the state, by museums, or by private patrons, archaeologists now swarmed all over Asia, and began looking for artifacts other than the remains of classical antiquity (though these remained the prize finds). Their haul included – just to take a few spectacular examples – the wall-paintings of Minoan Crete and Chinese Turkestan ('Turfan'), the vast papyri cache unearthed at Oxyrhynchus (Egypt) and the huge manuscript collection found at Tun-Huang, the Code of Hammurabi and the Ishtar Gate, the Tell-el-Amarna letters and Tutankuman's treasures, the multi-cultural remains of Ephesus, Boghazkoi, Ktesiphon, and Palmyra. After 1880, Christian sites in Asia Minor, North Africa, and on the European continent received new scrutiny, and Wilhelm von Bode began to fill his early Christian Museum with booty.[20] In 1899, the Kaiser joined the *Deutsche Orient-Gesellschaft* and the *Deutscher Verein zur Erforschung Palästinas* – just one of many signs that the Reich's exclusive commitment to classicism was weakening. Though he and his administrators did heavily finance classical archaeology, by 1902, he was also contributing to the mapping of East Jordan, the study of Chinese Turkestan, expeditions to Africa, and the study of Germanic prehistory.[21]

There was, then, much more material to draw on, and new, direct testimony from worlds previously studied only from the outside. More new funding was available for research into

---

16 H. Hesse, *Aus Indien* (Berlin 1913); H. Graf Keyserling, *Reisetagebuch eines Philosophen* (Darmstadt 1919).

17 On American intellectuals, see T. J. Lears, *No Place of Grace. Antimodernism and the transformation of American Culture, 1880-1920* (New York 1981).

18 L. von Schroeder, 'Buddha und unsere Zeit' [1905] in his *Reden und Aufsätze vornehmlich über Indiens Literatur und Kultur* (Leipzig 1913) 216.

19 See E. J. Sharpe, *Comparative Religion: A History* (London 1975) 125.

20 On Christian archaeology, see W. H. C. Frend, *The Archaeology of Early Christianity: A History* (London 1996) 83-86.

21 Documentation for his patronage can be found in, for example, BGStA Rep 76Ve, Sekt 1, Tit. XI, Teil I, Band II, vols 1-2; Turfan docs: see also S. Marchand, *Down from Olympus* (n. 5, above), chapters 3-6.

uncharted eastern territories. The study of Mesopotamia was just one such area in which new evidence overthrew nineteenth-century histories, based, almost exclusively, on Greek sources and the Bible. The testimony of the encyclopedic historian of the ancient world Eduard Meyer – in a 1908 elegy for the cuneiform specialist Eberhard Schräder – is telling:

> Today it is hard enough even for those who lived through the following development to call to mind what an enormous proportion of that which we now know of the history of the ancient Orient – which has now become almost an elementary common possession – was, but twenty years ago, still wholly unknown. Of the great political background against which the episodes recounted in the Old Testament took place, of the individual processes, from which the statements of the prophets were born, we knew pitifully little; and we were everlastingly engaged in the Danaiden task of trying to wrest from the information from Herodotus, Ktesias, Berossus and the historical remnants preserved in the Old Testament an overview of the history of the ancient Orient. Then the Assyriological information arrived. Everywhere – that it was accessible – it brought unimagined data, but above all it came into flagrant contradiction with the conventional presentation of Israelite history (but in no way with the most important historical material which the Old Testament provides) as well as with the information given by the Greeks and the systems that had been constructed from it.
>
> Small wonder that one resisted accepting [this new information]: how much we had erred, how much the Greek information, above all – apart from the fragments of Berossus – turned out to be historically worthless data, one could not until then have imagined.[22]

More proof can be found in the claims of Egyptologist Adolf Erman, who noted that to write his *Ägypten und ägyptisches Leben im Altertum* (1885), he had had to abandon completely the style and substance of earlier nineteenth-century treatments, which still depended much too much on Herodotus and the Old Testament.[23]

This does not mean, however, that this new visual world and new specialized studies were readily blended with the institutionalized neo-classical tastes of the middling and upper classes. As Gustave Le Bon described in 1895, it was hard to admit to being bored by the Greeks: 'For a modern reader the perusal of Homer results in immense boredom; but who would venture to say so? The Parthenon, in its present state, is a wretched ruin, utterly destitute of interest, but is endowed with such prestige that it does not appear to us as it really is, but with all its accompaniment of historic memories'.[24] This neoclassical nimbus of 'historic memories', passed on institutionally in the *Gymnasien* and universities, made the process of incorporating oriental texts into familiar classical narratives difficult. So too did disciplinary barriers, which cordoned off oriental philology and history, and kept it, for the

---

22 E. Meyer quoted in J. Renger, 'Die Geschichte der Altorientalistik und der vorderasiatischen Archäologie in Berlin von 1875-1945', in *Berlin und die Antike: Aufsätze*, ed. W. Arenhövel and C. Schreiber (Berlin 1979) 154. The Danaides were the daughters of Danaus, king of Argos; as punishment for having killed their husbands on their collective wedding night, they were sentenced to spend eternity pouring water into bottomless vessels.
23 A. Erman, *Mein Werden und mein Wirken: Erinnerungen eines alten Berliner Gelehrten* (Leipzig 1929) 273.
24 G. Le Bon, *The Crowd: A Study of the Popular Mind* [1895], 2nd edn (Atlanta 1982) 129-30.

most part, confined to theological faculties. The liberal classicists tried as long as possible to ignore developments in *Orientalistik*, but orientalists increasingly impinged on their territory from both ends, that is, from Babylonian, Persian, and Egyptian precursors of the Greeks to the Hellenistic successors of the Romans. As information and artifacts from the Orient poured in, the uniqueness of classical antiquity – and Christianity – began to look rather more questionable.

II The Origins of Religionsgeschichte

Clearly, these challenges to the 'liberal' worldview came not only from classics, or from new, secular studies of the Orient, but also from the ever-deepening historicization of the study of Christianity. As Thomas Howard has recently shown, nineteenth-century theology did not experience historicization as an assault from without, but rather as a continuing process, with its roots in the late Enlightenment.[25] Of course, this was a period of intense philosophical as well as philological criticism of the Churches as well as of the Bible. What is interesting about German Enlightened criticism, however, is its strong Protestant cast, which made scholars here reluctant to adopt an ahistorical pantheism or outright atheism. Though Old Testament critics, following in the tracks of Herder and J. D. Michaelis tended increasingly to turn Jewish texts into folkloric literature, the spiritual and much of the historical content of the New Testament, it was thought, could be saved. Impetus, then, was given to a kind of positive historicization of the New Testament, and negative historicization of the Old; while, as early as 1805, the radical Old Testament scholar W. M. L. de Wette claimed that the Jewish holy books had no historical value whatsoever (though they might be used to understand the spirit of the ancient Israelites), the quest for the historical Jesus went on, with high hopes that he could be saved from the wreckage left by increasingly specialized philological criticism.

The 1820s and 1830s saw considerable turmoil, as Romantic philosophy waned and historicist criticism, too, fell afoul of the restored regimes. In 1821, de Wette lost his position at the University of Berlin, and fled to Basel; but his Old Testament criticism, together with Hegel's analysis of the progress of the *Weltgeist*, left an important legacy for those who would gather around F. C. Baur at the small southern university of Tübingen. Here, the emphasis would be on understanding the crystallization of Christianity in the context of the languishing ancient (and Jewish) worlds, rewriting Gibbon, as it were, with a positive twist. The most famous biblical critic to come out of this world was the Young Hegelian, D. F. Strauss, whose *Leben Jesu* created huge controversy in the 1830s, and who, like de Wette, proved to be much too radical for the theological mainstream. Yet, as Susannah Heschel demonstrates in her excellent book on the Jewish biblical scholar Abraham Geiger, the work of the Tübingen school proved extremely influential, both in pioneering historical studies of the early Church and in perpetuating a sharp distinction between Judaism and Christianity. Baur's descriptions of the struggle between Pauline ('Greek') Christians and Jewish Christians in the first two centuries CE would both historicize the emergence of the new religion and retain an older Christian aversion toward adopting Jewish points of view (and using rabbinic sources). The

---

25 T. A. Howard, *Religion and the Rise of Historicism: W. M. L. de Wette, Jacob Burckhardt, and the Theological Origins of Nineteenth-Century Historical Consciousness* (Cambridge 2000) 14-15 and 38-39.

Tübingen School thus bequeathed to the *fin de siècle* a lopsided and incomplete view of the world of Jesus and the 'Greek' founder of his Church, the apostle Paul.[26]

But if the Tübingen school was influential, especially before about 1860, in the period of high liberalism (*c.* 1860-1900), the dominant theologians were those who hailed from the school of Albrecht Ritschl (1822-1889). Ritschl, who taught at the universities of Bonn (1846-64) and Göttingen (1864-89) had himself been heavily shaped by Tübingen historicism, though he saw his mission as chiefly a religious one, namely, that of preserving the power of Christian faith, and the practice of Christian ethics, in an era of scientific materialism and legalistic Lutheranism. If he believed that recuperating the essence of Christianity was, necessarily, a historical task, a goodly part of that task lay in identifying oneself (the inquirer being always imagined as a Christian) with Jesus' original followers, and thereby understanding the personal, and ethical, power of the apostles' faith. Again, Jewish sources were ignored. Moreover, in stressing the uniqueness of Christianity, he turned the creative, 'Jewish' elements Baur had adumbrated as essential to the early movement (if ultimately sublated) into remnants of a foreign faith which Jesus and his followers sought to strip away, he pushed Protestant theology, at least in the universities, further away from Judaism and Jewish scholarship, and into (said his critics) pagan arms.[27]

Controversial at the outset, Ritschl's work proved highly influential in academic circles, despite repeated accusations from orthodox believers that his search to find Christianity's 'essence' had resulted in stripping away the textual authority of the New Testament. This accusation was certainly leveled at his most important student, Adolf von Harnack (1851-1930), whose early career took him from Leipzig to Gießen to Marburg. In the 1880s, Harnack's critical discussions of the authorship of the Gospels and his rationalist scepticism about miracles, the virgin birth, and even resurrection, impressed the liberal members of the Prussian *Kultusministerium*, but caused the Prussian Church establishment to launch a crusade against his proposed appointment to the chair of New Testament theology at the University of Berlin. In 1888, Wilhelm II finally broke the standoff between churchmen and bureaucrats and appointed Harnack to the chair, and Harnack quickly became an influential lecturer, academic organizer, and even political force.[28] Committed, like Ritschl, to uncovering the 'essence' of Christianity, he also, like his mentor emphasized the importance of what was now a highly hellenized history for the restoration of personal, Christian faith.

Another significant member of Harnack's generation of liberal historicists was Julius Wellhausen (1844-1918), in many ways heir to de Wette's radical Old Testament criticism. But unlike de Wette, even unlike Ritschl and Harnack, Wellhausen was a historicizing philologist rather than a theologian; indeed, he gave up his position in the theology faculty at the University of Greifswald for a lesser one in the philosophy faculty at the University of

---

26 See S. Heschel, *Abraham Geiger and the Jewish Jesus* (Chicago 1998) 106-26.
27 *Ibid.*, 123-26; and C. Welch, *Protestant Thought in the Nineteenth Century*, vol. II, *1870-1914* (New Haven CT 1985) 1-30.
28 Harnack became one of the chief editors of the Academy of Sciences's edition of the Church fathers. He eventually became director of the Royal Libraries and the Kaiser Wilhelm Gesellschaft, in the founding of which he was a major player. He dabbled, too, in anti-socialist politics, and, as he grew closer to the Kaiser, advised him in various matters (though not, after 1903, in religious matters). See W. Döbertin, *Adolf von Harnack: Theologe, Pädagoge, Wissenschaftspolitiker* (Frankfurt a. M. 1985) 16-32.

Halle in 1882, signaling directly that he had no interest in theological controversies, or desire to train pastors. More interested in the national political history of the Israelites than in theological questions, Wellhausen replaced the Herderian aestheticism of de Wette with a *realpolitisch* orientation similar to that of Theodor Mommsen.[29] This allowed him to rewrite the history of the Israelites, and make numerous important contributions to the study of Hebrew and Arabic philology, while also reviving Herder's highly unflattering portrait of Hellenistic Judaism. Again, space prevents a thorough investigation of the work of this great Old Testament scholar, which, beginning with his *Geschichte Israels* of 1878 made an enormous impact on the study of ancient history and theology in Germany and beyond. What is striking here is that, unlike de Wette, Wellhausen moved quickly from a position as iconoclast to that of establishment figure. By 1900, his 'literary-historical' Old Testament scholarship, like Harnack's philhellenist historicism, had become widely practised and well-respected schools of thought, with far-reaching institutional clout and – especially in the case of Harnack – political influence.

Confident that historical rationalism along Harnack's lines would eventually restore the authority of the Bible – as well as the Greeks – and create a scientific Christianity, the liberal generation does not seem to have found this criticism threatening to their own religious convictions. For the next generation, however, their work, and the rationalist dogmatics of Ritschl and Harnack, had clearly not gone far enough. Bourgeois Protestantism would not suffice; theirs was a generation thrilled by mystical phenomena, from Jakob Böhme to the Upanishads, from Bayreuth to Eleusis, from the Kabbalah to the occult.[30] Their generation also recognized that historicist biblical criticism had reached a dangerous impasse, and that Christianity's uniqueness had been all but destroyed by the work of liberal philologists and theologians. One effect of these new cultural obsessions and professional pressures was the rebirth of the Creuzerian quest for the origins of the religion and religions, a quest which provoked an extremely fruitful series of interdisciplinary departures, but also a highly speculative set of publications, some of them all too tainted with the hyper-nationalism and racism shared by the *völkisch* movement and the conservative elite.

The sheer variety of these new attempts to find the origins and essence of religion are stunning, and range from Max Weber's sociology to the Pan-Babylonian theory that stars shaped Babylonian mythology, and Babylonian mythology shaped everything else. English and French scholars – beginning with Charles François Dupuis's late Enlightenment radical classic, *Origines de tous les cultes*, and including the nineteenth-century works of Max Müller, J. G. Frazer, Ernest Renan, and Fustel de Coulanges – had opened this quest: but they were outsiders to the world of specialized theological criticism, and unlike most Germans operating in the field, were confirmed non-believers. In Germany, on the other hand, the

---

29 See F. Boschwitz, *Julius Wellhausen: Motive und Maßstäbe seiner Geschichtsschreibung* (Darmstadt 1968) 24-25; 52-54. In 1892, Wellhausen received a new chair (at the University of Göttingen) in the philosophical faculty. For more on Wellhausen, see Heschel, *Abraham Geiger* (n. 26, above), 209-13; C. Hoffmann, *Juden und Judentum im Werk deutscher Althistoriker des 19. und 20. Jahrhunderts* (Leiden 1988); Momigliano, 'Religious History without Frontiers', in *New Paths of Classicism* (n. 9, above).

30 On German fascination with the occult, see C. Treitel, *A Science for the Soul: Occultism and the Genesis of the German Modern* (Baltimore 2003).

pursuit of such ideas in the Romantic period (by, for example, Creuzer, Friedrich Schleiermacher, Friedrich Schlegel, and Friedrich Schelling) remained heavily Christian. When Romanticism waned in the academy, a few materialist linguists and folklorists took up the study of what George Williamson has called 'the accidental, even mundane origins of ancient mythology',[31] but during the period 1860-1890, that is, precisely when other Europeans were developing the study of comparative religion, the Germans, for once, lagged behind.

By the 1890s, however, several 'religious-historical' schools of younger scholars were forming, centered at the universities of Göttingen, Tübingen, Marburg, Leipzig, and Bonn. Recognizing the need to go beyond liberal boundaries, this group investigated similarities between different religious traditions and delved deeply into the 'decadent' – and multicultural – 'oriental' world so despised by liberals. Profiting by drawing on convergent work in classics, oriental philology, and ethnology, many members of this school were highly self-conscious of their intellectual departures from the liberals.[32] Wilhelm Bousset, for example, distinctly disapproved of Wellhausen's anti-theological, secular orientation;[33] others defined themselves as strict historicists against the residual dogmatics of the school of Ritschl. In 1898, Ernst Troeltsch argued that a new, more historicist orientation in theology was now, thankfully, the order of the day, and would prepare for the actual realization of Ritschl's goal of establishing Christian uniqueness:

> The impact of the new intellectual atmosphere on theology consists in the following, that historical studies have risen significantly and dogma has almost completely receded ... Above all, under new pressures the old boundaries between the Christian and the non-Christian, between the areas of natural and supernatural events have disappeared ... The 'young' theologians ... have arrived at the notion of unifying the present-day meaning of Christian-religious life with the knowledge that the same methods of research must underlie the study of the whole religious life of mankind, and that the evaluation of Christianity as the deepest religious truth given to us cannot be separated from the methods and directions of specialized historical research that was created to analyze other analogous developments ...[34]

A new, more historicist orientation was certainly called for, one which, very clearly, took account of the second Oriental Renaissance – but still saw itself, ultimately, as serving the purpose of reviving Christian belief for an increasingly diverse set of German cultural consumers.

---

31 See G. Williamson, *The Longing for Myth in Germany: Culture, Religion and Politics from Romanticism to Nietzsche*, (Chicago, forthcoming); quotation here is found on manuscript p. 384.
32 On the *Religionsgeschichtliche Schule*, see G. Lüdemann and M. Schröder, *Die Religionsgeschichtliche Schule in Göttingen: Eine Dokumentation* (Göttingen 1987); also much valuable material is summarized and collected on a website, Archiv 'Religionsgeschichtliche Schule' at www.gwdg.de/~aoezen/Archiv_RGS. Thanks to JoAnn Cho for these references. H. G. Kippenberg, *Die Entdeckung der Religionsgeschichte: Religionswissenschaft und Moderne* (Munich 1997), also contains much helpful material on the origins and effects of the study of *Religionsgeschichte*.
33 Momigliano, 'Religious History Without Frontiers', in *New Paths of Classicism* (n. 9, above) 55.
34 E. Troeltsch, 'Zur theologischen Lage', *Christliche Welt* 12 (1898) 629; reprinted in http://www.gwdg.de/-aoezen/Archiv-Ritschl.html.

In pursuit of these goals, the proponents of *Religionsgeschichte* were neither so able, nor so willing, as their liberal forebears to use the traditional cultural institutions of the *Reich*, namely, the universities, *Gymnasien*, and academic publishing houses. Instead, they eagerly sought to cultivate non-academic audiences by launching popular ventures like the *Religionsgeschichtliche Volksbücher*, a series of short books for lay readers which were intended especially for students and women.[35] They were aided materially by the fact that a group of publishers – Eugen Diederichs Verlag and B. G. Teubner Verlag, to cite only the most important – now eagerly sought out modernist iconoclasts, especially those peddling experimental or revitalized religious orientations, while others – like the publishers of the *Volksbücher*, Gebauer-Schwetschke Verlag, then P. Siebeck Verlag, saw potential profits in these popularizing endeavours.[36] This was a revolt against the liberal fathers not only in ideas, but also in cultural tactics.

III Liberal Response

As in the case for most generational revolts, the 'fathers' were not at all unaware of the trouble brewing in their households: as noted above, many liberals had themselves helped to stack the intellectual timber for their own, collective, pyre. In the 1860s, 70s, and 80s, men like Wellhausen, Renan, and Eduard Meyer had been enormously important in launching the new Oriental Renaissance. But none of the three were willing to learn to read cuneiform, or to break entirely from the Bible, despite the fact that two of three (Renan and Meyer) did not consider themselves Christians at all. Theodor Mommsen persisted in endorsing the unconventional work of young scholars like Richard Reitzenstein, and apparently was once heard to utter, after an hour and a half digression on the Revelation of St John, 'Yes, often one wishes that one had been more than just a mediocre jurist.' But, recognizing that Reitzenstein had thrown himself into the camp of the historians of religion, the aged historian, just before his death in 1903, gave his former student the following advice: 'He who must, for many years, walk down a poplar-lined road at some point will climb up a tree in order to see further. But, R[eitzenstein], he who is clever, climbs down and walks on'.[37] This metaphor captures beautifully the scholarly as well as emotional self-restraint so prized by the liberals; the neo-Romantic 'sons', on the other hand, exhibited a quite different set of affective and scholarly drives.

It is instructive that two of the most influential of 'liberal' German scholars opposed comparative work: Wilamowitz in classics, and Adolf von Harnack in theology.[38] Friends,

---

35 See N. Janssen, *Theologie fürs Volk: Eine Untersuchung über den Einfluß der Religionsgeschichtlichen Schule auf die Popularisierung der theologischen Forschung vor dem Ersten Weltkrieg unter besonderer Berücksichtigung des kirchlichen Liberalismus in der lutherischen Landeskirche Hannovers* (Göttingen 1993), esp. 156-57.

36 On Eugen Diederichs's interest in religion, see G. D. Stark, *Entrepreneurs of Ideology: Neo-conservative Publishers in Germany, 1890-1933* (Chapel Hill 1981) 61-76. On the involvement of the publishers Gebauer-Schwetschke and P. Siebeck, see Janssen, *Theologie fürs Volk* (n. 35, above) 154-60.

37 R. Reitzenstein, 'Erinnerungen an Theodor Mommsen', in *Theodor Mommsen: Eine Biographie*, ed. L. Wickert, vol. IV (1980) 351.

38 In a 1912 letter to Hans Lietzmann, Harnack insisted that he was not against the religious-historical school as a whole, simply against bad scholarship – but it is hard to find evidence of his positive opinions, especially before the war. See Harnack to Lietzmann, 5 March 1912, in K. Aland, *Glanz und Niedergang der deutschen Universität: 50 Jahre deutscher Wissenschaftsgeschichte in Briefen an und von Hans Lietzmann (1892-1942)* (New York 1979) 309-10.

though they had their personal and political differences,[39] both were committed to historicist interpretations – Harnack emphasized Greek philosophy's contribution to Christianity, Wilamowitz relentlessly stressed the *historical* importance of the Greeks – but both, too, were ardent partisans of Protestant philhellenism, and certainly did not believe other nations or faiths were equal in the eyes of God.[40] Both also examined the past with philologically trained eyes, which may have made them less sensitive to the importance of social structures and rituals, and certainly made them less receptive to comparative perspectives.

Both Harnack and Wilamowitz opposed moving towards the full historicization suggested by Troeltsch – with mixed success. In 1901, Harnack delivered a *Rektoratsrede* insisting that there was no need to study religions other than Christianity. 'He who doesn't know this religion [Christianity], knows none, and he who knows all of its history, knows all [religions].' 'What is the significance of Homer, of the Vedas, of the Koran next to that of the Bible?' he asked.[41] 'Not much' was clearly Harnack's answer; the historian of religion needed to devote all his energy and attention to the all-absorbing history of the Christian Church. 'Why should the Church historian, even if he has the liveliest interest in religion in the widest sense of the word, be tempted to devote himself to the Babylonians, Indians, and Chinese, or even to the Negroes and Papuans?' It was possible, Harnack noted, to observe living faith among Buddhists or Muslims; '... but at best, we would see here only unclearly what we can observe better and with more certainty at home.'[42]

A violent letter of protest soon arrived from Hans Blüher, later to be a leading philosopher of the youth movement. The Bible, Blüher wrote, was not an organic whole, and could not compete philosophically with the works of Plato, Kong-tsu, or Laotse. Answering Harnack's claim that every age learned something new from the Lord's book, Blüher raged: 'But does the ever-new lie in the Bible or the age? Isn't it really that the European man of culture has lain 1500-2000 years in chains, and these chains are the Bible, to which man has had to accommodate himself, often with considerable misery? ... For centuries one had to make the new, which one carried in his own breast, fit into an interpretation of the Bible, and that is no great claim to fame for the history of the Bible'.[43]

Others may not have shared Blüher's scathing criticisms of the Bible, but they clearly could not buy Harnack's line, either. Among the prominent theologians of the next two decades were many scholars with comparative interests, among them Rudolf Otto (whose important *Das Heilige* was published in 1917), Hermann Gunkel, Albert Schweitzer, Rudolf Bultmann,

---

39 Harnack was, on the whole, less politically conservative than Wilamowitz, rallying, for example, to the Weimar Republic in its early years (though he became a Hindenburg supporter later). There were also personal rivalries between the two, centered chiefly on who was to be Theodor Mommsen's legitimate 'son'. See Wilamowitz to Eduard Schwartz, 10 January 1925, and 15 September 1901, and notes, in *The Preserved Letters of Ulrich von Wilamowitz-Moellendorff to Eduard Schwartz*, ed. W. M. Calder and R. L. Fowler (Munich 1986).
40 This is to underline the ways in which *fin-de-siècle* liberal historicism did *not* live up to Ranke's promise to treat all nations as equal under the eyes of God.
41 A. Harnack, *Die Aufgabe der theologischen Facultäten und die allgemeine Religionsgeschichte* (Giessen: J. Ricker'sche Verlagsbuchhandlung 1901) 11.
42 *Ibid.*, 15-16.
43 Blüher to Harnack, 21 November 1901, BSB Nachlass Harnack, K. 45.

Martin Buber, and Ernst Troeltsch.[44] But there was still no chair of *Religionsgeschichte* in Germany in 1909, though Switzerland, Holland, Sweden, and France had established positions, and the first two chairs in Germany (Berlin 1910 and Leipzig 1912) were filled by Scandinavians. As late as 1915, Julius Wellhausen voiced his amazement that Rudolf Otto, to whom he was rather sympathetic, 'had become an all-embracing scholar of religion on the basis of relatively short trips, without knowledge of the literatures and languages. These men', he concluded, speaking of the religious-historical school as a whole, 'have a predilection for the whole. One must let them play themselves out, the bubble will certainly burst soon.'[45] As Eric Sharpe has observed, in Germany, 'it was axiomatic, that a man could not be a *Religionsgeschichtler* and a respectable theologian at one and the same time. It was equally open to doubt, in the eyes of some, whether a man could be a *Religionsgeschichtler* of the wider variety and a scholar at the same time.'[46]

The same attitude was very much the rule in classics, though the neo-romantic and ethnographic study of religion began to flourish in some quarters, most notably at the universities of Bonn and Heidelberg. But elsewhere, classical philologists remained sceptical of outsiders, ethnographic comparisons, and religious questions. One can find the same situation in the reaction of British classicists to the Cambridge School, many of whose innovative approaches and topics resembled those of the German neo-Romantics.[47] If our historiography, especially as concerns Britain, emphasizes the mavericks, this should not lead us to conclude that they were, even by the 1920s, the dominant shapers of classical scholarship.

This caution is less pertinent for Germany, where the predominance of Wilamowitz has been demonstrated, thanks, particularly, to the energies of William M. Calder III. Calder's many editions of Wilamowitz's letters and writings, and the essays he has collected or written himself on the great man, have given us a clear picture of the diversity of his interests and correspondents, and his central role in shaping both the ideas and institutions of his generation. What is not quite so clear, here, however, is the great philologist's increasing resistance, cultural and political, to a world that was changing very quickly around him. Even more than Harnack, Wilamowitz was a cutting-edge historicist in the 1890s; indeed, as professor at the University of Göttingen from 1883 to 1897, he taught most of the young historians of religion their Greek. Yet, though he advocated the pursuit of a sort of *Altertumskunde* in which philology, archaeology, history, and other auxiliary sciences could be combined, the study of religion seems to have been vigorously sidelined, if not entirely excluded.[48] Wilamowitz may have been intrigued, from time to time, by studies of Greek rituals, like Rohde's *Psyche*, and did agree in 1897 to co-edit (with Harnack, of course), the

---

44 It should not be forgotten that the ultra-nationalist orientalist Paul de Lagarde had insisted on the importance of the study of comparative religions; Lagarde seems to have had a great deal of influence on this generation of scholars (e.g., Troeltsch). See U. Paul, 'Paul de Lagarde', in *Handbuch zur 'Völkischen Bewegung'* (n. 1, above).
45 J. Wellhausen to E. Littmann, 21 January 1915, quoted in G. Lüdemann and M. Schröder, *Die Religionsgeschichtliche Schule in Göttingen* (Göttingen 1987) 33.
46 Sharpe, *Comparative Religion* (n. 19, above) 125-26.
47 On the Cambridge School, see, for example, R. Schlesier *Kulte, Mythen und Gelehrte: Anthropologie der Antike seit 1800* (Frankfurt 1994) 123-92.
48 See Lüdemann and Schröder, *Religionsgeschichtliche Schule* (n. 32, above) 33-35.

Berlin Academy's Church Fathers project; but he was ultimately reluctant to abandon the traditions of *Kulturprotestantismus* and specialized philology for the dubious rewards of dabbling in the world of the irrational; although he was not, in any serious way, a Christian, as Momigliano rightly notes, 'thoughout his long life he was involved in the business of keeping his classicism within an undogmatic, vaguely Christian, religious tradition'.[49] Already in his scathing response to Nietzsche's *Birth of Tragedy* in the 1870s, he had shown that he did not care at all for speculative plunges into Dionysian prehistory;[50] nor, though he had studied with Usener, did he share the great Bonn professor's interests in myth, folklore, or religion.[51]

Travelling in small circles, linked together by profession, national-liberal politics and familial intermarriage, Wilamowitz, Usener, and Harnack had multiple connections and similarities, but Usener's interests, and cross-disciplinary daring, set him apart; and if Wilamowitz disapproved of the penchants of his teacher, he disapproved even more strongly of the unorthodox work of Usener's students. This would have a powerful impact on German classical scholarship, for Wilamowitz's verdicts were exceedingly influential in the years 1890-1931. They may also have been rather hasty. Of a summer's evening, the philologist's son in law (Hiller von Gaetringen, another classicist, of course) reported, Wilamowitz could be seen seated by an open window, impatiently slicing open books with his fingers; those he didn't like were flung into the garden, to be collected the next morning by a gardener wielding a large laundry basket.[52]

One can well imagine that the volumes produced by Usener's students figured heavily in the gardener's haul – and they certainly came in for much criticism in his book reviews and his letters of advice to the Cultural Ministry. Wilamowitz, as Albert Henrichs has shown, had little time for one of the Usener school's greatest fascinations, the Greek mystery cults; he described the worship of Aesclepios as '*Asklepiosschwindel*', trivialized Dionysian frenzy, and generally denounced what he called '*Panorphismus*' – the school of Reitzenstein, Dieterich, and Otto Kern.[53] Like Eduard Meyer, he could not believe the well-educated Greeks had swallowed such 'priestly deception and childish nonsense',[54] and he was even less willing than Meyer to entertain anthropological explanations. They and their fellow members of the philosophical faculty were deeply hostile, too, to Kurt Breysig's proposal to found a

---

[49] Momigliano, 'Religious History Without Frontiers', in *New Paths of Classicism* (n. 9, above) 55.
[50] Wilamowitz, *Zukunftsphilologie! Eine Erwiderung auf Friedrich Nietzsches 'Geburt der Tragödie'* (Berlin 1872).
[51] As a student, Wilamowitz had written a satirical poem about his mentor, and never really liked him, or his work; though Usener apparently forgave Wilamowitz, he did not always back him; in 1883, Usener apparently conspired with his brother-in-law Karl Dilthey to block Wilamowitz's appointment at the University of Göttingen. Momigliano, 'Usener' in *New Paths of Classicism* (n. 9, above) 35; on the attempt to block Wilamowitz's appointment, see Wilamowitz to Eduard Schwartz, 26 November 1901, in *Letters of Ulrich von Wilamowitz-Moellendorff to Eduard Schwartz* (n. 39, above) 43, n. 177.
[52] O. Skutsch, 'Recollections of Scholars I Have Known', ed. A. Bierl and W. M. Calder, *Harvard Studies in Classical Philology* 94 (1992) 396.
[53] A. Henrichs, '"Der Glaube der Hellenen": Religionsgeschichte als Glaubensbekenntnis und Kulturkritik', in *Wilamowitz nach 50 Jahren*, ed. W. M. Calder, H. Flashar, and T. Lindken (Darmstadt 1985) 290-305.
[54] Eduard Meyer, *Geschichte des Altertums*, vol. IV, 4th edn, 215, or 1st edn, 504; quoted in Kerenyi, *Eleusis: Archetypal Image of Mother and Daughter*, trans. R. Mannheim (New York 1967) 105.

seminar for comparative history at the University of Berlin in 1909, and implored the Minister to reject a programme that would lead only to *'Halbbildung'*, and not to any new insights.⁵⁵ The Ministry did, and the study of comparative cultural history languished, never again to rise.

In another academic culture, distaste for a particular direction of study might have remained purely personal, or factional, but in the hierarchical and state-monopolized educational institutions of the German Empire, the personal preferences of the chaired professors at the University of Berlin were tremendously influential, both informally and formally – for Wilamowitz, like Harnack, Wellhausen, and Meyer, had real clout with the Cultural Ministry as well as in the faculty senate debates. As Renate Schlesier argues, 'under the aegis of Wilamowitz's unimpeachable authority, anthropology (and comparative mythology as well) was laden with anathema'.⁵⁶ When at last – in the late 1920s! – Wilamowitz himself took up the question of Greek religion, he doggedly refused to introduce cross-cultural comparisons, though they had now become usual. The book, weirdly titled *Der Glaube der Hellenen (The Faith of the Hellenes)*, had not, as Walter F. Otto complained, transcended a Frazerian, utilitarian view of Greek religion,⁵⁷ and treated the gods as specifically 'hellenische Wesen'.⁵⁸ 'About other peoples', the author had written, 'I have no opinion. I know the Greeks.'⁵⁹

Implied in this position was clearly the claim that the now aged scholar knew the Greeks better than anyone else, and knew them not to be the irrational, half-oriental, sexualized beings others had begun to embrace. He had domesticated the Greeks, doing so in the image of his liberal generation – but he was not prepared to update the ancients for the sake of those coming after. No wonder Stefan George and his followers loathed the philologist; no wonder the hotheaded Hans Blüher, in a polemic of 1915, took on Wilamowitz, too, accusing him of leading the crusade to kill German creativity with scientific banality. 'Can there now be the slightest doubt', Blüher asked, 'that Herr von Wilamowitz would have chased the writer of *The Robbers* [Schiller] out of the university, because he was a revolutionary? And damned the writer of *Werther* and of *Satyros* [Goethe] because he wrote amoral books …? No one doubts that.' For Blüher, as undoubtedly for many contemporaries inside and outside classics, Wilamowitz represented the liberal 'father' – who stood in the way of the ascent of the sons.⁶⁰

It seems clear that Blüher was responding to many of the same discontents and longings expressed by Usener's students, their Western counterparts, and the Cambridge Ritualists. But much more than the English or French, the Germans were also looking for a new religion, and a deeper, more pristine set of cultural origins. Here in particular, by the century's end, the search for moral models in the ancient world was losing its appeal. The classicists who turned to *Religionsgeschichte* were not looking for ethical lessons, but rather for religious *experience* on the one hand, and a means to expose the superficiality of liberal classicism on the other.

---

55 Letter of the *Philosophische Fakultät* to the *Kultusministerium*, 27 February 1909, in BGStA, I, 76Va, Sekt 2, Tit. X, Nr. 182, Bd. 182.
56 See Schlesier, *Kulte, Mythen und Gelehrte* (n. 47, above) 195-213, and 314-15 (quotation 315).
57 W. T. Otto, *Dionysos: Mythos und Kultus* (Frankfurt 1933) 13-14.
58 See A. Henrichs, '"Der Glaube der Hellenen"' (n. 53, above) 274-75.
59 U. v. Wilamowitz-Moellendorf, *Der Glaube der Hellenen*, 4th edn (Darmstadt 1973), I, 288, and see also 10.
60 H. Blüher, *Ulrich von Wilamowitz und der deutsche Geist 1871/1915*, 2nd edn (Berlin 1916) 33.

'A focus on religion was chosen', Hans Kippenberg writes, 'because it promised to open the door to a world beyond the slick classical surface. It allowed not only the questioning of moral and aesthetic norms. The interpreters hoped in this way to systematically grasp another kind of life and to sensitize themselves to it.'[61] In what follows, I want to briefly sketch the careers of two scholars who took this path, and to show what perils and promises lay in this world below the slick surface of liberal classicism.

IV.i Case 1: Albrecht Dieterich

As Renate Schlesier has shown, most of the important early twentieth-century scholars of Greek religion were students of Hermann Usener at the University of Bonn. Between 1866 and 1905, Usener's combination of comparative ethnological analysis with phenomenological hermeneutics inspired an impressive list of students, which included Hermann Diels, Carl Robert, Eduard Norden, Hans Lietzmann, Aby Warburg, Franz Boll, Walter F. Otto, and even Wilamowitz himself.[62] Some of these figures – for example, Diels, Lietzmann, Norden, and Wilamowitz – retained Usener's 'liberal' rationalism and Christian apologetics: others looked more deeply into the darker side of the comparative religious history Usener pioneered. This holds for Warburg, Boll, Otto, Robert, and especially for Usener's favourite student, Albrecht Dieterich, who, as was remarkably common in German academic circles, bound himself even closer to his *Doktorvater* by marrying Usener's daughter Marie and naming both of their sons Hermann.

Filial-in-law piety was not hard for Dieterich, who had been extremely close to his own father after his mother's early death (Albrecht, an only child, was 7). Father Dieterich, a pious *Gymnasiallehrer*, tried to make his child a theologian – and half succeeded. Father Usener tried to make his son-in-law a philologist – and also had partial success. Much of the rest of Dieterich's make-up demonstrates the forces intruding on liberal philology at the *fin de siècle*.

Dieterich began his studies of theology at the University of Leipzig, but here he was already drawn to Germanic and classical philology. By 1886, he had decided upon philology, and a move to Bonn, where Usener's first lecture, he later reported, sketched the great problems to which he would devote his life.[63] Unlike philological converts of previous generations, Dieterich did not, however, leave his theological training at the door. His dissertation, based on Greek magical papyri, contended that many of these magical formulas were based on ancient Greek hymns and prayers – and displayed Gnostic, Egyptian, and Orphic resonances. For his teaching credential exam (*Staatsexamen*) he chose the theme: 'What do we know about Plato's theism or pantheism?' Wishing to write his *Habilitation* on another magical papyrus, he recognized the philologists' hostility to works on texts that did not belong to Greek '*Kunstliteratur*' – his alternative, however, was only slightly less objectionable: the Orphic hymns. By the early 1890s he was already planning what was to have become his *magnum opus*: a *Geschichte des Untergangs der antiken Religion*.[64]

---

61 Kippenberg, *Entdeckung* (n. 32, above) 161.
62 Schlesier, *Kulte, Mythen und Gelehrte* (n. 47, above) 195-96.
63 R. Wünsch, 'Albrecht Dieterich', in A. Dieterich, *Kleine Schriften*, ed. R. Wünsch (Leipzig 1911) xii.
64 *Ibid.*, xiii-xvi.

At Bonn, Usener detected in Dieterich the makings of a fine scholar, but insisted that he become a philologist first, then practice religious history afterwards; indeed Usener, probably arguing from his own experience, apparently believed that no *Religionsforscher* would ever be considered a true philologist. Yet Dieterich did manage to make his way among philologists. He sat in on Wilamowitz's lectures, and advised others to do the same; Georg Wissowa arranged for him to teach at the University of Marburg beginning in 1891, and he even contributed to the new edition of that grand liberal compendium, the *Pauly-Wissowa Realencyclopädie*, writing, however, only on Greek tragedy, and especially on Aeschylus. Yet Dieterich was also straying off the liberal path, publishing another papyrus study, *Abraxas* (1891), in which he linked this god-concept backward to Greek stoicism and forward to the gospels. *Nekyia: Beiträge zur Erklärung der neuentdeckten Petrusapokalypse* (1893) looked backward to Greek folk beliefs about the realm of the dead for sources of a newly excavated parchment fragment.[65]

What happened next seems to have exacerbated Dieterich's distance from the liberals: he travelled. Abandoning Marburg in March 1894, he roamed Greece, Asia Minor, and Italy, visiting numerous archaeological sites. He returned a year later, deeply impressed by the ruins, graves, and murals he had seen; he must have been reading, at the same time, Rohde's *Psyche* (1894), in which he discovered a kindred scholarly soul.[66] He began to incorporate art and northern folklore in his works – to the disapproval of his peers.[67] Nonetheless, he received a full professorship at Gießen in 1897: Usener attempted to use his influence to have his favourite appointed to a chair at the University of Göttingen, but his plans were foiled by the now more influential Wilamowitz, who succeeded in having the at least equally talented Eduard Schwartz appointed.[68] Still, Dieterich did receive, and accept, a call to Heidelberg, the center of comparative studies in Germany, in 1903. He continued to teach there until his death in 1908. Now safely chaired, he began his assault on liberal philology's taboos.

In many of his endeavours, Dieterich clearly felt himself to be assuming Usener's mantle – the Usener whose greatest work, *Götternamen* (1896) had been heavily criticized, and whose comparative and folkloristic interests had been scorned by Greek specialists.[69] In 1903, he founded the important series *Religionswissenschaftliche Versuche und Vorarbeiten* (1903) – which would be a major forum for Usener's and Dieterich's own students; in 1904, he reorganized Usener's own *Archiv für Religionswissenschaft*.[70] In 1902, following Usener's

---

65 *Ibid.*, xiii-xxxvii.
66 *Ibid.*, xvii-xx.
67 *Ibid.*, xxi-xxii; Wilamowitz wrote a devastating review of Dieterich's *Pulcinella* in the *Göttingische Gelehrten Anzeigen*, vol. LIX (1897) 505-15, which apparently affected Dieterich's production for years to come. See Wilamowitz to Schwartz, 23 November 1901, in *Letters of Ulrich von Wilamowitz-Moellendorff to Eduard Schwartz* (n. 39, above), n. 144, p. 35.
68 Wilamowitz to Schwartz 23 November 1901, in *Letters of Ulrich von Wilamowitz-Moellendorff to Eduard Schwartz* (n. 39, above), n. 144, p. 35.
69 See Dieterich, 'Hermann Usener', in his *Kleine Schriften* (n. 63, above), esp. 358-61, where he ardently defends Usener's philological credentials as well as describing him as 'Jacob Grimm's true heir' (361).
70 Burkert goes so far as to write: '... Dieterich established the history of religion as an independent discipline based on the study of religions of antiquity': he also notes that Martin Nilsson described himself as a descendant of this school, see W. Burkert, *Greek Religion: Archaic and Classical*, trans. J. Raffan (Oxford 1985) 2.

lead, he took philologists to task for their ignorance of new anthropological and folkloric literature and their hesitancy to engage in comparative studies. The objection that professional, specialized studies of myth and magic in each area had not yet been completed, he insisted, should not hinder scholars from profiting from the vast mass of new material and ideas now available. Unlike the genial Usener, however, Dieterich concluded his piece with an attack on liberal classicist mythography, insisting on the importance of home-grown empathy [*Nachempfinden*] for understanding the foreign. 'A man who has no inner feeling whatsoever for the thoughts and perceptions of the "*Volk*" [he is studying], who also knows nothing of the beliefs and customs of his own people and wants to know nothing [of this], is just as little able to study "mythology" or even understand a religion, as a man who possesses no inward religious sensibility at all'.[71] Dieterich's attack on liberal *Kulturprotestantismus* was underway.

He now, too, became vociferous in his advocacy of the use of unconventional, 'oriental', sources. In 1903, he claimed that a Greek magical papyrus he had discovered was the equivalent of a Mithraic liturgy. As suggested above, it was not easy, in his day, to make clear the importance of magical papyri; many classicists thought them unreliable and absurd, contaminated by Hellenistic emotionality and ignorance. In *Mithrasliturgie*, Dieterich himself complained that his earlier discoveries (especially *Abraxas*) had not been taken seriously because of their unconventional origin; had his documents not belonged to the magical papyri, he claimed, his work would have inspired great interest. 'But since [the Mithras liturgy] lies buried in the dark *Textmassen* of the great Paris magic book, the great men of literary history and scientific theology snatch back their clean hands to prevent them from being soiled. I wish they knew how many treasures lie hidden in this terrifying rubbish heap.'[72]

The object of the book was clearly to show parallels between this 'liturgy' and early Christian doctrine. Dieterich concluded by claiming that Christianity contains much that was not in Judaism – and by suggesting that hellenized Egyptian religion was at least part of the answer. A final footnote admitted that some of these unaccounted for ideas may have originated with the ancient Jews too – the documentation for this era of Jewish history remained thin. And indeed, one of the 'orientalist' fields to be revolutionized during Dieterich's career was the study of intertestamental Judaism.[73] It is instructive, however, that few members of Usener's school were eager to draw on this field, training their sights instead on ur-Hellas, Egypt, India, and Persia (Dieterich himself preferred the first two).

In 1905, Dieterich himself, now professor of comparative religions at Heidelberg, produced another interpretation of Christianity's origins that treated the problem from a completely different direction. In his hugely popular study of telluric cults entitled *Mutter Erde*, Dieterich sought the 'basic forms of religious thought' and the primeval 'ethnic substructure' from which all religions come, and into which they recede when their historical life has ended.

---

71 A. Dieterich, 'Über Wesen und Ziele der Volkskunde', *Sonderdruck aus den Hessischen Blättern für Volkskunde*, I.3, 1-26 [together with Hermann Usener's essay, *Über vergleichende Sitten- und Rechtsgeschichte* (Leipzig 1902)] 24.
72 A. Dieterich, *Eine Mithrasliturgie* (Leipzig 1903) 29.
73 Some inquiry into this area had already begun in the 1830s. See A. Momigliano, 'J. G. Droysen: Between Greeks and Jews', [1970] reprinted in his *Essays in Ancient and Modern Historiography* (Middleton Conn. 1977) 315-16.

Entering this realm through ethnology and folklore, Dieterich sought to understand prehistorical religious rituals of birth and death; in surviving customs like the laying of newborns on the earth, he found evidence of widespread belief in 'Mother Earth'. It was probable, he claimed, that there had been a prehistorical era of ur-promiscuity and rule of the mothers, during which time cults of the phallus and vulva had flourished.[74]

Dieterich sought to demonstrate the probability of his prehistorical case by showing that the Greeks, whatever their 'rational' convictions, had perpetually found solace in telluric cults. Using Hesiod and early tragedies, the Heidelberg scholar attempted to demonstrate the fundamental maternalism of ur-Greek folk religion, the key, he claimed, to the Eleusinian mysteries – and also to Plato's discussion of the soul.[75] The newer paternalist religions, like Christianity, Mithraism and Judaism – with their 'petrified male monotheism' – managed to suppress the age-old rites; but remnants of the violently orgiastic forms of the maternal survived, both in Christian and pagan practices.[76] Dieterich concluded by asserting that modern nature-worshippers should not be considered atheists, but as seekers quenching their thirst from the oldest and deepest springs of religious thought.[77]

Undoubtedly it was *Mutter Erde*'s proximity to Bohemian neopaganism that made the book something of a cult classic; we know that it had a deep impact on Carl Jung and Ludwig Klages, as well as on Walter Otto and Richard Reitzenstein. Dieterich, of course, was reviving Bachofen, but now as an explicit critique of Judaism and Christianity, 'the (liberal) fathers' and the neoclassically banal Greeks. His student Richard Wünsch attributed his late turning away from philological methods to a kind of prescience of his early death; we might more readily understand it as the gradual reassertion of his own penchants, suppressed by Usener's admonitions. In any event, the liberals were horrified; even his admiring biographer notes that many believed he had now ceased to be a philologist.[78]

If he terrified his elders, Dieterich had become, by the time of his early death in 1908, something of a cult figure for the next generation. His students seem to have felt an extremely strong reverence for their gifted teacher; on his death, the Heidelberg students reportedly claimed 'it is as if one's father had died'.[79] But Dieterich was a very different sort of 'father' from the Berlin *Doktorväter* Wilamowitz and Harnack, or even his own adopted father Usener. In his own work, the repressed – the Orient, the 'mothers', the *Volk*, and especially, religion – had returned; it was up to his students to make liberal classicism's *Id* professionally respectable – a task which seems, as yet, still incomplete.

---

74 Dieterich, *Mutter Erde: Ein Versuch über Volksreligion* (Leipzig 1905) 88-89. Dieterich drew not only on Bachofen, but also on the folklorist Wilhelm Mannhardt, who emphasized the origins of gods in organic processes and agricultural festivals. Mannhardt's work was a major source of inspiration for that of Frazer – whom Dieterich, remarkably, does not cite at all.
75 Dieterich, *Mutter Erde* 2, 55, 58.
76 *Ibid.*, 90-115.
77 *Ibid.*, 121.
78 Wünsch, 'Albrecht Dieterich' (n. 63, above) xxxvi.
79 *Ibid.*, xxxviii.

IV.ii Case 2: Richard Reitzenstein

If maternalism and folkloric comparisons seemed anathema to liberal classicists, so too did the post-Alexandrian age, with its syncretisms and 'silver' Greek, which terrified nineteenth-century students of good breeding and career-savvy mien. By the century's end, however, new interest was raised in the wake of the publication of the second edition of J. G. Droysen's *Geschichte des Hellenismus* (1877-78) and the Berlin Museums' acquisition of the Pergamon Altar (1879).

As Arnaldo Momigliano showed in an essay of 1970, Droysen was responsible for reconfiguring the term 'Hellenism', which had once referred to the Greek-speaking Jewish world, but after his *Geschichte des Hellenismus* (2 vols, 1st edn, 1836, 1843) began to signify the whole region conquered by Alexander and exposed to Greek influence. Even more crucially, as Momigliano demonstrates, Droysen believed that this larger region played the central intermediary role in the transition from Greek paganism to Christianity. Seeing the Hellenistic world as one in which Greek and oriental ideas intermingled in fruitful ways, he was, however, inclined to omit the Jews from his list of the great 'oriental' contributors to Christianity (preferring the Syrians, Babylonians, and Egyptians).[80] Curiously, given this perspective, Droysen completed only the political narrative he sketched out early in his career; even the second edition of his *Geschichte des Hellenismus* did not discuss the cultural (and religious) history of the era.[81] This was not a job the historians felt comfortable with, and it was left to the philologists and theologians to complete Droysen's work.

Having begun his training as a theologian, then shifted to secular philology, Richard Reitzenstein was – quite unwittingly, it seems – heir to J. G. Droysen's Hellenistic kingdom.[82] The younger man's politics, too, followed in Droysen's liberal nationalist line – the liberalism, however, being distinctly the weaker part of his credo. Late in life, Reitzenstein recalled an argument he had had with Theodor Mommsen in Rome in 1888; in response to Mommsen's impassioned outburst: 'Yes, that Bismarck, he has taught us to hate, as we never would have believed one could hate a foreign man', Reitzenstein replied, 'Herr Professor, not to contradict you, but to present my views honestly, I must add: "he also taught us to love, as we never believed we could love an unfamiliar man".'[83] That Reitzenstein remained one of Mommsen's favorite young scholars[84] suggests that at least until the time of Mommsen's death (November 1903), Reitzenstein had developed neither an ardent conservatism, nor his passions for eastern religions and erotic poetry, two subjects Mommsen surely did not find sympathetic.

It was, it seems, a trip to the Orient at about this time that propelled Reitzenstein's return to religious themes – and to Oriental origins. In 1904, the year after Mommsen's death, he published a book entitled *Poimandres*,[85] in which he looked to the *Corpus Hermeticum* as a source for the history and prehistory of Hellenistic religions (*Poimandres* is described in this

---

80 Momigliano, 'J. G. Droysen' (n. 73, above) 307-18.
81 For Momigliano's persuasive discussion of the incompleteness of this project, see *ibid.*, 312-20.
82 Momigliano describes Reitzenstein's first important book, *Poimandres*, as one 'written in Droysen's spirit'. *Ibid.*, 317.
83 Reitzenstein, 'Erinnerungen an Theodor Mommsen' (n. 37, above) 355.
84 O. Skutsch, 'Recollections of Scholars I Have Known' (n. 52, above) 388.
85 See R. Reitzenstein, *Poimandres: Studien zur griechisch-ägyptischen und frühchristlichen Literatur* (Leipzig 1904) vii.

group of Greek texts – from Hellenistic Egypt – as the teacher of the supposed prophet Hermes Trismegistus). In taking on this subject, Reitzenstein was already signalling his departure from liberal philology; the *Corpus Hermeticum* had been reviled by classical philologists since Isaac Casaubon's proof of its post-Christian origins. Undaunted by prejudices against non-classical Greek studies, Reitzenstein noted that he had been drawn to Hermetic documents by their literary form, but now believed them to be 'important documents of that powerful religious movement ... which overwhelmed the Orient, sending thence a flood across the West as well, preparing the way for Christianity ...'.[86] The main point of the book was to emphasize the importance of Egyptian hellenism for the religious history of the Near East: Reitzenstein suggested heavy Egyptian influence on Philo and the Jews, for example, as well as on Phoenicia, Persia, and possibly Mesopotamia.[87] Noting that in chapter two of the treatise, the writer states: 'I am Poimandres, the *nous* of *authentia*', Reitzenstein suggested that Egyptian sources lay behind what was essentially a Gnostic name for a god, translatable as Menschenhirt, or man-shepherd.[88] Here, he was not only reversing Casaubon's critique, but was also arguing for the existence of an Egyptian, non-Christian form of Gnosticism – a view which flew in the face of conventional attributions of this philosophical heresy to the post-Christian era and to the Greeks.

Reviews of the book were extremely critical; classicists were horrified by the idea that Reitzenstein would look outside Greek culture for keys to understanding this text. One reviewer expressed his 'fear of the damage that could be inflicted by the sickly vapours of Eygptian theology ...'.[89] They also took Reitzenstein to task for taking seriously – like Dieterich – magical and alchemical, as well as 'philosophical' texts.[90] But Reitzenstein had begun to look elsewhere for scholarly support and solace. He found confirmation for some of his views in a book published in 1902, Wilhelm Bousset's *Religion des Judentums im neutestamentlichen Zeitalter*. Bousset had concluded that the idea of 'Man' (*Mensch*) was foreign to ancient Judaism, and urged his colleagues to seek the *Urmensch* idea in Gnostic, Mandaean, Manichean, and medieval cabbalist speculations.[91]

Reitzenstein now commenced a series of excavations of the language and ideas of the New Testament, a task many contemporary classical philologists considered betrayal, and theologians considered usurpation.[92] As suggested above, he was not alone, however, in this

---

86 *Ibid.*, 2.
87 See, for example, *ibid.*, 161-88; 248-49.
88 R. Marcus, 'The Name *Poimandres*', *Journal of Near Eastern Studies* 8.1 (1949) 40-42. Reitzenstein himself translates ὁ τῆς αὐθεντίας νοῦς with 'der himmlische und daher zugleich der herrschende und der untrügliche Verstand', adding the footnote: 'Viel richtiger als Bernays, der an den selbstherrlichen Νοῦς dachte, übersetzte Ficinus: *de potestate atque sapientia divina*. Die αὐθεντία ist das Himmelreich.' *Poimandres*, 8.
89 T. Zielinski, in the *Archiv für Religionswissenschaft*, 1906, cited in P. Kingsley, 'Poimandres: The Etymology of the Name and the Origins of the Hermetica', *Journal of the Warburg and Courtauld Institutes* 56 (1993) 18.
90 *Ibid.*
91 C. Colpe, *Die religionsgeschichtliche Schule: Darstellung und Kritik ihres Bildes vom gnostischen Erlösermythus* (Göttingen 1961) 10-17.
92 As late as 1966, Friedrich Müller testified that the writings of the New Testament 'are treated by classical philologists almost as if they are taboo', F. Müller, 'Bultmann's Relationship to Classical Philology', in *The Theology of Rudolf Bultmann*, ed. C. W. Kegley (London 1966) 201-10 (201).

quest; his contemporary Adolf Deissmann (1866-1937) had already begun publishing studies of early Christian literature in which he emphasized the necessity of understanding these texts in the context of the prosaic linguistic forms and practices of the *Hellenistic* world.[93] In his highly influential first publications in the later 1890s, Deissmann showed that New Testament Greek was neither classical nor unique, but continuous with the world around it: the Greek Old Testament (of the Ptolemaic era) was a double sort of 'translation', into a kind of Egyptianized Greek, while the new texts breathed the spirit of Jews who had already been hellenized.[94] If Deissmann's claims initially rested chiefly on putting New Testament texts into the context of contemporary inscriptions, as the huge papyri cache from Oxyrhynchus became accessible after 1897, he delved more and more deeply into the 'oriental' aspects of this world; indeed, his most popular book would be titled *Licht vom Osten* (1908). In all of his studies, Deissmann, who was a pastor as well as a scholar, retained a rather curious, hyper-Protestant dislike for institutionalized Christianity and the book upon which it was built, both of which, he argued, tended to obscure the profoundly non-literary, personal message of Jesus's gospel.[95]

What Reitzenstein added to Deissmann's linguistic work was a new kind of religious history of the Hellenistic world. Now recognized as a full-fledged member of the school of *Religionsgeschichte* (despite the fact that he continued to work also on Latin love poetry), Reitzenstein plunged into the study of the religious ideas of the Hellenistic world, emphasizing in particular the 'irrational' or obscure ones; if this was a continuation of the historicizing trends of the past century, now, too, the 'illiberal' sensibility of his generation began to come to the fore. The book that was destined to be his masterpiece appeared in 1910, and was dedicated to his now deceased friend Albrecht Dieterich; titled *Die hellenistischen Mysterien-religionen*, it was the first major overview of the subject by a German since Lobeck's *Aglaophamus* of 1829. Again, he was not the only contemporary to come to some of these issues; the Belgian scholar Franz Cumont (who studied with Usener's student Hermann Diels) had begun to work on the 'oriental' religions in the Roman Empire by the 1890s,[96] and several theologians, beginning with Otto Pfliederer in 1887, had suggested parallels between Eleusinian practices and Christian sacraments.[97] Even more voluminous was the output of J. G. Frazer, whose *Golden Bough* threw mystery religions into the hopper with Near Eastern and classical mythologies, stirring in something notably missing from Reitzenstein's work, namely, modern anthropology. Two volumes of the *Golden Bough*

---

93 On Deissmann, see S. Neill and T. Wright, *The Interpretation of the New Testament, 1861-1986*, 2nd edn (Oxford 1988) 160.
94 See G. A. Deissmann, 'Contributions to the History of the Language of the Greek Bible' and 'Further Contributions to the History of the Language of the Greek Bible', in his *Bible Studies*, trans. A. Grieve (Peabody MA 1988; reprint of Edinburgh 1901 edn) 61-85; 171-80. The first essay was written in 1895, the second in 1897, but additions were made afterwards; still the full impact of the papyri is not yet felt in these essays.
95 See his brilliant essay, 'Prolegomena to the Biblical Letters and Epistles', in his *Bible Studies* (n. 94, above) 1-59, esp. 59.
96 F. Cumont, *Textes et monuments figurés relatifs aux mystères de Mithra* (Brussels 1896-1899); but Cumont's first major study appeared only in 1906: *Les religions orientales dans le paganisme roman* (Paris 1906).
97 See Neill and Wright, *Interpretation of the New Testament* (n. 93, above) 169-71.

appeared in 1890; by 1900 there were three volumes, and by 1915, twelve. Importantly, however, Reitzenstein's work was not intended, like Cumont's, to underscore the religious vitality of the Orient as against the backdrop of a declining Roman Empire, or, as Frazer's, to illustrate the common religious ideas and practices of mankind (and the need to supercede all of them). Rather, Reitzenstein's aims seemed essentially theological, that is, to understand the origins of the gospels. And in summing up his conclusions, he emphasized Paul's debts to a Greek world quite different than the one liberal theologians had championed: 'while very much indeed in the thought and perception of Paul may have remained Jewish, he had Hellenism to thank for his belief in his mission [*Apostolat*] and his freedom. Herein lies the greatest and most world-historically significant effect of the ancient mystery religions'.[98]

Reitzenstein's attempt to link Paul, and the language of the New Testament as a whole, to Greek mystery religions entailed the use of unconventional source materials like Egyptian papyri and obscure Hellenistic texts. He did not, however, like Cumont and later Fritz Saxl, incorporate material culture into his work; nor did he learn 'oriental' languages. In practice, Reitzenstein remained a Greek philologist. But he was one of the first to appreciate Deissmann's work on the Oxyrhynchus papyri, and the Jewish scholar Marc Lidzbarski's work on the Mandaens, an Aramaic-speaking sect from the Tigris/Euphrates region whose early medieval texts were thought to contain pre-Christian Gnostic ideas. Indeed, though Lidzbarski did the real linguistic and intepretive work, it was Reitzenstein's *Das mandäische Buch des Herrn der Grösse und die Evangelienüberlieferung* of 1919 that really sparked what one contemporary scholar called a '*fièvre mandéenne*'.[99] Even more important was his appreciation of the vast collection of manuscripts and artefacts discovered by a series of German expeditions to Chinese Turkestan between 1902 and 1914, and known as the 'Turfan' materials. The scholarly importance of the 'Turfan' expeditions has not yet been fully explored,[100] but certainly this cache of Manichean manuscripts and Graeco-Buddhist wall paintings had a powerful impact on many fields of study, beginning about 1905. 'We could almost say', argued Carsten Colpe some thirty years ago, 'that now [after the Turfan finds] a new form of humanism arose, this one arrayed under the sign of the inner-asiatic-European spiritual community [*Geistesgemeinschaft*]. One set oneself "On the Tracks of Greece in East Turkestan"'.[101]

By using these sources, Reitzenstein succeeded in expanding the study of Hellenistic religious ideas, and especially Gnosticism, much beyond the Mediterranean, a feat Hans Jonas would later applaud. Harnack, as Jonas showed, had taken a narrow, philhellenic view of Gnosticism, describing it as 'an acute Hellenising of Christianity'. Reitzenstein's *Poimandres* had led the way into non-Greek areas of thought, and at last, philology's monopoly was broken. 'The freeing of vision from humanistic exclusivity was the decisive act', Jonas wrote, 'it sharpened the eye for the radically un-Greek in Greek linguistic or conceptual clothing of

---

98 Reitzenstein, *Die hellenistischen Mysterienreligionen nach ihren Grundgedanken und Wirkungen* [1910], 3rd edn (Leipzig 1927) 91.

99 E. M. Yamauchi, 'The Present Status of Mandaean Studies', *Journal of Near Eastern Studies* 25. 2 (April 1966) 88-90, F. M. Braun quoted at 88.

100 I have made a start in this direction; see my essay 'Down from Olympus? The Turfan Expeditions between Classicism and Colonialism', in *Zeitschrift der Koldewey Gesellschaft: Bericht über die 40. Tagung für Ausgrabungswissenschaft und Bauforschung* (May 1998) 31-40.

101 Colpe, *Religionsgeschichtliche Schule* (n. 91, above) 31. 'Auf Hellas Spuren in Ostturkistan' was the title of Albert von Le Coq's popular account of the third Turfan expedition, published in 1926.

the age ... it opened the way to see the "barbaric" components as positive spiritual parts of the whole ...'.[102] But Jonas was writing from the standpoint of the early 1930s; in the 1910s, the older generation of liberals, both in philology and theology, were not yet ready for the 'radically un-Greek', and grew increasingly critical of Reitzenstein's inter-disciplinary endeavours. His poaching on the territory of the theologians earned him the disdain of Adolf von Harnack; his extensive dependence on orientalist scholarship made him suspicious to liberal classicists like Wilamowitz. His work did earn praise from younger classicists and theologians – though many, like Hans Lietzmann, expressed reservations about his methods.[103] As early as 1906, a few scholars, including Albert Schweitzer and Eduard Schwartz, complained about Reitzenstein's lack of attention to Jewish influences; but, as Schwartz himself noted, here he did not differ much from other New Testament scholars.[104] Reitzenstein defended himself, publicly and privately, but was deeply wounded by these not so subtle accusations of dilettantism, and continued to insist that in the theological realm, 'there are questions here that philology has the right and duty to discuss, too'.[105]

In the wake of the World War, Reitzenstein became an embittered patriot[106] – and also moved closer to the orientalists. In 1917, the maverick philogist first used Turfan documents to examine the mixing of Persian and Babylonian ideas in Mesopotamia and the birth there of the idea of man as a spiritual being, redeemed from matter. But from this time forward, Persia would begin to take on the central role in Reitzenstein's religious studies. In 1919, he suggested that Jewish hopes for the afterlife were shaped by Iranian ideas, and that Paul's anti-Jewish polemics were borrowed from Mandaean apocalyptical literature.[107] A 1926 essay underlined points of connection between Plato and Persian theology, and suggested that Plato's students had good reason for calling him the perfecter of Zarathustra.[108] Another written in the same year insisted upon an Iranian origin for the Icelandic saga, the Ragnarök.[109] Looking back at his 1910 opus from the vantage point of 1927, he insisted that

---

102 H. Jonas, *Gnosis und spätantiker Geist* (Göttingen 1934) 2-3 (quotation at 3).
103 For example, Lietzmann claimed that *Poimandres* had opened a new world for theologians, but that the latter shouldn't be careless in their embrace of his (often scanty or suspect) evidence, see Aland, *Glanz und Niedergang* (n. 38, above) 61-62.
104 R. Reitzenstein to E. Littmann, 14 March 1912, in BSB, Nachlass Littmann, K. 27. Schwartz to Lietzmann, 8 January 1906, in Aland, *Glanz und Niedergang* (n. 38, above) 229-30. Reitzenstein realized, by this time, that he had angered Jewish scholars, and wished Wilamowitz and Harnack would come to his defence, Reitzenstein to Lietzmann, 29 May 1906, in Aland, *Glanz und Niedergang*, 237.
105 Reitzenstein to Adolf von Harnack, 27 January 1914, in BSB Nachlass. Harnack, K. 40.
106 'If it were not for these terrific young men [former soldiers] and if a little ray of hope did not sleep in each of our breasts, that this misery will someday awaken the longing for a Messiah in our *Volk* – I don't want to think out the rest of this sentence, and would rather break off here.' R. Reitzenstein to E. Littmann, 4 February 1921, BSB, Nachlass 245 (Littmann), K. 27. It is clear from his letters that Reitzenstein and his family did suffer considerable ill-health and hardship as a result of the war.
107 Reitzenstein, *Das Mandäische Buch des Herrn der Größe und die Evangelienüberlieferung*, = *Sitzungsberichte der Heidelberger Akademie der Wissenschaften* (Phil.-hist. Klasse; 12. Abhandlung, 1919) 5-7, 40.
108 R. Reitzenstein, 'Plato und Zarathustra' [1926] reprinted in his *Antike und Christentum: Vier religionsgeschichtliche Aufsätze* (Darmstadt 1963) 30.
109 Calling on comparative mythographers to follow in the footsteps of comparative religion scholars, Reitzenstein here laid out a grand theory of the diffusion of Manicheism, from Iran westward. Acknowledging that Christianity played in many places a mediating role, he still believed that the chief question

no one would have dared to claim for Iranian religion the historical significance we now know it has.¹¹⁰ He emphasized in this edition the contribution Orientalists had made to his work, and he acknowledged the pioneering work of Usener and Dieterich, who, however, simply had not understood the oriental – and Reitzenstein now especially meant Iranian, not Egyptian or Jewish – origins of Christianity.¹¹¹ His 1921 *Das iranische Erlösungsmysterium* provoked a rebuttal from the Jewish scholar Isidor Scheftelowitz, in which Scheftelowitz disputed Reitzenstein's claim that Manicheism had evolved from a primeval Iranian religion and had nothing to do with Judaism. Scheftelowitz offered the more ecumenical position that Christianity was a syncretic religion, which contained Babylonian, Jewish, Buddhist, and Gnostic parts – Manicheism had evolved from it, and there was no reason to seek in ur-Persia the idea of salvation, of a God made flesh, or of the false Messiah.¹¹² Though profoundly illuminating, the Turfan finds, Scheftelowitz argued, did not give grounds for dispensing with traditional theology. Something else was going on, and Scheftelowitz clearly saw the road ahead: a history of Christianity that could do without the Jews entirely.

The years after 1918 witnessed extensive new studies of, and sympathy for, the Orient. Classicists, disillusioned by the collapse of the Wilhelmine Empire, gained new appreciation of antiquity's frailties – and of the Orient's spirituality and endurance. Pre-Socratic and Hellenistic Greece seemed suddenly more relevant than golden-age Athens, and mystery religions and mother goddesses gained new cachet. Theologians relaxed their attempts to prove Christianity wholly unlike paganism, and the long persistence of pagan cults – and their impact on Christian dogma and practice – was widely acknowledged.¹¹³ New attention turned to 'oriental' subjects: Manicheism, Gnosticism, mysticism. By 1920, one commentator argued, most scholars had taken Reitzenstein's point that Paul's theology was heavily influenced by the language of the mysteries; Harnack, however, among others, would not accept Reitzenstein's claim to have found the central Christian formula, faith, hope, love, in the orientalized rites.¹¹⁴ It was simply faddish, Harnack argued, to debunk Christianity's originality, and to credit as its main sources the mysteries rather than the Jews and the (rational) Greeks.¹¹⁵ What Harnack did not see was that this fad had its roots both in new evidence, and in the *Zeitgeist*, and that his younger colleagues – Ernst Troeltsch and Rudolf Bultmann, for example – were already looking for new, non-historicizing ways precisely to answer the question of Christianity's uniqueness.

---

about the poet of Völuspá was 'how much he owed to Iranian-influenced Christianity, and how much to Christian-influenced Iranian tradition', Reitzenstein, 'Die nordischen, persischen und christlichen Vorstellungen vom Weltuntergang', *Warburg Institut: Vorträge der Bibliothek Warburg*, vol. III [1923-24] 149-69 (168).
110 Reitzenstein, *Hellenistische Mysterienreligionen* (n. 98, above) 94.
111 *Ibid.*, ix. He did, however, also add a new discussion of the influence of heretical Judaism on Gnosticism in the third edition, see R. Bultmann, review of the third edition of Reitzenstein, *Hellenistische Mysterienreligionen*, and *idem, Die Vorgeschichte der christlichen Taufe, Historische Zeitschrift* 145 (1932) 372-76 (374).
112 I. Scheftelowitz, *Die Entstehung der manichäischen Religion und des Erlösungsmysteriums* (Gießen 1922) 80.
113 See J. Geffcken, *Der Ausgang des Griechisch-Römischen Heidentums* (Heidelberg 1920) 1-16.
114 *Ibid.*, 225-26.
115 A. v. Harnack, 'Über den Ursprung der Formel "Glaube, Liebe, Hoffnung"', *Preußische Jahrbücher* 164.1 (1916) 1-14 (3, 13-14).

Post-World War II scholarship has generally found Reitzenstein's orientalizing to be excessive; arguments tracing the origin of the idea of the Messiah or 'the son of man' back to Iran have been largely discredited. Most commentators take him to task for presuming diffusion where similarities may more readily be explained by independent invention, and for crediting early mystery religions and oriental religions with ideas that probably did not appear there until *after* the advent of Christianity (essentially, he had fallen into the Hermes Trismegistos trap!).[116] His contemporaries, and their successors, criticized him for not being able to read the 'oriental' documents himself – 'I warned him years ago', Eduard Schwartz said after Reitzenstein's death, 'not to deal with religious texts that he knew only in translation, but it didn't do any good.'[117] One of his great sins was that, like Dieterich, he knew (and perhaps cared) little about the Jewish tradition, and did not seek out scholars of intertestamental Judaism as he did scholars of other Near Eastern religions. Had he delved more deeply into Hellenistic Judaism, he would not, perhaps, have tried to credit the Greeks on the one hand and the Persians on the other, with the development of so many important New Testament ideas.[118]

In this, of course, he was not so different from his liberal theologian contemporaries who were, desperately, seeking 'the essence of Christianity' as an antidote to the text-destroying philological criticism of the last decades. Naturally, however, seeking the essence of one religion meant setting it off against the others – usually with benign intent, but sometimes with uncomfortable consequences. Hans Kippenberg has shown how those who tried to divide up religions into faiths with and those without the conception of salvation (including Reitzenstein, Wilhelm Bousset, and Ernst Troeltsch) drove a wedge between Christianity and Judaism – and led theology away from this-worldly morals in pursuit of purified, world-renouncing experience.[119] But it was the liberals, not the post-liberals, who began this process of historicizing self-justification, and they who developed most of the dismissive or perjorative rhetoric later applied to Hellenistic Judaism.[120]

Reitzenstein has often been taken to task for overemphasizing the mysteries and backdating Iranian Gnosticism. It should be said, however, that Scheftelowitz has also been criticized for his tendency to dismiss all outside influences on Jewish culture, and recent work on Franz Cumont has suggested that he too pushed his fragmentary sources too hard in the attempt to find Mithraism's sources exclusively in Iran.[121] In interpreting Manicheism, both Reitzenstein and Cumont were, to some extent, victims of the documents available which, as Peter Brown

---

116 See, for example, H. Maccoby, *Paul and Hellenism* (London 1991) 54.
117 Schwartz to Lietzmann, 12 December 1930, in Aland, *Glanz und Niedergang* (n. 38, above) 622.
118 One scholar, Eduard Grafe, who did know a great deal about Hellenistic Judaism, wrote of the maverick scholar: 'Reitzenstein inspired and taught me a great deal. But some things, I believe, still are more easily explained as originating in Judaism.' Grafe to Hans Lietzmann, *ibid.*, 296-97.
119 Kippenberg, *Entdeckung* (n. 32, above) 171-78.
120 It has been often noted how frequently nineteenth-century historians caricatured 'late' Judaism as sterile and arid, its God as a fierce, remote disciplinarian. Julius Wellhausen often takes the blame for this – but Ernest Renan surely deserves some, too. See Tal, *Christians and Jews* (n. 4, above) 191-201.
121 J. Duchesne-Guillemin, *The Western Response to Zoroaster* (Oxford 1958) 87. On Cumont, see R. L. Gordon, 'Franz Cumont and the doctrines of Mithraism', in *Mithraic Studies: Proceedings of the First International Congress of Mithraic Studies*, I (1971), ed. J. R. Hinnells (Manchester 1975) 215-47.

argued many years ago, presented Manicheism in its most 'Iranian' form.[122] Others in Reitzenstein's generation were similarly obsessed with Iranian origins, at least for a time; V. Gordon Childe and Mikhail Rostovtsev, are just two of many. Reitzenstein did not, to my knowledge, succumb to the 'Aryan Christ' theories backed by Wilhelm Schwaner and Friedrich Delitzsch.[123] He did overemphasize diffusion, but he did so against the backdrop of a discipline horrified by the idea of borrowing. 'We', he wrote of his fellow classical philologists, 'perceive acceptance of something borrowed in authentic *Hellenentum* to be tantamount to the injuring of belief in the originality of Greek intellectual life ...'.[124] His innovative approach in *Poimandres*, Peter Kingsley has recently suggested, still hasn't been given credit for the fruitful insights it offered into Egyptian-Greek relations.[125]

Reitzenstein's principle heresy in the eyes of liberal theologians was that he had given Christianity an irrational, oriental origin, not a rational Greek one, as had Harnack several decades earlier. Harnack's claim, he wrote, was 'that Greek philosophy, not Oriental belief, determined the first forms of [Christian] dogma.'[126] That was a claim Reitzenstein, whose heart belonged to the Hellenistic, not the neoclassical world, could not let stand. And his work, if deeply flawed, did at least create a wider and more complicated debate on Christian origins than that permitted by liberal philology. Rudolf Bultmann was clearly convinced by much of Reitzenstein's philological work; his historical reconstruction of Gnosticism resembles Reitzenstein's closely, and his commentary on the gospel of John is studded with references to Reitzenstein and Bousset. For Bultmann, one of the leaders in the theological revolt against Harnackian historicism, Reitzenstein's work had great significance for understanding the Hellenistic *homo religiosus* and the foundations of Christianity; he had gone far beyond philology to shed light on the greatest religious-historical questions.[127]

V Liberalism and neo-Romanticism after the Great War

In the wake of the war, interest in Greek religion, and especially mysticism, rose, and took some rather violent turns. The anti-intellectualism of most studies was palpable. As one classicist wrote in 1922: 'The unmistakable anti-intellectual drive [*Zug*] of our age corresponds to the tendency that has been growing especially since the war, to seek consolation for the lack of a world-view in all kinds of mystical practices. This trend is also visible in studies of Greek philosophy which assess the role intellectualism and mysticism

---

122 Brown notes that the discovery of coptic Manichean documents in Fayyum in Egypt in the early 1930s helped to correct this view, see P. Brown, 'The Diffusion of Manicheism in the Roman Empire', *Journal of Roman Studies* 59 (1969) 92-103 (92-93).
123 See K. Johanning, *Der Bibel-Babel Streit: Eine forschungsgeschichtliche Studie* (Frankfurt 1988).
124 R. Reitzenstein, 'Altgriechische Theologie und ihre Quellen', [1924/25] reprinted in his *Antike und Christentum* (n. 108, above) 2. Reitzenstein noted that only archaeologists had been able to prove the dependence of Greek art on the Orient.
125 Kingsley, 'Poimandres' (n. 89, above), esp. 18-20.
126 Reitzenstein, *Hellenistische Mysterienreligionen* (n. 98, above) 327.
127 Bultmann, 'Review' (n. 111, above). By no means did Bultmann agree with all of Reitzenstein's methods and conclusions, however; the second book under review here (*Die Vorgeschichte der griechischen Taufe*) came in for much serious criticism.

played in it.'[128] The lost war made for something of a dam-break, as scholars abandoned many liberal predilections and prejudices, and precisely the neo-Romantic themes sketched above – religiosity and the Orient's impact on the West – became common topics for investigation.

Space is too short here to discuss the Weimar era work of scholars like Ludwig Deubner and Robert Eisler, Otto Gruppe and Walter F. Otto, Karl Reinhardt and Karl Kerenyi. The neo-Romantic emphasis on the power of the Orient and the urgency of the religious quest continued to produce new insights, to challenge the liberal picture of the Greek past, and to erode the disciplinary structures that divided comparative religion, *Orientalistik*, and anthropology from classics. But the 'liberal' fathers held on a long time; if Wellhausen died in 1918, it would be 1932 before Wilamowitz, Harnack, and Eduard Meyer left the stage. If, after this point, the Oriental Renaissance went on, it went on chiefly outside Germany, for many of the great Orientalists, by this time, were Jews, and were compelled to leave Hitler's state. An examination of classical scholarship during the Nazi years is beyond the bounds of this already too long essay; but it is certainly clear that this period was in no way one of high accomplishment or innovation. An era of generational strife – and of German scholarly dominance – had come to an end.

In their receptivity to their environs, affective and evidentiary, the neo-Romantics opened up many new areas where nineteenth-century classicists for either prudent or chauvinistic reasons had feared to tread. In probing these areas, the postliberal generation exhibited both its creativity and its prejudices – and the worrying aspects of their work, from the evidentiary poverty of Dieterich's *Mutter Erde* to Reitzenstein's subtle anti-Semitism, must be underlined. It is indeed the case that neo-Romantic classicists tended to be reckless in their critiques of the old regime, and given to Germanophile effusions (though no more so than many of the conservative 'liberals'). More importantly, the neo-Romantics, in the war's wake, tended to ignore Anglo-French work, and failed, themselves, to create a new classicism that could incorporate the social and anthropological universalism of the Western schools. Finally, while they appreciated in a new way the Orient's entanglement with the West, the generation of the 1890s, and even more obviously, of 1914, failed to extend their embrace to one critical 'oriental' group – the Jews.

Still, I am not at all sure that this generation deserves all the blame for what went wrong in German classics in the 1920s, 30s and 40s. The Nazis certainly did not need Richard Reitzenstein to defend their racist policies, or Albrecht Dieterich to endorse their cult of motherhood. Aestheticizing classicism was, after all, just as potent a strain in Nazi ideology as was *völkisch* tellurism,[129] and as we have seen, liberal theology, even in its most radical phases, practised a kind of lopsided historicism, one which ignored Jewish sources and perspectives. Most certainly, the neo-Romantic generation deepened this contempt for Hellenistic Judaism, doing so, too, in the face of an oriental Renaissance with distinctly racialist tendencies. On the other hand, the maverick scholars of the *fin de siècle* did, indeed,

---

128 W. Nestle, 'Intellektualismus und Mystik in der griechischen Philosophie', in *Neue Jahrbücher für das klassische Altertum, Geschichte und deutsche Literatur* 25.4 (1922) 137-57 (137).
129 See Marchand, *Down from Olympus* (n. 5, above), chapter 9.

widen scholarship's scope, inspiring, for example, C. G. Jung, Joseph Campbell, Arthur Darby Nock, E. R. Dodds, Fritz Saxl, Hans Jonas, Karl Kerenyi, and Georges Dumezil.[130]

The creativity and fruitfulness of the work of many members of this third generation has not yet been properly assessed – in part because Anglo-French scholars have resisted acknowledging their debts to politically dubious German sources. When we have a good history of twentieth-century classical studies, we will certainly gain a fuller appreciation of the Germans' contributions – as well as their failures. Perhaps, too, we will then better recognize the necessity for present-day classics, in the wake of recent debates (on, for example, the usefulness of Martin Bernal and Michel Foucault), neither to turn back to liberal neoclassicism, nor to fall into neo-Romantic speculation. Rather, modifying Mommsen's advice, we should learn both to walk beneath the discipline's restraining poplars, and to scale the wider world's trees.

Louisiana State University

---

130 For Burkert's short but interesting discussion of the historiographical tradition, see his *Greek Religion* (n. 8, above) 1-4.

PHILOLOGIA PERENNIS? CLASSICAL SCHOLARSHIP AND FUNCTIONAL DIFFERENTIATION

INGO GILDENHARD

Introduction

In Rudolf Pfeiffer's *History of Classical Scholarship*, classical philology figures as 'one continuous undertaking' that began in Ptolemaic Alexandria and continues to-day: *Philologia perennis*, passed down by generations of 'Callimachean soldiers'.[1] The story has its kernel of truth, and is undoubtedly attractive: 'what a great tradition from the Alexandrian scholars to *Altertumswissenschaft* as *the* paradigm of all the "*historische Geisteswissenschaften*!"' as a contemporary scholar exclaims.[2] Yet in all this emphasis on continuity and exemplarity, a significant historical caesura tends to get glossed over. To adapt a famous phrase from Virginia Woolf, on or about 8 April 1777, the nature of the classics changed – first in Germany, then everywhere else.[3] And philology has been a hotly contested notion ever since.

The terms and the scope of the debate over the meaning and purpose of philology have of course shifted over time. Scholars in the 1980s (for instance) mainly argued over the place of philology within the professional study of language and literature: battle-lines emerged between philology and linguistics, philology and literary criticism, as well as philology and

---

* Embryonic versions of this paper were presented at the colloquium 'Verstehen vs. Erklären: Zu den Möglichkeiten der Erkenntnis in den Geisteswissenschaften nach der Krise der Hermeneutik' (Gerleve, April 1998, sponsored by the *Studienstiftung des deutschen Volkes*) and at the conference 'The Gods of Greece and their Prophets' (Princeton, April 1999). I wish to thank the participants at both events, in particular my co-organizers Andreas Pecar and Martin Ruehl, for stimulating discussions. I also owe thanks to Bettina Gildenhard and Michael Silk for their valuable feedback on draft-versions of this essay.

1 R. Pfeiffer, *History of Classical Scholarship: from the beginnings to the end of the Hellenistic age* (Oxford 1968), and *History of Classical Scholarship from 1300 to 1850* (Oxford 1976). See also his *Philologia perennis. Festrede gehalten in der öffentlichen Sitzung der Bayerischen Akademie der Wissenschaften in München am 3. Dezember 1960* (Munich 1961) 21, where he conceives of the individual philologists ('die Individuen, die die Wissenschaft fortführten') within a millennial context – together, they form 'über die Jahrtausende hin eine freie, die Welt umfassende geistige Gemeinschaft'.

2 E. A. Schmidt, 'New Approaches to Ancient Poetry – Theory and Practice', *International Journal of the Classical Tradition* 4 (1998) 433-49 (438-39).

3 See F. Nietzsche, *Wir Philologen* (= Nachgelassene Fragmente von Anfang 1875 bis Frühling 1876 3 [2]): 'Der achte April 1777, wo F. A. Wolf für sich den Namen stud. philol. erfand, ist der Geburtstag der Philologie' *Werke. Kritische Gesamtausgabe* IV 1, ed. G. Colli and M. Montinari (Berlin 1967) 90. But cf. E. Schröder, '*Studiosus philologiae*', *Neue Jahrbücher für das klassische Altertum* 32 (1913) 168, cited by Axel Horstmann, 'Die "Klassische Philologie" zwischen Humanismus und Historismus. Friedrich August Wolf und die Begründung der modernen Altertumswissenschaft', *Berichte zur Wissenschaftsgeschichte* 1 (1978) 51-70 (65 n. 55).

Out of Arcadia

(deconstructive) literary theory. As Jonathan Culler observed, '[p]hilology has a relational identity; it depends on what it is opposed to, so the question what is philology is the question of what are the relevant oppositions that divide, delimit, articulate the domain of the P's'.[4]

Culler is certainly right in stressing the relational identity of philology. But his assumption that the contests over philology are confined to the terrain of 'Language and Literature' is as blithe as it is unwarranted. Contrast the opening salvo of Friedrich Nietzsche's inaugural lecture at Basel 'Über die Persönlichkeit Homers' (18 May 1869).[5] Nietzsche starts out by noting that philology is, in and of itself, an 'inorganic aggregate', which he proceeds to pick apart. Within two pages, he distinguishes professional philologists from educated lay-persons; identifies three conflicting agendas within philology (scientific-historical understanding, artistic elements, and ethical and aesthetic imperatives); recognizes that it is the strong pedagogical mission of philology that accounts for some of its internal incongruities; and points out that the public perception of the field has much to do with strong 'philological personalities' (249-50). Patently, Nietzsche's frames of reference are broader than the 'P-shelves' of our libraries – and disconcertingly so: philology would be a much more manageable entity if we could simply subscribe to the sort of entrenchment that Culler performs.[6] But far from defining philology solely with reference to a specific object domain ('Language and Literature'), Nietzsche situates the pursuit in various social and intellectual settings: education; the research university; the classicizing tradition in literature and art; and society at large. His reflections on philology are outward looking and boast an impressively panoramic range: more is at stake than inner-academic trench warfare.

The contrast between Nietzsche's breadth of perception and Culler's comparative myopia is striking: it appears as if the classicists' descent from Mount Olympus in the past century has caused a drastic narrowing of vision of (even) those who, like Culler, look at the field from the outside.[7] It is therefore not merely out of historical interest that, in part I of this paper, I want to return to conceptions of philology in the age of Nietzsche, by reviewing the 'deferred dialogue' on this topic between Hermann Usener (1834-1905), Ulrich von Wilamowitz-Moellendorff (1848-1931), and Werner Jaeger (1888-1961). Between them, these 'Olympian figures'[8] (or, to speak with Nietzsche, 'philologische Maulwürfe') of German classics

---

[4] By which he means the 'P-section' of the Library of Congress catalogue system. See J. Culler, 'Anti-Foundational Philology', in *On Philology*, ed. J. Ziolkowski (= *Comparative Literature Studies* 27, 1, 1990) 49-52 (50).

[5] Later published under the title 'Homer und die klassische Philologie'. Page numbers refer to *Werke. Kritische Gesamtausgabe*, ed. G. Colli and M. Montinari (Berlin 1982), II.1, 247-69.

[6] Even if we stay within the confines of the LC cataloguing system, the issue that mattered most was not always the place of philology within 'Language-and-Literature'. In the Germany of the nineteenth and early twentieth centuries, the problematic relation of philology to history, or, more generally speaking, cultural studies, formed a primary source of scholarly disquiet. In Culler's terms, debates on philology implicated not just the domain of the *P*'s, but also those of the *H*'s and the *G*'s. A case in point is the tussle between Gottfried Hermann (1772-1848) and August Boeckh (1785-1867).

[7] For the full story, see S. L. Marchand, *Down from Olympus. Archaeology and Philhellenism in Germany, 1750 - 1970* (Princeton 1996).

[8] To quote Adele M. Fiske whose aim in editing and translating several essays of Werner Jaeger was 'to bring to life a vanished world of Olympian figures among whom the author early took a place', A. M. Fiske, trans., *Werner Jaeger. Five Essays. With a Bibliography prepared by Herbert Bloch* (Montreal 1966) viii.

endorsed widely divergent views on what philology is (or should be) all about; their tussling is therefore ideally suited to bring into focus the kinds of interests and investments that may underwrite perceptions of philology in modern times.

Then follows a change in perspective: if part I focuses on the ideas and the self-fashionings of individual scholars, part II relies on contemporary social theory to situate these scholars in their larger environment: modern society. This exercise in 'social physics'[9] is also meant to serve as bridge between 'then' and 'now', between, say, *Altertumswissenschaft* in the Germany of Bismarck and classics in the England of Tony Blair. It is true that, to quote from the anonymous reader's report for *BICS*, 'the social, political and politico-theological issues surrounding the practice of the subject were not and are not the same in all countries.' But just as the vastly different conceptions of philology put forward by Usener, Wilamowitz, and Jaeger can be shown to respond to the same historical importunities, so too it should be possible to identify certain structural problems that are common to *modern* classics wherever it is practised. The paper thus concludes with some reflections on the place of a discipline like classics in a 'functionally differentiated society' such as ours (part III).

I Philology and its inflections

In 1882, Usener delivered his *Rektoratsrede* at Bonn on *Philologie und Geschichtswissenschaft*.[10] Although virtually unread today,[11] the speech provoked some considerable controversy at the time: Wilamowitz, to whom Usener sent a copy, responded to it right away *per litteras*; and in due course, Jaeger joined the fray, devoting his inaugural lecture of 1914, which he allusively entitled *Philologie und Historie*, to a programmatic refutation of Usener's *Rektoratsrede*. We are dealing with three distinct voices – and three radically different conceptions of *philologia*:

I.i Hermann Usener: 'Philologia' demoted

Usener's basic thesis in *Philologie und Geschichtswissenschaft* is that philology is not a 'science' (*Wissenschaft*), but a method – the main method, in fact, of a comprehensive historical and cultural science. In this subordination of philology to history Usener's main interlocutor is August Boeckh, who conceived of classical philology as a com-prehensive *Altertumswissenschaft*, i.e. a *Wissenschaft* devoted to the investigation of all the facets that make up the life of a specific nation (or, in the case of classics, two: ancient Greece and Rome). Usener respectfully honours Boeckh's conceptual design as a significant achievement for its time; but, he contends, the progress of science has outdated the notion of philology as a *Wissenschaft* in its own right. Three developments in particular call for a reassessment of its place within disciplinary scholarship.

First of all, new archaeological discoveries have conclusively documented strong oriental influences on Greek culture; this rules out the organization of research along strict national

---

9 See P. Bourdieu and L. J. D. Wacquant, *An Invitation to Reflexive Sociology* (Chicago 1992), esp. 7-8.
10 H. Usener, *Philologie und Geschichtswissenschaft* (Bonn 1882), reprinted in, *Vorträge und Aufsätze* (Leipzig and Berlin 1907) 3-35. Page numbers refer to this edition.
11 See, though, B. Gentili, *Poetry and its Public in Ancient Greece. From Homer to the Fifth Century*, trans., with an introduction, by A. T. Cole (Baltimore and London 1988) 225.

boundaries (Greece, Rome) since nations do not form self-contained entities of study. Instead, a comparative approach is indicated that juxtaposes the evidence from other cultures to those of classical antiquity. Secondly, academic historians, once committed to a narrowly conceived political history, have recently broadened the scope of their interests: they now explore all manifestations of cultural life (customs, economics, geography, law, religion etc.). This shift in disciplinary outlook renders obsolete Boeckh's notion of classical *philology* as the comprehensive study of the Graeco-Roman past: the task now properly belongs to an overarching 'historical science' (*Geschichtswissenschaft*) that proceeds via cross-cultural comparison. And finally, there are the new data collected and prepared by ethnographic surveys, which were as yet unavailable to Boeckh's generation. These offer compelling reasons for redesigning the study of classical antiquity as part of a comprehensive science of humanity, which aims at the specification and analysis of general laws of human culture and their historical modifications, again *via* comparative procedures.

In light of these recent developments in scholarship, Usener proceeds to re-conceptualize the place and function of philology within the academy as follows:

1. His point of departure is the premise that the basic interest which drives philological endeavours is an *anthrôpinon* that comes into play whenever human beings try to understand and interpret a text: 'φιλολογεῖν', he says in a memorable passage, 'the quest to re-experience and re-think what important humans have experienced and thought before us, is an innate human need, no less than φιλοσοφεῖν, the search for truth; each human being exercises involuntarily and in however artless fashion the art of linguistic interpretation. Philology is as everlasting as the interest of the human in the human.'[12]

2. Professionally practised philology can no longer lay claim to the label 'science' (in Boeckh's definition of the term). For Usener, it makes no sense to speak of a special 'science of antiquity', in contrast to, say, a 'science of the Middle Ages' or a 'science of early modern times'. Scholars interested in any period of human history or culture use exactly the same tools of investigation and therefore belong and contribute to one science only, a universal *Geschichtswissenschaft*. Within this overarching enterprise, philology is a method: the *recensio* (critical sifting and restitution of the source material) and *interpretatio* (exegesis) of literary texts (cf. esp. 26 and 30).

3. The precondition for putting this method into practice is linguistic competence. Usener devotes several pages to a discussion of what anyone dealing with ancient sources must strive to attain (but never fully will): mastery of ancient Greek and Latin, or, as Usener puts it, the development of 'grammatical tact' or *Sprachbewußtsein*, which, in contrast to knowledge of textbook grammar, is based on talent and personal experience. In effect, this means that it is ultimately unteachable. Hence application of the philological method forms a *Kunstübung*, the creative practice of a special skill (in Greek: *technê*) (see 19-22).

4. Overall, this *Kunstübung* serves as a means to several ends:

---

12 *Philologie und Geschichtswissenschaft*, 23-24: 'φιλολογεῖν, das Streben nachzuempfinden und nachzudenken, was bedeutende Menschen vor uns empfunden und gedacht, ist ein dem Menschen eingeborenes Bedürfnis nicht minder wie φιλοσοφεῖν, das Suchen der Wahrheit; jeder Mensch übt unwillkürlich und wie kunstlos auch immer die Kunst sprachlicher Deutung. Philologie ist so ewig wie das Interesse des Menschen am Menschen.'

a. Usener concedes that the masterful restitution of a literary text may itself be considered a work of art, and he lists, *exempli gratia*, Hermann's Aeschylus, Ritschl's Plautus, Lachmann's Lucretius, and Scaliger's Festus. Still, he does not consider the critical edition an end in itself; its purpose consists in making possible the appreciation and enjoyment of literary texts in their original form (22-23).

b. Further, philology has a practical-pedagogical function, which Usener defines in strikingly Arnoldian terms: 'the education of the human being through the comprehending assimilation of all matters beautiful and great that human beings have thought and created.' Accordingly, the philologist has a role to play in the education of the young and the 'dwindling number of educated laypersons who are devoted to classical antiquity'. Yet while Usener acknowledges the role of the philologist as teacher and mediator of the Graeco-Roman past to a larger public, he does not dwell on 'die Bildung des Menschen': indeed, he brushes it aside in a paragraph-long *praeteritio* (23).

c. What preoccupies Usener most is the role of philology in research, as the fundamental (but not the only) method of a universal *Geschichtswissenschaft*. As master of textual criticism and literary exegesis, the philologist 'is and will remain the pioneer of historical research'. For only those scholars who analyze literature philologically are able to understand the intricate correlation of content and form that underwrites its (historical) meaning (26). At the same time, philological efforts must always be part of a wider 'science of culture'. Whereas all historical disciplines require a philological foundation (German history as well as jurisprudence and theology; cf. 33), the dynamic of scholarship does not stop with the critical assessment and restitution of our sources and their philological interpretation. These are basic operations, to be sure, but they acquire their meaning only if the results they yield are integrated into larger agendas of research. Thus Usener posits the subordination of philology to an all-embracing *Geschichtswissenschaft*.[13]

In his conception, then, philology is the methodical enactment of a basic human desire to understand what other human beings have thought and written. To realize this desire across distances of time and culture, one has to be proficient in the languages of the sources and be familiar with the critical procedures of recension and interpretation. But a text can never be fully understood in 'philological isolation'; rather, the application of philological interests must stand in dialogue with general bodies of knowledge and feed into agendas of enquiry that go beyond the interpretation of an individual text, author, or culture.

What we capture in *Philologie und Geschichtswissenschaft* is one of the most original and exacting metacritical minds in nineteenth-century German classics. With remarkable perspicacity, Usener realized that the way the first generations of modern scholars had divided up reality and assigned the individual segments to specific disciplines for investigation was a rather arbitrary exercise, shaped more by historical forces (including the state of knowledge

---

13 See *Philologie und Geschichtswissenschaft*, 29: 'Es werden immer, wenn nicht eine, doch nur einige Seiten des nationalen Lebens sein, deren Erforschung sich der Einzelne je nach Neigung und Anlage hingibt: für dieses Gebiet hat er den Zusammenhang mit der allgemeinen Geschichtswissenschaft zu suchen, in welcher der letzte Grund desselben enthalten ist, für Sprache in der vergleichenden Sprachforschung und weiter der Sprachwissenschaft, für Glauben und Sage in der Geschichte und Wissenschaft der Religion: er bebaut einen Kreisabschnitt, dessen Mittelpunkt außerhalb der Peripherie des nationalen Daseins liegt.'

at the time) and ideological commitments than by the internal logic of scientific enquiry. In contrast, his own conception of organized research follows criteria which the progress of scholarship itself made available. Usener thereby anticipated by over a century many impulses in cultural studies that have only recently come into their own, such as the pursuit of ethnography and anthropological perspectives, the use of comparative methods, and the transdisciplinary approach towards defining research agendas.[14]

Usener was clearly ahead of his times; few of his contemporaries were able to appreciate his new paradigm of an anthropologically grounded cultural science, partly, perhaps, because it was too demanding and difficult.[15] I suspect, however, that another reason was of at least equal importance: Usener's approach to the past, present, and future of classical scholarship saps philology of much of its extra-scholarly significance. Those who were heavily invested in an ideologically charged conception of philology could ill subscribe to its demotion from 'science' to 'method' that Usener proposed. Resistance was inevitable. The first critical rejoinder to *Philologie und Geschichtswissenschaft* that we know of came in the form of a letter by Wilamowitz.

I.ii Ulrich von Wilamowitz-Moellendorff: 'Philologia' as Revelation

In a letter written in February 1883, Wilamowitz included some comments on Usener's *Rektoratsrede*: a '*protreptikos*', he dubs it, a piece of stirring oratory. Most likely he has in mind the vision of scientific progress and the final note of exhortatory pathos on which Usener ended his speech: so much still remains to be done! Apart from these conventional touches of praise, however, with which Wilamowitz opens and closes his response, he utterly (if subtly) rejects the main premises on which his colleague based his argument:[16]

> ... so lebhaft meine sympathie auch die philology als 'kunst' anerkennt, so bin ich doch geneigt auf diesem wege weiter zu gehen und die methode demgemäß geringer zu schätzen. natürlich liegt der grund in der beurteilung von persönlichkeiten: für mich ist Gottfried Hermann ὁ φιλόλογος nicht in dem, was er geleistet hat; ich kann namentlich im Aischylos kein meisterbuch sehen, sondern in dem was er war. die alte poesie (und

---

14 For an appreciation of Usener's achievement, see M. Landfester, 'Ulrich von Wilamowitz-Moellendorff und die hermeneutische Tradition des 19. Jahrhunderts' in *Philologie und Hermeneutik im 19. Jahrhundert. Zur Geschichte und Methodologie der Geisteswissenschaften*, ed. H. Flashar, K. Gründer, and A. Horstmann (Göttingen 1979) 156-80 (160-61) and R. Kany, *Mnemosyne als Programm. Geschichte, Erinnerung und die Andacht zum Unbedeutenden im Werk von Usener, Warburg und Benjamin*, Studien zur deutschen Literatur, 93 (Tübingen 1987), who discusses Usener as a foundational figure in the establishment of a modern cultural science. (I owe this reference to Richard Simpson.) For current thinking on a 'transdisciplinary' approach to historical research, see, for example, J. Mittelstraß, 'Interdisziplinarität oder Transdisziplinarität?', in *Die Häuser des Wissens. Wissen-schaftstheoretische Studien* (Frankfurt a. M. 1998) 29-48.
15 So H. Lloyd-Jones: '... partly because of the immense difficulty of carrying out Usener's programme, most philologists preferred that of Wilamowitz', *Classical Review* n. s. 38 (1988) 136 (review of Kany, n. 14, above).
16 I cite the text as given in H. J. Mette, 'Nekrolog einer Epoche: Hermann Usener und seine Schule. Ein wirkungsgeschichtlicher Rückblick auf die Jahre 1856-1979', *Lustrum* 22 (1979/80) 5-106 (48). For the full correspondence, see *Usener und Wilamowitz. Ein Briefwechsel, 1870-1905*, ed. H. Dieterich and F. von Hiller, 2nd edn (Stuttgart and Leipzig 1994).

natürlich ebenso recht und glaube und geschichte) ist tot: unsere aufgabe ist, sie zu beleben, wenn man z.b. den Aischylos erklärt, und die sprache beginnt zu klingen und die rhythmen zu rauschen und die alten götter alloggiano sull' accesa fronte und die heroen handeln und leiden wieder, und dann die studenten ganz vergessen, daß da ein professor und ein text voll vocabeln und corruptelen und σχήματα διανοίας und σχήματα μετρικά ist, und nun den Aischylos und die Kassandra und das Dionysostheater mit der burg drüber, vor der seele haben: dann empfinde ich, daß philologie doch etwas für sich ist, oder wenigstens ihr τέλος hat, das ihr dann freilich die qualification als διδακτόν τι entziehen mag. was sie aber gemein hat mit jeder wahren wissenschaft, haben Sie so getroffen ὥστε οὐ μόνον προτρέπεσθαι ἐπ' ἀρετὴν ἀλλὰ καὶ προαγαγεῖν. und das ist's, wozu wir erziehen können ...

... vividly as my temperament acknowledges philology as an 'art', I am yet inclined to go further along this way and hence consider method of less importance. The reason for this lies of course in the assessment of personalities. For me, Gottfried Hermann is the Philologist par excellence: not because of his scholarly achievements – in particular, I do not regard his Aeschylus as a masterful edition – but because of what he was: the old poetry (and, of course, law and religion and history as well) is dead: it is our task to give it life; when one, for instance, explains Aeschylus and the language starts to ring and the rhythms to whisper and the old gods alloggiano sull' accesa fronte and the heroes act and suffer again, and the students then forget that there is a professor and a text full of vocabulary and corruptions and conceptual and metrical schemes, and now have in front of their souls Aeschylus and Cassandra and the theatre of Dionysus with the Acropolis above: then I feel that philology is something in and of itself after all, or at least has her telos, which, it is true, may divest her of the qualification as something that can be taught. But what she shares with every genuine science, you [i. e. Usener] articulated so well so as not just to turn people towards excellence but also to lead the way. And this is what we can teach ....

Under the guise of epistolary politeness, Wilamowitz articulates a conception of philology that is starkly opposed to that of Usener, 'to whom', as he put it in his Latin autobiography, 'he owed nothing'.[17] The peculiar mixture of fulsome flattery and hidden criticism that characterizes the letter is particularly apparent in the last sentence of the extract: there Wilamowitz manages to hail Usener's charismatic rhetoric, while simultaneously rejecting the main point of his argument. If Usener conceived of philology simply as a 'method of research', Wilamowitz reasserts its status as a 'genuine science'. He does not specify on the basis of what criteria he distinguishes the 'science of philology' from other sciences; still, it is fairly apparent that it is a specific object domain that for him delimits the remit of philology: 'Graeco-Roman civilization in its essence and every articulation of its life', as he puts it at the outset of his *Geschichte der Philologie*.[18] In effect, Wilamowitz reaffirms

---

17 '*quibus nihil debeo. inter philologos: Usener.*' See W. M. Calder, 'Ulrich von Wilamowitz-Moellendorff: An Unpublished Latin Autobiography', *Antike und Abendland* 27 (1981) 34-51 (48). For the strained relationship between the two scholars see also S. Marchand's paper in this volume.
18 'Die Philologie ... wird durch ihr Object bestimmt, die griechisch-römische Kultur in ihrem Wesen und allen Äußerungen ihres Lebens.' *Geschichte der Philologie*, ed. A. Henrichs (Stuttgart und Leipzig 1998, reprint of the 1st edn (1921)) 1.

Boeckh's notion of a comprehensive *Altertumswissenschaft* under the label of 'philology' and thereby performs just the kind of arbitrary slippage from data to discipline to science that Usener deemed antiquated and tried to supersede with a more satisfactory model.[19]

What is more, the *telos* Wilamowitz ascribes to his science of philology is rather far removed from Usener's conception of *Wissenschaft* as organized research aimed at the production of a specific type of knowledge. For Wilamowitz, the ultimate purpose of philology is to effect a moment of historical revelation. He vividly evokes the psychological shift that he imagines to take place as students are transported away from textual problems and out of the classroom, into an encounter with the ancient world itself.[20] Positivistic scholarship, the critical restitution and interpretation of the ancient sources, is merely a stepping-stone on the way to a truly transcendental experience. The practice of philology is meant to enable students to participate spiritually in the sublime grandeur of crucial aspects of ancient life, such as an original Aeschylus-performance. The language that Wilamowitz here employs is unmistakably that of mystic initiation: in leading his students into philological wonderland, he (as it were) steps down from the lecturer's desk, picks up a *thyrsos*, and joins his erstwhile opponent Nietzsche in the quest for an other-worldly experience.

Two further aspects of Wilamowitz's vision of philology go hand in hand with his insistence that the (unteachable) end and essence of this science reside in a leap of faith beyond the confines of evidence, scholarly techniques, and rational argumentation: his dismissal of method, and his emphasis on personalities.[21] While Usener had endorsed a balanced notion of philological practice as a *Kunstübung* that involves a combination of teachable and learnable skills as well as (unteachable) individual talent and experience, Wilamowitz, in his response, sets up a somewhat diffuse contrast between method and art, seeming to endow the latter with romantic connotations. The link he draws between 'art' and the 'assessment of personalities', suggests that he appears to conceive of philology primarily as a mode of being: it is a way of life, a calling of sorts, and Wilamowitz evaluates those who

---

19 For Wilamowitz, Graeco-Roman civilization (and hence the science of it?) sometimes forms a unity (even if it is impossible to specify its precise beginning and end), and sometimes it does not. Contrast the keynote of *Geschichte der Philologie* '[Die griechisch-römische] Kultur ist eine Einheit' (1) with 'Die Antike als Einheit und als Ideal ist dahin; die Wissenschaft selbst hat diesen Glauben zerstört' ('Der griechische Unterricht auf dem Gymnasium', in *Kleine Schriften* VI (Berlin and Amsterdam 1972) 77-89 (79) [delivered in 1901]). J. Bollack suggestively links the many inconsistencies or even outright contradictions in Wilamowitz's *oeuvre* to a disinterest in theory: 'Die Abwesenheit einer Theorie ist bei Wilamowitz nicht zufällig, sondern notwendig, d.h. jeder Versuch einer theoretischen Bestimmung seiner Position würde Widersprüche aufzeigen, die mehr als Widersprüche, nämlich eine Art von Falschheit sind' (Discussion of M. Landfester, 'Ulrich von Wilamowitz-Moellendorff und die hermeneutische Tradition des 19. Jahrhunderts', in *Philologie und Hermeneutik* (n. 14, above) 377).

20 The same conceptual two-step recurs in the programmatic opening paragraph of his *Geschichte der Philologie*. There Wilamowitz defines the task of philology as the revival of a bygone world through the strength of science; but its ultimate goal is the pure pleasure of contemplating (*Anschauen*) matters that have been understood in their truth and beauty. With a look ahead to Jaeger, it is worth stressing that the sort of understanding Wilamowitz advocates is, despite its mystic underpinnings, still always meant to be historical (or better: historicist) in nature.

21 His foregrounding of personalities manifests itself with particular force in his *Geschichte der Philologie*, which, in patches, reads remarkably like a Homeric catalogue of heroes or the roll-call of a Roman censor. The Catonic tag at the end of this work – the philologist as *vir bonus, discendi peritus* – is no coincidence. See A. Henrichs's 'Nachwort' in the 1998 reprint (n. 18, above), 84-85.

practice it not just, or even primarily, by scholarly standards, but on his own criteria of what a genuine philologist should be. His characterization of Hermann as ὁ φιλόλογος – not because of his scholarly attainments, but his 'ontological status' – has Platonic connotations.[22]

At the core of Wilamowitz's notion of philology is the historicist resurrection of Graeco-Roman civilization, in what amounts to a peculiar mixture of science and religion. His contemporaries had already identified the basic contradiction that compromises this project. As Werner Jaeger observes in his obsequy, with an apposite allusion to Goethe: 'Two souls perpetually wrestled with each other within his breast: the historian, who wishes to know nothing else but what has been, and the humanist and philologist, who must adore and preach what is great and eternal'[23] – an appraisal of Wilamowitz that is as perceptive as it is self-serving.

I.iii Werner Jaeger: 'Philologia Platonica'

A more studied response to Usener's treatise than Wilamowitz's epistolary remarks is Werner Jaeger's Inaugural Lecture *Philologie und Historie* (1914).[24] Its topic is identical to that of Usener's *Rektoratsrede*: the relation of history and philology. In the first part of his speech, Jaeger grants that, in certain respects, there is little difference between historical and philological scholarship: both deal with texts, and both need to apply the shrewdness and imagination of a detective (*'kombinatorische Phantasie'*) to restitute fragmentary evidence in the endeavour to reconstruct a lost world. At the same time, Jaeger posits essential differences (*'innere Wesensmerkmale'*), which set apart the *born* historian from the *born* philologist. These differences manifest themselves in the special relationship of philology and language:[25]

> Die Kraft des Philologen wurzelt in seinem Können der Sprache, und kein anderer Sinn – auch keine Sprachwissenschaft und theoretische Grammatik – kann den Mangel an feinem Ohr und rhythmischem Gefühl, an Beherrschung der einzelnen Sprachperioden und

---

22 It is worth pointing out that Usener picks up on Wilamowitz's endorsement of Hermann in his response (letter of 15 February 1883), which in turn leads Wilamowitz to provide a more 'scholarly' assessment of Hermann in the following letter (18 February 1883), as a great pioneer of historicizing criticism ('Damit Aeschylus wieder wirkte, mußten die Bedingungen seines Verständnisses, Sprache, Metrik, Religion, Athenertum zugänglich werden. Daß sie es wurden, dazu hat Hermann während seines langen Lebens soviel wie irgendeiner beigetragen').
23 'Zwei Seelen rangen in seiner Brust unaufhörlich miteinander: der Historiker, der nichts anderes wissen will als was gewesen ist, und der Humanist und Philologe, der anbeten und verkünden muß was groß und ewig ist.' W. Jaeger, 'Ulrich von Wilamowitz-Moellendorff' [1932], in *Humanistische Reden und Vorträge* (Berlin and Leipzig 1937) 209-15 (213-14).
24 Reprinted in *Humanistische Reden und Vorträge* (n. 23, above) 1-17. Page numbers refer to this edition.
25 On the task of rendering Jaeger's prose into intelligible English, see E. Badian, 'Jaeger's Demosthenes: An Essay in Anti-History', in *Werner Jaeger Reconsidered. Proceedings of the second Oldfather Conference, held on the campus of the University of Illinois at Urbana-Champaign, April 26-28, 1990*, (= Illinois Classical Studies, Supplement 3), ed. W. M. Calder (Atlanta 1992) 289-315 (296): 'Admittedly, there are, in Jaeger's style, flights of German mysticism which can perhaps not be turned into credible English at all. As Momigliano quotes Salvemini as saying, "English is an honest language".'

Stile ihm ersetzen, so wenig wie Tiefe des Gemüts und Lebhaftigkeit der Phantasie oder feine Psychologie beim Philosophen das fehlende Organ für begriffliches Denken ersetzt, oder der Vollbesitz der theoretischen Anatomie und Physiologie dem Arzt über den Mangel an sicherer Hand und scharfem Auge weghelfen mag. Das Wurzelreich philologischer Arbeit bleibt, mag man sie sonst definieren wie man will, stets die Literatur und ihr sprachlich-geistiges Verständnis. (*Philologie und Historie*, 9)

The strength of the philologist is rooted in his mastery of language, and no other type of perception – or linguistics and theoretical grammar – can compensate him for not having a keen ear and a feeling for rhythm, a grasp of each period of language and each style, just as in the case of the philosopher a profound soul and lively imagination or subtle psychology cannot compensate for a missing organ for conceptual thought, or as a complete comprehension of theoretical anatomy and physiology may not compensate the doctor for a lack of a sure hand and a keen eye. The roots of philological work, however one may wish to define it, remain always literature and its linguistic-spiritual understanding.

To some extent, the argument will sound familiar. In places, it is virtually identical to what Usener had to say about '*Sprachbewußtsein*'. But what was, for Usener, simply a precondition for excelling in a specific type of research, Jaeger, with a conceptual sleight of hand, turns into a distinctive feature that 'grounds' philology (note his repeated use of 'root' metaphors) and distinguishes it from history. Onto 'the feel for language', which Usener considered of equal importance for anyone working on texts, historian and philologist alike, Jaeger grafts an epistemological experience reserved for the philologist alone: the linguistic-spiritual understanding of literature. Therein Jaeger sees the special aim and objective of philology, and in this the philologist differs from the historian, who 'seeks in all expressions of the past the nexus of a great development'.[26] That Hegelian creature is not primarily concerned with individual pieces of evidence, but their place within the totality of historical events: 'Every preoccupation of the historian with the individual only comes to rest in a total view of the past, wherein his preoccupation resides as in its *telos*.'[27]

Jaeger then goes on to develop further the essential differences between his Historian and his Philologist (with a capital 'H' and 'P' respectively): they represent 'two autonomous ways of life that reside in themselves' ('*in sich ruhende selbständige Lebensrichtungen*') and are 'forces of value' ('*Wertkräfte*') 'in the realm of our spiritual existence' ('*im Bereich unserer geistigen Existenz*') (11). In elaborating this point, Jaeger introduces the distinction between '*Erkennen*' ('cognition') and '*Verstehen*' ('understanding'):

Das Erkennen bezieht sich auf Zusammenhänge von Tatsachen kausaler und zeitlicher Art, deren Verknüpfung aus bestimmten Data synthetisch zu erheben ist. Das Verstehen erstreckt sich nicht auf solche realen Beziehungen (γεγενημένα), sondern auf geistige

---

26 *Philologie und Historie*, 10: 'Worin prägt sich nun die historische Begabung aus? Der Geschichtsforscher sucht in allen Äußerungen der Vergangenheit den Zusammenhang einer großen Entwicklung.'
27 *Philologie und Historie*, 10: 'Alle Beschäftigung des Historikers mit dem einzelnen kommt nur in einer größeren, wenn nicht totalen Anschauung der Vergangenheit zur Ruhe, sie quiesziert in ihr als in ihrem Ziel.'

Gegebenheiten (ὄντα) und Werte, die als solche anerkannt und vom Verstehen angeeignet werden. Das Wesentliche ist die Wertbetontheit des Wortes Verstehen, die beim 'Erkennen' fehlt. (*Philologie und Historie*, 13)

Erkennen pertains to causal and temporal connections of facts, the intertwining of which is to be abstracted synthetically from specific data. *Verstehen* does not involve such actual relations (*gegenêmena*), but spiritual facts (*onta*) and values which are recognized as such and assimilated by (the process of?) understanding. The essential point is the emphasis on value in the word *Verstehen*, which is missing in '*Erkennen*'.

At first sight, it might appear as if Jaeger is here recapitulating an argument of Dilthey, who had claimed that *Geisteswissenschaft* employs a method distinct from those applied in the natural sciences: that of the empathetic-divinatory 'understanding' of authors and their works.[28] Dilthey is indeed in evidence throughout *Philologie und Historie*. But Jaeger is not concerned with examining the differences between the humanities and the natural sciences; rather, he wishes to assert an unbridgeable gulf between two disciplines – history and philology – that share the same data: literary texts. His project thus differs decisively from Dilthey's, whose aim was to develop a systematic and methodical account of historical understanding in general. For Jaeger, though, philological 'understanding' is, ultimately, precisely *not* historical: it culminates in the perception and assimilation of recognized spiritual facts and values.[29]

In other words, Jaeger argues that historians and philologists approach classical literature with two distinct epistemological agendas. The Historian wants to establish and explain facts; the Philologist wishes to view eternal truths. This undertaking Jaeger describes in an idiom strongly reminiscent of Plato's theory of ideas: the task of the Philologist is to bring about a Platonic enlightenment of sorts, as he illuminates for his contemporaries the great masters of our Graeco-Roman past. Jaeger explicitly calls this task 'scientific' (*wissenschaftlich*), but for him, the essence of a *Wissenschaft* and its status in society is inextricably tied up with aspects of values ('*Wertgesichtspunkte*');[30] it therefore has 'unimaginable, if incontrollable, impact on modern spiritual culture, education, and the ideals of a people (*Ideale des Volkes*)' (15).[31]

In the concluding part of his lecture, Jaeger specifies the vital importance of the Philologist's mission within Western Civilization. No longer, so Jaeger laments, do we have

---

28 See W. Dilthey, *Der Aufbau der geschichtlichen Welt in den Geisteswissenschaften*, Abhandlungen der Preußischen Akademie der Wissenschaften, Philosophisch-Historische Klasse 1910 (Berlin 1910) 1-123, reprinted in *Gesammelte Schriften*, vol. VII, ed. B. Groethuysen (Leipzig 1927) 79-188.

29 See *Philologie und Historie*, 15: 'Vom Standpunkt der Methode und des methodischen Betriebes aus mag also die Interpretation bloß ein Mittel sein zu "höheren" Schlüssen, vom Standpunkt der Idee unserer Wissenschaft aus sind die "höheren" Schlüsse, ja, das ganze historische Erkenntnismaterial nur Gerüst, ein θέατρον ἱερώτατον καὶ κάλλιστον zur Schau der "unbegreiflich hohen Werke".'

30 See *Philologie und Historie*, 11: 'Das Wesentliche an einer jeden Wissenschaft ist aber gerade der Wertgesichtspunkt, durch den sie sich dem Getriebe einer Kultur einfügt, und die Würde, die sie eben dadurch in ihm empfängt.'

31 When Jaeger ponders the Platonic 'idea' of classical philology, he thinks above all of Germany: 'Die oberste Aufgabe und Idee der Philologie ist, den ältesten und zugleich formsichersten Elementen der Gesamtkultur Europas, die keiner modernen nationalen Kultur tiefer als der deutschen mit Bewußtsein einverleibt sind: den Gütern der antiken Geisteswelt, zugewandt zu bleiben' (15).

the kind of unified culture that characterized antiquity, the Middle Ages, or even, still, the eighteenth century. Nowadays enlightenment, individualism, and the banishment of the comprehensive spirit of religion and the church from state and society are ceaselessly generating new forms of instability in personal and public life. Jaeger puts the blame for this squarely at the door of science: 'Es war der Weg der Wissenschaft, der uns so führte' (16). In this perilous state of affairs, Jaeger's Philologist, as legatee of classical literature, a domain of universal and immutable truths, emerges as the guardian of cultural continuity. The ardent worship of the ancients is the core of a *Lebensphilosophie* that opens a path into the realm of permanence and freedom ('*das Reich der Dauer und der Freiheit*') (17).

As these flights into the metaphysical indicate, Jaeger's discourse may have started out as a critical disquisition but it ends as a sermon. Philology turns into theology: Jaeger preaches the gospel of (neo-)classicism. The main articles of this faith are, first, an essential distinction between history and philology; secondly, the embodiment of eternal verities and values in classical literature; thirdly, a calling of the (German) Philologist as cultural missionary in modern society; and, finally, the promise of salvation.[32] Towards the end of his lecture Jaeger emerges as the stereotypical 'Philhellenic German': 'In the culture of ancient Greece, as they (sc. the Germans) saw it, man was the "whole man", with precisely that integrity of experience and that experience of physical integrity which they missed in the world around them.'[33]

Jaeger's *imago* of philology, while ideologically distinct, is in one crucial respect almost identical to that of Wilamowitz: both ardently believe (and invest heavily) in a transition from the realm of empirical research into another sphere of being that ultimately grounds both scholarship and life. Wilamowitz endorses a historicising version of this pattern; Jaeger opts for a classicising one.[34] Both elevate 'philology' into a way of life and a source of meaning, capable of endowing human existence with larger significance. Conversely, neither has much time for the sober conception of philology that Usener proposed, for whom it is simply a method of research.

At the end of this survey, then, we have a baffling outcome: three almost contemporary philologists, who worked in the same university system and are renowned for their redoubtable achievements in empirical research, endorsed radically different notions of philology. Our seemingly stable *Philologia perennis* has turned into a curious shape-shifter: it poses as a method of research and as a science, as the calling of a human sub-species (the Philologist *vs.* the Historian) and as the facilitator of a transformative experience in the seminar room, as an epistemology of understanding literature and as a crucial force of high culture within Western civilization – a plethora of views, which differ drastically in terms of their personal commitments, internal consistency, and ideological underpinnings. Still, I

---

32 For philology as a substitute for religion, see also W. Schadewaldt, 'Begriff und Wesen der antiken Klassik', in *Das Problem des Klassischen und die Antike. Acht Vorträge gehalten auf der Fachtagung der Klassischen Altertumswissenschaft zu Naumburg 1930*, ed. W. Jaeger (Leipzig 1931) 15-32 (31): 'Und indem die klassische Form, wie eben bei Vergil, den Drang seelischen Erlebens in vergeistigender Formung bindet, vermag sie zu erlösen. Klassische Form als erlösendes Gebundensein an das Gute, das heißt: Klassik vermag schon hier, lange vor Goethe, die Funktion des Religiösen anzunehmen.'
33 M. S. Silk and J. P. Stern, *Nietzsche on Tragedy* (Cambridge 1981) 4.
34 The fact that Wilamowitz had nothing but scorn for Jaeger's neo-classicism does not affect the striking formal analogies in their respective models of philology.

should like to submit that these conceptions, idiosyncratic as they are, share at least one common feature: they are all distinctly *modern*, insofar as they react to one and the same problem which no *premodern* classicist had had to face: how best to practise (and profess) the study of ancient Greece and Rome in a functionally differentiated society.

To pursue this line of argument beyond the obvious we need a working model of modern society, and the most promising place to look for such a model is, surely, contemporary social theory. True, social theorists relish a critical idiom that classicists and historians often find hard to countenance. In the language game they take pleasure in playing, off-putting tongue-twisters such as 'functional differentiation of society', 'the code and programmes of scientific exchange', or 'the internal and external environment of academic disciplines within the subsystem science' are par for the course – atrocious verbal *monstra*, no doubt, which are almost as shocking to the non-initiate as, say, textual critic-speak, permeated as it is by such disagreeable entities as 'positive *vs.* negative *apparatus criticus*', '*lectio difficilior*', or 'reconstruction of the hyparchetypes and their respective families'.

Still, there are distinct advantages in taking on board their critical idiolect (or at least the insights it affords): clusters of theoretically coordinated concepts are not simply haphazard collections of chic buzzwords ('jargon'); rather, they enable us to make 'scientific' (not common) sense of empirical data.[35] And just as one set has proven to be of great service in sorting out messy manuscript traditions, so the other should come in handy for analyzing the figuration of modern society, as well as the place of classics within it. By and large, it pays dividends to consider what the disciplinary experts have to say on any given issue, and the analysis of society (broadly defined) happens to be the territory of social theorists.

II Professor Janus – Classics between Science and Significance

There is a broad consensus among sociologists that the basic hallmark of modernity is a historically unprecedented type of societal organisation. What sets modern society apart from all previous societal orders is its high degree of 'functional differentiation'.[36] In a long evolutionary process – the origins of which can be traced back to the late Middle Ages – clusters of social practices, such as art, education, science, politics, and economics, gradually began to differentiate themselves from the larger societal whole and, over time, acquired a

---

35 On this topic, see J. Habermas, 'Umgangssprache, Bildungssprache, Wissenschaftssprache', in *Die Moderne – ein unvollendetes Projekt. Philosophisch-politische Aufsätze* (Frankfurt a. M. 1981) 9-31; and N. Luhmann, 'Unverständliche Wissenschaft: Probleme einer theorieeigenen Sprache', in *Soziologische Aufklärung 3 (Soziales System, Gesellschaft, Organisation)* (Opladen 1981) 170-77.

36 See, for example, A. Hahn, 'Funktionale und stratifikatorische Differenzierung und ihre Rolle für die gepflegte Semantik. Zu Niklas Luhmanns *Gesellschaftsstruktur und Semantik*', in, *Kölner Zeitschrift für Soziologie und Sozialpsychologie* 33 (1981) 345-60 (347): 'Daß der zentrale Aspekt der gesellschaftlichen Veränderungen der europäischen Neuzeit in der Ausdifferenzierung funktionaler Teilsysteme besteht, ist nun sicher nicht neue Erkenntnis, sondern Wiederholung eines einschlägigen Konsenses', or S. J. Schmidt, *Die Selbstorganisation des Sozialsystems Literatur im 18. Jahrhundert* (Frankfurt a. M. 1989) 16: 'In der umfangreichen soziologischen und geschichtswissenschaftlichen Literatur über das 18. Jahrhundert wird der soziale Wandel, der sich in diesem Zeitraum vollzieht, weithin übereinstimmend gekennzeichnet als Übergang von einer *ständisch geordneten* (stratifizierten) zu einer *funktional differenzierten* Gesellschaft.'

certain level of internal autonomy.[37] Modern society is said to feature 'subsystems' (Luhmann) or 'fields' (Bourdieu) that operate according to their own intrinsic 'code' or 'logic'.[38]

This process of differentiation, which picked up increasing momentum in the second half of the eighteenth century, varied from country to country. As George Steinmetz explains:[39]

> Contemporary social theory rejects the notion that one can determine a priori a 'normal' set of distinct social subsystems for all modern societies, or that each of the subsystems should evolve in the same direction or at the same pace. Instead, the number of distinct subsystems, their character, and their degree of closure will vary as a function of contingent struggles, accidents, and histories.

In Germany, for reasons too complicated to explore here, the differentiation of the two subsystems that Usener, Wilamowitz, and Jaeger would call their professional domains anticipated similar developments in other countries by several decades: science and education.[40]

II.i Science

Already the founding father of modern philology, Friedrich August Wolf, insisted on the 'scientific' aspirations of his *Alterthumswissenschaft*, an undertaking that he defined in contradistinction to the contemporary English conception of 'classics'. At the outset of his *Vorlesungen über die Alterthumswissenschaft*, he considers and discards several possible names for his novel pursuit:[41] first, *humaniora*: 'Dieser Ausdruck ist völlig unlateinisch und führt ins vage Feld. Er kommt bei keinem alten Schriftsteller vor. Was soll der Comparativ?' (6). Secondly, *Philologie*: 'Dieser Name scheint besser zu seyn, denn er kommt von λόγοι, complura, d. h. bei den Alten historische Kenntnisse, welche litterae hiessen.' But: 'die Alterthumswissenschaft fasst mehr in sich, als Sprachkenntniss; daher führt der Ausdruck Philologie irre' (10). Thirdly, *classische Gelehrsamkeit*; this will not do either:

---

37 Though it is worth emphasizing, with Luhmann, that the increase in reciprocal independencies coincides with an increase in reciprocal dependencies. See, for example, *Ausdifferenzierung des Rechts. Beiträge zur Rechtssoziologie und Rechtstheorie* (Frankfurt a. M. 1981) 155-56: 'Wer hier von Entdifferenzierung spricht, hat die Eigenart von Systemdifferenzierung, wechselseitige Unabhängigkeiten und wechselseitige Abhängigkeiten zu steigern, nicht begriffen.'
38 This is not to say that the theoretical architectures of, say, Luhmann and Bourdieu do not differ in crucial respects; but, depending on one's heuristic interests, it is often possible to use their models interchangeably. See, for example, G. Steinmetz 'German Exceptionalism and the Origins of Nazism: the career of a concept', in *Stalinism and Nazism: Dictatorships in Comparison*, ed. I. Kershaw and M. Lewin (Cambridge 1997) 251-84 (I owe this reference to Jan Plamper).
39 'German Exceptionalism' (n. 38, above) 269.
40 *Ibid.*, 267, and R. Stichweh, *Zur Entstehung des modernen Systems wissenschaftlicher Disziplinen. Physik in Deutschland 1740-1890* (Frankfurt a. M. 1984).
41 *Fr. Aug. Wolfs Vorlesungen über die Alterthumswissenschaft I-V*, ed. J. D. Gürtler *et al.* (Leipzig 1831-35) I, 11. See C. J. Classen, 'Über das Alter der "Klassischen Philologie"', *Hermes* 130 (2002) 490-97. See further *Friedrich August Wolf e la Scienza dell'Antichità. Atti del Convegno Internazionale (Napoli 24-26 maggio 1995)*, ed. S. Cerasuolo (Naples 1997), a collection in celebration of the bi-centenary of Wolf's *Prolegomena ad Homerum*, and *Friedrich August Wolf. Studien, Dokumente, Bibliographie*, ed. R. Markner and G. Veltri, *Palingenesia* LXVII (Stuttgart 1999).

Die Engländer pflegen beständig zu sagen: classische Gelehrsamkeit. Dieser Name 3) *classische Gelehrsamkeit* soll die Gelehrsamkeit bezeichnen, welche auf den Classikern beruht und diese sollen die Schriftsteller des Alterthums seyn. Allein dies ist unbequem. Wenn Classiker die ausgewähltesten Muster im Alterthume sind, so können sie nicht alle Classiker seyn. Dieser Ausdruck ist also auch nicht adäquat, dass man dadurch die Tendenz dieses Studiums anzeigen könnte (11).

The English are constantly in the habit of saying 'classical learning'. This name, 3) *classical learning*, is supposed to signify the learning that is based on the classics and these are supposed to be the authors of antiquity. However, this is awkward. If the classics are the most highly selected models of antiquity, not all of them can be classics. This term is therefore also not suited for indicating the tendency of this area of study.

So in the end, Wolf settles on *Alterthumswissenschaft*: 'Wir wollen diese Wissenschaft nennen 4) die *Alterthumswissenschaft* oder *Alterthumskunde*, oder auch das *Studium der alten Litteratur und Kunst*, doctrina antiquarum litterarum et artium. Dies ist der besste Ausdruck' (11).

That Wolf distinguishes his *wissenschaftlich* study of antiquity from 'classics' is significant. The very etymology of the word 'classics' flags affiliation with the idea that culture is, to quote Matthew Arnold's famous definition, 'a pursuit of our total perfection by means of getting to know, on all the matters which most concern us, the best which has been thought and said in the world'.[42] Historically, 'the classics' designated a canon of exemplary authors that formed one of those 'Great Traditions' that manage to preserve, within ever-changing times, their own, seemingly timeless presence – being attended to by castes of experts who take care of the selected texts and cultivate their cultural import: brahmins and mandarins, rabbis, monks, and theologians, or, in the case of classics, grammarians and critics.[43] Wolf's notion of *Alterthumswissenschaft* signals a conscious break with this tradition.

But what, exactly, is *Wissenschaft*? The question conjures up the spectre of long-standing debates, ranging from *Geisteswissenschaften* versus *Naturwissenschaften* à la Dilthey, to C.P. Snow's and F. R. Leavis's tussle over the 'two cultures' in the university, to more recent brouhahas triggered by philosophers of science such as Thomas Kuhn, Richard Rorty, and Mary Hesse, most of which revolve around the epistemological status of scientifically produced knowledge. From an anglophone point of view, the very notion of a scientific approach towards the ancient world sounds eccentric. After all, the term 'science' brings to mind research into nature (as opposed to historical events or products of the human spirit), *experimental* testing of hypotheses (predictability), technological advances (the use of

---

42 M. Arnold, *Culture and Anarchy*, ed. S. Lipman (New Haven and London 1994) 5 (= 1st edn 1865, viii). While, presumably, few classicists would still define their subject in such terms, an Arnoldian view of the discipline seems yet to prevail in some quarters *outside* our field. I quote from a call for a classics-themed guest issue by the 'international cultural-studies journal' *parallax* (e-mail of 26 June 2002): 'How can a self-consciously interdisciplinary field like cult. studs. take on the profoundly canonized discipline of classics with the whole institutional history (class, colonization, etc) that goes along with it?'

43 See *Kanon und Zensur. Archäologie der literarischen Kommunikation II* ed. A. and J. Assmann (Munich 1987) 'Introduction' 12-13.

research results in the applied sciences), or the reliance on a unified method (Kuhn's post-paradigmatic state). Indeed, in many quarters the suggestion that we may study the past (or literary texts) in scientific fashion is bound to elicit nothing more than a brief, postmodern cackle – a short articulation of disbelief at the absurdity of the thought.

Are we, then, merely dealing with a lexical crux, the German '*Wissenschaft*' connoting a broader semantic range than the English 'science'?[44] Or is it, on the contrary, unreflected and amenably obfuscating sentiments about science that have led to a widespread acquiescence in the belief that the phrase 'the natural sciences' is tautological? Prominent theorists of modern science suggest that the latter is indeed the case. For some time now, they have ceased to regard differences in type of data or methodology as indicative of a great and unbridgeable gulf between the sciences and the humanities. Theorists such as Niklas Luhmann and Pierre Bourdieu have put on the table conceptions of science that lay claim to *universal* validity, in being applicable to all types of data – be it the structure of an atom, social behaviour, or a literary text.[45]

Thus Luhmann takes for granted the post-Kantian truism that we 'construct' our world as well as our knowledge about it (which, one may add, is not the same as denying that a reality exists independently of human constructs);[46] and one way of doing so can be called scientific, in that it evaluates information according to the code 'true/not true', rather than, say, 'beautiful/ugly', 'moral/immoral', 'interesting/uninteresting', or 'advantageous/disadvantageous'. This scientific code, it is worth stressing, functions without foundations: whether a statement is to be regarded as – always provisionally, of course – 'true' (and hence to be made the basis for further acts of communication and research), or as – equally provisionally – 'not true', depends on theories and methods (the two main scientific 'truth-makers'), which are themselves the result of scientific reflection and are therefore also subject to constant critique and revision.

Luhmann specifies several consequences of organized scientific communication: first, research communities, with the help of the analytical tools (concepts, theories, methods) they generate to carry out their enquiries, are, over time, able to handle – to detect and explain – increasingly complex phenomena in their respective object domains. This involves the ever more refined ability of critical reflection to decompose and reconceptualize the intuitive and culturally conditioned assumptions we make about the world. Secondly, science is institutionalized unrest: there is nothing more ephemeral than scientifically produced knowledge. And each answer or solution to a question or problem invariably provokes a plethora of further questions and possibilities in need of exploration.[47] Thirdly, science

---

[44] The coinage '*Geisteswissenschaften*' seems to indicate as much – many a theorist insists on their radical differences in aims and methods, if not in epistemological outlook, from '*Naturwissenschaften*'.
[45] See N. Luhmann, *Die Wissenschaft der Gesellschaft* (Frankfurt a. M. 1990); P. Bourdieu, *Méditations pascaliennes* (Paris 1997).
[46] On this crucial distinction, often blurred in postmodern discourse, see the salutary pages of J. R. Searle, *The Construction of Social Reality* (New York 1995) 149-97. Since the implications of constructivist epistemologies for science have given rise to substantial misunderstandings, it seemed useful to discuss this aspect of Luhmann's conception of science in further detail: see Appendix A.
[47] In the words of Max Weber: 'Jeder von uns dagegen in der Wissenschaft weiß, daß das, was er gearbeitet hat, in 10, 20, 50 Jahren veraltet ist. Das ist das Schicksal, ja: das ist der *Sinn* der Arbeit der Wissenschaft, dem sie, in ganz spezifischem Sinne gegenüber allen anderen Kulturelementen, für die

inexorably erodes certainties: what we may consider plausible *hic et nunc* we may well have to archive as an outdated truth tomorrow. In all, science produces a type of knowledge that, while not bringing us any closer to the Truth, certainly moves us away from the sort of ordinary common sense that prevails in everyday life.[48]

There are certain distinct advantages to Luhmann's conception of science. First of all, it conveniently outflanks the rhetoric of those who posit an essential difference between *Geistes-* and *Naturwissenschaften*: his theoretical vantage point is abstract enough to accommodate both branches of enquiry within an overarching conception of science, notwithstanding their obvious differences in data and methodologies. This is extraordinarily helpful in discussing the function of scientific communication in modern society. Conversely, by distinguishing scientific communication from such entities as academic disciplines (the two are related but distinct), Luhmann's definition allows for the fact that some disciplines in the academy (classics, for instance), are, for better or worse, not exclusively (perhaps not even primarily) invested in the code 'true/ not true', but have legitimate stakes in modes of communication that do not aim at the production of scientific knowledge. [49]

With Luhmann's definition as foil, it becomes possible to see that the first generations of modern philologists indeed set in motion a scientific (re-)processing of classical data on an unprecedented scale and across a wide range of scholarly interests. In 1865, the year Matthew Arnold published his *Culture and Anarchy*, F. A. Wolf's 'science of antiquity' had already evolved into a pursuit that was, in many ways, the exact opposite of classics as traditionally conceived.[50]

Editors of classical texts were now expected to collate systematically many, if not all, surviving manuscripts of a given work. The purpose? To sift the material for, above all,

---

es sonst noch gilt, unterworfen und hingegeben ist: jede wissenschaftliche "Erfüllung" bedeutet neue "Fragen" und *will* "überboten" werden und veralten', in *Gesammelte Aufsätze zur Wissenschaftslehre*, ed. J. Winckelmann, 7th edn (Tübingen 1988) 582-613 (592) (emphases in the original). For illuminating comments on the historical context of this speech, see H. U. Gumbrecht, 'Live Your Experience – And Be Untimely! What "Classical Philology as a Profession" Could (Have) Become', in *Disciplining Classics* (n. 50, below) 256-63.

48 See A. Giddens, *The Constitution of Society* (Berkeley and Los Angeles 1984) 334-36; N. Luhmann, *Soziale Systeme* (Frankfurt a. M. 1984) 88.

49 This is a crucial point, virtually ignored by theorists of modern science, but it has important implications for understanding modern classics and its place within the topography of modern society. I shall return to it in part III. Cf. further J. Mittelstraß, 'Die unheimlichen Geisteswissenschaften', in *Häuser des Wissens* (n. 14, above) 110-33, for some reflections on the uneasy place of the 'truth-code' in the humanities.

50 The following paragraphs look at trends within nineteenth-century German classics through the wide-angle lens of Luhmann's notion of modern science. This is not meant to contest the validity of approaches which discuss the same phenomena from a more closely focused point of view, under such labels as 'the rise of the research university' (see, for example, L. O'Boyle, 'Learning for its own sake: the German university as nineteenth-century model', *Comparative Studies in Society and History* 25 (1983) 3-25); 'professionalization' (see, for example, C. A. Stray, *Classics transformed: schools, universities and society in England 1830-1960* (Oxford 1998)); or 'disciplinization' (see, for example, *Disciplining Classics – Altertumswissenschaft als Beruf*, ed. G. W. Most, *Aporemata* 6 (Göttingen 2002)). In fact, it is precisely the synergetic processes of disciplinization, institutionalization, and professionalization that have created, and continue to underwrite, the social context in which scholars enact the scientific code in pursuing their research: a functionally differentiated subsystem science.

discrepancies, errors, and inconsistencies, in an effort to reconstruct the history of transmission. What a bizarre way of approaching the classics, that is, texts to which previous generations had awarded iconic status on account of their stylistic exemplarity or the moral edification and aesthetic pleasure they were thought to afford! Not that modern editing invalidates such approaches, but, surely, no 'common-sensical' person would ever try to get hold of as many copies of the same script as possible and then scrutinize them for mistakes; and no one really did so systematically until the nineteenth century.[51] Yet this ostensibly eccentric pastime of the expert philologist makes perfect sense in scientific terms: we are dealing with a comprehensive collection of the available evidence, its programmatic investigation along self-generated models of analysis, with the aim of producing knowledge safeguarded by standards that the community of scholars deems right and proper.[52]

A similar point can be made about the rise of historicizing modes of interpretation.[53] Why should classical scholars be concerned with trying to (re-)construct the meanings of a world long gone? An intuitive attitude towards a piece of literature is to read it for its contemporary significance; a historicizing approach tries to do the exact opposite: instead of bringing the object of attention up close ('co-opting it'), its professed aim is to identify a meaning that is past, ultimately emphasizing difference, even alienness, over proximity and relevance.[54]

---

51 See A. Grafton, 'Polyhistor into *Philolog*: Notes on the Transformation of German Classical Scholarship, 1780-1850', *History of Universities* 3 (1983) 159-92. Historically speaking, this approach towards the classics acquired its full complexion only in the early nineteenth century, which is not to deny the existence of Alexandrian, Renaissance, and early-modern precursors to the disciples of Lachmann. The standard work on this revolution in philology is S. Timpanaro, *La genesi del metodo del Lachmann* (1966, reprinted, with corrections, Padua 1985) with the important qualifications by P. L. Schmidt, 'Lachmann's method: On the history of a misunderstanding', in *The uses of Greek and Latin. Historical essays*, Warburg Institute Surveys and Texts 16, ed. A. C. Dionisotti, A. Grafton, and J. Kraye (London 1988) 227-236 (= *Traditio Latinitatis. Studien zur Rezeption und Überlieferung der lateinischen Literatur* (Stuttgart 2000) 11-18). See now also G. Fiesoli, *La Genesi del Lachmannismo* (Florence 2000). For current, state-of-the-art thinking on the complexities of editing Greek and Latin texts, see the editor's preface and the contributions in *Editing Texts – Texte edieren*, ed. G. W. Most, *Aporemata* 2 (Göttingen 1998).

52 Classicists at the time were well aware that they were part of a 'scientific revolution'. Franz Bücheler, for instance, in 1878, recalls the editorial practices that still prevailed at the beginning of the century with horrified fascination: 'Noch zu Anfang dieses Jahrhunderts pflegten die Herausgeber alter Schriftsteller, von der Unfehlbarkeit des Preßbengels überzeugt, den letztgedruckten Text einfach zu wiederholen, oft genug mit allen dessen und mit einem Schock neuer Druckfehler.' *Philologische Kritik* (Rede, gehalten beim Antritt des Rektorats der Rheinischen Friedrich-Wilhelms-Universität am 18. Oktober 1878) 1-13 (3) [= *Kleine Schriften II* (1927) 239-50].

53 Interesting reflections on this phenomenon are now available in *Historicization – Historisierung*, ed. G. W. Most, *Aporemata* 5 (Göttingen 2001), see esp. Most's preface and H. U. Gumbrecht's epilogue 'Take a Step Back – And Turn Away from Death! On the Moves of Histor-icization' (365-76). The work reached me too late to take the individual contributions fully into account, but it seemed useful to add a discussion of Most's and Gumbrecht's views, see Appendix B (195-203, below).

54 For an intriguingly multi-layered reflex of this paradox, see H. Lloyd-Jones' review of Jones, *On Aristotle and Greek Tragedy*, in *Greek Epic, Lyric, and Tragedy. The Academic Papers of Sir Hugh Lloyd-Jones* (Oxford 1990) 205-9. In reaction to Jones' telling regret that 'It turns out to be our bad luck that Greek tragedy is superficially intelligible in a modern way', Lloyd-Jones counters: 'That sentence might almost imply that the fifth-century Greeks inhabited a world of thought mysteriously different from our own, like that of primitive savages whose cast of mind is strangely remote from that of normal civilized beings' (209).

Historicizing procedures ask readers of literary texts or students of history to minimize, as far as this is possible, personal involvement with the sources, an odd sort of self-denial that requires serious conceptual labour, i.e. theoretical reflection, adherence to an elaborate set of methodological rules, and a willingness to interrogate and discard cherished assumptions – 'artificial' restraints and worries that arguably detract from the immediate enjoyment and 'innocent' appreciation of historiography, art, and literature in their own right, apart from requiring years of professional training.[55] (That awareness of cultural differences might have important pedagogical implications is another matter: at issue here is the emergence of a mindset that is able and willing to perceive (constitute?) such differences in a systematic and methodical fashion and make their study the focus of a 'knowledge industry'.)

Furthermore, there is the closely related emphasis in a historicizing *Altertumswissenschaft* on studying *all* aspects of Graeco-Roman antiquity, irrespective of differences in the 'intrinsic' value of the source material. Any scrap of evidence potentially counts, and a genuine *Altertumswissenschaftler* will apply himself with the same self-denying enthusiasm to the Elgin Marbles and pieces of pottery, to Homer's *Iliad* and the charred shopping list on a papyrus-fragment from Hellenistic Egypt. *Prima facie*, this is decidedly odd and makes sense only from a scientific, that is, not a 'common-sensical', point of view. 'The true philologist must be a knight without fear', declared Usener in his *Rektoratsrede*, 'one willing, that is, to take on any text, no matter how arcane, unappealing, or intractable.'[56]

An antithesis begins to emerge, between classics (as traditionally conceived) and the novel pursuit of *Altertumswissenschaft*, that verges on the paradoxical: for science not only marginalizes moral and aesthetic criteria; by breaking down seemingly solid and meaningful essences into contingent relations, it also pulverizes the belief that a canonical body of texts and artifacts may contain permanent standards of excellence and can therefore serve as an enduring and authoritative source of transhistorical value. In other words, by approaching the classics scientifically scholars were sawing away the proverbial branch on which they were sitting: a strong belief in the special value and wider, non-scientific significance of the data of which they were in charge. This paradox made itself felt with particular force in the other societal subsystem in which 'classical' philology remained heavily implicated: education.

---

55 The paradox is well identified by N. Lowe, in his review of *Author and Audience in Latin Literature* ed. T. Woodman and J. Powell (Cambridge 1992), *Journal of Roman Studies* 84 (1994) 200-02 (201): 'If it takes a lifetime's training in the nuances of Augustan "etymology, oenology, topography, politics, and history" (Cairns, 106) before one can learn to read a seemingly ingenuous ode of Horace correctly ..., what kind of future has the reading of Latin poetry?'

56 S. Marchand, in this volume, 134. When G. Most, in his editor's preface to *Collecting Fragments – Fragmente Sammeln* (Göttingen 1997) writes that an author who has only survived in fragments, i.e. had once been within, but then fell out of, the canon, 'must once again become canonical, if scholars will be willing to undergo the enormous exertions involved in collecting, editing, and commenting on his texts' (vi), he confuses the logic of the canon with the logic of science. Scholars who devote several years of their lives to an edition of the fragments of, say, Androtion, Cassius Hemina, or Timotheus, hardly do so under the impression that their chosen author is due for a 're-canonization'; on the contrary, it is the very *absence* of any canonical standards that makes possible such prodigious expenditure of scholarly energies: its justification resides in the comprehensive remit of science, not the criteria of selectivity enacted by a canon.

II.ii Education

First, some (crude) generalizations: in the pre-modern era, the induction of the young into roles of social responsibility, a concern at the very heart of societal reproduction, rested primarily with the family and the church; the benefits of advanced schooling were by and large restricted to members of the social elite, and it reached only a tiny proportion of the population. In contrast, modern societies rely on comprehensive school systems that aim at exposing everybody to some form of general education. A new profession emerged: teaching. Yet whereas parents and preachers can rely on some sort of intrinsic authority as educators, the same is not the case for the modern pedagogue: 'Jene "natürlich-diffusen Autoritätsgrundlagen", die das Verhältnis von Eltern und Kindern bestimmen, stehen für den schulischen Erziehungsprozeß nicht zur Verfügung.'[57]

Educational authorities resorted to another 'Gewißheitsgrundlage': science. The special appeal of science in didactic contexts resides in its ability to manufacture a 'universal' view of things, beyond particular, especially religious, interests.[58] The rise of the classical philologist to special status in the schools (education) and universities (science) of late eighteenth- and early nineteenth-century Germany had a strong anti-clerical thrust.[59] At the same time, science and education are, in many ways, uneasy bedfellows. Even if educational discourse relies on science as a point of reference and source of legitimacy, educational practice is bound to retain a strong ideological investment, as a means and medium by which privileged sectors of society can establish, or preserve, socio-political distinctions. In contrast to the universal aspirations of science, education is much more context-specific, inevitably tailored towards the production of a particular brand of human being.

In nineteenth-century Germany, the notion that was supposed to bridge the strictures of science and the ideological preferences of the educational authorities was '*Bildung*'. Studies of the term are legion.[60] In one way or other, they all revolve around the tension between *Bildung* as a utopian ideal and *Bildung* as an elitist political programme, between the axiomatic premise that all human beings have the potential to ennoble themselves through lifelong learning, and the reality that *Bildung* could petrify into an acquired possession of those who belonged to a new social elite, the *Bildungsbürgertum*, that is, doctors, lawyers, high

---

[57] R. Stichweh, *Entstehung* (n. 40, above) 80, with reference to N. Luhmann and K. E. Schorr, *Reflexionsprobleme im Erziehungssystem* (Stuttgart 1979).
[58] *Ibid.*
[59] See H. Cancik and H. Cancik-Lindemaier '"Philologie als Beruf". Zu Formengeschichte, Thema und Tradition der unvollendeten vierten Unzeitgemäßen Friedrich Nietzsches', in *Philolog und Kulturfigur. Friedrich Nietzsche und seine Antike in Deutschland* (Stuttgart and Weimar 1999) 71: '"Philologie als Beruf" heißt: Der Beruf des Lehrers löst sich vom Klerikerstand und gewinnt aus dem Begriff der Erziehung und der Klassizität der Antike eine eigene normative Begründung'; and, most recently, M. Baumbach, 'Lehrer oder Gelehrter? Der Schulmann in der deutschen Altertumswissenschaft des 19. und frühen 20. Jahrhunderts', in *Disciplining Classics* (n. 50, above) 115-42 (118) with further bibliography.
[60] See, apart from the *Handbuch der deutschen Bildungsgeschichte, Vol. 4: 1870-1918*, ed. C. Berg (Munich 1991), the very different studies of A. Assmann, *Arbeit am nationalen Gedächtnis: eine kurze Geschichte der deutschen Bildungsidee* (Frankfurt a. M. 1993); G. Bollenbeck, *Bildung und Kultur. Glanz und Elend eines deutschen Deutungsmusters* (Frankfurt a. M. and Leipzig 1994); and M. Fuhrmann, *Bildung. Europas kulturelle Identität* (Stuttgart 2002).

ranking civil servants, priests and teachers, who had graduated from a *Gymnasium*, long a prerequisite to attend a university.[61] And while *Bildung* should ideally take place within the context of science, it maintained a strong, extra-scientific nimbus, as the epitomy of 'high culture', which included familiarity with a (necessarily idealized) version of classical antiquity.[62]

Rudolf Stichweh explains the special status of classical philology in nineteenth-century Germany with reference to this 'structural coupling' of science and pedagogy in modern times under the banner of *Bildung*, drawing attention to the fact that, ironically, the chair which F. A. Wolf occupied in Halle to teach his *Altertumswissenschaft* had just recently been created as a professorship in *Pädagogik*.[63] Indeed, what makes nineteenth-century German classics so remarkable is the fact that just as the *wissenschaftlich* investigation of the ancient world took off within the newly established research university, certain constructions of classical data acquired a special status in a national *Bildungsreligion*. The ideals of Phil-hellenism and secular humanism contributed much to this phenomenon, in particular since German thinkers fostered a belief in the special affinity between Germany and ancient Greece, a historical *Wahlverwandtschaft* with a decidedly anti-French undercurrent.[64]

But *Wissenschaft* and the religious aspects of *Bildung* are irreconcilably at odds with each other. Few had a keener sense of the contradictions inherent in the double role of philology as both science and pedagogy than Nietzsche:[65]

Dass diese durchaus verschiedenartigen wissenschaftlichen und aesthetisch-ethischen Triebe sich unter einem gemeinsamen Namen, unter eine Art von Scheinmonarchie zusammengethan haben, wird vor allem durch die Thatsache erklärt, dass die Philologie ihrem Ursprung nach und zu allen Zeiten zugleich Pädagogik gewesen ist.

---

61 See most recently H. Cancik and H. Cancik-Lindemaier, '"Das Gymnasium in der Knechtschaft des Staates". Zu Entstehung, Situation und Thema von Friedrich Nietzsches "Wir Philologen"', in *Disciplining Classics* (n. 50, above) 97-113, esp. 101-04.
62 Stichweh, *Entstehung* (n. 40, above) 80-81: '... man [interpretiert] Erziehung als Bildung und Bildung als etwas, das idealiter im Medium von Wissenschaft geschieht.' 'Bildung ... gewinnt ihre Suggestivität noch aus anderen Zusammenhängen. So reichert sich der Begriff "Bildung" semantisch an durch die Verbindung mit einer idealisierten Vergegenwärtigung der klassischen Antike.'
63 *Ibid*.
64 See, for example, Burckhardt, *Griechische Kulturgeschichte* I [= GW V] 10: 'Seit Winckelmann, Lessing und dem Voß'schen Homer hatte sich das Gefühl gebildet, zwischen dem hellenischen und dem deutschen Geiste bestehe ein ἱερὸς γάμος (heiliger Ehebund), ein ganz spezielles Verhältnis wie bei keinem anderen Volke des modernen Abendlandes.' The earliest programmatic endorsement of the special affinity between the national character of ancient Greek and modern-day Germany seems to have come from Humboldt's pen. See M. Fuhrmann, 'Die "Querelle des Anciens et des Modernes", der Nationalismus und die deutsche Klassik', in *Classical Influences on Western Thought AD 1650-1870*, ed. R. R. Bolgar (Cambridge 1979) 107-29 (124).
65 'Homer und die klassische Philologie' (n. 5, above) 250. Cf. also *Wir Philologen* 3 [3] (n. 3, above) 90: 'Gegen die Wissenschaft der Philologie wäre nichts zu sagen: aber die Philologen sind auch die Erzieher. Da liegt das Problem, wodurch auch diese Wissenschaft unter ein höheres Gericht kommt. – Und würde wohl die Philologie noch existieren, wenn die Philologen nicht ein Lehrerstand wären?'. See further H. Cancik and H. Cancik-Lindemaier 'Philologie als Beruf' (n. 59, above).

That these rather diverse scientific and aesthetic-ethical drives have come together under a common name, under a sort of false monarchy, finds its explanation above all in the fact that philology, in terms of its origins and throughout its history, has simultaneously been pedagogy.

Instead of a 'unified empire', we have – to elaborate on Nietzsche's imagery – a civil-war situation that all but forced the philologist to perform in the paradoxical role of priest and homicide: as revered impresario of learning, he married off the spirit of Hellas to a fledgling *Germania* at the altar of *Kultur* (Burckhardt's 'holy union'), while driving analytic stakes through the bridegroom's heart in his research seminar. Or, to use a more contemporary idiom, *Wissenschaft* was killing Homer.

The rise of modern science, then, compelled classical scholars to negotiate the crucial tension between '*Wissenschaftsanspruch*' (i.e. the claim to do science) and '*Orientierungsbedürfnis*' (i.e. the need for orientation).[66] And it is, I submit, this tension, itself an epiphenomenon of the peculiar order of modern society, that ultimately accounts for the widely diverging conceptions of philology that we looked at in part I. When Usener, Wilamowitz, and Jaeger reflected on the meaning of their professional practice, they operated from competing premises, endorsed diverse aims and objectives, and came up with incompatible answers. But this confusing diversity begins to make somewhat more sense once we regard their idiosyncratic views as highly individual responses to a problem they all shared: how to cope with the specific logic and demands of modern science.[67]

II.iii Usener, Wilamowitz, and Jaeger: a second look

Of the trio, the one arguably most at ease with the intrinsic logic of scientific research was Usener. His willingness to let go of an 'essentialist' conception of philology in *Philologie und Geschichtswissenschaft* indicates as much. He must have been quite aware of the fact that his view of philology as a method was bound to decentre classics, at least within the context of the research university; but, instead of harnessing ideological bluster in defence of outdated positions, his proposals for the future organization of scholarship on Graeco-Roman antiquity are based entirely on the implications of recent scientific findings. Nowhere in his *Rektoratsrede* is there any intimation that he sacrifices the stringency of his argument in the interest of a personal quest for meaning. In *Philologie und Geschichtswissenschaft*, at any rate, philology remains entirely a part of the subsystem science: a method, if an extraordinarily important one, of scientific research. Usener's shockingly mundane view of philology could not differ more drastically from the responses it elicited from Wilamowitz and

---

66 See G. Scholtz, *Zwischen Wissenschaftsanspruch und Orientierungsbedürfnis. Zu Grundlage und Wandel der Geisteswissenschaften* (Frankfurt a. M. 1991).

67 For the uneasy correlation between science and education in the nineteenth-century *Gymnasium*, see M. Baumbach, 'Lehrer oder Gelehrter?' (n. 59, above): whereas at the beginning of the century, schoolteachers were still expected to contribute actively to *Wissenschaft*, the inherent dynamic of *Wissenschaft* itself rendered this increasingly impracticable: the *Gelehrter* became more and more a *Lehrer*, a development with inevitable consequences for instruction at university level. If science cast an imperial shadow over education in the nineteenth century, education, in the form of *Pädagogik*, is exacting its revenge on the research universities in the twentieth: see J. Mittelstraß, 'Vom Elend der Hochschuldidaktik', in, *Häuser des Wissens* (n. 14, above) 213-31.

Jaeger, who kept insisting on philology as a means and medium of ascending to higher, non-scientific spheres of privileged insight.

If one broadens the range of sources, however, it is possible to present a more composite picture of Usener. For elsewhere he specifies that his scientific research had its motivational centre in extra-scientific concerns. In a letter to the catholic theologian Ignaz Doellinger, president of the *Bayerische Akademie der Wissenschaften*, Usener identifies a reunited Christianity as the ultimate aim of his scholarly efforts. Unsurprisingly, his work on ancient religion manifests a noticeable 'Christian-apologetic' thrust.[68] In addition, Usener coped with science by infusing science itself with outright religious import. His fervent endorsement of Plato's Academy is a case in point:[69]

> Niemals ist die Hoheit und Menschenwürdigkeit des Strebens nach wissenschaftlicher Wahrheit so tief, so glühend empfunden worden. Es ist die wahre Religion für diesen Kreis. Nach der Wahrheit forschen, heißt Gott ähnlich werden, heißt die Fesseln des Irdischen brechen, das Unsterbliche in uns befreien und seinem Lebenselement zuführen.

> Never was the majesty and human dignity of the striving for scientific truth so deeply and ardently felt. For this circle, it is the true religion. To search for truth is to become similar to God, means to break the bonds of the terrestrial, to liberate the immortal in us and to unite it with its source of life.

Secondly, Wilamowitz. He, too, was wont to accord science the status of a personal creed, a source of ultimate and transcendent meaning. Consider his Platonic vision towards the end of his lecture on 'Das Griechentum als lebendige Kraft':[70]

> Und da kommen die vielen, ängstlich und kläglich und rufen: 'Ja die schwere Wissenschaft mit allen ihren Relativitäten und ihrem Wechsel in geschichtlichen Einsichten und Kunsturteilen, wie soll denn diese in der Schule bestehen? Der alte Lehrer, der jetzt vor seiner Klasse steht, der kann doch das alles nicht verfolgen?' Gewiß nicht. Aber die Antwort liegt nicht fern. O, ihr Kleingläubigen! Jeder Lehrer, der lehrt, was in ihm lebendige Kraft ist, der eine Seele hat, die zu dem Ewigen emporstrebt, der wird in der Seele der Knaben schon Resonanz finden und wird wieder Leben schaffen. Wissenschaft ist schön und heilig, ewig und unsterblich gegenüber uns Sterblichen, die wir alle wissen, daß unser Wissen Stückwerk ist. Die fordert immer den ganzen Einsatz der Person, auf daß diese selbst darin aufgehe und vergehe. Wissenschaft fordert Resignation. Aber ein Hochgefühl ist es, das erkannte Wahre und Göttliche zu verkünden, und mit dem Einsatze der eigenen ganzen Person unmittelbar anderen Seelen zuzuführen.

---

68 See R. Schlesier, *Kulte, Mythen und Gelehrte. Anthropologie der Antike seit 1800* (Frankfurt a. M. 1994) 197-200 for the argument, references to the most important primary sources, and further bibliography.
69 'Die Organisation der wissenschaftlichen Arbeit. Bilder aus der Geschichte der Wissenschaft' (1884), reprinted in *Vorträge und Aufsätze* (Leipzig and Berlin 1907) 69-102 (101).
70 'Vortrag gehalten in der 3. ordentlichen Versammlung des Vereins der Freunde des humanistischen Gymnasiums in Wien am 27. März 1909', printed in *Mitteilungen des Vereins der Freunde des humanistischen Gymnasiums in Wien*, 8 (Vienna and Leipzig 1909) 3-12 (11).

And then there come the many, timorous and wretched, and call out: 'But science is so difficult, with all its relativities and its changes in historical insights and judgments about art, how is it supposed to survive in school? The old teacher, who now stands in front of his pupils, he is surely unable to keep up with all that?' That is true. But the solution is not far off. O ye of little faith! Each teacher, who teaches what is a living force within himself, who has a soul that strives upward towards the eternal, will appeal to the soul of the boys and will regenerate life. Science is beautiful and sacred, eternal and immortal in contrast to us mortals, who all know that our knowledge is incomplete. Science always demands the full commitment of the entire person, so that the person lives entirely for it and passes away. Science demands submission. But it is an inspired feeling to preach what has been apprehended as true and divine, and to instil this with an all-out effort directly into other souls.

Wilamowitz here starts with the realization that scientific insights are utterly contingent and constantly in flux (a point he strategically places in the mouth of the rabble[71]), only to end with a hypostasis of science as a source of revelation, to be administered by charismatic individuals. By endowing science itself with divine connotations, Wilamowitz manages to sublimate (and thereby counterveil) the utter contingency he has rightly identified as a hallmark of modern, scientific research. The view of science as a source of religious fulfilment permeates the rhetoric of nineteenth-century historicism. Few scholars, however, went so far as Wilamowitz, who, at the end of his life, professed to philosophy and science 'as a religion of the heart, more immortal than all divinities.'[72]

Apart from turning science into a religion, Wilamowitz relied on other antinomies to salvage significance: a scientific patriotism; an ahistorical historicism; and a non-classicizing classicism. Let me briefly illustrate each of these aspects:

On patriotic occasions, Wilamowitz was fond of insisting that the pursuit of scientific truth and spiritual satisfaction formed an inner unity within the larger context of German nationalism.[73] At times, he forged an explicit link between mental and military efforts: just as every German happily gives his heartblood for his country ('dafür sind wir Deutsche!'), so those Germans equipped with the swords of the mind, the '*Schwerter des Geistes*', contribute to national strength by cultivating unconditional patriotism at the university.[74] Exposure to

---

71 In all likelihood those, who, like F. Aby, argued against Wilamowitz's attempt to replace a 'classicizing' approach to antiquity with a 'historicizing' one in secondary education. See F. Aby, *Humanismus oder Historismus* (Marburg 1902) 19, '... die Wissenschaft ist in beständigem Flusse; was heute als feststehend gilt, kann morgen durch die Entdeckung einer Handschrift, eines Monuments umgestossen werden. Man kann aber nicht seine Lebens- und Weltanschauung, man kann nicht den Lehrgang einer Schule alle paar Jahre umwerfen.' (Cited by Baumbach, 'Lehrer oder Gelehrter?' (n. 59, above) 137.)

72 *Der Glaube der Hellenen* (Berlin 1931), I, 44.

73 This aspect of Wilamowitz's outlook on science and education has received detailed attention. See L. Canfora, 'Wilamowitz: Politik in der Wissenschaft', *Wilamowitz nach 50 Jahren*, ed. W. M. Calder, H. Flashar, and T. Lindken (Darmstadt 1985) 56-79.

74 'Ansprache an die Studierenden. Gehalten zur Feier des 150 jährigen Jubiläums der Universität Göttingen am 9. August 1887 vor der Aula', in *Reden und Vorträge*, 3rd edn (Berlin 1913) 86-90.

genuine German *Wissenschaft*, Wilamowitz thought, was apt to produce good citizens and to strengthen the moral fibre of the nation.[75]

Further, Wilamowitz was, in theory, an ardent proponent of a strictly historicizing approach to Greek and Roman antiquity. Yet in practice, he frequently opted for a breezy hermeneutics of identity. As Hellmut Flashar has acutely observed, Wilamowitz lacked any sense of a 'hermeneutics of difference'.[76] His version of historicism was, despite its comprehensive reach, devoid of historical depth. Owing in part, perhaps, to his aversion to method and to self-critical reflection, once he started to shape the vast amount of empirical evidence that he commanded so effortlessly into interpretive visions, Wilamowitz tended simply to let loose his 'free formative imagination'. In effect, this meant applying to the task of historical interpretation his common sense, i.e. *his* preconceptions, preferences, and prejudices, quite unchecked by critical reflexivity and other scientific strictures. As a result, his analyses of Greek literature and culture are to an unusual degree impregnated with his personal background and experiences:[77] they sport an apodeictic immediacy and contemporaneity that extend from the personal to the political.[78]

At some level, of course, it is inevitable (and the irreducible *aporia* at the heart of the historicist enterprise) that one projects the present into the past when one brings the past into the present.[79] All of us are situated in history, and this 'situatedness' forms the only ground from which we can advance claims about reality. Wilamowitz saw the dilemma and captured it in a striking image: the need to give one's heart-blood to revive the ghosts of antiquity, but

---

75 *Ibid.*, 89. What Wilamowitz considers peculiarly German is 'die Art und Weise ..., die an den deutschen Universitäten und sonst bei keinem Volke gilt, die Jugend durch die Teilnahme an wissenschaftlicher Arbeit für die praktischen Berufe in Staat und Kirche auszubilden'.

76 'Wilamowitz heute? Zur Situation der Geisteswissenschaften', in *Wilamowitz in Greifswald. Akten der Tagung zum 150. Geburtstag Ulrich von Wilamowitz-Moellendorffs in Greifswald, 19. – 22. Dezember 1998*, ed. W. M. Calder *et al.* (Zurich and New York 2000) 667-91 (690). See already V. Pöschl (Discussion of M. Landfester, 'Ulrich von Wilamowitz-Moellendorff und die hermeneutische Tradition des 19. Jahrhunderts', in *Philologie und Hermeneutik* (n. 14, above) 376: 'Es ist in der Tat merkwürdig, wie wenig historische Distanz ein historischer Forscher wie Wilamowitz besitzt.'

77 As the studies of W. M. Calder show, Wilamowitz was, by inclination and schooling, a prototypical 'personal voicer', see esp. 'Ecce Homo: The Autobiographical in Wilamowitz' Scholarly Writings', in *Wilamowitz nach 50 Jahren* (n. 73, above), 80-110, for example, 80 'During his most impressionable years Wilamowitz learned from his beloved teacher an intensely personal approach to a text, to find something there that would make him better', and 90, for aunt Emma von Schwanenfeld influencing Wilamowitz's interpretation of Phaedra's character in Euripides' *Hippolytus*.

78 As M. S. Silk and J. P. Stern note in their balanced assessment of Wilamowitz's talents, he lacked 'the sureness of touch in any area of cultural interpretation that he showed elsewhere' (i.e. in textual criticism, in metrics, and in various techniques of editorial interpretation), *Nietzsche on Tragedy* (n. 33, above) 100. Silk and Stern also draw attention to the telling split in British reactions to Wilamowitz: hailed as the greatest classicist of his era by Housman (in his incarnation as textual critic), he was dismissed as getting the proverbial wrong end of every stick in cultural studies by James Frazer.

79 Not exactly a new insight, see Friedrich Schlegel, 'Jeder hat noch in den Alten gefunden, was er brauchte oder wünschte, vorzüglich sich selbst' (quoted by E. Friedell, *Kulturgeschichte der Neuzeit. Die Krisis der europäischen Seele von der Schwarzen Pest bis zum Weltkrieg*, vol. II: *Barock und Rokoko / Aufklärung und Revolution* (Munich 1928) 371, as one of his motti for the chapter on 'Die Erfindung der Antike').

then to cast it out again in the name of truth.[80] But he only went so far in performing this surgery on his own interpretations of Graeco-Roman antiquity, ignoring, even despising, many of the critical instruments that scholarly research had already made available for precisely this purpose (such as the strict definition of concepts or the importance of method, esp. cross-cultural comparison).[81] Just as his vision of public pedagogy involved grudging nods towards the subversion and contingency that inheres in science, followed instantly by the sublimation of the problem within broader ideological constructs, so too Wilamowitz recognized the arduous demands of historicizing research, but then proceeded to disregard many of them in his personal appropriations of ancient culture.

Likewise, Wilamowitz was very much aware of the impact of modern science on classicizing tenets. He was, generally speaking, adamant that the adjective 'classical' could no longer be applied to antiquity in good faith. That science had destroyed many a cherished belief about ancient Greece and Rome formed a basic premise of his work.[82] Yet while Wilamowitz realized that the kind of historical criticism which he himself advocated had significantly deflated the mythopoetic philhellenism of earlier generations, he still insisted that the great work of art, the great idea, or the great human being inspire an immediate form of worship:[83]

Dann bleibt immer noch das große Kunstwerk, der große Gedanke, der große Mensch. Vor dem Tempel von Pästum, im Pantheon, auf der Burg Athens wird der Mensch immerdar eine innere Erhebung erfahren, ein Geist wird zu ihm reden, der ihn zu Andacht zwingt.

What always remains is the great work of art, the great thought, the great man. In front of the temple of Paestum, in the Pantheon, on the acropolis of Athens, the human being will always experience an inner elevation, a spirit will speak to him and compel him to worship.

In addition to a Science, conceived as religion, Wilamowitz here marshals Art and Genius as further rhetorical bulwarks to keep at bay the corrosive implications of scientific research. Again, the religious dimensions of his 'scholarly' self-fashioning are unmistakable. Karl Reinhardt thus continues Wilamowitz's own imagery when he calls him first and foremost the 'berufene Künder des Ewigen in griechischer Größe', using an apt description that would fit Jaeger and his classicizing Third Humanism equally well.[84]

---

80 See *Greek Historical Writing and Apollo. Two Lectures delivered before the University of Oxford, June 3 and 4, 1908*, trans. G. Murray (Oxford 1908) 25.
81 For Wilamowitz's terminological inconsistencies and its consequences, see Bollack's view (n. 19, above) and the paper by Egon Flaig 'Towards "*Rassenhygiene*"' in this volume (105-27), which also highlights the racist underpinnings of Wilamowitz's dismissal of cross-cultural comparison.
82 See 'Die Geltung des klassischen Altertums im Wandel der Zeiten' [1921], in *Kleine Schriften* VI (Berlin and Amsterdam 1972) 144-53: 'Eben durch den Feuereifer, mit dem sich die deutsche Wissenschaft auf die Erforschung von Hellas und Rom warf, entstand die historische Kritik, die manchen lieb gewordenen Glauben zerstörte, aber jeder Zeit und jedem Werke und Personen das Seine gab oder geben wird' (150).
83 *Ibid.*, 152.
84 K. Reinhardt, 'Ulrich von Wilamowitz-Moellendorff 1848-1931', in *Die Grossen Deutschen. Deutsche Biographie*, ed. H. Heimpel, T. Heuss, B. Reifenberg, 4 vols (Berlin 1957) 415-21 (415).

Throughout his career, then, depending on occasion, audience, and, no doubt, changing biographical circumstances, Wilamowitz responded in various ways to the challenge posed by modern science: he elevated science into a religion; he fervently believed in the moral value of scientific research; he practised a historicist hermeneutics of identity that allowed him to see existentially important parallels and draw meaningful analogies between periods of ancient history or characters in ancient literature and his own world; and he endowed certain entities of Greek and Roman antiquity with an aura of transcendence. In all four strategies of salvaging significance, we capture a Wilamowitz who is surprisingly 'Nietzschean' in outlook, one who attempts 'to purvey wisdom about the ancient world attained by some non-scholarly, intuitive means' – as M. S. Silk and P. Stern characterize Nietzsche's approach in *The Birth of Tragedy*.[85]

Finally, Jaeger. We already had occasion to notice that his attitude towards *Wissenschaft* was decidedly ambivalent. After all, he thought that science had destroyed the unity of culture he so yearned for. Throughout his career, Jaeger endeavoured to reconcile his commitment to scholarship with public proselytizing for his personal faith in classical antiquity, a life-long quest that culminated in the Naumburg-conference on classicism and his study of Greek *paideia*.[86] As he himself explains in his autobiography, ancient Greece early on acquired both existential and professional significance for him: 'Although Rome was historically the prerequisite for the existence of the Greek element in this union [sc. of the classical and Christian worlds], nonetheless Hellas became the real source for my spiritual needs and the field of my scholarly activity.'[87]

In the end, he was unable to resolve in any convincing fashion the paradox between spirituality and science that defined his attitude towards antiquity. Emblematic of this 'schizophreny' was his tragi-comic relationship with the poet and self-proclaimed classical scholar Rudolf Borchardt. As E. A. Schmidt has shown in his edition of the correspondence, Borchardt looked to Jaeger for his approval in matters philological, whereas Jaeger, who apparently could not care less for Borchardt's philological pretensions, wished to recruit the poet, with his conservative, humanistic outlook, for his classicizing agenda. Schmidt concludes: 'The correspondence, then, was allowed to lapse because – to put it in a nutshell – Jaeger, who wanted the poet Borchardt, was given the scholar, and Borchardt, who wanted the scholar Jaeger, found the programmatic educator'.[88]

In all, then, Usener, Wilamowitz, and Jaeger are prime incarnations of 'Professor Janus': all were thoroughly committed to the production of scientific knowledge and practised classical scholarship at the highest level; yet, simultaneously, they were desperate to salvage significance. By trying to endow their research with special, non-scientific meaning, purpose, and value, they all sought to counterveil, in one way or other, the inexorable logic that inheres in modern science – a quest that resulted in all three cases in some sort of religious

---

85 *Nietzsche on Tragedy* (n. 33, above) 96.
86 *Das Problem des Klassischen*, ed. W. Jaeger (n. 32, above); *Paideia: die Formung des griechischen Menschen* (Berlin 1934).
87 Introduction to *Scripta Minora*, 'An Intellectual Autobiography', cited in the translation of A. M. Fiske, *Werner Jaeger. Five Essays* (n. 8, above) 27.
88 'Werner Jaeger and Rudolf Borchardt: Correspondence 1929-1933', in *Werner Jaeger Reconsidered* (n. 25, above) 161-208 (203).

mystification. Still, there are useful differences to be observed between the scholarly self-fashioning of Usener on the one hand, and of Wilamowitz and Jaeger on the other: the perspicacious, down-to-earth, and internally coherent theorizing Usener offers in *Philologie und Geschichtswissenschaft* contrasts sharply with the ideologically driven responses of his two 'interlocutors', thereby illustrating the benefits to be gained from reflecting critically on the historical evolution of scholarship in modern times – even if that may entail the need to jettison some cherished assumptions.

Part III Back to the Future

If one surveys the stories which classicists and historians of classical scholarship tell about the current state, or the history, of their discipline, it is possible to observe a widespread penchant for binary patterns: thus we find pitched against each other *Bildung* and *Wissenschaft*, Renaissance learning and technical skills,[89] humanism and historicism, teaching and research, popular education and sterile theory, or a living classical tradition and 'pure' scholarship.[90] Such binary patterns yield a captivating plot: the Manichean struggle of two monoliths, one good, the other evil, in a dialectical quest for supremacy. The story ends in either tragedy (often including the neat causalities of a classic murder mystery: a corpse and a culprit), triumph, or a facile truce.[91] Yet, what these plots gain in terms of narrative appeal and coherence, they lose in complexity[92] – apart from coming dangerously close to violating one of Suzanne Marchand's and Anthony Grafton's 'non-controversial rules' of how to do intellectual history, that is not to imitate 'first-year undergraduates' in presenting historical tussles along 'two or three easily identifiable party lines which can be described as "conservative" or "progressive," "orthodox" or "radical".'[93]

---

[89] Grafton locates the reasons for the crisis that he perceives in German classics around the middle of the nineteenth century in the triumph of positivist and historicist research over humanistic traditions of scholarship. For him, it is a story of loss and decline: technical questions, in particular textual criticism, had driven out the more comprehensive ideals of *Bildung* (see 'Polyhistor into *Philolog*', n. 51, above).
[90] Silk and Stern construct the confrontation between Rohde and Wilamowitz over Nietzsche's *Birth of Tragedy* with the help of this opposition: 'We have here a classic confrontation, the epitome of all controversy between the defenders of "pure" scholarship and the spokesmen for learning in the service of art and life' (*Nietzsche on Tragedy*, n. 33, above, 100). As the foregoing pages have shown, Wilamowitz was, in many ways, much more Nietzschean in his outlook on the classical past than this neat dichotomy allows for, even though his defiant and vitriolic rhetoric in *Zukunftsphilologie!* obfuscates the affinities.
[91] See D. Light, 'The Structure of the Academic Professions', *Sociology of Education* 47 (1974) 2-28 (5): 'Training future teachers conflicts with training future researchers, unless one assumes that the way to train college teachers is to make them good researchers. This, in fact, is the dubious assumption by which such conflicts are "resolved".' See already Weber, *Wissenschaft als Beruf* (n. 47, above), who denies any intrinsic correlation between the charismatic teacher and the productive scholar.
[92] On complexity in scholarship, see H. Willke, *Systemtheorie: eine Einführung in die Grundprobleme der Theorie sozialer Systeme*, 4th edn (Stuttgart 1993) 4: '... vielmehr geht eine sehr ermutigende Entwicklung dahin, die Wissenschaftlichkeit jeglicher Disziplin daran zu messen, inwieweit sie die Komplexität ihres jeweiligen Gegenstandsbereiches nicht künstlich – und allzu oft bis zur Trivialität ihrer Fragestellungen – reduziert, sondern diese Komplexität ernst nimmt und kontrollierbare Verfahren zur Bearbeitbarkeit dieser Komplexität entwickelt.'
[93] S. Marchand and A. Grafton 'Martin Bernal and his Critics', *Arion*, 3rd series 5.2 (1997) 1-35 (6).

It is, furthermore, evident that the dichotomies set out above tend to endow the second term (sc. *Wissenschaft*, technical skills, historicism, theory, pure scholarship) with pejorative connotations – these entities are viewed as encroaching upon a humanistic conception of education, in which 'life' and 'learning' form a wholesome unity. But in presenting the process of 'scientification' in negative terms, scholars reproduce a partial view found in their sources: it is not difficult to spot the affinities of this evaluation with the '*Wissenschaft-anteportas*' rhetoric of an Aby or a Jaeger. This seems to prejudge the issue: instead of unearthing the factors that shaped this rhetoric and assessing its validity, such accounts turn a subjective point of view into a factual statement about historical reality. And finally, even if one considers the pursuit of scientific interests in the humanities ultimately misguided, this does not answer the question why the insistence on scientific standards, procedures, and rationality has acquired such astounding prominence in the first place; or, to put it more generally, why modern society is willing to invest an unprecedented (some would say: inordinate) amount of resources in the production of information about the Graeco-Roman past that many outside a narrow circle of specialists would consider entirely superfluous.

In short, conceiving of classics as an entity at the mercy of a procrustean tug-of-war between *Bildung* and *Wissenschaft* (or their respective equivalents) without asking what forces are behind this constellation, evinces certain explanatory deficits. This calls for a fresh perspective. Theories of modern society arguably offer one, in that they afford the chance to place both the rise of science and the field of classics within a broader context. Not that, to prevent a common misunderstanding, social theory offers a ready-made blueprint of how best to deal with the challenges posed by the peculiar order of modern society. This is not its task. But it offers a more abstract and comprehensive account of the societal environment in which classicists are asked to perform and may thereby help us better to understand the factors behind the tensions and tussles that have come to define our field and to clarify the options and choices we have (to make) in shaping its future. This is especially true for gaging the importance of scientific considerations in humanities subjects and, more generally speaking, education.

An excellent point of departure for rendering this claim plausible is a quotation from M. Beard's and J. Henderson's 'very short introduction' to our discipline. In one place, the authors state categorically that there is 'no alternative' to approaching, at least to some extent, our primary data in what we may call, with Luhmann, scientific fashion:[94]

> You can see why the business of producing editions of Greek and Roman authors has traditionally carried great prestige among professional scholars. It carries risks too; for the vast majority of attempts to produce a 'better' text are destined to win only temporary approval and are quickly forgotten. All the same, there is no alternative to taking the risk and *trying*, at least, to reach as accurate a view as possible of what ancient authors wrote.

Beard and Henderson have here chosen to present editorial efforts in the idiom of the 'correspondence-theory of truth': to approximate, as accurately as possible, to what the author wrote. Some would consider the theory behind this idiom a sort of 'metaphysical hangover'; but, as I suggest in Appendix A (194-95, below), such criticism is quite beside the point: one

---

[94] M. Beard and J. Henderson, *Classics. A Very Short Introduction* (Oxford 1995) 57.

could easily rewrite this paragraph in constructivist terms. Rather, what deserves to be foregrounded is that the authors present the commitment to a scientific study of primary data as both fundamental and without alternative, quite irrespective of the fact that most endeavours fail to win the lasting approval of the scientific community. Beard and Henderson here pinpoint a crucial aspect of the logic of scientific research: the constant testing, critique, and overhaul of previous findings. In his lecture on *Wissenschaft als Beruf*, Max Weber identified this process as the very purpose of science. We may add, as consolation to those scholars whose views do not even find *temporary* approval, that, within science, errors, too, have their function.[95]

But is it really true that there is 'no alternative' to scientific efforts at establishing the outlook of primary data? Evidently not. Joseph Farrell, for instance, has recently started to experiment with creating a 'Communal Text' of Virgil, i.e. a text that features those readings that receive the most votes from its users.[96] His visionary project would offer us a democratic alternative to the 'elitist' efforts of professional scholars. Or one could simply choose to 'opt out' of the scholarly paradigm evoked by Beard and Henderson, which is, at any rate, the product of a specific time and place (nineteenth-century Germany), and return to the more free-spirited approach to empirical accuracy of the early modern period, so well evoked by Franz Bücheler,[97] thereby freeing up time and energy for more important pursuits. Some scholars seem indeed to be heading that way, with predictable polemics against nineteenth-century German scholarship and its delusory belief in the possibility of objectivity.[98]

Arguably, they have a point. Accuracy comes at a price. As mentioned in part II, editing a Greek or Latin text nowadays involves an elaborate and complicated set of programs, procedures, and precautions, is to be undertaken only by well-trained experts, and is, at any rate, far removed from the quotidian reality of the classroom. *Pace* Beard and Henderson, one could decide that the investment we have to make in order to constitute our data scientifically is far too high, apart from being quite unnecessary: to maintain the contemporary relevance of Greek and Latin texts, to teach lessons in ethics and aesthetics, to create personal, if imaginary, encounters with the ancient world, there is no need of trying 'to reach as accurate a view as possible of what ancient authors wrote.' In fact, one could argue that the commitment to scientific truths *obstructs* other, more personally enriching, experiences to be had with classical literature. Why should we be obsessively concerned with the odd, unmetrical line, a couple of interpolated verses, or relatively minor variants in the manuscript tradition, in particular since, as Beard and Henderson point out, efforts at fixing such problems are historically contingent and their results bound to be ephemeral?

In all, then, it is at least conceivable for classicists to relinquish commitment to the scientific truth-code altogether. On the other hand, most of us would probably (still?) agree with Beard and Henderson that one should make the effort and approach primary data at least *also* with scientific interests in mind. But why?

---

95 See J. Mittelstraß, 'Vom Nutzen des Irrtums in der Wissenschaft', in *Häuser des Wissens* (n. 14, above) 13-28. For Weber, see n. 47, above.
96 See http://vergil.classics.upenn.edu/project.html#text, s.v. 'The Communal Text' (last changed 8/23/95).
97 See n. 52, above.
98 See Appendix A (194-95, below).

Beard and Henderson do not back up their assertion that there is 'no alternative' to the discourse of science, with its internal hierarchies, strictures of accuracy, and seemingly wasted efforts – I suspect because the reasons are too obvious. Still, it is worth spelling them out. The advantages of basing our view of things on the mercurial foundation of what expert communities regard as plausible at any one point in time – be it in editorial criticism, medicine, quantum physics, or cultural studies – emerge if one starts to compare scientific knowledge to possible alternatives: instead of basing one's views of the world on scientific findings, one could, for instance, rely on such sources of authority as the charisma of gurus, holy scriptures and their exegetes, the principle of seniority, or the persuasive qualities inherent in various forms of socio-political power (the fiat of the tyrant or the rhetoric of the demagogue, the consensus of the (oligarchic) in-group or the vote of the majority). In contrast to these options, communities of experts who talk about the world in scientific fashion are expected to give reasons for the validity, or at least plausibility, of their opinions, in compliance with certain sets of formal criteria that are shared by other members of their profession, even though these criteria are themselves open to contestation and change.[99]

On a very basic level, then, adherence to the scientific truth-code in establishing, or contesting, claims about reality (a conjecture, an interpretation, a theory) has certain advantages that one should not lightly dismiss – even in humanities disciplines and the age of constructivist epistemologies. (As argued in Appendix A, the scholarly procedures which, say, underwrite textual editing, retain their validity as means of manufacturing scientific truth, even if we abandon (as we should) belief in the possibility of ever reaching an 'objective' account of the ancient world.) We only have to imagine a society where such claims are assessed by other criteria than those made available by scientific reflection to see that to suspend the logic of science is a *political* decision with dogmatic and authoritarian implications.

The consequences of abandoning commitment to scientific efforts would indeed be drastic, both in scientific and educational contexts. Within the subsystem science, the field of classics would lose the ability to communicate meaningfully with other disciplines. And forsaking scientific efforts and their outcomes as common standards in education would raise the question of what might take the place of 'the better argument'. As suggested above, possible alternatives seem unattractive: the practice of majority vote in the classroom, for instance, would put the teacher at a distinct disadvantage (he or she could easily get outvoted on an unmetrical conjecture proposed by a student[100]), whereas such criteria as age or any other type of authority, while likely to favour the pedagogue, would smack suspiciously of indoctrination.

All this is not to deny that alternative sources of authority have been, and will always be, part of the field of classics as a socio-political configuration and are bound to influence the enactment of the scientific code, both in its practice and its outcomes. It is perfectly obvious,

---

99 See Mittelstraß's point that the unity of science lies in the unity of scientific method: 'Unter wissenschaftlicher Methode ist dabei ganz allgemein die Art und Weise bezeichnet, wie in der Wissenschaft Geltungsansprüche begründet werden' ('Interdisziplinarität oder Transdisziplinarität?', in *Häuser des Wissens* (n. 14, above) 29-48 (38).
100 Contrast J. Farrell's experiment of creating a 'Communal Text' of Virgil (n. 96, above) with J. Mittelstraß, 'Legitimation der Wissenschaft. Warum es in der Wissenschaft keine Mehrheitsentscheidungen geben kann', in *Häuser des Wissens* (n. 14, above) 190-202.

and requires constant vigilance and investigation, that scientific practice is inevitably implicated in very real struggles for prestige, influence, and power, in mechanisms of inclusion and exclusion, and in the accumulation and preservation of social, symbolic, and financial resources. But this holds true for both the natural sciences and the humanities; and it neither proves the impossibility of scientific communication as a manufacturer of a specific type of 'truth' nor the undesirability of pursuing it. Quite the contrary.

These observations may sound banal, but they strongly suggest that the dichotomy between 'scientific' or 'scholarly' approaches and education is, at a very basic level, misconceived. Scientific truths as well the codes and programmes by which they are manufactured do not only form the basis of meaningful communication within the subsystem science; they also contribute crucial aspects to modern education. In fact, it could be argued that an education at university level that does not induct students into the principles of scientific rationality (for example, methodological awareness and empirical accuracy, conceptual precision and appreciation of complexity, critical reflexivity, the relentless undoing of the impostures of common sense, and a sound scepticism of all non-scientific authority) would be deficient, not least in denying students an understanding of how a very powerful field or subsystem of modern society operates.

In all, then, induction in, and practice of, the scientific code has a special function in forming the ground for discursive interactions, not only in highly specialized research, but also in general education. Yet this does not imply that the production of scientific knowledge has to be the *only* preoccupation of classicists. And here Luhmann's definition of science as a specific mode of communication offers a potentially more relaxed attitude to the apparent tensions and contradictions within the discipline. For classics is quite able to accommodate a variety of different 'codes' within its remit. To return to Nietzsche's 'philological trinity': apart from scientific-historical understanding, the field harbours natural interests in artistic appropriations of Graeco-Roman antiquity ('the classical tradition') as well as ethical and aesthetic imperatives ('values').[101]

To put this point in a more contemporary idiom: learning scientific facts about the ancient world (and how to manufacture them) is only one facet of an educational experience in classics. There are other concerns: guidance in how to view art and read literature, encouragement to sharpen moral-political awareness, the provision of 'frame conditions that make it *possible* for aesthetic experience to happen',[102] or even basic help in acquiring fluency

---

[101] See M. Silk, 'Pindar meets Plato: theory, language, value, and the classics', in *Texts, Ideas, and the Classics. Scholarship, Theory, and Classical Literature*, ed. S. J. Harrison (Oxford 2001) 26-45.
[102] H. U. Gumbrecht, 'Live Your Experience' (n. 47, above) 268. The paper makes an interesting case for the connection between (postmodern reading) 'experience' and 'complexity', which, in suggestive ways, complements the increasing appreciation of complexity in science. See Wilke (n. 92, above) with Gumbrecht's claim that the exhilarating moment of 'lived experience' in a university setting can happen 'by confronting ourselves and our students with objects of a complexity that defies easy structuring, conceptualization, and interpretation – especially if such a confrontation happens under conditions of low time-pressure' (267).

in oral and written expression.¹⁰³ Briefly put, despite the rise of science, the Renaissance version of a 'liberal education' has lost none of its appeal.

In all, then, it seems misguided to construct the tension between *Wissenschaft* and *Bildung* in outright antagonistic terms – apart from precluding a considered assessment of the *relative* importance of scientific and other concerns *in relation to* the various contexts in which classicists are asked to perform. In a functionally differentiated society, the environment classicists inhabit is composite, including various scientific and educational contexts, from undergraduate lectures to postgraduate seminars to scholarly conferences and publications to society at large (outreach). The challenges that ensue as classicists travel from one context to another elude the heuristic grasp of binary schemes. To be sure, pressing the history of the field and debates about its future into a Manichean straitjacket may be useful to peddle an argument, in the same way as, for instance, mystifications of science as a religion or objectifications of philology. But such rhetorical manoeuvres are *theoretically* inadequate.

I would like to conclude with a reference to a new institution in the European university system: the European College of Liberal Arts (ECLA). The founders, a group of young German scholars and entrepreneurs who all went abroad in search of educational experience, trace their vision 'to both the Angloamerican liberal arts tradition and to the neohumanistic ideas of Wilhelm von Humboldt and his circle – for both programmes stem from a single source, the humanistic philosophy of education developed in classical Greece and Rome.'¹⁰⁴ Four terms are inscribed on ECLA's programmatic logo: Πράξις, *Humanitas*, *Liberté*, and *Wissenschaft*.

King's College London

---

103 See M. Fuhrmann, *Der europäische Bildungskanon des bürgerlichen Zeitalters* (Frankfurt a. M. and Leipzig 1999), who stresses the importance of teaching 'den je Heranwachsenden zuallererst einen hohen Standard von Sprachbeherrschung in Wort und Schrift und hiermit zugleich den Zugang zur Literatur, zur Philosophie und zur Geschichte' (p. 10).
104 See http://www.ecla.de.

Appendix A: On constructivism

There is a tendency among scholars in the humanities to link (the possibility of) science to certain epistemological preconceptions, such as the existence of, and search for, objective truths or the need and necessity to approximate 'reality'. A corollary of such hypothetical connections is the assumption that the constructivist epistemologies that have gained ever greater acceptance in the humanities over the last four decades, have put into question, if not completely undermined, the type of scientific scholarship pioneered in nineteenth-century Germany. The insight of twentieth-century physics that the observer influences the outlook of the data (Einstein, Heisenberg), thereby collapsing 'the gap between the "objective" world and its formulation in the mind of the knower' is frequently adduced to corroborate the point. This train of thought often culminates in the assertion that in the age of constructivism, 'personal', reader-response approaches to classical texts are the only viable ones.[105]

This line of argument does not stand up to closer scrutiny. To begin with, the appeal to the insights produced by natural scientists as an argument against the possibility of science is rather curious, if not outright contradictory. The realization that there is no gap between the phenomenon under consideration and the act of its apprehension has clearly not inaugurated the demise of quantum physics, so why should it have such drastic consequences for scholarship on ancient Greece and Rome? Put differently, working within a constructivist paradigm does not *entail* the impossibility to talk about the world in scientific fashion; it follows that the assumption that science *requires* a foundationalist epistemology is wrong.[106]

In fact, social theorists such as Luhmann and Bourdieu are quite happy to dispense with any 'correspondence-theory of truth' or the belief in foundations.[107] In their conceptions of

---

105 So, for instance, T. Van Nortwick, 'Conclusion: what is classical scholarship for?' in *Compromising Traditions. The personal voice in classical scholarship*, ed. J. P. Hallett and T. Van Nortwick (London 1997) 182-90 (quotation at 185).

106 A related misconception is the view that the 'turn towards science' that occurred in the nineteenth century was the misguided attempt of classical scholars to imitate the natural sciences, owing to anxieties about their subject losing ground in status and prestige (see Van Nortwick, 182-83, who thinks that 'the notion of objectivity as an ideal in scholarship' came into being in nineteenth-century Germany as a reflex of 'the anxieties of scholars not working in the so-called "hard sciences"'.) This ignores the crucial role that the development of *Altertumswissenschaft* initially played in defining the modern research university: in nineteenth-century Germany, classicists were not latecomers on the scientific scene, but part of its vanguard. Cf. Grafton, 'Polyhistor into Philolog' (n. 51, above) and Stichweh, *Entstehung* (n. 40, above). The point here is that the formal principles of scientific communication that were developed then (and have further evolved since) do not depend for their validity on – now outdated – nineteenth-century epistemological assumptions.

107 See N. Luhmann, *Die Wissenschaft der Gesellschaft* (n. 45, above) 173 n. 13: 'Hiermit überschreiten wir zugleich die Grenzen der traditionellen Definition der Wahrheit als *adequatio*, die in ihren beiden Anwendungsmöglichkeiten (*adequatio intellectus ad rem* und *adequatio rei ad intellectum*) auf beiden Seiten etwas vorausgesetzt hatte, was der Attribuierung von Eigenschaften standhalten konnte. Wir müssen statt dessen nach dem Verfahren der Attribuierung selber fragen' and 177: 'Entgegen einer verbreiteten Auffassung führt jedoch das Kappen der Fremdreferenz und der Verzicht auf jede Art Adäquations- oder Korrespondenztheorie der Wahrheit keineswegs zum Relativismus oder gar zum "anything goes". Das Gegenteil trifft zu.' For the 'post-empiristische Wende in der Wissenschaftstheorie', see further A. Reckwitz, *Struktur. Zur sozialwissenschaftlichen Analyse von Regeln und Regelmäßigkeiten* (Opladen 1997), who lists her most important representatives in various fields as follows:

science, it does not matter whether we are *constructing* or *re*-constructing a text, authorial intentions, a pot, or any other aspect of Graeco-Roman antiquity. It is adherence to (historically contingent) programs (theories, methods) and formal criteria of rendering claims about the world plausible, not any epistemological premises, that constitutes science. In other words, those who question the possibility of science on epistemological grounds do not engage the reality of scientific practice and its most up-to-date theoretical modelling. Instead, they delight in setting strawmen afire. Finally, it is worth pointing out that the emergence of constructivist epistemologies owes itself to a crucial scientific principle: the willingness to subject any findings to reflexive critique. From this point of view, constructivism is only the most radical realization of scientific reflexivity in matters epistemological. In short, attempts to show the impossibility of science on epistemological grounds are misconceived.

All this should not be misconstrued to imply that the *possibility* of a scientific approach towards Greek and Roman antiquity is also *necessary* and the only one that classicists should practise. Just as pleas for a personal take on classical literature do not invalidate the option to profess classics in scientific fashion, the option of doing so does not constitute a challenge to the validity of, say, reader-response approaches. The question, rather, is: when, where, and why does it make sense to practise the one rather than the other?

Appendix B: On historicization

The fifth volume of G. W. Most's inspiring series *Aporemata. Kritische Studien zur Philologiegeschichte* tackles 'historicization'.[108] The immense value of the collection as a whole, and of Most's preface and H. U. Gumbrecht's epilogue in particular, is the problematization of a practice that tends to be taken for granted. The fact that Most and Gumbrecht set forth conceptions of historicization that are strikingly different, at times mutually exclusive, adds to the appeal (or, to speak with Gumbrecht, it agreeably 'complexifies' matters). In what follows, I wish to rehearse and critique their arguments in some detail, both to give 'historicization' a sharper profile and to throw into better relief the heuristic value of viewing the emergence and evolution of this cognitive procedure through the lens of Luhmann's or Bourdieu's theory of modern society. The tensions between preface and epilogue, as well as Most's and Gumbrecht's musings on the morbidity of historicizing research, also re-enact in salient ways some of the rhetorical fault lines in the self-fashionings of nineteenth-century scholars, traced in parts I and II of this paper.

In an attempt to delimit the theme of the volume, Most distinguishes between historicity, historicism, and historicization.[109] *Historicity* he defines as the universal, if more or less developed, awareness which human beings have of the temporal dimension of their existence. *Historicism* is taken 'to designate a mode of academic research into the human past which eschewed grand philosophical schemes in favor of detailed causal analysis of events and processes'. According to Most, this mode was 'highly local' (European and North American) and came and went: he situates its heydays in the period of ca. 1850-1930 and underscores

---

L. Wittgenstein, H. Putnam, N. Goodman, P. Lorenzen, M. Hesse, T. Kuhn, K. Knorr-Cetina, H. G. Gadamer, Ch. Taylor (16 n. 18).
108 *Historicization – Historisierung* (Göttingen 2001).
109 Preface, vii-viii.

that the precise meaning of the term has become 'obscure in the extreme', partly because of the pejorative connotations it acquired in time. Finally, *historicization*: 'something neither as universal and platitudinous as [historicity] nor as local and confused as [historicism]', 'historicization can be defined as a specific mode of cognitive activity which defines a body of knowledge and in so doing determines that it is constituted in its essential meaning by its temporal structure.' As the defining characteristics of historicization, Most specifies 'defamiliarization', 'recontextualization', and 'narrativization'. He conceives of these moments as a three-step process in which elements in the world around us first lose their intrinsic and unquestioned validity, creating the need of new explication and justification. This need is then satisfied by resituating the element in its context of origin, and the temporal gap between the present and the past that thereby ensues is, finally, bridged by a narrative that links that origin to the present.

Most's model of historicization is impressive, but not without flaws. By way of critique, I should like to single out the following four aspects: first of all, what Most sets up as 'historicization' is, on a formal level and in theory, almost indistinguishable from the agenda of historicism. Historicist criticism, too, aimed at defamiliarization and recontextualization; it, too, viewed 'the past as being not ontologically different from the present and future'; it, too, was critical of 'genesis and eschatology' and worked with a 'humanized' conception of time (ix). In fact, Most's definition of 'defamiliarization' as 'the Enlightenment project of taking every element and subjecting it to the analysis of reason' (ix) is virtually identical to his definition of historicism as a mode of research that aims at the 'detailed causal analysis of events and processes' (vii). None of this invalidates his strictures against the obscure semantics of the term 'historicism'; but it does raise questions about the precise relationship between 'original' historicism and his own concept of 'historicization'. What Most does not provide is a comparative explication of how his model of historicization differs from and improves upon, rather than simply replicates under a new label, central premises of historicist research.

Secondly, Most's model of historicization features some conceptual soft spots, in particular in how it configures the 'origin'. Specific to the act of historicization, Most claims, is the assertion that the 'essence' of each element 'is determined by where it came from historically, its moment of origin' (viii).[110] This smacks strongly of a secularized metaphysics of origin, in which the Romantics may have been invested, but which creates some odd ruptures in Most's own theoretical architecture: for the emphasis on origins seems to contradict one of his other claims, namely that historicization 'disqualifies genesis'. To take it as axiomatic that 'the essence' of an entity is determined by its moment of origin is, rather, to privilege genesis.

Here the fact is crucial that in its heavy investment in the moment of origin, Most's theory of historicization does not correspond to current historicizing practice: three decades of reception studies have long since put paid to any notion that the origin determines the essence of an entity, and, I submit, most historicizers nowadays are Nietzschean enough to go about their business without committing themselves to any such *Ursprungsmythologie*:[111] while

---

110 The point finds elaboration on the following page, where Most traces the origins of his theoretical axiom: '... recontextualization in terms of the situation of origin corresponds to a Romantic nostalgia for the origin as what determines the essence of a thing.'
111 See the paper by A. Sommer in this volume (87-103).

reconstructing the meaning an element may have had in its context of origin is part of the project of historicization, it does not follow that historicizers view this meaning as being in any way 'essential'; rather, being good genealogists, they take it for granted that the meaning of an element is relative to its context, changes over time, and continually evolves.[112]

A very similar point can be made about Most's third aspect, i.e. the need of narrativization: if historicization involves bridging a temporal gap between the moment of origin and the present, this seems to define (and legitimate?) the present with reference to the past. Again I am unsure of how many current historicizers actually 'feel the pressure' (viii) to provide such narratives, which, by definition, seem to be narratives of identity. Quite a few nineteenth-century *historicists* were committed to this exercise, but in the age of genealogy such narrativization has suffered a drastic loss of credibility. Put differently, in important respects, the practice of contemporary historicizers (including Most himself) is more radical and sophisticated than the theory by which he wishes to capture it.

Thirdly, Most suggestively links the success of historicization to 'deeply seated, widespread cultural needs of the *modern* period' (ix) and draws attention to the fact that 'the *discourse of science* in particular turned out by reason of its special claim to truth to raise different kinds of problems for the project of historicization than those posed, for example, by literature' (xi) (my italics). Yet the precise relation between historicization, modernity, and science remains by and large obscure.

And finally, Most draws attention to the fact that (hitherto) historicizers have tended to be reluctant to historicize themselves, a reluctance which he interprets via a series of open-ended questions as potentially arising from our desire 'to overcome our dread of our own mortality' (xii). These questions deftly prefigure Gumbrecht's epilogue, but are hardly an adequate explanation of the phenomenon of self-historicization in the modern academy – a project, one may point out, that is already fully underway.[113] To summarize: in Most's conception of historicization certain problems are left hanging: the affinities between nineteenth-century historicism and historicization; the tendency to essentialize origins in his notion of recontextualization; the assertion of the need of filling the gap between past and present through narrativization; the precise connection between historicization, science, and modernity; and the challenge of how to confront the task of self-historicization without 'embarrassment'.[114]

---

112 See, for instance, D. C. Feeney, *Literature and Religion at Rome* (Oxford 1998) 115-16: '... the interest in origins is correspondingly far more muted in recent scholarship; as Versnel puts it, "*origin is not to be identified with meaning*". The idea that the power or meaning of a rite is necessarily linked causally to its origin is, after all, as misplaced as the idea that the power or meaning of a myth or a word is linked causally to their origin.'
113 See, for example, T. Mergel and T. Welskopp, 'Geschichtswissenschaft und Gesellschaftstheorie', in, *Geschichte zwischen Kultur und Gesellschaft. Beiträge zur Theoriedebatte*, ed. Mergel and Welskopp (Munich 1997) 9-35 (9): 'Auch in anderen Disziplinen scheinen die Kulturanthropologie, die Linguistik und konstruktivistische Ansätze der Philosophie die Rolle des Leitwolfes übernommen zu haben. Das steht für einen Schub an Selbstreflexivität, der die Konstruktionsarbeit der Wissenschaft anstatt der "Wahrheitsfindung" betont.'
114 Apparently, during the conference on which this collection of papers is based, 'invitations made to speakers ... to position themselves historically led to astonishing, and memorable moments of shared embarrassment' (xii).

I would like to submit that these problems may be solved if one changes the theoretical architecture and approaches the rise of historicizing research as part of the modern preoccupation to investigate and explain data scientifically. From this point of view, it is possible to conceive of nineteenth-century historicism and the phenomenon that Most describes under the label 'historicization' as more or less evolved versions of scientific endeavours to explain (construct) reality according to a specific logic. The best way to render this claim plausible is by taking a look at a yet further evolved version of 'explanatory defamiliarization' than that of historicism or historicization, i.e. Bourdieu's 'praxeological history'. Egon Flaig captures its quintessence thus:[115]

> Praxeological history is faced with the laborious task to counteract the effects of cultural practice, to make them undone intellectually. The social world reproduces itself ceaselessly in objectified form so that those socialized in this world perceive, without questioning, the objects of their social investments and strategies as 'entities' – as finished results, whose constructedness remains unnoticed. All objectification is a forgetting. Praxeological history therefore endeavours to counteract scientifically the spontaneous objectifications by decomposing wherever possible the substance of 'the state', of 'pleasure', of 'festivals', of 'politization' etc. into their respective practices through which these 'entities' acquire the semblance of existence in the first place. The conceptual apparatus of praxeological history untiringly transforms substances into relations.

This procedure of decomposition and reconstitution of data with the help of a highly evolved theoretical and conceptual apparatus is the hallmark of science.[116] In more or less developed form, we can see this logic at work in historicism and Most's model of historicization: the insistence on questioning the objects around one ('defamiliarization'); the endeavour to explain entities *in relation to* their contexts of origin; or the willingness to relinquish objectifications, such as investing historical time with ontological priorities or eschatological patterns. But against the backdrop of current theory and practice in the cultural sciences, it is also possible to spot where historicism and Most's model of historicization still perpetuate commitments to entities and their objectifications that a praxeological history would pulverize – in Most's case the traces of *Ursprungsmythologie* or the insistence on the vague concept of 'narrativization'.

In other words, I would like to suggest that it is possible to conceive of historicism and historicization as schools of thought and cognitive procedures that are part of the (on-going) re-interpretation of the world along scientific principles which acquired such startling

---

115 E. Flaig, *Den Kaiser herausfordern: die Usurpation im Römischen Reich* (Frankfurt a.M. 1992) 32-33.
116 See N. Luhmann, 'Unverständliche Wissenschaft' (n. 35, above) 174: 'I want to call [this special characteristic of modern science] the capacity to decompose and reconstitute. Gaston Bachelard demonstrated this tendency in exemplary fashion with respect to our notion of physical matter. What was initially conceived as a unity and endowed with attributes, is reconceived as relational. What functioned as element, is located on a deeper level – only to be decomposed in turn at the next stage of scientific evolution. Counterconcepts emerge which articulate a recombination corresponding to the level of decomposition – for instance, emergence, evolution, system. The proper scientific statements now refer to relations or correlations, or rather relations of covariation: how does a variable change if other variables change, and under what additional conditions are these correlations true or not true.'

momentum in modern times.[117] While it would be wrong to conceive of this process as smooth and straightforward, or, even, irreversible, it is possible to specify certain general principles at work by which one may assess (and critique) less developed stages of this process and to detect a trend towards radicalization. A good example of such radicalization is the adoption of constructivist epistemologies (see Appendix A) as well as modes of self-reflexive critique by which cultural scientists have started to bring into view the conditions of possibility for their own activity. In so doing, they have started to attack the last bastion of objectification: the ground on which they themselves are standing.[118]

Most is able to show that historicization has been laying waste to entire provinces of (premodern) 'meaning', such as a notion of time deeply rooted in metaphysics. One has to look very hard for places where his model still allows for operations of '*Sinnstiftung*' or for thresholds of scientification not yet crossed.[119] In short, his view of the phenomenon places it squarely within the brave, new world of modern science. Enter Gumbrecht and his epilogue.

The first few sections of Gumbrecht's paper set forth a possible correlation between various political configurations and waves of historicization in nineteenth- and twentieth-century Europe and America, building up to the thesis of a causal nexus between 'an interest in historicization' and a commitment to 'the critique of a political present' (369). Then Gumbrecht switches gears and offers some phenomenological musings on the deeper philosophical significance of historicization. It is this second part that I wish to focus on since it furnishes a rather interesting complement to Most's preface.[120]

---

[117] This is not to deny that (German) historicism, as a historical configuration, did not also have strong political discontents, see, most recently, E. Flaig, 'Identität gegen Autonomie. Vexierspiel mit der Individualität', in *Historismus in den Kulturwissenschaften*, ed. O. G. Oexle and J. Rüsen (Vienna, Cologne, Weimar 1996) 221-38.

[118] In the field of classics, reflexive critique is often narrowly conceived in (auto)biographical terms – an invitation to personal exhibitionism which, I suspect, might have caused the moments of shared embarrassment at Most's conference. But instead of asking for the personalized conditions of possibility that apply to one individual only (and are therefore of rather limited relevance and applicability) one may conceive of the challenge of self-historicization as a call to investigate the *structural* conditions of possibility that underwrite the knowledge industry of which historicization is a part, more generally speaking: modern science. This is precisely the agenda of Bourdieu's *Méditations pascaliennes* (n. 45, above). Such a project is still uncomfortable (for instance, it requires extensive reading in social theory), but, arguably, no longer embarrassing.

[119] See E. Flaig, 'Verstehen und Vergleichen. Ein Plädoyer', in *Historismus in den Kulturwissenschaften* (n. 117, above) 263-87 (277): 'Je mehr Sinn die Historie für uns aus der Vergangenheit herausschlägt, desto mythogener wird sie selber. Je sinnentleerter die Vergangenheit, desto größer die Erkenntnischancen. Das Verdikt Henry Fords – "Geschichte ist Müll" – eröffnet diese Chancen. Die Vergleichgültigung, die dem Gegenstand zustößt, wenn man ihn wie Müll behandelt und niemand sich mehr um seinen (politischen, identitätsfördernden) Tauschwert streitet, erlaubt uns allererst, ein reiches Inventar von Kategorien und Differenzen zu erstellen.'

[120] A couple of observations on the first part: it is unclear whether Gumbrecht conceives of the nexus between 'historicization' and 'critique of a political present' as a necessary one, or whether 'waves' of historicization could also be due to other factors; secondly, is it accurate to see the same *political* logic at work in early nineteenth-century Prussia, where, so Gumbrecht, historicization served to furnish 'the image of a past that would set standards for a desired national future' (366) and post-Vietnam America, even though both countries were recovering from a military disaster? Apparently, waves of historicization may serve opposite political programmes (mythopoiesis and 'subversive' critique), which raises questions about centering its logic (entirely) in politics; a third (and related) point concerns the

Most and Gumbrecht agree on the crucial role of defamiliarization in historicizing research. For Gumbrecht, historicization first and foremost requires 'the beholder's readiness to overcome a primary inertia, the inertia, that is, to assume that (s)he knows enough to make good (or "adequate") use of an object (s)he encounters' (370). It follows that one precondition of historicization is 'the willingness (or the spontaneous reaction) to take a step back from the paradigmatic orientation that permeates our everyday life' (*ibid.*). But then the two part company. For Gumbrecht takes a religious turn that, as we shall see, is strongly reminiscent of the self-fashioning of a Jaeger or a Wilamowitz. In other words: he opts for *Sinnstiftung*. As we have seen, such efforts are often woolly, and Gumbrecht's is no exception; still, it is possible to identify the following train of thought: first, Gumbrecht argues that the defamiliarization of elements against our quotidian inertia endows these elements with a certain 'aura' and turns them into 'objects of desire'; this, so Gumbrecht, is tantamount to saying that historicizers create, quite literally, 'sacred objects': 'Through our skills of historicization we produce sacred objects, and I want to avoid any metaphorical undertones in this proposition (as much as I want to avoid any other effects of being *geistreich* here).'[121]

These sacred objects are at the centre of a religion (quite without 'inverted commas') – the religion of historicization:

> ... I want to claim that 'our' sacred objects, the sacred objects produced by (cultural) historians, are as legitimately sacred as the sacred objects produced by any other religion. For there are no sacred objects without specific frames of staging and scaffolding (such as our *historisches Bewußtsein* for example), i.e. without priests, theologians, and specialists in any other field capable of exempting such objects from the everyday sphere and capable of explaining why they require (or, to say it in a more sophisticated way: why they deserve) special treatment. (372)

Gumbrecht here tries to render plausible his claim that 'historicization' is a religion and 'historicizers' priests *via* some rather suspect reasoning: first, he implies that the (uncontroversial) proposition 'there are no sacred objects without specific frames of staging and scaffolding' entails its (highly controversial) inverse, i.e. 'every frame of staging and scaffolding generates sacred objects'; and secondly, he posits that every act of exempting objects from the everyday sphere and subjecting them to some special treatment by experts *must* have religious motivations and consequences. At closer inspection, neither one of these moves turns out to be particularly persuasive. There are frames of defamiliarization that do not generate sacred objects (for example, science); and there are expert communities that

---

precise relation between political and other aspects of the phenomenon, in particular the processes of professionalization, including the high degree of specific skills, which, as Gumbrecht rightly stresses (366), came to be standard in the modern period in historically oriented disciplines. And finally, there is the uneasy shift between the historical and the philosophical part of the paper: in the former, historicization figures as a mode of (subversive) critique; in the latter as a (religious) means of defying mortality. It remains unclear how we are supposed to reconcile these two rather different conceptions. These problems could arguably be solved if we conceive of historicization as an (evolving) commitment to scientific interpretation, a project that features its own logic, but may be highjacked for purposes of *Sinnstiftung*.

121 372. It is, of course, difficult to determine how serious to take his protestations of seriousness, especially since the entire paper *is* very *geistreich*.

subject elements of the world to special treatment without endowing them with special meaning or worshipping them as objects of desire (for example, scientists). In fact, the same two aspects that Gumbrecht uses to identify religious activities, i.e. (a) the defamiliarization and special framing of the everday by (b) a group of experts, are also hallmarks of science.[122] Unless one wishes to identify science with religion, it follows that Gumbrecht's notion of religion is undertheorized, i.e. in need of further specification through differentiating characteristics.

So all Gumbrecht has shown is that the moves of historicization *may* amount to a religion, not that they *have to*. This raises the obvious question – which Gumbrecht never poses, let alone answers – under what conditions this is the case, and under what conditions it is not, and by which criteria we may distinguish historicizing moves which are 'religious' from those which are 'scientific'. The quotation from Flaig (above, n. 119) furnishes us with such a criterion: we may differentiate between a historicization that aims at (religious) *Sinnstiftung* and one that aims at (explanatory) *Sinnentleerung* ('depletion of meaning'). For defamiliarization, scaffolding, and special treatment are characteristic enabling conditions for both, the charging of elements thus treated with special meaning and significance *and* their complete dissolution into 'meaningless' relations via theories and methods and related professional procedures.[123] The former is the work of religion; the latter that of science.

Gumbrecht, however, simply ignores the second possibility and goes on to specify what the high priests of historicization (among whom he includes himself) nowadays set out to achieve. Surprisingly, one of their main aims turns out to be the very elimination of the gap between the present and the past that constitutes their religion. Historicization consumes itself:

> There is a style of writing and of staging history today whose main (if not only) ambition lies in making us forget that the past is no longer present. Making material objects from the past present and tangible – or at least pointing to them – often seems to produce the truly magic effect of eliminating the temporal distance that separates us from the desired past (or, to be more precise, it helps us produce the illusion of this effect).[124]

This quotation generates an interesting experience of déjà vu. Here is Wilamowitz again, in his letter to Usener:[125]

> the old poetry (and, of course, law and religion and history as well) is dead: it is our task to give it life; when one, for instance, explains Aeschylus and the language starts to ring and the rhythms to whisper and the old gods alloggiano sull' accesa fronte and the heroes act and suffer again, and the students ... now have in front of their souls Aeschylus and Cassandra and the theatre of Dionysus with the Acropolis above: then I feel that philology is something in and of itself after all ...

---

122 This partial overlap of science and religion is not coincidental. Modern science took over many of the functions that religion had in premodern societies, in particular the generations of 'truth-claims' about our world. But this does not mean that science *is* (a special kind of) religion (*pace* Wilamowitz).
123 Such as abstraction, formalization, specification, and generalization: see G. W. Most, 'Preface' to *Disciplining Classics* (n. 50, above) vii.
124 374. For an example of this magic at work, we are referred to his book *In 1926. Living at the Edge of Time* (Cambridge MA 1997).
125 See 166 n. 16, above.

Through the magic powers of the historicizer the past miraculously comes alive. Historical and cultural differences fall by the way. Immediate encounters with the thought and sensibilities of a bygone age become possible. We may take unmediated hermeneutic strolls through vanished realms of history, talk to the dead, and partake in an original Aeschylus performance. In their desire for, and belief in the possibility of, a miraculous resurrection of the past and the attending experience of sublimation and transcendence, the old historicism and the new historicism turn out to be remarkably alike[126] – apart from one telling difference: in contrast to the old, the new historicism is no longer epistemologically naiv. Unlike Wilamowitz, Gumbrecht considers this experience an 'illusion' that we may 'indulge' in 'for our pleasure' (374).

The argument that hedonism justifies intellectual fraud is an interesting one, and there is, arguably, much to be said for experimenting with recreational uses of history. Gumbrecht, for one, sees the main value of such trips into the past in affording us the chance to turn away from death, to either cowardly or defiantly eschew confrontation with the *factum brutum* of our own mortality: 'For turning to the past, making the dead "speak" in order to overcome the threshold of death, unavoidably implies a turning away from that future in which our own death will lie.'[127]

Guided by the high priests of historicization, i.e. humanities professors, we may 'overcome the threshold of death', dodge our mortality, encounter sacred objects, and thereby cross into another world – the idiom of self-ordainment and religious mystification that Gumbrecht here employs makes yet another *déjà vu* impossible to avoid: his rhetoric recalls very similar evocations in the writings of Wilamowitz and Jaeger, most strikingly, perhaps, the ending of Jaeger's inaugural lecture, in the course of which we ascent through the auratic view of classical literature to a realm of permanence and freedom. In terms of content, politics, and ideological commitments, Jaeger's and Gumbrecht's respective conceptions of scholarship as religion are very different; in their formal outlook, even their idiom, they are virtually identical.[128]

By comparing, or, rather, assimilating, museums to temples and historians (and litterateurs?) to priests, Gumbrecht manages to capture important aspects of their function in contemporary society. His is a most suggestive, postmodern attempt to revitalize canonical value and classicizing import in an age of historicization.[129] But also very much in evidence is the fact that such attempts ultimately turn out to be conspicuously *anti*-historicizing (in Most's conception of the term). They are meant to generate an 'illusion' of ahistorical immediacy and special significance, partly by charging specific objects with a religious aura and thereby turning them into sources of pleasure and identity. Put differently, Gumbrecht's

---

126 Gumbrecht, in this section, relies much on Stephen Greenblatt's famous fascination with 'speaking to the dead'.
127 374-75, where Gumbrecht, with reference to Heidegger, also explains why this may be a 'cowardly' move.
128 There are some interesting lexical parallels between Gumbrecht's and Jaeger's attempts to turn the study of the past and of literature into a religious experience. Both use the metaphor of the scaffold (*Gerüst* in German; see n. 29, above) as an enabling device for the encounter with 'the sacred objects of our desires'.
129 See his Gadamerian take on '*klassisch*' at 371 and see his assimilation of historicizers to priests with J. and A. Assmann's definition of the canon and its exegetes (175, above, with n. 43).

religious take on historicization offers an antipode to the radical secularization that Most places at the centre of the phenomenon. There are two ways of dealing with a proposal such as his: one can either critique it on logical grounds; or join the faith.

In all, then, in Most's preface and Gumbrecht's epilogue we have an intriguing re-enactment of the tension between 'science' and 'significance', a tension which has produced the figure of Professor Janus. The poles of this tension seem destined to perform as tweedle-dum and tweedle-dee in discussions on the meaning and purpose of classics in modern society. What remains to be seen is whether the complementary pairing of waves of scientification and religious backlashes, of *Sinnentleerung* and *Sinnstiftung* can be sublimated in any convincing fashion, not just in practice (where it often is), but also in theory.

THEMATIC INDEX

Aestheticism, aestheticizing 3, 6, 27-39, 41-44, 84, 133
Agon 2, 31, 65-66, 76, 77-78
Alteuropa 4, 7, 8, 21, 27-28, 36, 50, 63, 78, 80, 111, 117, 120-121, 159, 171-72
Antisemitism 5, 75, 82, 129, 155, 159
Athens 11, 14, 24-25, 28-29, 37, 50-51, 58, 71, 76, 81-82

Basel 39, 47-59, 75-79
Bildung, Bildungsbürger, Bildungsreligion 1, 79, 126, 131, 135, 165, 180-81, 188, 193

Christianity 5, 23, 88-96, 110, 112, 114-122, 130, 138-140, 143, 149-50, 151-53, 156-58, 183
City-state (ancient) s.v. *polis*

Democracy 4, 8-26, 27, 44, 57-59, 66, 75, 76, 78, 86, 123
Dionysus, the Dionysian 4, 61, 83-84, 88, 145

Fascism, fascist 4, 34-39, 41, 43 n.5, 44, 45, 105, 114, 115 n.22, 116, 121, 122-127, 129, 135 n.13, 140, 159

Graecophilia 1, 3, 6, 51, 52, 65, 69-71, 74, 84, 93, 130-133, 140, 143, 154, 172, 181, 186

Historicism, historicization 5, 20, 130-134, 138-140, 143, 144, 153, 158, 159, 168 n.20, 169, 172, 178-79, 184-87, 188-89, 195-203

Judaism 91, 94, 110, 112, 114-122, 130-132, 138-140, 149-50, 151-53, 156-57, 159

Kultur 1, 27-39, 49-50, 63, 65, 67, 79, 88, 111

Liberalism, liberal 1, 3, 4, 7, 10, 13, 23, 31, 41-45, 55, 57, 59, 63, 66, 67, 71, 83, 86, 115 n.22, 129-160

Method, methodology 2, 3, 6, 7-8, 11, 98, 102, 105, 116, 120, 122, 131, 142-143, 144-46, 148-49, 163-73, 176-79, 186, 191 n.99, 195

Nationalism 33, 41, 44, 49-51, 75, 184-85
National Socialism s.v. Fascism, fascist
Neo-humanism s.v. Graecophilia

Orient, Orientalism, *Orientalistik* 129-160, 163
Origins 5, 87-103, 146, 149, 152, 196-98

Philhellenism s.v. Graecophilia
Polis 4, 7, 11, 12-16, 19-23, 25, 33, 47-59, 65, 67, 68, 70, 74, 76, 78, 85, 106, 108

Racism, racist 3, 5, 35, 38-39, 105-127, 129, 140, 159
Religion 5, 14, 57, 87-96, 102, 111, 112-122, 129-160
Revolution 9, 13, 58, 63, 70, 72, 73, 78-80, 86, 94-95, 111 n.11, 123

Slavery 4, 7, 63, 67, 70, 71, 73, 94-95, 99
Sparta 33, 36, 38, 54, 57, 71, 76

Ursprungsmythologie s.v. Origins

War 3, 28-39, 48, 67, 82, 85
Western Civilization (continuity of) s.v. *Alteuropa*
Wissenschaftsgeschichte 2, 105, 131, 188-89

INDEX OF NAMES

Arnold, M. 45, 165, 175

Bachofen, J.J. 6, 44, 50, 79, 135
Bakunin, M. 74, 79
Beethoven, L.v. 84, 86
Boeckh, A. 52, 70 n.41, 162 n.6, 163-64, 168
Böcklin, A. 132, 135
Bousset, W. 141, 152, 157, 158
Burckhardt, J. 2, 5, 7-39, 41-45, 47-59, 66, 75-84, 107, 112, 113, 116, 117, 130, 135, 182 *Briefe* 8 n.3, 10, 25; *Die Kultur der Renaissance in Italien: Ein Versuch* 2 n.9 41, 77, 82-83; *Die Kunst des Altertums* 21 n.22, 121 n.28; *Die Zeit Konstantin des Großen* 4, 20, 21; *Griechische Kulturgeschichte* 3, 4, 10 n. 7, 12, 14-17, 19-20, 22, 24-26, 27, 28-29, 33, 38, 39, 41, 48, 49, 51, 53-58, 76 n.85, 77 n.91, 93 n.35, 109 n.9, 111 n.12, 181 n.64; *Historische Fragmente* 23-24, 78 n.103; *Jacob Burckhardt Archiv* 36, n.33; *Über das Studium der Geschichte* 18-19, 29-31, 33, 34, 35, 36-37, 38 n.36, 48, 77, 80-83, 85 n.155, 111 n.12

Clausewitz, C. v. 31-32, 34
Clement of Alexandria 91-93, 95
Constant, B. 10, 11, 42, 45, 51, 55, 57, 59
Creuzer, F. 133, 140

Darwin, C. 30, 107, 135
de Lagarde, P. 88, 144 n.44
de Wette, W.M.L. 138-140
Dieterich, A. 5, 6, 130, 145, 147-150, 153, 156, 157
Dilthey, W.: 171, 175
Donoso Cortés, J. 3, 9, 14 n.12, 20, 23, 24
Droysen, J.G. 4, 5, 11, 49, 52, 56 n.23, 70 n.41, 107, 112, 117, 151

Foustel de Coulanges, N.D. 11, 20, 23, 26, 42, 43, 44; 140; *La cité antique* 3, 12-16, 20, 22, 23
Frazer, J. G. 140, 150 n.74, 153, 154, 185 n.78

George, S. 105, 122, 146
Gibbon, E. 94, 138
Gobineau, J.A. 41, 72 n.62
Goethe, J.W. v. 1, 42, 51, 52, 53, 71 n.51, 83, 146, 169, 172 n.32
Grote, G. 48-49, 53, 59

Harnack, A.v. 5, 90, 113, 117, 121, 139, 140, 142-46, 150, 154, 155, 156, 158, 159
Hegel, G. W. F. 11, 63, 67 n.25, 70, 71 n.53, 80, 138, 170
Herder, J.G. 42, 50, 111 n.11, 138, 140
Hermann, G. 162 n.6, 165, 166-67
Hobbes, T. 25, 67
Humboldt, W.v. 1, 45, 69-70, 111 n.11, 181 n.64, 193

Jaeger, W. 6, 162-63, 168 n.20, 182, 183, 186-88, 189, 200; 'Philologie und Historie' 163, 169-72, 174, 202
Jünger, E. 34, 41, 126 n.39, 127

Lassaulx, E.v. 20, 21 n.20
Ludendorff, E. 32-33

Mann, T. 43, 81 n.122
Meyer, E. 6, 131, 136-137, 142, 145, 146, 159
Michelet, J. 50, 51 n.11
Mommsen, T. 11, 36, 49, 107, 112, 140, 142, 151, 160
Montesquieu 4, 7, 42, 45, 59
Montherlant, H.de 41, 43
Müller, K. O. 70 n.41, 133

Nietzsche, F. 2, 4, 5, 6, 29, 34, 38, 39, 49, 61-86, 87-103, 121-122, 132, 135, 162, 168, 187, 192, 196; *David Strauss der Bekenner und Schriftsteller* 81; *Der Antichrist* 85, 95, 99; *Der Fall Wagner* 65 n.13, 72 n.56, 72 n.57; *Der Griechische Staat* 4, 61-86; *Die Fröhliche Wissenschaft* 72 n.62, 85, 97; *Die Geburt der Tragödie aus dem Geiste der Musik* 4, 61-86, 87, 88, 97, 100, 101, 145, 187, 188 n.90; *Einführung in das Studium der platonischen Dialoge* 67 n.31; *Fünf Vorreden zu fünf ungeschriebenen Büchern* 4; *Geschichte der griechischen Literatur* 68, n.37; *Homer und die klassische Philologie* 162, 181-82; *Jenseits von Gut und Böse* 68 n. 33, 84, 85; *Menschliches, Allzumenschliches* 66 n.20, 84, 97-102; *Morgenröthe* 84; *Schopenhauer als Erzieher* 85; *Sokrates und die Tragödie* 69, n.40; *Über die Genealogie der Moral* 85, 89, 99-101; *Über die Zukunft unserer Bildungsanstalten* 79, 85; *Vom Nutzen und Nachtheil der Historie für das Leben* 97, 98, 100; *Wir Philologen* 71 n.49, 81, 84, 161 n.3, 181 n.65; *Wissenschaft und Weisheit im Kampfe* 76 n.88.

Otto, F.W. 113, 116, 121-122, 131, 146, 147, 150, 159

Overbeck, F. 5, 76 n.81, 87-103

Plato 67-68, 85, 118, 147, 150, 171, 183

Ranke, L.v. 33, 50, 52, 53, 111 n.11

Reitzenstein, R. 5, 6, 117 n.25, 130, 131, 142, 145, 150-58

Renan, E. 117, 140, 142

Ritschl, A. 139-141, 165

Rohde, E. 74, 75, 93 n.35, 96, 135, 145, 148, 188

Rousseau, J.-J. 9, 11, 17, 43 n.5, 67 n.25, 71 n.53, 73 n.64, 80, 84

Schiller, F. 1, 4, 51, 52, 69-70, 71 n.52, 86, 146

Schlegel, F. 141, 185 n.79

Schmitt, C. 31, 41

Schopenhauer, A. 53, 65, 69, 80, 83, 84 n.141, 98, 132

Schwartz, E. 148, 155, 157

Sieyès, E.J. 9, 17

Spengler, O. 32, 33, 34, 127

Taine, H. 38, 107

Tocqueville, A.d. 11, 13, 15, 18 n.17, 20, 23, 28, 41, 45

Troeltsch, E. 141, 143, 144 n.44, 156, 157

Usener, H. 5, 6, 113, 122, 123 n.29, 145-50, 153, 156, 162-72, 174, 182, 187-88, 201; *Rektoratsrede* 'Philologie und Geschichtswissenschaft' 134, 163-73, 179, 182, 188

Vischer-Bilfinger, W. 49, 50-51, 74, 79

Wagner, R. 4, 61-86, 97

Weber, M. 51, 112, 118, 135, 140, 176 n.47, 190

Wellhausen, J. 139-142, 144, 146, 159

Winckelmann, J. 1, 4, 51, 69, 70 n.42, 71 n.51, 135

Wilamowitz-Moellendorf, U.v.: 2, 5, 6, 93 n.35, 105-127, 131, 142-46, 147, 148, 150, 155, 159, 162-69, 172, 174, 182, 183-88, 200, 201-02; *Der Glaube der Hellenen* 5, 105, 112-127, 146, 184

Wolf, F.A. 51, 68 n.34, 131, 161 n.3, 174-75, 181